AMERICA'S
"CRIME PROBLEM"

An Introduction to Criminology

AMERICA'S
"CRIME PROBLEM"

An Introduction to Criminology

Joseph F. Sheley

Tulane University

Wadsworth Publishing Company

Belmont, California
A Division of Wadsworth, Inc.

Sociology Editor: Sheryl Fullerton

Production Editor: Ron Newcomer

Cover Designer: Steve Renick

Interior Designer: Ron Newcomer

Copy Editor: Perry Ewell

Technical Illustrator: Irene Imfeld

Printed in the United States of America
1 2 3 4 5 6 7 8 9 10—89 88 87 86 85

ISBN 0-534-04251-1

Library of Congress Cataloging in Publication Data

Sheley, Joseph F.
     America's "crime problem."

     Includes index.
     1. Crime and criminals—United States.   2. Criminal
     statistics—United States.   3. Criminal justice,
     Administration of—United States.   I. Title.
HV6789.S518   1984   364'.973   84–16133
ISBN 0-534-04251-1

CONTENTS

PREFACE

America's "Crime Problem" began as a revision of my earlier book, *Understanding Crime*, but became something more. The change occurred because my reading of the recent criminological literature indicates that much is different about the discipline since my mid-1970s work on the earlier book. Crime trends have changed; crime has "cooled down." More is known about the dimensions of crime and about the characteristics of criminals and victims due to our ability to compare official statistics with victimization and self-reported criminality survey data. Causal analysis has regained some lost popularity after about fifteen years of stagnation. We now know more about deterrence. Criminal justice practices are better understood; we can now say more about alleged sentencing biases, for example. The impact of the conflict perspective upon criminology has been tremendous. It has brought the study of law into the mainstream and, thus, has increased our awareness of the role of interest groups in shaping laws and public perceptions of crime. It has also brought a renewed and stronger interest in white-collar crime.

In short, we hardly *understood* crime in the 1970s and, though we know much about it now, we still really cannot say that we understand it. What we legitimately can profess to understand well are the dimensions of public concern about our "crime problem" and what structures it. Hence, *America's "Crime Problem."* The quotation marks in the title exist for a reason. They reflect the fact that, as a society, we do not confront crime as a real object but as a set of perceptions which we have strung together to form what we define as problematic. We construct our "crime problem." This is a theme carried over from *Understanding Crime* and with it the notion that this construction has very important implications for the average citizen.

In *America's "Crime Problem,"* I have tried to address the manner in which crime touches the reader. Most people reading this book are neither perpetrators nor victims of serious crime nor do they know personally many victims of serious crime. However, like most members of our society, they exhibit a great deal of fear of "street crimes," both attitudinally and behaviorally. Most make personal decisions that are potentially costly—as an extreme example, keeping guns in the home for protection, which often can lead to accidental shootings. More importantly, fear of crime leads to demands for "law and order," encouragement of legislation and criminal justice system efforts to curb crime through restraints on individual rights, and approval of tax spending for anticrime research and programs. Since tax dollars spent on crime represent dollars not spent on other pressing problems and since individual rights, once forfeited, are not easily regained, we owe it to ourselves to formulate as accurate a picture of the "crime problem" as possible before supporting various anticrime policies. Hopefully, readers will develop a critical approach to all they hear and read about crime ("How can I be mislead by these statistics?" "What negative effects may follow policy based on this theory?").

America's "Crime Problem" is able to employ this critical framework while still permitting coverage of most traditional and recent criminological concerns. All bear, in one way or another, on public attitudes toward crime and its prevention.

Chapter 1 provides an overview of criminology with a special emphasis upon the application of criminological findings to both personal and governmental anticrime policy decisions.

Chapters 2 and 3 constitute Part I of the book: "Structuring a 'Crime Problem.'" Chapter 2 reviews the recent history of public concern with crime and the sources of that concern. Chapter 3 examines the role of major interest groups in determining who and what come to be labeled criminal in this society and in shaping the content of our perceptions of crime as a social problem. In line with the book's emphasis on the costs of responding to crime fears, the impact of these fears on personal habits, social solidarity, the economy, and procedural rights is discussed.

Part II explores crime statistics. Chapter 4 elaborates the many problems encountered in trying to develop an accurate picture of crime through examination of official crime statistics, self-reported criminality survey findings, and victimization survey data. Chapter 5 examines a range of types of criminal behavior (from homicide to fraud to vice to white-collar crime) and raises questions about our priorities in allocating resources to fight crime.

Part III is devoted to descriptions of criminals and their victims. We stress the fact that common stereotypes of who victimizes whom often are inaccurate. Chapter 6 pays special attention to links between criminal behavior and the sociodemographic variables of gender, age, social class, and race. Chapter 7 offers an analysis of aspects of victim characteristics which is absent from most criminology texts. Not only is victimization often a non-random occurrence, but it is also not always simply a matter of the active criminal preying upon the passive victim. Various patterns of victim-offender interactions are examined for anticrime policy implications.

Chapters 8 and 9, Part IV of the book, address the always difficult question of crime causation. The former chapter outlines the notion of cause and the scientific approach to searching for it. It reviews espoused biological and psychological links to criminal behavior as well as examining sociological variables popularly thought to influence crime. The latter chapter evaluates the merits of a number of more formal sociological theories of crime causation and suggests two general directions for future research.

In Part V, we examine yet another dimension of the "crime problem"—namely, the extent to which it is created by criminal justice system interests within our society. In Chapter 10, this theme is more specifically applied to the police and courts. These segments of the criminal justice system are not simply processors of criminal suspects; rather, they are producers of such products as official crime rates and official criminals. Chapter 11 examines the corrections system and its negative role in the crime situation.

America's "Crime Problem" concludes with a reemphasis of the need for a critical approach to crime statistics and theories in an attempt to avoid costly "knee-jerk" anticrime policies. The positive and the negative potential of a number of possible policy responses to the crime situation—limiting procedural rights, pretrial preventive detention, capital punishment, increasing penalties for crimes, incarcerating career offenders, and instituting gun-control laws—are examined in light of what we know and, more importantly, what we do not know, about crime in this society.

Throughout the book, the reader will encounter a number of *boxes* ("Newsprint and Comment") which contain newspaper excerpts concerning various aspects of crime. These are followed by commentaries tying the excerpt to a theme explored in the book. The idea for this feature comes directly from my students who constantly bring me clippings which "make sense" of the material they confront in class. What I often take for granted in the morning paper has special significance for people just introduced to new ways of viewing America's "crime problem."

ACKNOWLEDGMENTS

A number of people helped me with this book. Sheryl Fullerton of Wadsworth shepherded the project. Constructive counsel and criticism at several points came from the following individuals: Howard C. Daudistel, of the University of Texas at El Paso; Frederick R. Eisele of Pennsylvania S⸱

University; Kerry K. Fine, formerly at the University of Minnesota; John D. Hewitt, at Ball State University; Peter K. Manning, at Michigan State University; Katheryn M. Mueller, of Baylor University; David G. Peck, at Shippensburg University; Ross L. Purdy, of Corpus Christi State University; Don Taebel, of Georgia State University; and Mervin F. White, of Clemson University. Jane Kuroda and Marionita Williams assisted in typing and library research. My special thanks to all of them.

AMERICA'S
*"CRIME
PROBLEM"*
An Introduction to Criminology

1

ISSUES FOR CRIMINOLOGY

Most people swimming at our seashores do not know about riptides. Riptides occur when waves hitting a beach at two points converge inward as they ebb, thus forming a sudden, very rapid undertow. Swimmers caught in riptides likely will panic. Finding themselves being carried out to sea, they will flail against the current, trying to fight it. But they will make no headway. Arms become blocks of cement plunging through the water, pulling the swimmer downward instead of forward. The magnet tugs relentlessly. The shoreline within seconds grows distant. The struggle is short.

Experienced swimmers respect riptides, but they are not killed by them. They know the key to survival is to conserve strength, avoid panic, and assess the situation rationally. They do not fight a riptide head-on. Instead, they allow the current to carry them out a short distance until it weakens. Then they swim across it—perpendicular to the current—until they are out of it. Thus, they find themselves free to swim to shore.

The cover of this book indicates that its subject is crime, not tides and swimming. But the riptide concept is useful in beginning a book about crime in America. As we shall see repeatedly throughout this book, the American public often views crime as a riptide (the common term is *crime wave*), overwhelming them, sapping their strength, pulling them under. What is the appropriate response? As against the riptide, panic is inappropriate. Panic in the face of our "crime problem" is not likely to kill us literally. (This is not unheard of, of course. In 1976, a New York couple in their late seventies, victims of an assault in their own home, frightened of another attack and of relocating elsewhere, laid out their best clothes on their bed and hanged themselves; see *New York Times*, 1976). But, as coming chapters indicate, panic at our "crime problem" can devastate our society economically and socially as we spend income and tax dollars on wars on crime, as we draw away from others in our society, and as we try to fight criminals by sacrificing our own legal rights.

This book is about not panicking in the face of crime. Since tax dollars spent on crime represent dollars not spent on pressing problems, self-imposed individual isolation erodes community solidarity, and legal rights, once forfeited, are not easily regained, we owe it to ourselves to formulate as accurate a picture of the "crime problem" as possible before engaging in such anticrime measures. Hopefully, criminologists can contribute in this direction.

Traditionally, the sociological subfield of *criminology* has addressed crime-related issues. Criminology is the scientific study of crime as a *social* phenomenon (as opposed, for example, to a legal, historical, psychological, economic, or forensic phenomenon). That is, crime is a matter of sociological interest because it violates social rules and draws a social response, because a criminal act is a social, though generally not a sociable, act occurring in a social setting, and because crime is implicated in a society's cultural and structural framework.

Criminal behavior is implicated in the most basic of sociological problems, that of social order and disorder. The sociologist is concerned with the collective aspects of human life, how one collective aspect (rapid social change, for example) influences another (suicide rates, for instance). In a more social-psychological vein, the sociologist seeks to know how societal conditions influence individuals so that they engage in behaviors which produce societal rates of behavior—how poverty influences individuals' perceptions of the world to the extent that they contribute to the society's crime rate, for example.

These interests translate into questions of order and disorder:

What is social order?
How is order created?
How is it maintained?
What spells the difference between orderly change and collapse into disorder?

The study of criminal behavior springs directly from these questions. Some sociologists have viewed crime as a sign of a weakened or socially disorganized society. Others have noted that, paradoxically, criminal behavior in tolerable amounts may actually serve to strengthen the existing social order. Others have studied crime as the means toward understanding societal members' assumptions about order, the assumptions upon which the members base decisions which contribute to everyday order and disorder. Finally,

NEWSPRINT AND COMMENT

A Cut Eye, a Hole in the Wall: Brutality Charge Kills a Case

By Russell Goodman

Within hours of the senseless killing last fall of Melanie Asquith, headlines blared the tragedy of another tourist murdered in New Orleans and of police groping for a lead in the case.

Nine days later, New Orleans Police Department homicide investigators announced the case was solved. Three suspects were arrested and admitted that they shot the 24-year-old Houston artist to death and wounded her companion, Matt Borel, 28, as they hunted for their car at about 1:30 a.m., Sept. 27, on a dark street in the Central Business District.

Now, almost 10 months after the fatal shots were fired, the chances of bringing the three to trial appear almost nil.

Charges have been dismissed by the district attorney, the three defendants have been released and the officers who broke the case may themselves become targets of a federal investigation into alleged beatings used to wring confessions from the suspects.

The first break in the case came at about 11:30 p.m., Oct. 6, when a police radio dispatch interrupted several police officers drinking coffee in a Canal Street restaurant. The police department dispatcher said a robbery had just occurred in the 800 block of Carondelet Street.

Police scuffled with three suspects on the streets, officers said, the arrests were made and by midnight 17-year-old Epher-iam Williams, 21-year-old Kenneth Robinson and 27-year-old Lawrence C. Johnson were in the 1st District police station on Rampart Street being questioned about the holdup.

Sgt. Clement Desalla later testified he had to subdue Robinson. "It was a wrestling match," the sergeant said. "We were rolling around in the street."

After Robinson was handcuffed, Desalla said he noticed a cut below Robinson's right eyebrow. "It was nothing serious," Desalla said.

Ten hours later, however, the Carondelet Street robbery had been forgotten and all three were booked at Central Lockup with the first-degree murder of Melanie Asquith.

When motions to suppress the suspects' confessions began in December, Detective Ronald F. Brink testified Williams' "effeminate" appearance after his arrest in the robbery sparked the break in the case.

Though he was only peripherally involved in the Asquith murder investigation, Brink testified, he said he recalled an unidentified witness near the murder scene had told him a black man was seen fleeing the scene in the company of another man who had feminine features.

Brink said he thought Williams might have been the man the witness described. When he told the suspects that October night he wanted to question them about a murder, he said Robinson and Johnson began accusing Williams of "killing that lady" and declaring they had played only minor roles in the shooting.

When the hearing to suppress the confessions began, the suspects claimed they had nothing to do with the murder and they confessed only after police beat and kicked them inside the 1st District station.

The cut above Robinson's eye occurred during the beatings, the suspects said.

That kind of allegation is heard quite often . . . but rarely is there any evidence to support the contentions. This time there was what court-appointed defense attorneys called "scientific evidence": two photographs of Kenneth Robinson which corroborated his claim that he was injured while in police custody.

The first photograph of Robinson, a Polaroid snapshot, was taken by Brink one hour and 15 minutes after his arrest. The picture shows no injury like the one Desalla described Robinson sustained during his arrest. The second photograph, taken when Robinson was booked with murder at Central Lockup, clearly shows a one-inch hairline cut just below the suspect's right eyebrow.

The defense was unaware of the photographs, but when Assistant District Attorney Jack Peebles found them in the files handed to him by police, he recognized the importance they would play in the supression hearing.

Peebles, a long-time defense attorney . . . also knew the law compelled him to turn over to the defense that kind of evidence.

Peebles was praised as a "man of integrity" by defense counsel for giving them the evidence. Defense attorney Clyde Merritt . . . said many prosecutors would have just "submarined" the evidence, meaning to hide it from defense attorneys.

Police acknowledged the suspects were held for 10 hours before they were booked at Central Lockup.

Williams, accused of pulling the trigger that killed Asquith and wounded her companion, gave the most graphic testimony during the supression hearing.

"Tell the judge what happened to you . . . at the 1st District," Merritt told his client.

"Well, I was whipped," Williams answered. "I was questioned about a murder. I had plastic bags put over my head where I couldn't breathe. I bit through two and got two more put on.

"I was hit with a stick wrapped in some type of plastic covering, punched in the mouth, my head was pushed into the wall that I was sitting by and I was kicked and everything else and questioned."

"Were any books used, too?" Merritt asked.

"Yes, sir. That was I believe what you call a log book, about maybe three inches thick, and was used. One officer got on top of the desk and jumped down on my head with it four or five times," Williams said.

Criminal District Court Judge Jerome Winsberg, who presided over the hearing, and Williams and attorneys for both sides visited the 1st District station Feb. 13, looking for a hole in the wall that Williams described.

Efforts to find it were futile and the group was prepared to leave when Merritt raised a calendar from its position on a wall just above a desk and discovered an opening.

Williams said he was seated when officers pushed his head through the wall. A photograph was taken of him as he sat in a chair and attorney John Lawrence pushed his head into the hole.

Police said the hole was created more than a year ago when furniture was being rearranged and something was accidentally rammed into the wall. The calendar was placed over the opening, officers said, because the hole was unattractive.

The prosecution's case had been built around the incriminating statements given by the suspects and when the confessions were suppressed, it was

only a matter of weeks before the case fell apart.

Since Williams allegedly did the shooting, the prosecution hoped to snare him with the testimony of Johnson, the alleged lookout man.

Charges were dropped against Johnson July 2 and he was granted immunity from prosecution in return for his testimony before a parish grand jury. Johnson spent nearly an hour with the jurors the day the murder charge was lifted, but apparently no information was gleaned from him.

On July 9, the state dismissed charges against Robinson, who was accused of trying to snatch Asquith's purse. Robinson was taken before the grand jury the same day. He stayed with the jurors only 15 minutes.

Efforts to gain evidence against the accused teen-age gunman apparently failed again. Time was running out. The trial was scheduled to start July 14.

The day of trial came and went, but business that day consisted of only routine matters and not a murder trial.

Charges against Williams were dropped July 14 and he was released from prison, just as Robinson and Lawrence were freed before him.

Source: © Times-Picayune Publishing Corp., 1982. Reprinted by permission.

Comment: Painful Choices

It is difficult to read the above news story without being outraged. It is clearly possible that three criminals (one a killer), once in the clutches of the law, have been freed because the court ruled their confessions invalid as trial evidence. The average citizen's anger likely is directed toward the "technicality" that permitted the defendants' release. But let us look a bit closer at this "technicality."

History has instilled in us a healthy fear of allowing our criminal justice officials to go about their business unchecked. Power corrupts, and we find example after example of police abuses of power and overzealous or politically motivated actions by prosecutors. In fact, we are hard-pressed to find a society that relies wholly on the good will of its criminal justice functionaries and has its faith rewarded. Our founding fathers seemed acutely aware of this when they drafted the Bill of Rights. We may quarrel about specific applications of the Bill of Rights, but we can hardly dispute its intent: to protect the individual citizen from the state. Thus, we may speak our minds without fear of prosecution; the police cannot enter our homes without warrants, nor search or arrest us without probable cause; we have the right to a trial if we are accused of a crime; and the state cannot impose cruel and unusual punishment upon us. The "technicalities" against which the public so often rails are the substance of the freedom the same public cherishes.

Clearly, we cannot allow the police the discretion to beat citizens to obtain evidence, no matter how important the case or odious the citizen. Such discretion opens the door to the kinds of abuses the Bill of Rights seeks to check. If we all are not protected, none of us is.

Therefore, with whom are we angry regarding the case described above? The rules did what they were intended to do. The police did what they were not allowed to do. The rules did not cost the case; the police did. Obviously, we do pay a price in adhering to the Bill of Rights. Sometimes criminals cannot be prosecuted. But we pay a dearer price when the Bill of Rights pertains only to some of us.

---

some sociologists have viewed social order as the socially constructed result of competition and conflict among various groups in society. Crime thus is viewed as endangering the interests of some groups while promoting those of others.

Within this general framework, criminologists study these more specific issues:

1. *The Creation and Use of Laws.* Criminology is concerned in part with the development of laws, the function of law in a society, law as an instrument of social change, and the functions of legislation and law enforcement for interest groups within a society.

2. *Patterns of Crime.* Some criminologists study patterns of crime for a society or community at a given point in time and over various time periods. This area of criminology, also known as the *epidemiology* of criminal behavior, involves the study of trends and the impact of crime on a population. It examines as well the way criminal behavior is distributed among us—by gender, age, race, and so forth.

3. *Causes of Crime and Criminality.* Criminologists also study the conditions affecting societal crime rates and the causes of individual and group involvement in crime. This study of causes, known as *causal analysis,* also attempts to identify distinctive types of criminal careers

and their development. Traditionally, a major goal of causal analysis has been the formulation of strategies for crime prevention.

4. *The Societal Reaction to Crime.* Criminological theory and research focus on the forces influencing a society's definitions of certain behaviors as criminal, the ways in which a society reacts to individuals and their acts, the process by which individuals come to be called criminals, and individuals' reactions to society's definition of them.

5. *Criminal Justice Administration.* Criminologists are interested in the criminal justice system and its organizational and bureaucratic processes; the police and the legal profession as occupational categories; and, importantly, the criminal justice system as the primary producer of a community's criminal population and crime rates.

6. *Custody, Punishment, and Rehabilitation of Criminals.* A final branch of criminology is the study of society's methods of dealing with criminals. Most research in this area is designed to evaluate the success and deterrent effects of correctional programs, from the point of view of both the public and the individual offender. Much of this research concerning prisons and other correctional agencies also is used in developing theories of bureaucracy.

POLICY RESEARCH

Criminology generally has tried to be responsive to the crime concerns of its day. However, traditionally it has directed its responses less at immediate than at long-range solutions to crime. As a subfield of sociology, criminology has channeled its efforts primarily toward building a general body of knowledge about societal norms (rules, laws), deviance (rule violation), and social control (restraining individual pursuit of self-interests thought to be detrimental to society or thought by groups in power to represent a threat to their social and economic positions). Thus, crime is studied as a form of deviance and methods of combatting crime as forms of social control. The ultimate goal of such an approach is the development of a sophisticated set of sociological principles to allow broad-based solutions to problems like crime, rather than reliance on ad hoc, patchworklike remedies.

As public concern about crime has grown, public patience with searches for long-range solutions to the problem of crime has worn thin. Shifting with public sentiment in recent years and spurred by the availability of government and private foundation grants (money which grows constantly scarcer in the 1980s), criminologists now are more willing to address more specific crime questions, with an eye to more immediate crime-control strategies. For example, much research has been conducted to provide criminal justice planners with knowledge about community-based rehabilitation programs for juvenile offenders. Empey and Erickson's *The Provo Experiment* (1972) serves as a landmark for such research. The authors used sociological theory and methodology to investigate the claim that probation and supervised treatment in the community are superior to incarceration in discouraging future delinquencies. They found no basic differences in the success of these types of corrections. More recently, Rossi et al. (1980) conducted a large-scale controlled experiment to determine whether or not the recidivism rate(i.e., the rearrest rate) of ex-convicts could be reduced or slowed by giving the former prisoners monthly financial aid. While interpretation of the study's results is debatable (see Zeisel, 1982; Rossi et al., 1982), the results do seem to indicate that the payment method employed in the experiment did not influence the recidivism rate of the subjects. Results aside, this study and *The Provo Experiment* provide research models by which future correctional innovations can be evaluated.

Research of the type just described is called *social policy research*. It attempts to identify or better conceptualize social problems, map strategies to combat the problems, and conduct research to evaluate the costs and the effects of the strategies. Policy research assumes that criminologists can, and should, make immediate, significant contributions to the solutions of major social problems. Most policy studies are large-scale, governmentally funded projects. While many have involved experimentation with various correctional programs, the list of topics for study seems to be growing. Studies of the degree of effectiveness of police patrols in lowering crime rates serve as examples (Kelling et al., 1974). So also do evaluations of programs designed to make the bail process less class-biased (Bynum, 1982), and studies of the effectiveness of juvenile deinstitutionalization and diversion programs that channel youths upon arrest into various educational and treatment programs rather than into the traditional prosecution process (Selke, 1982; Sheley and Nock, 1982). The question of reducing robbery and burglary rates through decriminalization of narcotics also represents a policy-research problem (Inciardi, 1981).

Through policy research, criminologists seem able successfully to claim that they at least partially are addressing public demands for solutions to the crime problem. Yet, criminology's impact on the average citizen's concern with crime is questionable. Crime touches most people through the fear it instills; people are anxious about their safety and that of their possessions. Most citizens are unaware of the governmental policy research in which sociologists participate. From the citizens' point of view, criminological theory and research that do not address directly and visibly their fears are interesting but largely irrelevant. Indeed, when criminologists suggest that "common sense" anticrime remedies may not succeed or point to possible damaging side effects of a given remedy to certain lower income groups, they are accused of "coddling" the criminal element and thus failing in their responsibility to society.

Criminology need not change radically to become more responsive to public concerns. Basically, it must accurately assess public perceptions of crime and the content and quality of crime fears. People base decisions on these perceptions and fears. Some decisions involve organizing one's personal life to minimize the chances of being a crime victim: buying a gun, barring windows, or, in the extreme case mentioned earlier, taking one's life. Other decisions concern the citizen's involvement in legal and political responses to crime. Even in as power-differentiated a society as ours, few governmental decisions can forego at least tacit public approval. Directly or indirectly, the public approves or disapproves the spending of the tax dollar on crime-control programs. More importantly, the public explicitly or implicitly condones or condemns crime control measures that limit such individual rights as those guarding against unlawful search and protecting one against self-incrimination.

THREE QUESTIONS

Whether at the personal or governmental level, decisions about potential crime solutions like those just described carry important consequences. They therefore must be based on the most accurate knowledge available. Three important questions should be addressed in any personal or governmental policy decision:

1. What are the nature and scope of the problem at hand (that is, how accurate are the assumptions and figures relating to the problem)?
2. Will the proposed remedy actually aid in solving the problem?
3. What incidental side effects may accompany implementation of the proposed remedy?

Criminology can be made relevant for the average citizen by providing information that can aid in both asking and answering these three questions. The goal of this book is to summarize current criminological thought on crime in this society in such a fashion that its readers can make better sense of the crime situation as it affects them, better formulate personal decisions concerning the crime situation, and better evaluate general governmental anticrime policies. Surveys indicate, for instance, that the public increasingly favors capital punishment for certain crimes and that it supports at least some form of gun control (Gallup, 1981a, 1981b). Thirty percent of the American public support electronic surveillance of suspected criminals, and nearly half would allow police to stop and search anyone on suspicion (*Newsweek,* 1981). These attitudes apparently are based on perceptions of crime as being highly troublesome for society. Yet we can be certain that most citizens systematically have not assessed the crime situation they see as threatening, the potential effectiveness of the preventive measures just mentioned, or their potential negative side effects.

This book will disappoint readers who are looking for ready solutions to the problem of crime. It has none to offer. Instead, it tries to provide a framework for asking questions about crime and solutions for it. Those who read the book, it is hoped, will become very skeptical of all they hear about crime and will begin to ask questions first and to act later. Hopefully, they will gain a sense of the *complexity* of the crime situation and proposed responses to it. Nothing is simple; nothing is black and white; every benefit carries a loss. The ever-controversial debate concerning the plea of insanity in criminal trials highlights this theme.

AN EXAMPLE: THE INSANITY PLEA DILEMMA

Historically, our concept of legal responsibility for a criminal act rests on the notion of *mens rea,* the guilty mind. That means that when persons have violated the law, they must have done so intentionally in order to be found guilty in a court of law. Children who have not yet attained the age of reason cannot commit a crime in the legal sense because they cannot appreciate the consequences of their own behavior; senile persons cannot commit crimes for the same reason. If one is physically coerced to violate the law, one is not a criminal, for criminal intent is lacking. Accidents and mistakes cannot be crimes, for intent is not present (though we are responsible for the foreseeable consequences of our actions, such as accidents resulting from speeding). Finally, legal insanity can free one from responsibility for a criminal act.

The issue of legal insanity always is controversial, but it becomes especially so when it is implicated in a highly publicized court case such as that of John Gacey; who killed thirty-three young men in Chicago, or that of John Hinkley, who attempted to assassinate President Ronald Reagan in 1981. At issue always is the fear that criminals "fake" insanity and are set "scot-free" by gullible juries. Let us look at this complex problem.

Insanity is a legal, not a medical, term. It means in simplest terms that a person could not avoid committing the crime in question because he or she had a mental defect. Exactly how insanity is defined in court trials varies by court system. Most states utilize a formula based on the *M'Naghten rule,* a definition of insanity established in England in 1853 during a murder trial. In essence, the M'Naghten rule states that a person is legally insane if he or she could not understand the nature and quality of the act in question or could not understand that the act was wrong at the time the act was committed. Over the years, some states have added an "irresistable impulse" rule whereby criminal responsibility is negated if the person who committed the act can demonstrate that he or she was unable to control an impulse to act in a manner he or she knew was illegal. The M'Naghten rule is known as the *prosecutor's rule* since it is extremely difficult for a defendant to demonstrate insanity under its terms.

The 1940s and 1950s witnessed a growing national respect for psychiatry and with it some doubts about the fairness of M'Naghten-type formulas. These formulas cannot accomodate the person who can distinguish right from wrong and is not acting under impulse, but who is somehow emotionally compelled to violate a law. The mad bomber who cannot help himself, or a "Son of Sam" who is driven to kill for years, even though knowing that killing is wrong, serve as examples. Thus, in 1954, a judge for the U.S. Court of Appeals in the District of Columbia handed down the *Durham formula* whereby persons may be found insane if their criminal act is a product of a mental disease or defect. Knowing right from wrong and acting impulsively are not necessary elements within this formula. Following other appeals court decisions, some states adopted a modified version of the Durham formula proposed in 1955 by the American Law Institute. Under this proposal, criminal responsibility is negated if, due to mental defect or disease, persons cannot appreciate the nature of their criminal behavior or cannot act in accord with the law. Mental defect or disease must be demonstrated independent of the criminal act. At present, about one-third of our states employ a variant of this formula; the others hold to the M'Naghten rule.

The Durham-type rule is known as a *defendant's rule* because critics argue that it is too easily employed in the defendant's behalf. In fact, insanity is a rarely employed plea under any formula for its determination; the majority of those using it are charged with lesser offenses, and most do not use the plea successfully (*New Orleans Times-Picayune/States-Item*, 1982; *Newsweek*, 1982). Yet, it is also true that the Durham-type rule makes the state's case more difficult. Defendants can attempt to link their crimes to more nebulous mental problems. Prosecutors find such pleas harder to rebut "beyond a reasonable doubt." Where once psychiatrists simply could state whether, in their opinions, a defendant could distinguish right from wrong, psychiatrists now deal in far fuzzier diagnoses of mental defect and even fuzzier links to criminal behavior. Defense attorneys may call several psychiatrists to establish insanity. Because psychiatry is a highly inexact science marked by disagreement among its practitioners, the prosecution can find an equal number of psychiatrists to contradict those employed by the defense. The jury, a group of lay persons, is left to decide which of these experts is correct.

A number of solutions have been offered to remedy the problems created by Durham-type rules. Some argue for eliminating the insanity plea and allowing the jury to return a verdict of "guilty but insane"—a nonsensical suggestion since persons who are insane by definition cannot be legally responsible for (guilty of) the crime in question. Others would allow the defendant to enter a plea of "diminished capacity" (the inability fully to premeditate the offense) and be found guilty of a lesser offense. Yet, this proposal still requires complicated psychiatric testimony. Some critics desire to eliminate or restrict psychiatric testimony in trials, but this still leaves jurors to decide the difficult question of mental defect and its link to behavior. Most critics simply call for a return to the narrower M'Naghten rule.

In short, we are faced with a general belief that people can possess mental defects which influence them to commit crimes. We are also faced with an inexact psychiatry which has difficulty distinguishing those persons mentally defective from those who are not. We have a public that worries that criminals may escape punishment by pretending to be insane. Finally, barring some new advances in psychiatric diagnoses, we have two general formulas for determining insanity, each with a major liability. The M'Naghten rule is the more common and the narrower. By limiting insanity to lack of ability to distinguish right from wrong, it insures that fewer criminals can feign insanity. However, it also insures that persons who can distinguish right from wrong but who are nonetheless mentally defective may be held responsible for their crimes. The less common and considerably broader Durham-type rule insures that mentally defective persons will less likely be held responsible for their crimes. However, its broadness means that it is open to pretenders. One's choice in the matter rests with one's priorities: a legal net so tight that it catches all who enter it, both guilty and not guilty—or a net so loose that some guilty escape along with those who are not guilty.

The insanity plea dilemma illustrates the complexity of crime-related issues in our society. As noted above, the problem does not involve large numbers of offenders. Nonetheless, the public is concerned about it, and politicians find in it the opportunity to gain credibility as "crime fighters." Choice of formula in determining insanity may mean the difference in whether or not persons not guilty of crimes are punished as criminals. The choice is important, therefore, and should be exercised only after a critical review of the issue.

COMING CHAPTERS

Most responses to crime involve choices like the one just described. Given their possible negative consequences, we must avoid knee-jerk reactions to our "crime problem." We owe it to ourselves to formulate as accurate a picture of that problem as possible before structuring our lives (or allowing the government to structure them for us) in avoiding or attacking the problem. To this end, we will devote the coming chapters to assessments of major interest groups' involvement in shaping the dimensions of our "crime problem," the content and accuracy of public views on crime, statistical dimensions of crime, apparent offender and victim characteristics, causal explanations, and the role of the criminal justice system in producing and controlling crime.

REFERENCES

Bynum, T. S. 1982. Release on recognizance: Substantive or superficial reform? *Criminology* 20:67–82.

Empey, L. T., and M. L. Erickson. 1972. *The Provo Experiment: Evaluating Community Control of Delinquency*. Lexington, Mass.: D. C. Heath & Company.

Gallup, G. H. 1981a. *The Gallup Poll, March 1, 1981*. Princeton, N.J.: The Gallup Poll.

———. 1981b. *The Gallup Poll, January 22, 1981*. Princeton, N.J.: The Gallup Poll.

Inciardi, J. A. 1981. Marijuana decriminalization research: A perspective and commentary. *Criminology* 19:145–59.

Kelling, G., T. Pate, D. Dieckman, et al. 1974. *The Kansas City Preventive Patrol Experiment—A Summary Report*. Washington, D.C.: The Police Foundation.

New Orleans Times-Picayune/States-Item. 1982. Hinckley's plea would have had a hard time in Louisiana. June 23, sect. 1, 11.

Newsweek. 1982. The insanity plea on trial. May 24, 56–61.

New York Times. 1976. Couple, recently robbed, take their own lives, citing fear. October 7, sect. 1, 15.

Rossi, P. H., R. A. Berk, and K. J. Lenihan. 1980. *Money, Work, and Crime: Experimental Evidence*. New York: Academic Press.

———. 1982. Saying it wrong with figures: A comment on Zeisel. *Am. J. Sociol.* 88:390—93.

Selke, W. L. 1982. Diversion and crime prevention: A time-series analysis. *Criminology* 20:395–406.

Sheley, J., and S. Nock. 1982. Deinstitutional efforts in Louisiana. In *Neither Angels Nor Thieves: Studies in Deinstitutionalization of Status Offenders*. Edited by J. Handler and J. Zatz. Washington, D.C.: National Academy Press.

Zeisel, H. 1982. Disagreement over the evaluation of a controlled experiment. *Am. J. Sociol.* 88:378–89.

SUGGESTED READINGS

A picture of what criminologists currently seem to be doing can be gained by looking through recent issues of journals such as *Criminology, Journal of Research in Crime and Delinquency, The Journal of Criminal Law and Criminology*, and *Law and Society Review*. An examination of some more traditional texts is also helpful: Sutherland and Cressey's *Criminology*, 10th ed. (Philadelphia: J. B. Lippincott Co., 1978), and D. C. Gibbons, *Society, Crime, and Criminal Careers*, 3rd ed. (Englewood Cliffs, N.J.: Prentice-Hall, 1977). Just as important are critiques of mainstream criminology, such as *The New Criminology* (New York: Harper & Row, Publishers, 1973) by Taylor, Walton, and Young.

PART I

STRUCTURING A "CRIME PROBLEM"

Both individually and collectively, people address social problems according to what they *think* they know about them. But, as we shall see, there are great dangers in many of today's "gut reactions" to crime. Chapters 2 and 3 examine some of the forces that shape our view of crime in this society and our ideas about how to fight it.

2

CRIME FEARS

The fact that most persons would answer in the affirmative when asked whether or not crime is a serious problem for this society should surprise no one. Americans nearly always have felt threatened by immorality, deviance, and crime; however, never so much as during the past fifteen years. This chapter analyzes concern about crime as a "social problem" and explores the shape, sources, and costs of the public's fear of crime and its influence on criminal justice policy. Fear of crime is more complicated than it appears at first glance.

DEFINING SOCIAL PROBLEMS

What are "social problems"? They are social phenomena that, at base, people perceive as threats to society. That is, social conditions become "problems" for society when significant numbers of people define them as such.

The definition of a situation as a social problem—whether crime, drug abuse, alcoholism, or any of a seemingly endless list of potential social maladies—generally does not occur overnight. It begins with an alarm sounded by a few, is then given coverage by the mass media, and finally creates widespread public concern and elicits governmental attention. Whether or not the perception of the problem moves beyond the alarm sounded by the initial few depends greatly on the social identity and legitimacy of those few. Doomsday prophets, for example, do not gain the public's attention as easily as do scientists, religious leaders, legislators, or government administrators. The development of the problem depends as well on the crusaders' organizational abilities to lobby key government figures, to employ the media in their behalf, and to construct and publicize stereotypical cases of the "problem" and vocabularies that catch the public's fancy. Much of this process of defining social problems for the public is governed by the political struggles of various interest groups in this society. This theme is pursued in detail in Chapter 3.

If we understand that social problems are socially constructed, then we can also see that perceptions of situations as threatening or harmless may or may not be accurate. For instance, with hindsight we can see that some very real dangers, such as early deaths of chemical plant workers due to chemically induced cancer, were not recognized as social problems when they first occurred. By contrast, other situations once considered threatening, such as the "witches" of colonial Salem or the 1950s "Red scare," now can be viewed as having been considerably less harmful than they seemed when they were frightening people. In any case, whether correctly or incorrectly diagnosed, a situation defined as a social problem precipitates alarm, fear, and demands for solutions.

CRIME AS A SOCIAL PROBLEM

Crime currently is defined as particularly threatening by the majority of Americans. Although there is little consensus among experts about *objective* measures of social threat from crime—that is, agreement as to how many crimes really constitute a danger for society—there is a great deal of public consensus that life in America is hampered by fear of crime (Garofalo, 1977:70). During the past decade numerous surveys have found crime consistently rated as a major concern in most communities (Flanagan et al., 1982:177–189; Garofalo, 1977:17–23; Hindelang et al., 1977:4). A 1973 survey of New York City residents, for instance, reported that crime was considered *the* most threatening of nineteen social problems (*New York Times,* 1974). In 1977 and 1978, 70 percent of this nation's urban residents rated crime as severe a problem as drugs, unemployment, housing, and medical care (U.S. Department of HUD, 1978). In 1981, between 58 and 68 percent of the U.S. population viewed crime as increasing in their areas of residence (Harris, 1981; *Newsweek,* 1981). Forty-five percent of the respondents of one national survey feared walking alone at night; 16 percent felt unsafe in their own homes at night (Gallup, 1981a). One in four persons expressed a concern about being robbed, and one in six worried about becoming a murder victim (Research and Forecasts, Inc., 1980).

Crime fears are higher in larger cities than in smaller ones. Within cities, fear of crime among whites is related to level of property crime rates and the proportion of whites who are victimized by nonwhites. Nonwhites' fear of crime varies as city size, segregation level, and proportion of nonwhites in the city increase (Liska et al., 1982). Overall, females report higher levels of crime fear than do males, and nonwhites display higher levels than do whites. Crime fear is greater among lower than among higher income groups (Alderman et al., 1981; Gallup, 1979; Research and Forecasts, Inc., 1980).

In general, crimes that appear to concern the public the most are the eight crimes the yearly *Uniform Crime Reports* by the Federal Bureau of Investigation (1982) label the *Index Crimes*. They are:

1. Homicide
2. Aggravated assault
3. Forcible rape
4. Robbery
5. Burglary
6. Larceny
7. Motor vehicle theft
8. Arson

On the one hand, fear of such crimes reflects a natural human desire to be safe from attack on one's person or property (Nettler, 1974:3). On the other hand, the fact that the FBI reports detailed information for these offenses only—and we have displayed them prominently above because we will return to this list in coming chapters—helps structure the form of crime concern within this society. Why these crimes and not others? Larceny (theft), for example, touches fewer victims and entails lower losses than does Medicare fraud (not an Index crime). Notably, arson is a newcomer to the list of Index crimes, first appearing in 1979. It is a crime which causes greater property losses than do any other property crimes in the Index. Its incidence has increased dramatically since the mid-1960s. But the national public and governmental response to arson has been low-key (Garofalo, 1977:38). Only firefighters' associations and activist groups in such burned-out cities as New York and Boston have pushed for tougher anti-arson legislation (Brady, 1982). One means to legitimize that push is to draw public attention to the crime. Its inclusion among the Index crimes serves this function. Reported along with other "major" crimes, it becomes, by definition, a major crime. In short, the crimes we fear seemingly are frightening crimes. Ours is an understandable concern. Yet, it is also a concern that is shaped by organized segments of the public.

Whether natural or cultivated, crime fear is, at base, a fear of "street crimes," especially of violent attacks with weapons while one is out at night. More than a decade ago, a special President's Commission on Law Enforcement and Administration of Justice suggested that current fear of crime is essentially a fear of strangers (President's Commission, 1967a:50). The public tends to view criminals as a special class of people who live outside of law-abiding neighborhoods and communities and enter them to commit crimes.

Most major crime today is attributable, the public believes, to a relatively small number of hardened criminals—villainous public enemies who necessitate a "war on crime" or, more precisely, a "war on criminals." Interestingly, these offenders also are seen as products of environmental and developmental deficiencies, such as bad companions and poor family supervision (Gallup, 1981b; *Newsweek*, 1981:47), though this aspect generally is downplayed in the public mind. Whatever its causes, once criminality is achieved, the public considers it a permanent individual condition. As we shall see shortly, this view greatly colors responses to the "crime problem."

THREE SOURCES OF PUBLIC CONCERN

The way people think and act stems partly from their own experiences and partly from others' accounts of experiences that may be transmitted, for example, through politicians campaigning for office or through the mass media independent of the political campaign. Let us examine these sources.

Personal Experience

The relation of personal experience to crime fear is difficult to ascertain. We gain some sense of the average household's chances of having a member become a crime victim in a given year by reviewing the information in Figure 2–1. These data are presented along with those concerning other forms of negative life events in order to put crime victimization chances into some perspective (U.S. Department of Justice, 1982a:3). An important caveat is necessary here. None of the types of events reported here is distributed equally among U.S. households. That is, not every household has the same chance of falling victim to these events. Therefore, the chance that the average person (in the true as opposed to statistical sense) will experience any given type of event listed in Figure 2–1 is exaggerated in the illustration.

The data in Figure 2–1 quickly make clear that homicide, the most feared of crimes, represents far less a problem for the average citizen than do most other of the event-types enumerated in the figure. Robbery and rape likewise touch relatively few homes. But the data also indicate that crime, especially property crime, occurs much more frequently than do the other negative events. Seven percent of American households experience a burglary, for example, while less than 2 percent house a victim of heart disease. Further, when burglaries are combined with rapes, robberies, and assaults by strangers—"high concern crimes"—it appears that about one in ten households contain victimized members. Again, it is important to note that these percentages do not reflect an equal distribution of crime across households. But the percentages are sufficiently high to enable average citizens understandably to imagine themselves as crime victims, or to know a victim of a crime.

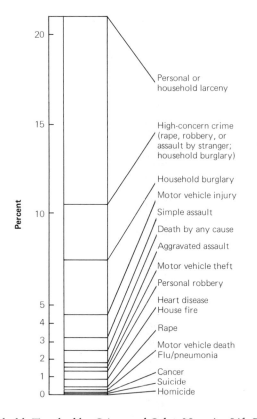

FIGURE 2–1
Percent of Households Touched by Crime and Other Negative Life Events in a Year
(Source: U.S. Department of Justice, *Bureau of Justice Statistics Bulletin:
Households Touched by Crime, 1981.* Washington, D.C.: Bureau of Justice
Statistics).

Are those victimization chances the primary determinant of crime fears?
Perhaps not. Research has indicated generally that an individual's personally
witnessing a crime, being the victim of a crime, or having an acquaintance
who was victimized is unrelated to fear of crime. Garofalo (1977:34–58) reports, for example, that crime victims differ little from non-victims in perceptions of crime trends, chances of being attacked or robbed, and fear of
walking alone in one's neighborhood during the day or night (see also Bid-
ermen et al., 1967). Reports suggest that most people, even those living
in high crime areas, view their own neighborhoods as safe as or safer than
other neighborhoods (President's Commission, 1967b:87–88; Garofalo,
1977:68). These results suggest that even objectively measurable danger may
not influence attitudes toward crime. Further, victimization surveys consistently indicate that crime fears seem disproportionate to victimization rates
(DuBow et al., 1979).

Somewhat skeptical, Balkin (1979) argues that studies of the type which measure danger in terms of crime rates computed from police reports or victimization surveys underestimate danger. He contends that an actual high victimization rate may cause a high level of crime fear which in turn influences people to limit their exposure to potential situations of victimization (by locking themselves in their homes, for example). Thus, the victimization rate decreases but the fear does not, making people seem needlessly afraid when victimization rates are low.

Balkin's thesis necessitates some caution regarding the link between fear and personal experience (victimization or threat of victimization). Nonetheless, victimization survey results suggest that victims may soon forget their victimization. Recall of even major victimizations (assault, larceny, burglary, robbery) decreases rapidly over the course of a year. Eighty-five percent of crime victims recall the crime after three months, 77 percent after six months, and 63 percent after a year (Dodge, 1981; Murphy and Dodge, 1981; Turner, 1981). Details become fuzzy within a year: date of the crime, characteristics of offenders, extent of injuries and losses. People tend to "telescope" crime events; that is, they remember them as having occurred more recently than is in fact the case. One in four burglary, robbery, and assault victims "telescopes" in this manner (Dodge, 1981). One study reports that when asked to recall the worst crime they had ever experienced, 79 percent of the respondents said it had occurred during the past five years, 60 percent within the past two years, and 50 percent within the previous eighteen months (President's Commission, 1967b:86–87). However, statistical probabilities indicate the chances are slim that this is when they actually happened, which suggests that even serious crimes committed against us do not shape our attitudes for a long time. Perhaps political campaigns and the mass media are more important than personal experience in generating public concern about crime.

Political Campaigns

The presidential election year of 1968 fostered many slogans about "law and order," "war on crime," and "safe streets," and public concern about crime consequently became particularly noticeable. It is misleading to suggest that a political campaign manufactured our "crime problem." However, American political campaigns search out issues that reflect public and media attention, and otherwise legitimize them. Edelman (1964:172) writes:

> [M]ass publics respond to currently conspicuous political symbols: not to "facts," and not to moral codes embedded in the character or soul, but to gestures and speeches that make up the drama of the state.
>   . . . [Thus] the mass public does not study and analyze detailed data about [social problems]. It ignores these things until political actions and speeches make them symbolically threatening or reassuring, and it then responds to the

cues furnished by the actions and the speeches, not to direct knowledge of the facts.

It is therefore political actions that chiefly shape men's political wants and "knowledge," not the other way around.

If crime was not a true social problem before the 1968 campaigns, it certainly was one during and after them. The 1968 anticrime platforms continue to inspire politicians. As Conklin (1975:25) points out, promises to reestablish law and order and to make streets safe are especially effective in mobilizing political support for a candidate, for crime arouses deep-seated fears for personal safety and for the preservation of the social order. Part of a speech by President Ronald Reagan (*New York Times,* 1981a) illustrates the point:

> It's time for honest talk, for plain talk. There has been a breakdown in the criminal justice system in America. It just plain isn't working. All too often repeat offenders, habitual lawbreakers, career criminals, call them what you will, are robbing, raping, and beating with impunity and, as I said, quite literally getting away with murder. The people are sickened and outraged. They demand that we put a stop to it.

Mr. Reagan's remarks were not novel, as evidenced by quotes from two former presidents that appeared in the *New York Times* (1981b):

> As murder is on the increase so are all offenses of the felony class, and there can be no doubt that they will continue to increase unless the criminal laws are enforced with more certainty, more uniformity, more severity than they now are. I presume it is useless to expect that courts will turn from their present tendency to amplify technicalities in behalf of defendants until legislatures shall initiate the change.
>
> William Howard Taft, 1905

> It is time for some honest talk about the problem of order in the United States. Let us always respect our courts and those who serve on them. But let us also recognize that some of our courts in their decisions have gone too far in weakening the peace forces as against the criminal forces and we must act to restore that balance. I pledge to you that our attorney general will be directed to launch a war against organized crime in this nation.
>
> Richard M. Nixon, 1968

Crime seems the most enduring issue yet discovered by policitians.

The Media

Like political campaigns, the media respond to and stimulate fears of crime, and are therefore probably the single greatest influence on public attitudes about the topic. Basically, control of information to the public represents, in many ways, control of the public, since people structure much of their views of the world around media information and crime dramatization. Gerbner and Gross (1976) argue, for example, that the entirety of television programming (not news alone, nor drama alone, and so forth) must be viewed as a system of messages which cultivates a given world view.

The media tend to influence public perceptions of crime in three important ways: (1) by making it a national problem, (2) by selectively reporting crime news to the public, and (3) by perpetuating criminal stereotypes in the entertainment media. Let us discuss each of these.

1. Crime as a National Problem. Once primarily a community problem, crime only recently has become a matter of national concern—that is, defined by the public as a nationwide problem. The shift in concern from community to society has meant that rural, as well as urban, areas have been included among those communities with "crime problems." Mass communications networks are especially implicated in this shift. News once was slow-traveling; word of Abraham Lincoln's death, for example, did not reach many people in the western states for weeks. John F. Kennedy's assassination, however, was news within minutes. His brother Robert's killing was broadcast practically as it occurred. The graphic pictures of the attempt on Ronald Reagan's life in 1981 were unprecedented. Crimes of all kinds now gain national interest by being televised to nearly all members of society simultaneously. In the mid-1970s, the Watergate coverup crimes and the exploits of Patty Hearst and the Symbionese Liberation Army were daily news. National news bulletins concerning hostage situations are common today. Everyone receives much the same details of a crime. Everyone is afforded the same chill when a gruesome crime occurs.

As mass communications increasingly "shrink the globe," those in relatively crime-free areas become involved in and identify with the drama of crime as never before. On-the-spot coverage has shown, for example, that participants in a crime situation, especially victims and witnesses, usually are ordinary people rather than a strange breed of city dweller. All this has transformed what once may have been community problems (for example, routine vandalism) into one major problem—a national trend toward lawlessness. In other words, what once were small, isolated problems now are perceived as being interrelated symptoms of a larger crime problem.

2. Selective Crime News Coverage. The news media often are accused of distorting the picture of crime in America. Critics contend that the media select crime news items primarily on the basis of their sensationalistic features. Actually, one study (Roshier, 1973:34–35) reports that the factors influencing crime news selection are the seriousness of the offense, whimsical or unusual elements connected with it, sentimental or dramatic elements of it, and the involvement of famous or high-status persons in any aspect of it. Some argue that the more trivial the motive for a crime, the more likely its inclusion in the news. Sutherland and Cressey (1974:246) contend that "crime waves" generally are fabricated by the press. A sensationalistic crime occurs, receives coverage in one community, and before long editors in other communities begin giving attention to hitherto unnoticed similar crimes.

Although the news media do not ignore the question of their obligations to the public, neither do they grant these obligations the same importance as "selling news." As business enterprises, the media cannot devote their energies to discerning and communicating a *representative* picture of crime to the public. Thus, representative crime—that is, property and white collar offenses—is not the "news" the public receives. Nor does the government consciously attempt to persuade or employ the news media to present a full picture of crime in America. Instead, the government generally restricts itself to offering data on a few selected offenses, primarily violent crimes and a few property crimes, and leaves presentation of the data to the media.

Because the media are relatively free to pursue and report most aspects of crime, a "crime wave" may be perpetuated or diminished in line with the manner in which the media choose to cover the subject. Fishman (1978) makes precisely this point in his analysis of a crime wave against the elderly in New York City in 1976. The city's newspapers and television stations reported increases in acts of violence against elderly citizens. National media soon picked up the story. The crime reports outraged the public and caused some reorganization of criminal justice services. And yet, Fishman notes, crime rose no more for the elderly in 1976 than for other age categories. In his view, the crime wave occurred when news reporters became aware of a few crimes against the elderly and began to search for and to highlight such crimes. Ironically, the major source of crime news for reporters is the police wire service that signals reporters only about certain sensational offenses, crimes in which the police have an interest, or types of crime about which reporters have expressed an interest.

Thus, the news of crime we receive from the media is anything but representative. Indeed, numerous studies report disproportionately high coverage of violent offenses by the news media and an overrepresentation of older and higher-status offenders in their stories (Antunes and Hurley, 1977: Graber, 1980; Jones, 1976; Sheley and Ashkins, 1981).

Does news media coverage actually influence public views of crime? In an often-cited article written thirty years ago, F. James Davis (1952) presented evidence indicating that official crime rates and crime news coverage are unrelated, and that the public's conception of crime more accurately reflects the picture of crime presented in the newspapers. Garofalo (1977:42) reports that 86 percent of the residents of eight major cities feel crime is as serious as, if not more serious than, its presentation in the news media. Countering the influence implied in these findings, Warr (1980, 1982) reports considerable accuracy in public estimates of the number of offenses reported to the police, the percentage of juveniles committing offenses, and the sex ratio among juvenile offenders. He concludes that the media must be offering more accurate assessments of crime incidence than is often suspected, and that the public retains this knowledge. Yet, Warr's thesis flies in the face of the evidence cited above, which points to substantial crime picture distortion by the media.

In addressing the problem of media influence on crime views more systematically than other researchers, Graber (1980) reports that public estimates of offender age reflect estimates based on official statistics more than that provided by newspapers. Public estimates of offender occupation more closely approximate the newspaper image. Estimates of gender and race distribution among offenders differ from both official statistics and newspaper accounts. Similarly, public images of the sex and race of crime victims differ from the images found in newspapers and victimization surveys. Public images of the victim's age are similar to the image provided by newspapers.

A comparison of New Orleans official crime statistics, television and newspaper crime stories, and public attitudes regarding crime trends, the relative frequency of occurrence of Index crimes, and the characteristics of offenders during a three-month period (Sheley and Ashkins, 1981) indicates that:

1. The public felt that crime increased over time though the media and official statistics showed no change.
2. There was no agreement among official statistics, television and newspaper reports, and public estimates regarding the relative frequency of offenses, though the correlation between the public's view and that presented by the newspapers narrowly missed statistical significance.
3. Few differences existed among the various images of the race and sex characteristics of offenders, but public views of offender's age better reflect the image supplied by official statistics than that presented in the media.

In sum, the evidence concerning the relation between the media portrayed and public images of crime is inconsistent. The strongest of links appears to be between newspaper reports and public views. Television news reports do not seem to influence public estimates of crime trends, crime frequency, and offender characteristics. Considerable research remains to be done, not only regarding the influence of the media but also concerning the interaction of the media with other sources of information used by the public to develop a picture of crime (Graber, 1980; Warr, 1982).

3. *Media Stereotypes of Crime and Criminals.* Crime-related shows constitute as much as one-third of television entertainment offerings (Dominick, 1978). There is much discussion about the extent to which the entertainment media promote violence or, at least, promote indifference to violence. Yet, less is written concerning how these media shape public attitudes about the amounts and types of crime in this society.

If the public *is* influenced by the entertainment media, it is clearly in the wrong direction. Research indicates that the least committed offenses (violent crimes such as murder and assault) appear most often in television dramas, but that property crime (burglary and larceny) receives little coverage though it constitutes the bulk of real-life crime (Dominick, 1978; Barrile, 1980). In addition, violent crimes as portrayed on television generally are pictured as resulting from greed or attempts to avoid detection for offenses, whereas most violent crimes in our society are crimes of passion committed during arguments (Barrile, 1980). The racial, age, and socioeconomic characteristics of criminals and victims also are distorted. Victimization of poor blacks (common in real life), for example, rarely is seen in television dramas. In television, white middle-class offenders over thirty years of age prey upon victims of the same background—a rare occurrence (Barrile, 1980; Dominick, 1973; Pandiani, 1978). Finally, television shows also exaggerate the necessary use of violence in police work and seemingly sanction the use of illegal police tactics (Arons and Katsh, 1977). Television's police officers and detectives are unfettered by procedural law and nearly always capture the "bad guys," usually in violent confrontation (Barille, 1980; Culver and Knight, 1979).

Firm documentation of television crime dramas' influence on public attitudes about crime remains to be developed. Gerbner and co-researchers (1976, 1978, 1979) posit an influence based on the cultivation of a "television world view" among those who view television programs regularly. Their research indicates that "heavy" television viewers tend to respond to questions about crime and violence in a manner more in line with television portrayals than do "light" viewers of television. Yet, Teevan and Hartnagel (1976) report only mixed results in a similar investigation. It seems plausible that some segments of the population—for instance, the aged, the very young, recent immigrants—would be more susceptible to the influence of television's crime shows. Yet, more research in this area clearly is necessary before this assertion can be accepted uncritically.

THE COST OF CRIME FEARS

Whatever their causes, public fears about crime have three major types of detrimental consequences: personal, social, and economic.

Personal Consequences: Withdrawal and Retreat

Whether based on fact or fiction, fear of crime colors the thoughts and actions of many Americans, and most responses to this fear involve some form of social withdrawal. One recent national survey indicates that 64 pecent of the American public try to remain off the streets at night for fear of criminal attacks (*Newsweek, 1981*). Excluding family constraints and economic problems, crime fear is given as the major reason people choose to go out less (Garofalo, 1977:84). One of every four people takes something along—a dog, a weapon, a whistle—when out at night. One in three takes along another person (Research and Forecasts, Inc., 1980). Within the home, 51 percent have installed extra locks to fight crime; 15 percent use burglar alarms; and 8 percent have barred at least some windows. Forty-four percent of the public keep a dog for protection (*Newsweek, 1981*). Between 43 and 52 percent keep guns in the house for protection (Cambridge Reports, Inc., 1978; Research and Forecasts, Inc., 1980).

The ultimate response to fear is actual retreat. The most often-cited reason by urban dwellers for desiring to move from one's home is fear of crime. Twenty-four percent of urban residents and 30 percent of central city residents would move to avoid crime if they had the opportunity (Gallup, 1981c).

Social Consequences: Erosion of Solidarity

Emile Durkheim (1933) and G. H. Mead (1918) postulated that crime may unite and strengthen a community as its members come together to counter the lawbreaker's actions (see Chapter 3). Yet, crime which continues over time may have more negative consequences. As mentioned earlier, fear of crime is primarily a fear of strangers, which results in suspicion, withdrawal, and a weakening of societal unity and informal mechanisms of social control. Conklin (1971, 1975) reports that perceptions of high crime levels are related to low levels of interpersonal trust of others and general satisfaction with one's community. Hartnagel (1979) finds perception and fear of crime in a Canadian city negatively related to general satisfaction with neighborhood and city, and unrelated to relationship with neighbors and to social activity.

To the extent crime breaks down social solidarity, *more* crime may be created. Retreat from strangers to avoid victimization represents a breakdown in interaction among people and a breakdown in citizens' informal surveillance and correction of potential offenders. When people desert the streets and become aloof and indifferent to the plights of others as they try to seal themselves off from crime, they actually may make the streets *safer* for criminals, who are then relatively free to attack the people who venture out. Cohen and co-researchers (1979, 1980, 1981) report that extent of "guardianship" by ordinary citizens of one another and of property as they go about routine activities is a key to predicting crime rates. They note that a "decrease in the density of population in physical locations occupied by persons having primary-group relationships" increases the risk of crime within those physical locations (Cohen et al., 1980:91; see also Washnis, 1976). Thus, we observe a possible self-fulfilling prophecy: fear of crime that, as suggested above, may not be wholly realistic may produce the very situation that makes it realistic.

Economic Consequences: Billions of Dollars

Millions of dollars are spent each year on private security guards for homes and businesses (that pass the costs on to consumers). Theft insurance, burglar alarms, and other security systems and devices cost millions more (Clotfelter and Seeley, 1979). While it is difficult to ascertain how many guns people buy annually for self-protection, they no doubt cost further millions of dollars. It is equally difficult to estimate how much communities with a so-called "crime problem" lose when new industries decide to avoid them, but here again, millions, perhaps billions, of dollars are involved.

Despite these costs (perhaps seeking to alleviate them), the public is willing to devote a large share of its tax dollars to fight crime. Indeed, 74 percent of the American public desire *increases* in federal spending to fight crime (Alderman et al., 1981). Government legislators and administrators apparently listen—whether in agreement as to the necessity of spending, in vote-seeking efforts, or in response to interested parties such as weapons manufacturers and police and prosecutors' associations. In terms of lobbying efforts, Quinney (1980:126–138) notes the growth of what he terms the "criminal justice-industrial complex." He argues that in recent years crime-fighting has become big business as the demand for such modern police "necessities" as computers, radio systems, helicopters, surveillance devices, antiriot equipment, and sophisticated weaponry has increased (President's Commission, 1967c). Much of the cost of developing this new technology has been borne by the taxpayer through the Law Enforcement Assistance Administration (LEAA), a federal agency founded in response to the first major public fears about crime in the late 1960s. Operating from 1969 to 1980, LEAA spent $7.7 billion.

LEAA no longer exists. Yet, the 1982 federal budget for reorganized assistance to local justice systems remains high—$128 million (U.S. Department of Justice, 1982b:1). Federal, state, and local government statistics indicate that 1,275,031 persons are employed in criminal justice system jobs, a 37 percent increase over the number employed in 1971. In 1971, federal, state, and local governments spent $10.5 billion in criminal justice activities. In 1975, the figure was $17.2 billion. Four years later, 1979, spending reached $28 billion (U.S. Department of Justice, 1981a). Figure 2–2 displays the distribution of 1979 criminal justice spending across governmental levels and by types of expenditure. Police services consume the greater part of the dollar at the federal and local levels. Corrections programs account for the

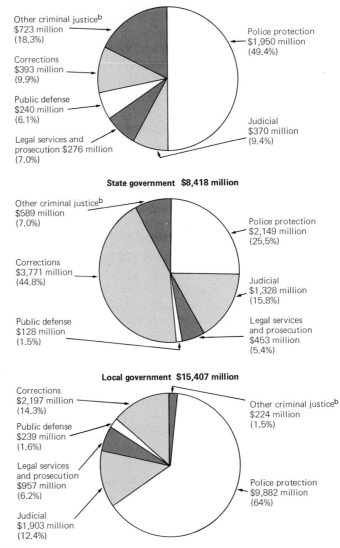

Federal government $3,951 million[a]

Other criminal justice[b] $723 million (18.3%)

Corrections $393 million (9.9%)

Public defense $240 million (6.1%)

Legal services and prosecution $276 million (7.0%)

Police protection $1,950 million (49.4%)

Judicial $370 million (9.4%)

State government $8,418 million

Other criminal justice[b] $589 million (7.0%)

Corrections $3,771 million (44.8%)

Public defense $128 million (1.5%)

Police protection $2,149 million (25.5%)

Judicial $1,328 million (15.8%)

Legal services and prosecution $453 million (5.4%)

Local government $15,407 million

Corrections $2,197 million (14.3%)

Public defense $239 million (1.6%)

Legal services and prosecution $957 million (6.2%)

Judicial $1,903 million (12.4%)

Other criminal justice[b] $224 million (1.5%)

Police protection $9,882 million (64%)

FIGURE 2–2

Expenditures for Criminal Justice Activities, by Type of Activity and Level of Government, United States, Fiscal Year 1979

[a]Because of approximating, detail does not add to total.

[b]Other = educational spending, crime commissions, and so forth.

(Source: Flanagan, T. J., D. J. van Alstyne, M. R. Gottfredson. 1982. *Sourcebook of Criminal Justice Statistics—1981*. Washington, D.C.: U.S. Government Printing Office).

major spending at the state level. State expenditures generally are related to state population size. California and New York thus spend the most. The smallest spender is Vermont (U.S. Department of Justice, 1981a). Obviously, public fear of crime has expensive consequences.

RESPONSES TO CRIME: PRESSURES ON LEGISLATURES AND CRIMINAL JUSTICE SYSTEMS

The public response to crime fears is focused on criminals, not on the causes of crime. This response reflects peoples' frustration with alleged "liberal coddling" of criminals and the seeming inability of scholars and scientists to find "cures" for the crime problem. As a result, the public has developed a "lock'em up" philosophy, feeling crime can be combatted best by isolating for extended lengths of time those "few hardened criminals who commit most of the serious crimes in this society."

State legislatures respond to these ideas by passing bills designed to make control of criminals easier: lengthening prison sentences, eliminating parole for some offenses, and developing "multiple billing" procedures so that sentences of repeat offenders may be doubled or tripled (see Chapter 12). At present, some social critics are concerned that America is overreacting to the "crime problem." They argue that before truly drastic measures are considered, there must be much research into the nature of the crime problem and the potential effectiveness of crime prevention measures (for example, see Pearl, 1977). As in television westerns in which the new sheriff rids the town of hoodlums and then himself becomes a dictator, solutions to problems sometimes cause more damage than the problems themselves. Often the damage is irreparable; once a solution is implemented, it may be impossible to offset its undesirable effects. An inaccurate picture of crime or a poorly researched "remedy" may go beyond wasting tax dollars. It may also vastly alter individual rights.

LIMITING CIVIL LIBERTIES

One way to deal with crime is to restrict public freedom of movement in order to limit the opportunities for criminal behavior. Curfews may be instituted, certain areas placed off limits, prominently displayed identification required, and homes and persons routinely searched. The precedent for such measures exists in the concept of martial law—that is, rule by the military and suspension of civil liberties when civil authority fails. The implementing of such radical techniques may occur when the public (or, more precisely, its representatives) perceive crime as being wholly beyond normal means of control. In the United States at present, however, the situation is not perceived as being so desperate that it requires such drastic measures.

NEWSPRINT AND COMMENT

Doctors Threaten to Cancel Meeting, Say [New Orleans] Isn't Safe

By Walt Philbin

A national association of dermatologists, upset by what it calls excessive street crime during a recent convention in New Orleans, says it will cancel a 1986 convention planned for here unless the safety of its members and guests is guaranteed by the city.

The American Academy of Dermatology said inadequate lighting and police protection around river-area hotels and the Rivergate Convention Center were partially responsible for several crimes committed against academy members and their guests during the group's Dec. 4–9 convention attended by 9,537 dermatologists, and spouses and guests.

During the convention the academy voted to cancel its 1986 convention and all future conventions here unless the city guarantees it will:

"1. Maintain full lighting in the walking corridors between the Marriott and the Hilton hotels to include the River Exhibition Center.

"2. Maintain greater police protection until 2 a.m."

Many of the group's convention activities last until 1 a.m., a spokesman said.

The executive director of the dermatology academy said he also will file a copy of the group's resolution with the Professional Convention Management Association, a clearinghouse used by medical and health-related associations in choosing convention sites.

Bradford Claxton, executive director of the dermatology academy, said most of the street lights in the Rivergate area went off just after midnight during the first few nights of the convention.

James Prigmore, director of the city's Department of Utilities, confirmed that the lights went off just after midnight in a two- or three-block area near the Rivergate, partly to save energy. He said that, since the complaint, the lights are left on until 2 a.m.

Claxton said there were at least eight crimes committed against people attending the convention. He said they included one armed robbery, two attempted holdups, purse snatchings, and theft of jewelry from a hotel room.

New Orleans police said only three crimes were reported. Claxton said he does not know why the other crimes were not reported.

The motion to cancel plans to hold its 1986 convention in New Orleans was made by Dr. Theodore Tromovitch of San Francisco on Dec. 6.

Tromovitch reported to police an armed robbery attempt on him and his wife.

A copy of the resolution was included in a Dec. 16 letter from Claxton to Ed McNeil, executive vice president of the tourist commission.

According to the letter, this "extraordinary action was taken following a series of incidents that included attempted robbery at gunpoint, assorted robberies (pickpocketings and purse snatchings) in elevators and lobbies of the Hilton, Marriott and Sheraton hotels, accostments and street harassments between the headquarters hotels (Hilton and Marriott) and the Rivergate exhibition center, French Quarter and adjacent areas."

Claxton said that, after receiving the copy of the Dec. 6 resolution, McNeil contacted city and police officials who increased police protection and street lighting for the rest of the convention.

However, Claxton said, even with these precautions there were still reports of street crime.

McNeil said many things are being done to alleviate the problem.

He said Police Superintendent Henry Morris recently added 10 officers to the 1st Police District, which includes the Rivergate hotel area.

Lt. Forest Craig, assistant commander of the 1st District, said he and other police officials attended the Dec. 6 session at which Tromovitch's motion was approved.

He said one police car normally patrols streets near the Rivergate-area hotels between 11 p.m. and 6 a.m. This patrol is paid for by the hotels, he said.

After the complaint, Craig said, a second police car and two or three mounted policemen were assigned to the area.

Tom Hewitt, general manager of the Sheraton, said he thinks the situation "was unfortunate but that steps are being taken in the right direction to remedy it."

Tom Vincent, general manager of the Marriott, said he is leaving for Chicago Thursday for the Joint Conference on Medical Conventions and will try to convince people there that New Orleans is doing something to correct the problem. "There are all kinds of stories going around now since this dermatology convention," he said.

Source: © Times-Picayune Publishing Corp., 1983. Reprinted by permission.

Comment: The Costs of Crime Perceptions

The economic well-being of many of our major cities has much to do with crime. This is not only in the sense that victims lose money to thieves and cities direct money toward crime control. Equally important to many cities is the impression outsiders have concerning the cities' crime levels. Perceived crime levels influence industries' decisions to locate in given areas; cities gain or lose jobs through such decisions. Perceived crime levels also influence tourists' decisions to visit cities like New Orleans, New York, and San Francisco. Such cities are highly image-conscious and very susceptible to pressure and threats from organized tourist interests.

Most of our major tourist cities have been subjected to bad press during the past decade. Miami, Houston, New Orleans, Los Angeles, San Francisco, New York, Boston, all have been characterized, usually unjustifiably, as cities that are unsafe for tourists. Each city breathes a sigh of relief when another grabs the negative spotlight. The damage done by such bad press is extremely difficult to overcome and generally forces cities to spend millions to recreate their images, though not necessarily to alter their actual crime levels.

Still, there are several examples of partial restriction of individual freedom designed to combat crime. Searches of boarding airline passengers and their baggage testify to the gravity with which we view airplane hijackings. Controversy over gun-control laws represents a debate over the seriousness of violent crime and the merits of preventing it through eliminating the freedom of private gun ownership. Both the hijacking precautions and the proposed firearms regulations reflect the sentiment that conventional prevention mechanisms cannot combat crime. In both cases, restriction of individual liberties is seen as being undesirable but necessary in order to regain control of the crime situation.

NARROWING PROCEDURAL RIGHTS

Measures that restrict the freedom of all citizens in order to curb the criminal behavior of a few generally are less acceptable than measures that apparently will affect only criminals and a few noncriminals. Hence, the demand for "law and order" often takes the form of proposals for altering those individual rights more directly linked to law enforcement and the administration of justice. To explore this theme, we first must examine criminal law and the public perception of it.

Criminal Law

Criminal law takes two forms, one clearly recognized by most people, the other less so. Substantive law defines acts (felonies and misdemeanors) that members of this society may not perform—for example, assault, use of heroin, corporate price fixing. Substantive law includes descriptions of specific penalties for violations. *Procedural law* governs actions of state officials in dealing with persons suspected or found guilty of criminal acts. This kind of law covers such phenomena as searches and arrests, the right to a fair and speedy trial, the right to counsel, admissibility of evidence, and the right to appeal. Through television crime shows, most people are familiar with at least one procedural law, the *Miranda* rule, whereby police must inform suspects of their legal rights at the time of the arrest. Generally, however, Americans are far less aware of and concerned about procedural than substantive law.

Law and Order

The oft-heard demand for "law and order" reflects society's current view of criminal law (see Skolnick, 1975:1–22). "Order" suggests control of law violations. The public, convinced that we are fast becoming a criminal society, is particularly concerned with such control. "Law" in this framework refers to substantive law that, it is argued, requires more stringent enforcement if crime is to be controlled. In addition to its dissatisfaction with substantive-law enforcement, the public—inspired by police and other agents of the criminal justice system—has come to view procedural law as being simply a set of "technicalities" that hinder law enforcement and encourage crime.

It is apparent there is an inherent tension between substantive and procedural law. *Substantive law* (the quest for order) strives for control of the population, but it is prevented from doing so completely by procedural law, or the rule of law, which traditionally in the United States has been placed above the enforcement of substantive law. Hence, total order is beyond reach, and perhaps the popular phrase "law and order" should read, "law or order" (or perhaps, "law and a degree of disorder"). We cannot presently have both total enforcement of substantive law and full protection of individual rights. Currently procedural law takes precedence, and until detection, prevention, and prosecution techniques are developed that work without violating individual rights, or until our priorities change, some apparent criminals indeed will go unpunished.

Eliminating "Technicalities"

Because laws, both substantive and procedural, are essentially social definitions of, or meanings given to, certain activities, they always are changeable.
Thus, what currently is not considered a right later may be defined as such.
Or current rights may be revoked or altered to become more liberal or more
conservative. In addition, many laws are not written clearly and therefore
constantly are open to changes in interpretation.

The way the public perceives a crime problem will affect how serious the
crime situation seems. Rights may be affirmed totally (no restrictions), liberally affirmed (limited restrictions), conservatively affirmed (major restrictions), or abolished. Because procedural law prevents substantive law from
being applied to every offender, it is theoretically possible that the crime
problem could become so uncontrollable that restriction of procedural law
might occur as a "necessary evil." Many now view crime as uncontrollable
and define procedural laws as "technicalities" that give criminals the freedom to violate the law without fear of punishment. However, because rights
are not easily reinstated once forfeited, it is important that two precautions,
described in detail in Chapter 1, take place. First, consideration of more conservative definitions of procedural rights must be acompanied by accurate information about the scope of our crime problem; and second, there must be
relative certainty that restriction of a particular right will accomplish its end
without undesirable side effects. Unfortunately, in the opinion of many experts, these precautions rarely are taken. Two examples will illustrate this
point.

Example 1: The Organized Crime Control Act of 1970. Organized
crime has been a source of major concern to the Justice Department since
early in this century. Most efforts to deal with the problem involve attempts
to jail major crime-syndicate figures, thereby depriving organized crime of its
leadership and deterring potential leaders from assuming control. Before
1970, Justice Department efforts in this direction had been stymied by the
refusals of underworld figures to divulge information when called before
grand juries. Claiming their Fifth Amendment right to withhold testimony
that might be self-incriminating, syndicate members had successfully
avoided being indicted or providing information about their colleagues. In
the minds of U.S. prosecutors, procedural law was hindering attempts to enforce substantive law. The important question was thus raised: Should procedural law be changed to deal with an apparent crime problem?

In 1970, the Justice Department, seeking a more efficient technique for
combatting organized crime, convinced Congress to pass the Organized
Crime Control Act (Public Law 91-452), which severely restricted the use of
the Fifth Amendment by grand jury witnesses (Cowan, 1973). In the 1960s,

prosecutors had developed the use of *transactional immunity* as a method of combatting organized crime. This form of immunity guaranteed freedom from all prosecution in return for testimony. Refusal to testify after the granting of immunity could result in a jail sentence. Transactional immunity was not widely used, however, because it appeared to most observers overly to compromise justice. The newer act of 1970 introduced the concept of *use immunity*, whereby witnesses might be granted immunity from prosecution on the basis of information they supplied the jury. However, immunity did not provide freedom from prosecution on the basis of evidence independent of the immune witnesses' testimony. Thus, members of organized crime were trapped: On the one hand, testimony did not automatically guarantee freedom from prison, though it did guarantee the wrath of other underworld figures; on the other hand, refusal to testify meant a jail sentence. The witness could be imprisoned for the duration of the grand jury proceedings or up to eighteen months. After release, the witness could immediately be recalled before the grand jury, granted immunity, and if he or she still refused to testify, be reimprisoned for up to eighteen months.

The example of the Organized Crime Control Act points up the urgent necessity for criminological research into the problem of crime control and procedural law. There has been considerable research into assessing the impact of organized crime in the U.S., though our knowledge is still undoubtedly superficial. The gathering of such information and, to some extent, its dissemination to legislative bodies and the public, are criminological problems. Whether the organized crime problem merits consideration of a restricted Fifth Amendment is a legislative-political problem, and, unfortunately, the extent to which such political decisions rely on criminological data is suspect.

If we assume for the moment that the organized crime problem is serious enough to require limitations on procedural rights, the next question is whether these limitations indeed can combat organized crime effectively. Before the Organized Crime Control Act was passed, no effort was made to determine systematically whether investigation and prosecution of crime-syndicate figures were actually hindered by an overly liberal definition of Fifth Amendment rights. While the Justice Department strategy was based on its experience with organized crime, there was no hard evidence that harassment of syndicate figures would alter significantly the impact of organized crime on this society. To date, there is no published research on the effects of the Organized Crime Control Act on syndicate activity since 1970. Though no easy task, this empirical question does seem researchable.

A final important problem that could and should have been addressed before the Organized Crime Control Act was enacted is the identification of possible less desirable effects that, if known, would have made the act less attractive to Congress. Again, no easy task, historical and comparative research into similar attempts at crime control might have addressed this problem. Critics contend that the Organized Crime Control Act was accompanied by at least one major drawback: It precipitated the use of the grand jury, originally developed to protect individuals from arbitrary state actions, as a Justice Department vehicle for gathering information about left-wing political activists of the early 1970s. Since grand-jury proceedings are less structured and controlled than trial proceedings, prosecutors simply subpoenaed witnesses, granted them immunity, and, under threat of citing them with contempt, attempted to coerce them to reveal information not pertinent to the alleged crime being investigated.

Only when such "fishing expeditions" began to occur did activists decry the new use of the grand jury. (Similarly, only when reporters were jailed for refusing to divulge news sources did editorials rail against the "misuse" of the grand jury.) Earlier, activists apparently had assumed the tactics developed in the Organized Crime Control Act would not be used against them, but against "crooks." Had the real facts been known, critics argue, the bill would not have been passed.

Ironically, the very same issue recently has surfaced in a slightly different guise. Following disclosures that the FBI had engaged in widespread domestic spying on persons belonging to various left- and right-wing political groups and civil rights organizations during the 1960s and 1970s, the Ford administration in 1976 created stringent guidelines concerning such spying. In 1983, the FBI under the Reagan administration revised these guidelines to make it easier for federal agents to investigate groups that attempt to "achieve political or social change" through violent tactics (*San Francisco Chronicle*, 1983a). The new guidelines permit federal agents to investigate statements advocating criminal activity or indicating "an apparent intent to engage in crime, particularly crimes of violence." Agents also are permitted to infiltrate political organizations in the preliminary stages of investigations of advocacy of violence (i.e., to gather evidence of violence advocacy rather than to keep tabs on persons already reasonably certain to be involved in violent activity).

According to the new guidelines, "a domestic security-terrorism investigation may be initiated when the facts or circumstances reasonably indicate that two or more persons are engaged in an enterprise for the purpose of furthering political or social goals wholly or in part through activities that involve force or violence and a violation of the criminal laws of the United States."

Critics contend that the new guidelines constrain First Amendment freedoms in the sense that mere advocacy of political violence as opposed to violent activity is grounds for government spying. They worry that the FBI will utilize very liberal definitions of *reasonable* suspicions and threaten political dissent (*San Francisco Chronicle*, 1983b). Yet, what the critics overlook is that the Justice Department has been using these same guidelines for several years in investigating suspected members of organized crime. Indeed, the new guidelines are defended by the FBI as an attempt to make uniform the standards for investigating general crimes, racketeering enterprises, and domestic security cases. As with the Organized Crime Control Act, no one objected to the earlier restriction of the First Amendment rights of "crooks." It is only when the government begins to apply the precedent established by that earlier restriction to the political arena that some citizens begin to understand how elastic is the label "crook."

Example Two: The Fourth Amendment and the Exclusionary Rule. Surely those who drafted the Fourth Amendment of the Bill of Rights could not have foreseen the turmoil surrounding the amendment in the 1980s. The Fourth Amendment states:

> The right of the people to be secure in their persons, houses, papers, and effects, against unreasonable searches and seizures, shall not be violated, and no warrants shall issue, but upon probable cause supported by oath or affirmation, and particularly describing the place to be searched, and the persons or things to be seized.

Most people support the Fourth Amendment in principle. No one wishes the government to conduct searches and seizures without sufficient cause and without guidelines. But people differ about how to make the Fourth Amendment work. In 1914, the U.S. Supreme Court in *Weeks* v. *United States* decided that federal law enforcement officials and prosecutors had been giving little thought to Fourth Amendment rights in the manner in which they accumulated evidence for prosecution. Thus, the Court created the *exclusionary rule,* which forbade the use in federal trials of evidence seized unconstitutionally by federal agents. In 1961, in *Mapp* v. *Ohio,* the Court extended the exclusionary rule to cover state court cases. It is important to note that the exclusionary rule not only forbids the use of illegally seized evidence in trials but also the use of any other evidence acquired as a result of the unconstitutionally developed evidence.

The thinking of the Supreme Court seems to be that without the exclusionary rule there is no way to enforce the provisions of the Fourth Amendment. Law enforcement officers cannot be trusted to obey the provisions of the Amendment to the letter without threat of penalty. This counters the "catch-the-bad-guys" spirit of law enforcement. Nor is it easy to prosecute officers who violate Fourth Amendment rights. They can argue that their unconstitutional behavior is the result of an honest mistake or accident, and it is unlikely that other police officers will contradict that claim. Thus, the Court has created a "necessary evil" in the exclusionary rule. It has sought compliance with the Fourth Amendment by placing police and prosecutors in a pressure situation. If they behave unconstitutionally, their cases will be jeopardized and perhaps lost. No public official can easily withstand such pressure. Beyond this, the Court has sought through the exclusionary rule to assure the public that there is no partnership between the judiciary and law enforcement officials in questions of unconstitutional behavior. The judiciary must show itself neutral (Kamisar, 1982).

Critics of the exclusionary rule argue that there is no evidence that the police will not obtain evidence illegally, despite the exclusionary rule, and then use that evidence to develop other evidence which can be disguised as "independently" obtained. They argue as well that evidence obtained through "good faith," unconstitutional means (that is, evidence obtained by officers who truly thought they were acting constitutionally) should be admissible in court—though "good faith" hardly makes an illegal search more constitutional. Finally, opponents claim that the costs of the exclusionary rule are too high: the truth-seeking process of the court is blocked and some persons who have committed crimes (provable by virtue of the excluded evidence) are set free.

Recently, the exclusionary rule issue has made good political copy. President Reagan has argued that the rule "rests on the absurd proposition that a law enforcement error, no matter how technical, can be used to justify throwing an entire case out of court, no matter how guilty the defendant or how heinous the crime" (U.S. Department of Justice, 1981b:1), and his anticrime task force has targeted the rule for modification to allow for "good faith" violations by police. Bills seeking to modify or abolish the exclusionary rule were brought before the Ninety-seventh Congress in 1982 and, having failed, are due for reintroduction in the Ninety-eighth Congress.

The Supreme Court, in two 1981 cases (*Robbins* v. *California* and *New York* v. *Belton;* for summaries see *U.S. Supreme Court Reports,* 1982), recently has narrowed the limits of the exclusionary rule. Both cases involved the use of evidence found in warrantless searches of cars and containers found in them after the occupants had been arrested for drug possession. Previously, the justices had ruled that warrantless searches could occur only in situations in which there was a legitimate fear on the part of an arresting officer that an arrestee could gain possession of a weapon or destroy evidence. In an effort to reduce ambiguity for police officers making arrests and searches of automobiles, the justices now have ruled that anything in the passenger area of a car (though not in the trunk) whether packaged or locked, whether visible or in a locked or unlocked glove compartment or console, always is able to be searched even if the arrestees are under police control to the extent that they could not gain possession of a weapon or destroy evidence.

In short, we see an assault on the exclusionary rule without an adequate substitute to enforce the Fourth Amendment. While many argue that police who violate the law in searches and seizures should be punished, no one has suggested an adequate means to accomplish punishment. The willingness to purge the exclusionary rule rests on the assumption that opening the door to police excesses is preferable to allowing criminals to go free on "technicalities." This in turn rests on the assumption that many criminals are, in fact, "cheating" the legal process through use of the exclusionary rule (Sachs, 1982).

The results of a U.S. General Accounting Office (GAO) study (1979) suggest that, as is often the case, critics of the exclusionary rule exaggerate the extent to which it turns criminals loose upon society. The GAO analyzed 2804 defendant cases handled from July 1 to August 31, 1978, in thirty-eight U.S. attorneys' offices. Its report indicates that search and seizure was an element in 30 percent of the cases studied. Only in one-third of these cases—11 percent of the 2804 cases—was a motion filed to suppress evidence based on Fourth Amendment rights. The vast majority of search and seizure cases in general and of cases resulting in Fourth Amendment motions do not involve violent offenses but instead involve narcotics, firearms, and immigration arrests. Most of the appeals to suppress illegally seized evidence are denied. Overall, in only 1.3 percent of the 2804 cases analyzed was evidence actually excluded because of Fourth Amendment violations. Fourth Amendment appeals may be costly and time-consuming and, in the few cases in which they succeed, reduce conviction chances from 84 percent to 52 percent. However, the GAO report clearly indicates that the picture of the exclusionary rule circumstances and danger currently given to the American public is far from accurate (for summaries of other studies of the effects of the exclusionary rule see Wicker, 1983).

A second study of California felony arrest during the years 1976–1979 (Stewart, 1982) indicates that, statewide, about 5 percent of arrest cases were rejected for prosecution due to search and seizure problems. In large urban areas the rejections ranged from 9 to 13 percent. About three-fourths of the rejected cases involved drug arrests. Only 14 percent involved index offenses. The study points out that these lost cases carried costs for the public in that defendants were allowed "back on the street." Statewide, 46 percent of those released were rearrested for other felonies within two years—three-fourths for drug violations. The study makes no official recommendations concerning the exclusionary rule, but its tone seems to suggest that it be abolished. Obviously, the report could have recommended as easily that police exercise more care in the use of search warrants and the seizing of evidence.

To the extent that the exclusionary rule is abandoned without an adequate substitute to enforce Fourth Amendment rights, the American public effectively has forfeited yet another of its rights for absolutely no gain in preventing crime. The state will possess considerably more freedom to disregard constitutional search and seizure constraints, a precedent will be set which later may lead to increased freedom for the state regarding other constitutional rights, and, in return, the public will be no safer from criminal activity.

A clearer example of the need and potential for criminological research in the area of crime prevention and procedural law could not have been invented. As the demand for "law and order" increases, we will see more "remedies" like those described in the above examples. It is hoped that criminological research in this social policy vein correspondingly will become visible.

SUMMARY

In this chapter we explored society's "crime problem" in terms of public definitions and fears of crime. We noted that during the past decade the "crime problem" has taken on a national, as opposed to community, flavor. Large segments of the public fear violent attacks from strangers and have altered their lives to cope with this fear. In addition, this fear has led to tremendous governmental and business anticrime expenditures. The increased fear of crime has led to the encouragement of anticrime proposals that call for restricted procedural rights, and many police and legislators have felt that crime best can be combatted through the elimination of the "technicalities" that supposedly block the arrest and prosection of criminals.

In Chapter 1 of this book, we suggested that criminology can make significant social policy contributions by identifying and examining the accuracy of public assumptions about crime, and Chapter 2 has expanded on this theme. The Organized Crime Control Act and the assault on the exclusionary rule illustrate the fact that legislatures are responding to public demands for law and order through conservative definitions of individual rights. The examples also demonstrate the urgent necessity for research about proposed crime solutions *prior* to passage of restrictive bills to determine if the proposed measures will accomplish their goals. Such precautions are extremely important, given the fact that reinstatement of restricted rights is nearly impossible.

In the next chapter, we will examine yet another facet of the way in which our view of crime is structured. Chapter 3 explores the issue of interests behind laws and notes inconsistencies in crimes which do and do not receive attention. Crime represents more than persons violating the Ten Commandments. Indeed, very little about law and our "crime problem" is so simple and straightforward.

REFERENCES

Alderman, J. D., L. A. Cranney, and P. Begans. 1981. ABC News–*Washington Post* Poll, Survey No. 0030. New York: ABC News, March 23.

Antunes, G. E., and P. A. Hurley. 1977. The representation of criminal events in Houston's two daily newspapers. *Journalism Q.* 54:756–60.

Arons, S., and E. Katsh. 1977. How TV cops flout the law. *Saturday Review* March 19, 10–18.

Balkin, S. 1979. Victimization rates, safety, and fear of crime. *Soc. Prob.* 26:343–58.

Barrile, L. G. 1980. Television and attitudes about crime. Ph.D. diss., Boston College.

Biderman, A. D., L. A. Johnson, J. McIntyre, et al. 1967. Report on a Pilot Study in the District of Columbia on Victimization and Attitudes toward Law Enforcement. Field Survey I: President's Commission on Law Enforcement and Administration of Justice. Washington, D.C.: U.S. Government Printing Office.

Brady, J. P. 1982. Arson, fiscal crisis, and community action. *Crime & Delinq.* 28:247–70.

Cambridge Reports, Inc. *An Analysis of Public Attitudes toward Handgun Control.* 1978. Cambridge, Mass.

Clotfelter, C. T., and R. D. Seeley. 1979. The private costs of crime. In *The Costs of Crime.* Edited by C. M. Gray. Beverly Hills: Sage Publications.

Cohen, L., and M. Felson. 1979. Social change and crime rate trends: A routine activity approach. *Am. Sociol. Rev.* 44:588–607.

Cohen, L. E., M. Felson, and K. Land. 1980. Property crime rates in the United States: a macrodynamic analysis, 1947–1977; with ex ante forecasts for the mid-1980s. *Am. J. Sociol.* 86:90–118.

Cohen, L. E., J. R. Kluegel, and K. C. Land. 1981. Social inequality and predatory criminal victimization: An exposition and test of a formal theory. *Am. Sociol. Rev.* 46:505–24.

Conklin, J. 1971. Dimensions of Community Response to the Crime Problem. *Soc. Prob.* 18:373—85.

———. 1975. *The Impact of Crime.* New York: Macmillan Publishing Co.

Cowan, P. 1973. The new grand jury. *New York Times Magazine,* April 29, 18 and *passim.*

Culver, J. H., and K. L. Knight. 1979. Evaluating TV impressions of law enforcement roles. In *Evaluating Alternative Law-Enforcement Policies.* Edited by R. Baier and F. A. Meyer, Jr. Lexington, Mass.: Lexington Books.

Davis, F. J. 1952. Crime news in Colorado newspapers. *Am. J. Sociol.* 57:325–30.

Dodge, R. W. 1981. The Washington, D.C. recall study. In *The National Crime Survey: Working Papers,* Vol. 1. Edited by R. Lehnen and W. G. Skogan. Washington, D.C.: U.S. Government Printing Office.

Dominick, J. R. 1973. Crime and law enforcement on prime-time television. *Pub. Opinion Q.* 37:241–50.

———. 1978. Crime and law enforcement in the mass media. In *Deviance and Mass Media.* Edited by C. Winick. Beverly Hills: Sage Publications.

DuBow, F., E. McCabe, and G. Kaplin. 1979. Reactions to crime: A critical review of the literature. Washington, D.C.: U.S. Government Printing Office.

Durkheim, E. 1933. *The Division of Labor in Society.* Translated by G. Simpson. New York: Free Press.

Edelman, M. 1964. *The Symbolic Uses of Politics.* Urbana, Ill.: University of Illinois Press.

Federal Bureau of Investigation. 1982. Uniform Crime Reports—1981. Washington, D.C.: U.S. Government Printing Office.

Fishman, M. 1978. Crime news as ideology. *Soc. Prob.* 25:531—43.

Flanagan, T. J., D. J. van Alstyne, and M. R. Gottfredson, eds. 1982. *Sourcebook of Criminal Justice Statistics—1981.* Washington, D.C.: U.S. Government Printing Office.

Garofalo, J. 1977. *Public Opinion about Crime: The Attitude of Victims and Nonvictims in Selected Cities.* Washington, D.C.: U.S. Government Printing Office.

Gallup, G. H. 1979. *The Gallup Opinion Index.* Report No. 172. Princeton, N.J.: The Gallup Poll, November.

———. 1981a. *The Gallup Poll.* Princeton, N.J., April 4.

———. 1981b. *The Gallup Poll.* Princeton, N.J., April 6.

————. 1981c. *The Gallup Poll*. Princeton, N.J., April 18.

General Accounting Office. 1979. *Impact of the Exclusionary Rule on Federal Criminal Prosecutions*. Washington, D.C.

Gerbner, G., and L. Gross. 1976. Living with television: The violence profile. *J. Communication* 26:173–99.

Gerbner, G., L. Gross, M. Jackson-Beeck, et al., 1978. Cultural indicators: Violence profile no. 9. *J. Communication* 28:171–207.

Gerbner, G., L. Gross, N. Signorielli, et al. 1979. The demonstration of power: Violence profile No. 10. *J. Communication* 29:177–96.

Graber, D. A. 1980. *Crime News and The Public*. New York: Praeger Publishers.

Harris, L. 1981. *The Harris Survey*. New York: The Chicago Tribune-New York News Syndicate, February 26.

Hartnagel, T. F. 1979. The perception and fear of crime: Implications for neighborhood cohesion, social activity, and community effect. *Soc. Forces* 58:176–93.

Hindelang, M. J., M. R. Gottfredson, C. S. Dunn, et al. 1977. *Sourcebook of Criminal Justice Statistics—1976*. Washington, D.C.: U.S. Government Printing Office.

Jones, E. T. 1976. The press as metropolitan monitor. *Pub. Opinion Q.* 40:239–44.

Kamisar, Y. 1982. How we got the Fourth Amendment exclusionary rule and why we need it. *Crim. Just. Ethics* 1:4–15.

Liska, A. E., J. L. Lawrence, and A. Sanchirico. 1982. Fear of crime as a social fact. *Soc. Forces* 60:760–70.

Mead, G. H. 1918. The psychology of punitive justice. *Am. J. Sociol.* 23:577–602.

Murphy, L. R., and R. W. Dodge. 1981. The Baltimore recall study. In *The National Crime Survey: Working Papers*, Vol. 1. Edited by R. Lehnen and W. G. Skogan. Washington, D.C.: U.S. Government Printing Office.

Nettler, G. 1974. *Explaining Crime*. New York: McGraw-Hill Book Company.

Newsweek. 1981. The plague of violent crime. March 23, 46–54.

New York Times. 1974. What New York thinks. January 20, sect. 4, 5.

————. 1981a. Reagan proposes revision of laws to combat crime. September 29, sect. 1, 1.

————. 1981b. Where they stood on crime. October 6, sect. 1, 24.

Pandiani, J. A. 1978. Crime time TV: If all we knew is what we saw. . . . *Contemp. Crises* 2:437–58.

Pearl, A. 1977. Public policy or crime: Which is worse? *Soc. Policy* 7:47–54.

President's Commission on Law Enforcement and Administration of Justice. 1967a. *The Challenge of Crime in a Free Society*. Washington, D.C.: U.S. Government Printing Office.

————. 1967b. *Task Force Report: Crime and Its Impact—An Assessment*. Washington, D.C.: U.S. Government Printing Office.

————. 1967c. *Task Force Report: Science and Technology*. Washington, D.C.: U.S. Government Printing Office.

Quinney, R. 1980. *Class, State, and Crime*. 2nd ed. New York: Longman.

Research and Forecasts, Inc. 1980. *The Figgie Report on Fear of Crime: America Afraid*. Willoughby, Ohio: A-T-O Inc.

Roshier, B. 1973. The selection of crime news by the press. In *The Manufacture of News*. Edited by S. Cohen and J. Young. Beverly Hills: Sage Publications.

Sachs, S. H. 1982. The exclusionary rule: A prosecutor's defense. *Crim. Just. Ethics* 1:28–35.

San Francisco Chronicle. 1983a. FBI gets wider powers for domestic spying. March 8, sect. 1, 1.

————. 1983b. Lawsuit filed against FBI spying rules. March 10, sect. 1, 11.

Sheley, J. F., and C. D. Ashkins. 1981. Crime, crime news, and crime views. *Pub. Opinion Q.* 45:492–506.

Skolnick, J. 1975. *Justice Without Trial.* 2nd ed. New York: John Wiley & Sons.

Stewart, J. K. 1982. *The Effects of the Exclusionary Rule: A Study in California.* Washington, D.C.: National Institute of Justice.

Sutherland, E. H., and D. R. Cressey. 1974. *Criminology.* 9th ed. Philadelphia: J. B. Lippincott Company.

Teevan, J. J., and T. F. Hartnagel. 1976. The effects of television violence on the perceptions of crime by adolescents. *Sociol. Soc. Res.* 60:337–48.

Turner, A. G. 1981. The San Jose recall study. In *The National Crime Survey: Working Papers,* Vol. 1. Edited by R. Lehnen and W. G. Skogan. Washington, D.C.: U.S. Government Printing Office.

U.S. Department of Housing and Urban Development. 1978. *The 1978 HUD Survey on Quality of Community Life.* Washington, D.C.

U.S. Department of Justice. 1981a. *Expenditure and Employment Data for the Criminal Justice System 1971–1979.* Washington, D.C.: U.S. Government Printing Office.

————. 1981b. *Justice Assistance News,* Vol. 2, No. 9 (November). Washington, D.C.: U.S. Department of Justice.

————. 1982a. *Bureau of Justice Statistics Bulletin: Households Touched by Crime 1981.* Washington, D.C.: Bureau of Justice Statistics.

————. 1982b. *Justice Assistance News,* Vol. 3, No. 1 (February). Washington, D.C.: U.S. Department of Justice.

U.S. Supreme Court Reports. 1982. Lawyers edition, second series, vol. 69. San Francisco: Bancroft-Whitney Company.

Warr, M. 1980. The accuracy of public beliefs about crime. *Soc. Forces* 59:456–70.

————. 1982. The accuracy of public beliefs about crime: Further evidence. *Criminology* 20:185–204.

Washnis, G. J. 1976. *Citizen Involvement in Crime Prevention.* Lexington, Mass.: D.C. Heath & Company.

Wicker, T. 1983. Attack on the Fourth. *New York Times,* March 4, sect. 1, 31.

SUGGESTED READINGS

Though now somewhat dated, the 1967 reports by the President's Commission on Law Enforcement and Administration of Justice remain most enlightening analyses of the crime problem and responses to it. See especially the commission's *Task Force Report: Crime and Its Impact—An Assessment* and *The Challenge of Crime in a Free Society* (both Washington, D.C.: U.S. Government Printing Office, 1967). John E. Conklin also offers a more recent investigation of these issues in *The Impact of Crime* (New York: Macmillan, 1975). James Garofalo's *Public Opinion About Crime* (Washington, D.C.: U.S. Government Printing Office, 1977), an analysis of victimization survey data, represents the best current source of information about citizens' attitudes toward crime. D. A. Graber offers a thorough review of media coverage of crime in *Crime News and the Public* (New York: Praeger Publishers, 1980).

In addition to the materials cited in the notes for this chapter, a number of readings point up the dilemmas of legal responses to the "crime problem." Herbert Packer's *The Limits of Criminal Sanction* (Stanford, Calif.: Stanford University Press, 1968) is widely considered one of the best descriptions of the competing interests of the due process and crime-control orientations. Jerome Skolnick examines the same law-and-order dilemma as it influences law-enforcement agencies in *Justice Without Trial,* 2d ed. (New York: John Wiley & Sons, 1975).

Finally, H. E. Pepinsky's *Crime Control Strategies* (New York: Oxford, 1980) provides a clear look at the sources of pictures of crime and the policy implications of each source.

3

CONFLICT AND LAW

We are cautioned often about "failing to see the forest for the trees"—focusing on parts without noticing the whole. Throughout this book we will deal with more traditional criminological questions, albeit with a somewhat different emphasis: How much crime? Who commits crimes and why? Who is victimized? What solutions are proposed to combat crime, and what dangers accompany them? These questions are the proverbial "trees." They are important, but there is an equally important "forest." Many criminologists during the past decade have insisted that we grant more critical attention to an issue often taken for granted in discussions of our "crime-problem": Why do we call certain acts and certain people "criminal"?

At first glance, this question seems to have a simple answer. We call acts "crimes" when they pose a threat to society. We label people "criminal" when we catch them committing these acts. Definitions of people and acts as criminal are not so neatly explained, however. A number of assumptions may be called into question. Can we speak of society as if all members are affected similarly by crime? Can we easily say what constitutes a threat for society or groups within it? Is breaking the law the only criterion for gaining criminal status? Will it assure this status?

In the previous chapter we examined various influences on our crime fears. In this chapter, we will explore criminal status as a definitional problem through discussions of interest groups, ruling classes, and definitions of crime. We suggest that the worth or quality of acts and persons is primarily a matter of the meanings we give them. The *conflict perspective* examines such meanings as they relate to various economic, status, and power interests in society. Who or what is called criminal at a given time reflects the socio-economic power relationship of that time.

Our look at what structures criminal labels—the "forest"—is important even though this book focuses primarily on more traditional questions—the "trees." The conflict perspective relates to public perceptions of the "crime problem" and its potential solutions, for it fosters a healthy skepticism about crime and its control. It tends to make people more cautious when confronted with proclamations about the "threat of crime" and proposals to outlaw certain acts. As noted in Chapter 1, this critical approach helps form a framework for asking questions first and acting later. Hence, potentially disastrous "knee-jerk" responses to crime are avoided more easily.

VALUE CONSENSUS AND CRIME'S FUNCTIONS

Until relatively recently, most sociological and criminological theory assumed that definitions of acts and persons as deviant or criminal reflect a value consensus within society. People were thought to hold much the same views of right and wrong because societies could not function long under constant moral conflict. Thus, law was viewed by traditional theorists as a reflection of custom and a codification of societal values, as an institution functioning to settle disputes arising occasionally when values and norms become somewhat cloudy, and as the organization of social control when the rare individual deviates too far from the normatively acceptable (for summaries of these positions see Rich, 1978). Indeed, deviance itself and the ensuing application of the legal process were seen by some as necessary to the proper functioning of a society. Emile Durkheim (1958:67; 1933:102) provides some classic statements in this vein:

> Crime is a factor in public health, an integral part of all healthy societies.

> Crime brings together upright consciences and concentrates them. We have only to notice what happens, particularly in a small town, when some moral scandal has just been committed. They stop each other on the street, they visit each other, they seek to come together to talk of the event and to wax indignant in common. From all the similar impressions which are exchanged, for all the temper that gets itself expressed, there emerges a unique temper, more or less determinate according to the circumstances, which is everybody's without being anybody's in particular. That is the public temper.

Both G. H. Mead (1918) and, later, Durkheim were pointing up a paradox about crime. While it has obvious dysfunctions for a community—cost, injury, disruption—it may also be functional in some important ways. Crime and other forms of deviance tend to remind members of a community about the interests and values they share. Community bonds are strengthened in the common outrage and indignation inspired by a deviant act. Further, deviance reassures individual members of a community of their own moral normality and forthrightness.

Some authors caution us not to emphasize the functions of deviance alone. While noting the unifying functions of punishment, Mead (1918:91) also points out that punitive reactions to deviance lead to repressive societal conditions that stifle the creativity that deviance often represents. Repressive hostility also will prevent societal self-examination and subsequent attempts at improvement. Finally, Coser (1956:87–95) notes that if solidarity is weak in the first place, deviance and reactions to it can divide a community into factions.

The "functions of deviance" theme continues to be explored, however. Some students of Durkheim suggest that a society actually encourages, or at least allows, a certain amount of deviance for its functional aspects. Obviously, the balance between functional and dysfunctional amounts of deviance is delicate. Too much would destroy a society, yet too little would mean the loss of societal unification derived from deviance. This unification function is considered so imperative that Durkheim (1958:67) once noted that if all present forms of criminal activity suddenly were eliminated, a society immediately would create new forms. Even in a society of saints, he wrote, "faults which appear venial to the layman will create the same scandal that the ordinary offense does in ordinary consciousness."

Kai Erikson's study (1966) of deviance in the early Puritan colonies has furthered Durkheim's work. He discovered three "crime waves" during the first sixty years of settlement in Massachusetts: the Antinomian controversy (a challenge to the community's religious establishment), the arrival of the Quakers from Pennsylvania, and the Salem witches hysteria. Each occurred at a time when unity in the colonies was waning. Each precipitated considerable turmoil. Erikson notes, however, that these crime waves were matters of shifts of public attention from one form of trouble to another. Other problems were forgotten as each new crime problem arose. In fact, despite the "crime waves," crime rates remained relatively stable over the six decades. In Erikson's mind, this suggests a deviance "quota"—that is, the encouragement or allowance by the social system of a sufficiently functional amount of deviance to produce unity through creation of a response to a "common enemy."

Erikson's study of the three Puritan "crime waves" also caused him to extend Durkheim's notion of the unification functions of deviance. He argues that crime in the colonies served certain boundary definition and maintenance functions. Deviance and reactions to it help set the boundaries of acceptable behavior and provide a sense of stability and direction for a fledgling society. As time passes, these boundaries tend to become somewhat vague and new possibilities of societal growth arise. Deviance again causes the society to refocus on its character and mission, to reemphasize the common beliefs and interests of its members. Deviance thus serves to maintain the social and moral boundaries of societies.

James M. Inverarity (1976) recently attempted to extend Erikson's work through a study of lynchings in Louisiana between 1889 and 1896. His thesis is essentially Erikson's: As a united group begins to lose its sense of solidarity, it seeks out and represses "enemies," thus reunifying itself. Inverarity argues that prior to the late 1800s, the South was a white-dominated, relatively closed, united society. Two general white classes existed, a wealthy planter-merchant-industrialist class and a larger, poorer, farmer-laborer class. Their relationship was fairly harmonious, even if economically unequal. Blacks at this time were considered inferior by both white classes. Yet, blacks did have the vote; laws created to exclude the black vote did not reach major proportions until the early 1900s. In the late 1800s, the black vote was controlled by the wealthy class who utilized this control to solidify its power position.

White solidarity collapsed briefly in the early 1890s with the advent of the Populist revolt, an abortive attempt to capture economic and political power by some members of the lower classes. Inverarity points out that this disunity coincided with an increase in lynchings, primarily of blacks but also of whites, in Louisiana parishes (counties). He posits that the lynchings were a societal mechanism to counter the lack of social unity by rallying people against their "common enemies." After the Populist movement collapsed in the 1890s, the white South reunited and lynchings declined in Louisiana. In Inverarity's opinion, the decline reflected the lessened need for a unifying mechanism, i.e., a decreased necessity to search out a common threat. In short, as in the early Massachusetts colonies, the societal response to deviance had functioned to strengthen a social system whose unity was threatened.

CRITICISMS OF THE CONSENSUS MODEL

It is important to realize that Erikson's Puritan colonies and, to some extent, Inverarity's southern communities represented small, apparently highly homogeneous societies. In general, the "functions of crime" thesis seems to apply to smaller societies far better than to larger, heterogeneous ones. As a society expands and becomes more differentiated, it tends to form clusters, smaller subcultures or groups that differ from each other in world view, social status, and economic interests. Generally, these groups compete for various scarce economic and status rewards in society. Crime and deviance within these *smaller* segments of society may serve the same unification and boundary maintenance functions as does crime in smaller societies, such as the Puritan colonies. More importantly, however, definitions of and reactions to crime and deviance in the larger society are tied integrally to competition and conflict *among* the smaller segments or interest groups.

But many critics of the consensus approach will not accept the notions of value consensus and functions of deviance even for the smaller society (see Chambliss, 1974; Turk, 1976). They argue that were consensus in the small society really present, deviance would be rarer and the use of legal threat to deter deviance rarer still. They note that "societal needs" and the functioning of social phenomena like deviance to meet those needs are impossible to document; they must be accepted on faith alone. According to these critics, it is as plausible that laws are created in the interests of a few and then shape public values as that public values shape law (see Figure 3–1). The consensus position assumes that the state (legal mechanisms and processes) represents the interests of the majority. Many historical studies can be found which trace a given law to the interests of a powerful minority. None is found that ties a law directly to an expressed will of a majority independent of the influence of some interested minority.

The possibility that the consensus approach underestimates political and economic conflict within smaller societies becomes clear with a second look at Erikson's study of "crime waves" in the Puritan colonies. As Chambliss and Seidman (1982:197–201) note, in each of the crime situations studied by Erikson, the interests of the major political figures in the community were at stake. The Antinomian controversy became a "crime problem" when the "different" religious views of a woman and a few of her followers began to be taken seriously enough that large numbers of people sought her counsel rather than that of established church leaders; the result: The leaders not only accused their rivals of heresy but of trying to overthrow the government. Similarly, Quakers became a "criminal element" rather than a nuisance when they began gathering converts to their notion that individuals should form their own covenant with God rather than seek that covenant through the intercession of church leaders. The result: Being a Quaker became a criminal offense severely punishable. Finally, Chambliss and Seidman note, the Salem witch problem was interwoven with a power dispute between political magistrates and leading clergymen.

Similar comments pertain to Inverarity's study of lynchings in Louisiana during the Populist revolt. Ignoring the harsh theoretical and statistical critiques his study has received (for examples, see Pope and Ragin, 1977; Bagozzi, 1977), we note that his findings at the very least are open to other

Societal needs ➡ societal values ➡ legislation

The Consensus Model

Group interests ➡ legislation ➡ societal values

The Conflict Model

FIGURE 3–1

Models of the Source of Legislation

interpretations as plausible as his consensus thesis. Inverarity's data (1976) indicate that 65 percent of the lynchings were responses to alleged homicides and rapes. If a rise in such serious crime coincided with the Populist revolt, it is difficult to link the two. The lynchings may have represented a common frontier-rural response to perceived heinous crimes. If lynchings declined after the Populist failure, it is possible that crime coincidentally declined or, more likely, was deterred by the lynchings. More important is the possibility of the political use of a "crime problem" by members of either or both white classes. The wealthier class, fearing success in the Populist's drive to unite blacks and poor whites as one working class, could easily have fomented racial unrest. More influential members of the poorer white class whose status was being eroded by new Populist leaders could have countered the erosion as easily by stirring up racial hatred. In either case, lynchings declined as the threat to these two elites decreased.

In general, there are few cases raised by consensus theorists which are not open to highly plausible reinterpretations that focus on conflicts among interested or threatened parties. These alternative interpretations do not rest on the undocumentable notion of "societal need." Rather, they rest on the documentable economic and political interests of specific persons and groups. This thought forms the basis of what is known as the *conflict perspective*.

THE CONFLICT APPROACH

If power struggles characterize smaller societies and shape law and its enforcement to the extent critics of the consensus model claim, it is difficult to conceive of a consensus model accurately describing the source of criminal definitions in larger societies. For this reason, an alternative conflict model has found increased popularity among criminologists. While not all conflict models are alike, three themes cut across all models: (1) the relativity of criminal definitions, (2) the role of control of major social institutions in maintaining interests, and (3) the definition of law (legislation and enforcement) as an instrument of power.

Criminal Definitions as Relative

At base, the conflict perspective argues that no act or individual is intrinsically moral or criminal, immoral or noncriminal. If a criminal label is attached to an act or a person, there is an underlying reason; such definitions serve some interests within society. If these labels are tied to interests, then they are subject to change as interests change. Thus, every definition of an act as immoral, deviant, or criminal (or as acceptable) must be viewed as tentative, always subject to redefinition.

NEWSPRINT AND COMMENT

Trial of Woman Accused of Rapes to Test Law's Intent

PITTSBURGH (UPI)

The trial of an elementary school teacher accused of raping two teen-age boys will begin Jan. 12, a case thought to be the first test of whether Pennsylvania's statutory rape law applies to female defendants.

The trial date was scheduled by Allegheny County Common Pleas Judge Robert Dauer. Defense lawyers also requested trial before a jury, a court official said Wednesday.

Kathleen Harden, 31, a teacher at Mount Vernon School in nearby Elizabeth Township, has been charged with five counts of statutory rape, three counts of corruption of minors and one count of involuntary deviate sexual intercourse. She is free pending trial.

County detectives said Harden has admitted to having intercourse with boys 13 and 15 years old in a variety of places beginning last December.

She is believed to be the first woman charged with statutory rape in the state's history. Her lawyer contends the law was never meant to apply to female defendants because its legislative intent was to protect only women from attack.

Source: © United Press International, 1981. Reprinted by permission.

Comment: The Tentativeness of Criminal Definitions

We treat most of our laws as nonnegotiable, almost as if they are carved in stone. It seems clear to us to what acts laws pertain. And the reasons given behaviors are outlawed generally seem obvious. But we should draw such conclusions cautiously. Indeed, in terms of understanding the dynamics of the legislative process, we probably should assume that *no* act is inherently wrong and that *no* law is etched in stone. We appreciate this position when we realize that laws regarding certain vices have changed over the years. But we negotiate the meaning of even more serious acts; today we debate the wrongfulness of taking another's life through mercy killing, for example.

The news item reprinted above illustrates some of these points. Statutory rape laws always seemed to pertain to the seduction of young girls by older men or boys. In a more traditional, sexist view, it seemed inconceivable that an older woman would seduce a young boy. In a yet more sexist view, it seemed that boys would not be harmed by such a seduction—at least not to the degree young girls were thought to be harmed by statutory rape. Indeed, boys were thought perhaps to benefit from such encounters.

Times have changed, and ideas with them—at least to some extent. We note in the news item that the state of Pennsylvania must cope with defining statutory rape in terms of the genders to which its law applies. In short, the traditional statutory rape law must be viewed as tentative, as subject to redefinition. So, of course, must the interpretation of the Pennsylvania statutory rape law after the trial of the woman involved in the above case.

Prime examples of the definition-redefinition process are seen in our perpetually changing attitudes, laws, and law-enforcement patterns concerning "vices." Several states recently have decriminalized certain sexual acts between consenting adults. At one time, possession of marijuana was legal in this country; currently it is not and the question of legalization shifts back and forth. Abortion, once illegal, has been given new legal definitions that are challenged constantly. Gambling once was illegal in Atlantic City, New Jersey; it is legal now. Prostitution is legal in certain counties in Nevada but outlawed in all other states. Being the customer of a prostitute likewise is legal in some states but not in others. For all of these acts, we may wonder which definition reflects their "true" quality or nature: evil (illegal) or good (legal). In practice, we must treat current meanings as "truth," for they are the meanings employed in a court of law. From a conflict perspective, however, we soon realize that nothing is inherently sacred or sacrilegious; all definitions are subject to change.

Some may argue that the emphasis of the conflict perspective on the relativity of moral and legal definitions is demonstrated easily with respect to "vices," about which there is little societal consensus, but may not apply so easily to acts that seem uniformly defined by most people over time. For example, cannot murder be called intrinsically wrong if nearly everyone considers it so and has so considered it for a very long time?

The conflict theorist likely will counter that universal acceptance of a criminal definition, even for a long time, may be mere coincidence. Whether or not universally accepted, a criminal definition almost certainly has its origins in the protection of some power group's interests. And the definition certainly need not be permanent. Radical structural changes such as those created by a severe famine or cultural changes like those fomented in Nazi Germany in the 1930s could cause changes in the value placed on human life (Hughes, 1962). Further, the conflict theorist might argue that definitions of homicide currently are being negotiated. Continual legislative and courtroom debates over the criminal status of abortion and euthanasia are, at base, debates about the limits of acceptable life-taking versus criminal homicide. The same holds true for the fight over capital punishment. Finally, history suggests that a revolutionary political assassin's status as hero or murderer depends on the success of the revolution, not on the intrinsic value of the act of assassination.

Control of Institutions

Conflict theorists argue that there are three basic means of maintaining and enhancing interests in a society: force, compromise, and dominance of social institutions. Force is the least desirable, for it calls attention directly to interest preservation and basically dares others to summon enough counterforce to alter the power structure. Compromise is preferred, since all parties involved somehow benefit. Concessions bear witness to the absence of absolute power in the hands of any one interest group. Yet, compromise, though preferable to force, still carries liabilities. It points up the weaknesses of certain parties and encourages others to organize further to exploit those weaknesses.

The strongest mechanism for gaining or holding power is dominance of social institutions. Control of such institutions as the law, religion, education, government, economics, and science means control of the world views of members of society, especially regarding questions of interests and power. With respect to the problem of crime and criminals, control of legal institutions means that more powerful groups gain legal support for their interests by outlawing behavior and attitudes that threaten them or by focusing attention away from their own wrongdoings. Control of other institutions, such as religion and education, is used to promote the interests of the more powerful by shaping the opinions of the less powerful concerning the legitimacy of the economic, political, and legal status quo. For example, we note, without arguing its validity, that the religious belief that rewards in the afterlife await those who suffer in this life serves to discourage this life's less powerful from more aggressively seeking the earthly rewards now in the hands of the more powerful. Similarly, an examination of textbooks used in most of our public and private elementary and secondary schools indicates how rarely serious questions are raised concerning the unequal distribution of wealth and power in this society.

Law As An Instrument of Power

While consensus theorists view law as an institution expressing common societal values and controlled by the majority in society, conflict theorists view law as an instrument of control or, in Austin Turk's (1976) words, "a weapon in social conflict." Whoever owns the law owns power. Those who own it fight to keep it; those who want it fight to get it. Indeed, Turk argues, rather than simply reducing conflict, law also produces it by virtue of its status as a resource to be won by some combatants and lost by others. This point is illustrated by the importance given to nominations of Supreme Court Justices. Presidents attempt to fill court vacancies with persons sympathetic to their views, i.e., persons more likely to decide cases in a manner protecting the interests of a given president and the parties that president represents.

The value of law as an instrument of power needs almost no explanation. Most obviously, control of the legal order represents the ability to use specified agents of force to protect one's interests. Beyond this, Turk notes that decisions concerning economic power are made and enforced through law; that is, control of the legislature represents control of the process that determines in part the distribution of economic rewards through such vehicles as tax laws. Further, control of the legal process means control of the organization of governmental decisions in general—decisions concerning the structure of public education, for example. Control of the law aids in determining much of culture; law grants legitimation to "right" views of the world and denies legitimation to "wrong" views. Finally, Turk notes that the attention commanded by the workings of law (policy, trials, and so forth) serves to direct attention from more deeply rooted problems of power distribution and interest maintenance. In sum, as Quinney (1970:13) suggests, laws that forbid particular behaviors and make others mandatory are passed by legislators who have gained office through the backing of various interest groups. The ability to have one's interests translated into public policy is a primary indicator of power.

If law is an instrument sought after and employed by powerful interest groups to enhance their position in society, and if criminal law states forbidden acts, it is reasonable to define *crime* as "acts perceived by those in power as direct or indirect threats to their interests." Conflict theorists (Chambliss and Seidman, 1982:174–75) note that most of our current criminal law follows directly from English common law. Jeffrey (1957) argues that acts such as murder, theft, and robbery, once considered dispute problems to be settled within or between families, became crimes against the state (wrongs against society) when Henry II, King of England, attempted to centralize his power in a politically divided country by declaring them wrongs against the crown. Jerome Hall (1952) has traced theft laws in their present form to their origin in the change from a feudal economy to a capitalist-mercantile economy. As a new economic class of traders and industrialists developed, the need to protect their business interests grew. Hall (1952:66) describes the creation of embezzlement laws:

> The patterns of conditions which gave rise to embezzlement may therefore be delineated as follows: (1) the expansion of mercantile and banking credit and the use of credit mechanisms, paper money, and securities; (2) the employment of clerks in important positions with reference to dealing with and, in particular, receiving valuables from third persons; (3) the interests of the commercial classes and their representation in parliament; (4) a change in attitude regarding the public importance of what could formerly be dismissed as merely a private breach of trust; and (5) a series of sensational cases of very serious defalcation which set the pattern into motion and produced immediate action.

The same conditions spawned laws governing the receipt of stolen property and obtaining goods under false pretenses. The conflict theorists' point is that our definitions of crime have their roots less in general beliefs about right and wrong than in perceived threats to groups with the power to legislate their interests.

Control of The Police

Law enforcement patterns as well as legislation reflect the attempts of the more powerful to protect their interests. Jacobs (1979:914) writes:

> . . .[T]he more there are inequalities in the distribution of economic power and economic resources, the more one can expect that the social control apparatus of the state will conform to the preferences of monied elites.
> . . . In this society, the major institution responsible for the coercive maintenance of stability and order is the police.

Jacobs argues that the greater the economic differences in a community, the more likely will poorer community members attempt forcefully to alter the inequality. Thus, economic elites utilize the police as protection and as a general stabilizer within a community. Jacob's analysis of police strength in metropolitan areas appears to support his thesis. Law enforcement personnel are more numerous in metropolitan areas where economic inequality is most pronounced.

In the same vein, Liska et al. (1981) report that following civil disorders in the South in the 1950s, 1960s, and early 1970s, whites in cities with larger percentages of nonwhite residents and less residential segregation perceived chances of crime victimization to be greater whether or not actual crime rates changed. Hence, the more powerful whites demanded and received greater police protection. Jackson and Carroll (1981) confirm this finding in their study of 90 non-Southern cities. To the extent that black population and political mobilization increased in cities in the late 1960s and early 1970s, cities' expenditures on police services increased—regardless of their crime rates. The authors conclude that police expenditures are a resource that is mobilized when minority groups appear to threaten the political and economic position of more dominant groups. They therefore echo Silver's (1967) characterization of the police as a mechanism designed to control "dangerous classes" in a way that protects wealthier classes but seems to do so in a manner not directly orchestrated by the wealthy. That is, police protect the wealthy while appearing to protect the poor as well—all under a "war on crime" umbrella.

RULING CLASS VERSUS PLURALIST THEORIES

Thus far, we have reviewed characteristics common to conflict theories. However, there are major differences among theorists concerning the distribution and use of power in this society. In terms of our present interest, the clearest difference revolves around the question of who is behind legislation and law enforcement: a single dominant class or a number of relatively powerful, competing interest groups?

Class Conflict

A number of prominent conflict theorists argue that law in this society is a major tool or power of a ruling elite of capitalists. Underlying this approach is the Marxian thesis of perpetual conflict between the two primary economic classes of capitalist societies, those who own the means of production (factories, machinery, investment capital) and those who work for these owners turning raw materials into salable goods. Owner-capitalists strive to minimize labor and production costs in order to increase the surplus value of production (profit), which then becomes capital to be invested in other capital-producing markets. If unchecked, the capitalist instinctively works constantly to mechanize labor, thereby reducing the costs of production, and to monopolize the production market, thereby eliminating competition and increasing the pricing potential of goods in the consumer market. This same instinct drives capitalists constantly to expand both the range of goods they produce and the markets to which they ship these goods.

To the extent that they understand the capitalist system, workers find themselves in conflict with owners. Both can lay claim to a portion of the profits from production; the owners by virtue of risked capital and the workers by virtue of the fact that they actually transform raw materials into usable and salable items. The issue is a matter of the degree of profit each deserves or, deservedness aside, the degree each can seize. Since capitalists always have held the upper hand in this matter, it is clearly in their interest to keep workers unaware of their potential for a greater share of the surplus value of production. In terms of its sheer advantage in numbers, an aware and organized worker population could dictate the terms of profit distribution and, one step further, could seize the means of production from the owners.

Law and the Capitalists

The methods by which owners maintain their advantage over workers were mentioned earlier in this chapter: force, compromise when necessary, and, most importantly, control of social institutions that shape the world view of workers, especially regarding their rights and duties within the capitalist system. There is no set combination of force, compromise, and control that owners may utilize to preserve their superior economic position. Crises within capitalism (unemployment due to increased mechanization, for example) appear constantly, forcing owners to devise new and varied solutions. The solutions in turn spawn new problems and crises (heavy government borrowing to support welfare programs designed to placate the unemployed, for example). Thus, the conflict between owners and workers is dynamic.

Capitalists wish to avoid appearing to control directly the political economy. Such visible control would invite worker wrath during capitalism's sporadic major crises. Thus, capitalists require a mechanism which appears free of direct owner influence, legitimizes the economic system, "holds things together" by defusing crises, and represses rebellious workers in the name of maintaining the general order. The *state* is such a mechanism. Its role is to organize and integrate economic, political, legal, and, occasionally, religious systems and processes. Thus, the legal order may be viewed as protector and enhancer of capitalist interests through tax legislation and incentives and through organization of and arbitration among various capitalist subgroups. At the same time, its apparent neutrality and the mystical quality provided by complicated legal ritual serve to convince workers that their general interests are maintained and protected.

The legitimation given to the "law" by the workers allows capitalists to use legislation to create repressive mechanisms without implicating themselves in the repression. Thus, political activism and worker strike activity is held in check by laws governing the shapes they may take. Violations of these laws are addressed by the state for the "common good," i.e., because "no cause justifies illegal activity." Workers in general become focused upon the law as sacred and fail to appreciate the interests and forces underlying both the law and the crises it addresses.

Instrumentalists and Structuralists

Clearly, law is an important tool in the preservation of economic interests. As noted earlier in this chapter, it is a resource worth fighting to gain and to keep. Yet, there is some disagreement among Marxian conflict theorists about the extent to which the law or, more generally, the state is controlled by capitalists. One camp, known as *instrumentalists,* argues that a core of "monopoly capitalists"—those heading the most powerful corporate and banking interests—totally control the state, orchestrate its every action, and utilize legal processes directly to preserve their interests. This approach has its modern roots in the writings of such theorists as C. Wright Mills (1956) and G. W. Domhoff (1967, 1978), who have demonstrated empirically very strong economic and social ties among industrial leaders and those appointed to high-level government positions regulating business, education, financing, and media. Quinney (1980:84) describes the ruling class:

> The capitalist class also is divided into several fractions. Two major fractions are those capitalists who own major units of the economy and those whose holdings and power are less than that of the uppermost sector of the capitalist class. The upper division, the "monopoly sector," as contrasted to the "lieutenant sector," owns the largest corporations and financial institutions. . . . The other segment . . . is largely delegated power by the monopoly sector.

So powerful are these major capitalists, in the eyes of instrumentalists, that they are able to hide from public view. Hill (1975:4) argues:

> [Monopoly capitalists] use all the resources at their command to keep secret the extent of their power, their decision, who they are, etc.

... [They] desire to perpetuate the myth that America is a free, classless society. As long as the existence of a ruling class is hidden, the chances of rebellion against it are small. The myth that America is a "pluralistic
democracy" is one of the greatest weapons in the arsenal that maintains their
class rule.

And so in control of the political process are the monopoly capitalists, in the
opinion of some instrumentalists (Balkan et al., 1980:8), that:

> [W]e can understand how even as powerful a person as President Nixon could
> have been forced to resign from the presidency. In spite of continued resis-
> tance from many powerful people to label the president a criminal, a sizeable
> majority of powerful elites came to the conclusion that, given the public
> knowledge of the president's "questionable" activities, it would be better for
> the long-term maintenance of their power to replace him with someone who
> inspired more public confidence.

The instrumentalist's position often is criticized. It fails to consider
noneconomic influences on political and legal processes. It cannot account
for the outlawing of certain behaviors seemingly in the interests of capitalists,
e.g., price-fixing. It cannot explain why, if capitalists control the law, they do
not simply change it to correspond to their interests rather than sometimes
violating it themselves. Finally, it fails to consider disagreements and conflict
among capitalists.

To counter these criticisms, a number of Marxian theorists espouse a
"softer" and more complex brand of ruling class theory. These theorists,
called *structuralists* (see Chambliss and Seidman, 1982; Greenberg, 1981;
Spitzer, 1979), argue that the state and the law are more than mere reflections of ruling class interests. Instead, the role the state plays in furthering
and legitimating capitalism negates its strict attachment to the monopoly-
capitalist sector. In short, structuralists feel that the state is relatively autonomous and, as such, protects the long-term interests of capitalists though not
always their short-term interests. Thus, in order to gain legitimacy in the eyes
of workers, the state indeed often does execute the law fairly and against capitalists' immediate interests. Chambliss and Seidman (1982:308) write:

> ... [T]he state and government must legitimize the existing political and eco-
> nomic arrangements in order to provide an atmosphere in which capitalist ac-
> cumulation and production can continue.... to serve the interests of the
> ruling class, the state must create [a sense of fairness] among the people....
> [T]he state and legal order best fulfill their function as legitimizers when they
> appear to function as value neutral organs fairly and impartially representing
> the interests of everyone.

Structuralists also are open to criticism. They have yet to document the
development of the short-term neutrality yet long-term bias represented by
the legal arrangement between the state and capitalists. They seem to under-
emphasize legal discrimination against segments of the worker population,

(e.g., blacks and women). They tend often to reify the "state," as if it has a life of its own, though Chambliss and Seidman (1982:309–16) do much to counter this problem by refining the notions of "state" and "autonomy." In short, while instrumentalists have given us a conspiritorial ruling class whose existence is hard to prove, structuralists have given us *two* powerful interests whose relationship is equally difficult to document: capitalists and the state.

PLURALIST THEORIES

Though starting from essentially the same point as Marxian theorists—that legislation and law enforcement have their roots in group conflict—another cadre of conflict theorists offers a broader approach to the explanation of the legal process. *Pluralist theorists* argue that the legal process is not controlled by one specific interest group but emerges from or is shaped by the conflicting interests of a multiplicity of groups, all seeking something different from a given legal issue (Troyer and Markle, 1982). The object of conflict is not always economic interest; it may reflect as well status concerns and moral and ideological commitments. Hence, much of what occurs in legal conflicts is symbolic rather than purely instrumental.

Pluralist theories have their roots in historical studies of the process by which issues are contested and resolved rather than in identification of the key parties involved in conflict (a theme pursued by Marxian theorists). Pluralists recognize the unequal distribution of wealth and power in this society and its importance in the negotiation of conflict. But they do not accord it the degree of significance given it by Marxian theorists (Friedman, 1972). Like Marxian theorists, pluralists consider conflict ongoing and ever-changing as new groups vie for power and as groups in power err through oversight, misdefinition of the situation, and miscalculation of policy effects. Like the Marxian approach, the pluralist approach stresses the importance of gaining and preserving power through control of the world view of groups whose explicit or implicit support is required. Pluralists also vary in the degree to which they feel the state has become an autonomous, interested party in conflict rather than simply a sought-after resource.

Multiple Interest Groups

Pluralists view society as composed partly of groups varyingly aware of their interests and organized in various degrees to maintain and enhance these interests. They view society also as composed partly of groups unaware of their interests and, therefore, unorganized (see Table 3–1). Although more organized groups vary in their power to benefit themselves, none is so well organized that it enjoys total freedom to promote its interests. Power relationships and, therefore, the positions of interest groups in the power

TABLE 3–1

Interest-group Awareness and Organization: Examples

Awareness of interests	Organization around interests		
	High	Moderate	Low
High	Major U.S. corporations	NAACP	Homosexuals
Moderate	Unknown*	California migrant farm workers	Women
Low	Unknown*	Unknown*	Urban poor

*Since awareness generally precedes organization, it is difficult to conceive of degrees of organization higher than degrees of awareness.

structure are continually subject to threat of change as groups increase or decrease in awareness and organizational might. New groups constantly are becoming conscious of and organizing around their interests and are posing threats to the traditional power structure (the women's movement is a recent clear case in point). All powerful groups require the support of other powerful groups above and below them in the power hierarchy. Further, no group can afford to arouse direct opposition from the unorganized. Failure to placate this group may result in discontent that breeds awareness of interests and organized threats to the staus quo. This same unorganized group provides a pool of potential support for the various organized and organizing groups.

State Agents

No law exists in a vacuum. Every law represents the intersection of interests of many groups, some cutting across socioeconomic classes. Among interested parties, many pluralists argue, are groups (or agencies) within the state. The creation of laws necessitates the creation of law enforcers (regulatory bureaus, prosecutor's offices, police departments, etc.). Once formed, law enforcement agencies themselves become interest groups whose existence may be threatened by other groups' attempts to decriminalize the behaviors they police, or may be strengthened through their own attempts to expand the realm of activities they monitor and the procedural powers needed for monitoring. Hence, law enforcement lobbies and public relations divisions attempt to sway legislators and public opinion to preserve or strengthen laws against such activities as drug use, prostitution, homosexuality, and gambling.

Howard Becker (1963:135–46) provides an illustration of law enforcement pressure groups in his discussion of the passage of the Marijuana Tax

Act. Prior to 1937, the American public and governmental agencies charged with policing drug use showed little concern about marijuana. In the mid-1930s, the Treasury Department's Bureau of Narcotics began pressing for marijuana legislation. Its crusade included cooperation with state agencies in drafting anti-marijuana laws and use of the mass media to sway public opinion against the drug.

Becker notes that numerous articles condemning marijuana suddenly appeared in popular journals and magazines of the time (for critical comments on Becker's work see Galliher and Walker, 1977). Many contained atrocious stories about the effects of the drug. Most appealed to the same sentiment that had earlier caused the prohibition of alcohol and opiates: Anything that causes the loss of self-control and is used purely for pleasure is evil.

In the spring of 1937, the Treasury Department approached Congress with "proof" of the popular sentiment that it had, in fact, helped to create. In the summer of the same year, Congress passed the Marijuana Tax Act, which allowed the Federal Bureau of Narcotics, under the auspices of revenue laws, to join with state agencies in arresting and prosecuting marijuana traffickers. In Becker's view, the fact that marijuana presently is outlawed in this country is the direct result of the work of an interest group, The Bureau of Narcotics, seeking to prepetuate its existence by creating its own "business."

Types of Interest

Pluralists note that the multiplicity of groups involved in a given legislative conflict often indicates a variety of *types* of interest in a given issue. Most obvious are economic concerns. Certain groups may stand to lose or to gain economically if a given law is enacted. The passage of antipollution laws clearly threatens some corporate economic interests. Laws allowing attorneys to advertise and set their own fee schedules threaten the economic interests of certain established law firms but enhance the economic interests of other law firms and certainly of the general public.

Ideological concerns also influence law. Laws often express political and moral values. The antipollution laws mentioned above may reflect the political ideologies of groups who feel that corporations should be accountable for the condition of the environment that they in part shape. Laws governing freedom to protest politically obviously are political in nature. The abortion issue now contested in the political arena is largely a moral issue. Finally, related to the ideology question, status may be at issue in the legal process. Certain groups obtain sufficient power to define in large part the character of our culture (the degree to which it is a religious or a secular culture, for example). Some are able to maintain that powerful status, while others lose it and new groups gain it. The passage of a given law may reflect the rising or falling sociopolitical fortunes of these various groups. The study by Zurcher et al. (1971) of antipornography campaigns, for example, indicates that those opposing pornography are fighting for a lifestyle or social climate, i.e., fighting for the power to define the cultural character of their particular region. The outcome of such a campaign is, therefore, a comment of the sociopolitical status of these crusaders. Of course, in line with the pluralist's view of intersecting types of interests, it must be pointed out that the economic interests of producers and sellers of pornography also are at stake in such campaigns. Similarly, those strongly against censorship have an ideological interest in the issue. Local politicians—prosecutors, legislators—may also be party to an antipornography campaign in order to better their election interests. Finally, it is important to note that status interests at stake in legislation need not involve large groups of persons nor status within the larger society. Pfohl (1977), for example, traces modern child abuse laws to the attempt of pediatric radiologists, a low-status specialty group in medicine, to establish their own area of importance within medicine. Rather than working in an area of specialization supplementary to that of the pediatrician, pediatric radiologists now can enhance their status by becoming partners with pediatricians and psychiatrists in the fight against an important illness syndrome.

Symbolism

The ideological and status interests behind some laws call attention to an important issue in most pluralist theories: *symbolic interests* (Edleman, 1964; Gusfield, 1963 [summarized below in Example 3]). Often the surface issue that is contested is less important to the parties contesting it than is some underlying, broader issue. Underlying issues cannot always be contested directly in legislatures and courts; such issues are too difficult to specify legally. Instead, some more specific issue, perhaps only vaguely tied to the underlying conflict, often becomes symbolic of the contest, mapping out an arena where it can be fought. At times, the groups involved only are concerned with legislation. They care not whether a law can be or is enforced (though the enforcement issue eventually may become symbolic as well). It is enough that their view of social, moral, or economic order be given the sacred stamp of the law.

Galliher and Cross (1982) provide an excellent illustration of the symbolic theme in their analysis of Nevada's penalty for possession of marijuana. The state's residents feel the need to convince the outside world, and perhaps themselves, that theirs is not a lawless and immoral world despite the fact that it permits casino gambling, prostitution, and easy marriages and divorces. Further, the state wishes to show the federal goverment that it can control unwanted aspects of its liberal laws, such as the intrusion of organized crime. Nevada's tough marijuana law addresses both needs. Nevada is the only state in which first-offense possession of even the smallest quantity of the drug constitutes a felony that can be punished by up to six years in prison. Yet, Galliher and Cross point out that the law seldom is enforced. They argue that its presence on the books signifies less a desire to stamp out marijuana than a symbolic statement to the outside world concerning Nevada's lawfulness and moral character.

Influencing Legal Outcomes

Within the pluralist model of the creation of law, the goal of any given group seeking to maintain or enhance its interests is to influence legislators to write laws and law enforcers to administer laws as the interest group sees fit. Since legislators and law enforcement officials are political beings whose jobs depend on a satisfied constituency, an interest group's immediate aim is to bring constituency pressure to bear upon the officeholder to the extent necessary to accomplish the desired outcome. Thus, an interest group must sway a public that is indifferent or hostile to a position to accept that position as valid and to pressure their political representatives to legitimate it.

Social identity clearly plays a key role in swaying public opinion (Spector and Kitsuse, 1977; Turner, 1969). Discredited individuals and groups find it difficult to gain a sympathetic ear. Prominent and "legitimate" persons (e.g., scientific experts and religious leaders) more easily capture an audience. Those attempting to reverse a criminal stigma, i.e., to alter the public's definition of a given practice, such as marijuana use or prostitution, find the task extremely difficult. For they appear to have a self-serving interest in changing the public's mind.

Assuming equal social respectability among interested parties in a contest to influence the legal process, the major factor in victory is the propaganda effort. Quality of organization and resources utilized in capturing media attention and in directing public sentiment to lawmakers and law enforcers are extremely telling variables. Interest groups attempt to employ symbols of the problem at hand—definitions and pictures of the problem and the people implicated in it that easily capture the public imagination. Thus, stereotypes are promoted (of the drug user, the rapist, the psychopath, the pornographer, and so forth) that fit the general public conception of evil and danger. Edelman (1977:14) argues that the ability to create a "personified" danger, i.e., to put a face to the problem even if that face is in reality a rarity, "marshals public support for controls over a much larger number of ambiguous cases symbolically condensed into the threatening stereotype."

Vocabularies also are created that subtly (and at times not so subtly) seek to bias the public (Edelman, 1977:26). For example, "pro-abortion" groups choose to characterize themselves as "pro-choice," while "anti-abortion" groups label themselves "pro-life." Homosexuals present themselves as "gay" while their opponents call them "perverts" (Spector and Kitsuse, 1977:13–16). Such tactics accomplish more than simply gaining a public forum for an issue. They transform the issue into a "good guy versus bad guy" contest that allows the public more easily to take a stand.

The result of the propaganda activity of groups contesting an issue often is public indignation about a fiction which has emerged from the competitive propaganda process. For the interest groups, the creation is symbolic. For the public, it is real. Gusfield (1981) offers an illustration in his study of "drinking-driving" laws, i.e., laws governing driving under the influence of alcohol. So effective were the "anti-drunk driver" campaigns by interested parties that the public now equates the notion of "drinking-driver" with that of "killer." Gusfield argues that this conception is at odds with reality, at least as it is measured by the types of cases brought before the courts, most of which generally are treated leniently.

Criticisms

The strength of the pluralist approach is essentially the weakness of the Marxian theories discussed earlier. Pluralists are able to demonstrate that much of the use of legal process involves the competing interests of many parties, not simply the maneuverings of an economic elite or of the state looking out for the long-term interests of that elite. Countering the pluralists, more radical instrumentalists argue that intergroup competition for both instrumental and symbolic legal support is a mirage, that ruling elites "allow" such competition (as long as it does not threaten specific ruling elite interests) in order to promote the impression that ours is a diversified, democratic society. Of course, this claim is untestable. Yet, it seems that pluralists may be open to the more modest criticism that they do not hear enough of the Marxian theorists' message. They pay lip service to power differentials, to the economic clout of corporations, and to a semiautonomous state. However, these elements are absent from most of their analyses.

In part, the absence of attention to elites is due to the types of law creation studied by pluralists. Pornography laws, for example, reflect the activity of groups of roughly equal power and organization; and such laws tend not to threaten any specified corporate interests. But how might pluralists explain tax law structure or weak legal control of corporations responsible for oil spills on our coasts despite very organized and strong efforts to gain such control (Molotch, 1970)? The problem lies in the pluralist penchant for defining elite involvement in the legal process as defensive, i.e., as reacting only to direct economic threat. Surely elites are sufficiently aware of their interests and sufficiently organized to pursue them that much of their activity is anticipatory and aimed not simply at protection of interests but at their enhancement as well.

THREE EXAMPLES

In sum, the conflict perspective seems more aggressively and more convincingly to address the issue of the workings of the legal process than does the earlier described consensus model. Despite criticisms of elements of the instrumentalist and structuralist Marxian theories and of pluralist theories, the conflict perspective's basic argument cannot be ignored: Laws do not simply appear miraculously on our law books and do not reflect "society's" values. Instead they reflect the activity of groups in this society seeking legal support for economic, ideological, and status interests. Sometimes only a few groups are involved in the struggle for legal support; other times many groups compete. The issue contested in a legal struggle may be explicit and instrumental or may be symbolic of some greater conflict. Three examples highlight these points.

Example 1: Vagrancy Laws and Economic Interests

Few people would look beyond the moral indignation that tramps arouse in a society that labels itself dedicated to work and prosperity for the inspiration behind vagrancy laws. Yet a historical look at these laws indicates that they have had very little to do with morality or the work ethic. Rather, as William Chambliss (1964) argues in an analysis of vagrancy statutes in Anglo-American law, the laws generally have been designed and used to protect special economic interests and to control "undesirables."

Chambliss notes that the first known law related to vagrancy was a 1274 statute in England that forbade religious houses from giving food or shelter to travelers. So many persons, rich and poor, had taken advantage of these houses that they faced financial ruin. The new law was designed to give them economic relief.

The first specific vagrancy laws in England were passed around 1350. These statutes made it a crime to give alms to anyone who was unemployed but healthy. Further, they made unemployment among the healthy illegal if work at the standard wage of the time was available. Finally, they prohibited movement from one county to another to find work for higher wages. These laws represented attempts by rural landowners to maintain cheap labor in the face of drastic labor reductions caused by the Black Death, a plague that struck England in 1348 (Orcutt, 1983:39). The unemployment status effectively prohibited workers from economically "black-mailing" the landowners. The ordinance making it criminal to move in search of work was designed to prevent laborers from fleeing to rapidly industrializing larger towns, which offered higher wages.

England eventually recovered its economic footing, and revisions of the vagrancy laws did not appear again until 1530. New laws called for whippings, maimings, and imprisonment for beggars, transients, and people engaging in "unlawful games" (for example, peddlers and con men). Chambliss points out that these changes coincided with increased threats to England's movement toward international commercialism. Foreign merchants were becoming hesitant to enter the country because they were constantly being robbed on English roads. In an attempt to better control the "criminal classes" that undoubtedly included the robbers, the government passed harsher vagrancy laws.

The control pattern established by the 1530 laws continued into modern-day England and into the United States, until the U.S. Supreme Court in 1972 struck down vagrancy laws. Vagrancy statutes have been used to control members of undesirable groups—the lower classes, racial and ethnic minorities, student radicals—and were used extensively in the Great Depression and Dust Bowl era to prevent migrants from taking jobs or joining the welfare rolls of towns throughout the country.

In sum, Chambliss's examination of the history of vagrancy laws indicates that morality and law do not exist in a vaccum. At no time have the vagrancy laws been directed at vagrancy alone. Instead, they have been written and enforced to protect special economic interests. The analysis of the vagrancy laws should prompt us to take less for granted when faced with any legislative attempt to "control crime."

Example 2: Prostitution Laws and Diverse Interests

In September 1967, a law took effect in the state of New York which made prostitution (the exchange of sexual favors for a fee) and patronizing a prostitute violations, i.e., acts less serious than crimes yet still illegal. A violation is punishable by a maximum of fifteen days in jail as opposed to the maximum one-year jail term for prostitutes under the previous state law. Prior to the 1967 revision, patronizing a prostitute was not illegal.

According to Pamela Roby (1969), the new law emerged from the work of a state governor's commission appointed in 1961 to revise the state's penal code. Following other states' penal code revisions and at the urging of a former Supreme Court justice, the commission proposed that prostitution be considered a violation but did not address the issue of patronizing prostitutes in their proposed code revision. However, when the proposed revision was presented at a public hearing, certain interested parties apparently caught opponents unaware and persuaded the commission to amend the proposal. An organization called the American Social Health Association argued that patronizing prostitutes should be outlawed in an effort to help prevent the spread of venereal disease. Others argued that patronizing should be outlawed in simple fairness—if prostitution is wrong, both parties to it are wrong. The new law, enacted in 1965 and effective in September 1967, radically altered the legal status of prostitutes and their customers.

Before the new law took effect, another interest group exerted itself. Police and prosecutors argued that they would not be able to combat prostitution since customers of prostitutes would now be unwilling to testify against them in court and plainclothes officers now would face legal problems in arresting prostitutes. To force the issue, the police apparently relaxed their enforcement of prostitution laws in downtown Manhattan just before the new law was to take effect. Rumors flew concerning an "invasion" of prostitutes into the area, and this brought yet another group into the legal battle—downtown merchants and hotel owners who claimed that businesses were being hurt by rampant street prostitution. Their political representatives began pressuring the police for more arrests. At this point, the commission which drafted the new law reentered the fray to defend it.

Just as the new law became effective, the police jammed the courts with massive arrests of women charged with loitering. They argued that this was their only means to combat prostitution. This tactic brought yet another interest group into the conflict: the New York Civil Liberties Union and the Legal Aid Society who protested the dragnet as a violation of the arrested women's civil rights. To end the conflict, the New York City mayor appointed a new committee that accepted the police and prosecutors' proposal that prostitution be made a misdemeanor (a crime) punishable by up to a year in jail. The new proposal was presented to the appropriate state senate committee for review.

In a surprise move, the state senate committee effectively killed the proposed revision for at least a year, ostensibly because they felt a year in jail too harsh a penalty for prostitution. Yet, Roby notes that members of the senate committee had very close ties to the original commission that drafted the prostitution statute causing the conflict. One coalition had outfought the other. The process by which certain parties had structured and then protected the new law represents the classic pluralist approach example of the legal process. It underscores perfectly the pluralist notion of the multiplicity of groups and interests (instrumental and symbolic) that shape the law.

Example 3: Prohibition Laws and Symbolism

We noted earlier that not all interest group conflicts are economic in nature. Nowhere is this made clearer than in Joseph Gusfield's *Symbolic Crusade* (1963), a historical analysis of the temperance movement in America. In addition to arguing persuasively that the fight over the prohibition of alcoholic beverages was primarily a cultural and status conflict, Gusfield suggests that contested behaviors often reflect deeper-rooted, less distinct issues.

According to Gusfield, nineteenth-century America was controlled primarily by rural, white, middle-class Protestants. The dominant cultural views of the era stressed moderation and hard work. Nondrinking was characteristic of higher-status groups, drinking a sign of lower status. The dominant position of the more powerful, higher-status groups was challenged in the late nineteenth and early twentieth centuries by the influx of new cultural values and lifestyles accompanying massive European immigration into this country. America's newcomers—lower-class, predominantly Catholic, urban dwellers—placed different values on work and leisure, including drinking behavior. Alcoholic beverage consumption played an important role in their leisure activities.

The focus of life in America began to shift. The traditional status position of rural, Protestant America began to erode. These general shifts were undoubtedly imperceptible. Inevitably, some more tangible issue would rise to the surface and force a conflict symbolic of the deeper status and cultural problems. Gusfield argues that Prohibition became this symbolic issue. A primary method of maintaining a group's status position is the translation of the group's views into public law. Enforced or not, a law represents a symbolic stamp of approval for the group it favors. Thus, the Prohibition laws of 1919, banning the importation, manufacture, and sale of alcoholic beverages, represented a symbolic victory for traditional higher-status Americans. Life in America seemed destined to remain as it had been for these people. The dream faded with the repeal of the Eighteenth Amendment of 1933, a symbolic defeat for the traditional higher-status groups. The end of Prohibition signaled the coming of major political and cultural changes in America.

Gusfield's analysis of the symbolic content of an interest-group-initiated law might also be applied to more recent legal debates over such issues as pornography, abortion, liberalized homosexual laws, and gun control. The legislation and enforcement of drug laws in the 1960s may have symbolized an attack on "New Left," "unpatriotic," anticapitalist, antiwar college youth by "middle America" seeking to preserve traditional values. These examples suggest that we always look beyond contested behaviors in the larger, more complex society for the underlying issues they may mask.

SUMMARY

This chapter stressed the theme that law does not exist in a vacuum. The acts and people we call "criminal" and our concern with crime at any given time reflect the work of various interest groups within society's current power structure. The ebb and flow of law is the ebb and flow of interest groups. Laws emerging from this process must be viewed as tentative and negotiable and as potentially highly symbolic. The key issue now for conflict theorists concerns the political strength of the major economic interests in this society. Do they stand alone or do they share power with other relatively weaker groups?

We introduced this chapter by noting that there is a "forest" (the forces which structure definitions of law and crime) behind the more traditional "trees" (who commits crimes and why?) studied by criminologists. We will not devote the rest of this book to relating every issue we encounter to America's power structure. This issue is extremely important, but so is the danger of forgetting about the trees while we study the forest. We can become so focused upon underlying interests that we forget that crime itself is real and hurts many people. Crime fears are real too, and they victimize most of us. Proposed solutions to our "crime problem" also are real and potentially very costly. In terms of our present interest, the conflict perspective is not an end in itself but a means to grasp better the issues confronted in this book. It is tied to the first of the three questions raised in the previous chapter's discussion of responses to the "crime problem": What is the nature and scope of the "crime problem"—what are our assumptions about it?

In this chapter we have raised questions about the sources of the definitions of criminal behavior that shape our concern with crime. Coming chapters are devoted to evaluating various aspects of the "crime problem," which we have described in Part I of this book. In Chapters 4 and 5 we will review crime statistics to determine how many and what types of crimes seem to be occurring today. In Chapters 6 and 7 we will analyze research on basic sociodemographic characteristics of criminals and victims in order to develop a picture of who victimizes whom.

REFERENCES

Bagozzi, R. P. 1977. Populism and lynching in Louisiana. *Am. Sociol. Rev.* 42:355–58.

Balkan, S., Berger, R., and Schmidt, J. 1980. *Crime and Deviance in America.* Belmont, Calif.: Wadsworth Publishing Company.

Becker, H. S. 1963. *Outsiders.* New York: Free Press.

Chambliss, W. 1964. A sociological analysis of the law of vagrancy. *Soc. Prob.* 12:67–77.

———. 1974. The state, the law, and the definition of behavior as criminal or delinquent. In *Handbook of Criminology.* Edited by D. Glaser. Chicago: Rand McNally & Co.

Chambliss, W., and R. Seidman. 1982. *Law, Order, and Power.* 2nd. ed. Reading, Mass.: Addison-Wesley Publishing Co.

Coser, L. 1956. *The Functions of Social Conflict.* Glencoe, Ill.: Free Press.

Domhoff, G. W. 1967. *Who Rules America?* Englewood Cliffs, N.J.: Prentice-Hall.

———. 1978. *The Powers That Be.* New York: Random House.

Durkheim, E. 1933. *The Division of Labor in Society.* Translated by G. Simpson. New York: Free Press.

———. 1958. *The Rules of Sociological Method.* Translated by S. A. Soloway and J. H. Mueller. Glencoe, Ill.: Free Press.

Edelman, M. 1964. *The Symbolic Uses of Politics.* Urbana, Ill.: University of Illinois Press.

———. 1977. *Political Language.* New York: Academic Press.

Erikson, K. 1966. *Wayward Puritans.* New York: John Wiley & Sons.

Friedman, W. 1972. *Law in a Changing Society.* Harmondsworth, England: Penguin Books.

Galliher, J. F., and J. R. Cross. 1982. Symbolic severity in the land of easy virtue: Nevada's high marijuana penalty. *Soc. Prob.* 29:380–86.

Galliher, J. F., and A. Walker. 1977. The puzzle of the social origins of the Marihuana Tax Act of 1937. *Soc. Prob.* 24:367–76.

Greenberg, D. 1981. *Crime and Capitalism: Readings in Marxist Criminology.* Palo Alto, Calif.: Mayfield Publishing.

Gusfield, J. 1963. *Symbolic Crusade.* Urbana, Ill.: University of Illinois Press.

———. 1981. *The Culture of Public Problems: Drinking-Driving and the Symbolic Order.* Chicago: University of Chicago Press.

Hall, J. 1952. *Theft, Law and Society.* 2nd ed. Indianapolis: The Bobbs-Merrill Co.

Hill, J. 1975. *Class Analysis: United States in the 1970s.* Emeryville, Calif.

Hughes, E. C. 1962. Good people and dirty work. *Soc. Prob.* 10:3–11.

Inverarity, J. 1976. Populism and lynching in Louisiana: A test of Erikson's theory of the relationship between boundary crises and repressive justice. *Am. Sociol. Rev.* 41:262–80.

Jackson, P., and L. Carroll. 1981. Race and the war on crime. *Am. Sociol. Rev.* 46:290–305.

Jacobs, D. 1979. Inequality and police strength: Conflict theory and coercive control in metropolitan areas. *Am. Sociol. Rev.* 44:913–25.

Jeffrey, C. R. 1957. The development of crime in early English society. *J. Crim. Law Criminol. & Pol. Sci.* 47:647–66.

Liska, A., J. Laurence, and M. Benson. 1981. Perspectives on the legal order: The capacity for social control. *Am. J. Sociol.* 87:413–26.

Mead, G. H. 1918. The psychology of punitive justice. *Am. J. Sociol.* 23:577–602.

Mills, C. W. 1956. *The Power Elite.* New York: Oxford.

Molotch, H. 1970. Oil in Santa Barbara and power in America. *Sociol. Inq.* 40:131–44.

Orcutt, J. D. 1983. *Analyzing Deviance.* Homewood, Ill.: Dorsey Press.

Pfohl, S. J. 1977. The "discovery" of child abuse. *Soc. Prob.* 24:310–23.

Pope, W., and C. Ragin. 1977. Mechanical solidarity, repressive justice, and lynchings in Louisiana. *Am. Sociol. Rev.* 42:363–68.

Quinney, R. 1970. *The Social Reality of Crime.* Boston: Little, Brown and Company.

———. 1980. *Class, State and Crime.* 2nd. ed. New York: Longman.

Rich, R. M. 1978. Sociological paradigms and the sociology of law. In *The Sociology of Law.* Edited by C. E. Reasons and R. M. Rich. Toronto: Butterworths.

Roby, P. A. 1969. Politics and criminal law: Revision of the New York State penal law on prostitution. *Soc. Prob.* 17:83–109.

Silver, A. 1967. The demand for order in civil society: A review of some themes in the history of urban crime, police and riots. In *The Police.* Edited by D. Bordua. New York: John Wiley & Sons.

Spector, M., and J. I. Kitsuse. 1977. *Constructing Social Problems.* Menlo Park, Calif.: Benjamin/Cummings Publishing Company.

Spitzer, S. 1979. The rationalization of crime control in capitalist society. *Contemp. Crises* 3:187–206.

Troyer, R. J., and G. E. Markle. 1982. Creating deviant rules: A macroscopic model. *Sociol. Q.* 23:157–69.

Turk, A. 1976. Law as a weapon in social conflict. *Soc. Prob.* 23:276–91.

Turner, R. 1969. The public perception of protest. *Am. Sociol. Rev.* 34:815–31.

Zurcher, L. A., R. George, R. G. Cushing, et al. 1971. The anti-pornography campaign: A symbolic crusade. *Soc. Prob.* 19:217–38.

SUGGESTED READINGS

A number of books provide an understanding of legislation and law enforcement as a product of interest group conflict. Charles E. Reasons and Robert M. Rich offer an overview of the sociology of law in *The Sociology of Law: A Conflict Perspective* (Toronto: Butterworths, 1978). Richard Quinney's *Class, State and Crime,* 2nd edition (New York: Longman, 1980) expresses the Marxian instrumentalist position well. David F. Greenberg's *Crime and*

Capitalism (Palo Alto, Calif.: Mayfield Publishing, 1981) and William Chambliss and Robert Seidman's *Law, Order and Power,* 2nd edition (Reading, Mass.: Addison-Wesley Publishing Co., 1982) make the Marxian structuralist approach understandable. Finally, the pluralist approach and the meaning of symbolism in legislation is demonstrated in Joseph Gusfield's *Symbolic Crusade* (Urbana, Ill.: University of Illinois Press, 1963) and *The Culture of Public Order: Drinking-Driving and the Symbolic Order* (Chicago: University of Chicago Press, 1981).

PART II

THE STATISTICAL PICTURE

Most of what we hear and read about crime represents condensations and distortions of official crime statistics. How reliable are these statistics? Chapters 4 and 5 review what we have learned about crime from official and unofficial sources.

4

CRIME FACTS
AND FIGURES

Official crime statistics obviously are important for governmental anticrime policy, but their importance in our everyday lives rarely is considered. As noted earlier, a realistic assessment of crime statistics is mandatory if sound decisions are to be made about crime prevention.

For most people, the "reality" of crime is, in great part, a matter of news media summaries of official crime statistics—crimes reported, arrests, convictions, persons imprisoned, and so forth. Most of these statistics, as we have stated, are for the "major" FBI Index offenses of homicide, assault, rape, robbery, burglary, larceny, motor vehicle theft, and arson. Statistics on "lesser" offenses, organized crime, white-collar crime, and similar activities, are available only on a limited basis, if available at all.

Before we review current crime data, we should discuss certain problems with official statistics that according to some critics render these statistics worthless or at least suggest the need for cautious interpretation.

STATISTICS AS SOCIAL CONSTRUCTS

In the present context, the term *statistic* refers to a description of some social phenomenon, usually expressed in terms of rates or percentages to facilitate geographic, cultural, and temporal comparison. Thus, we refer to a rate of twelve homicides per 100,000 persons in city A in 1982 and twenty per 100,000 in city B in the same year. Or we note that 15 percent of the population of city A was criminally victimized in 1981 while only 8 percent suffered the same fate in 1982. In short, a statistic provides a picture of some social situation—in this instance, a picture of a crime situation.

Artistic pictures do not simply appear. They result from an artist's activity. We often fail to view crime statistics in this fashion. Although we realize that we possess no radar that detects and records all crimes, we continue to act as if we do or as if the error in our perception is random or constant. That is, we act as if crime pictures paint themselves. However, crime statistics are better viewed as *social constructs*, the result of social activity whereby organizations and workers within them exercise varying degrees of discretion in choosing among behavioral options regarding their approaches to crime (Cicourel, 1968; Kitsuse and Cicourel, 1963). The notion of organization used here is broad. It includes both policy and citizens. Crime rates are *produced* through the interaction of police departmental crime classification policy, the crime-reporting behavior of policy officers in the field, and citizen crime-reporting. The end product of the use of discretion by these "agents" is the crime statistic or, more generally, a picture of crime for a region or community. The statistic or picture is a construct and, logically, could be constructed otherwise if other behavioral options were pursued by police or citizens.

This view of the production of pictures of crime in no way dismisses the possibility of behavioral changes among criminals altering the picture of crime provided by official crime statistics. If the migration, age, or economic patterns of a community were altered, for example, we could expect increases or decreases in certain types of crime. However, these changes may or may not be reflected in official crime statistics since we cannot be certain of the extent to which the criminal justice system perceives and adapts to the changes. Thus, before proceeding to the hypothesis that crime statistics reflect the activity of criminals solely or even in part, we must first examine the hypothesis that crime statistics reflect the discretionary activities of criminal justice agents and the citizenry.

McCleary et al. (1982; see also Sheley and Hanlon, 1978) provide some excellent examples of crime statistics as "organizational outcomes." They studied three cases of change (a drastic increase or decrease) in burglary statistics in two cities. In one city, numbers of officially recognized burglaries decreased drastically when detectives rather than uniformed officers began investigating and filing reports on burglaries. The difference, according to the authors, was a matter of definition. Uniformed officers often mistakenly classified simple thefts (stealing an item) as a burglary (breaking and entering a building). If a thief breaks through a fence and steals something from a yard, for example, no burglary has occurred. If the thief breaks into an enclosed garage or house, a burglary has occurred. Uniformed officers often failed to apply proper definitional criteria; detectives were more exact. The difference in precision accounted for a difference of about 150 officially recorded burglaries each month in the cities in question.

The same city experienced a major rise in reported crime, including burglaries, at a later date when administrators removed supervisory sergeants from the radio dispatch bureau. It is this bureau that takes incoming calls from citizens and decides whether or not to send an officer directly to the scene of the reported problem. Immediately dispatched service calls have a greater likelihood of resulting in an official crime report than do later responses to a call for assistance. When sergeants were supervising the bureau, they functioned to relieve dispatchers of the responsibility of determining the immediate need for an officer at a potential crime scene. When sergeants were absent, dispatchers were more likely to order an immediate service call in an effort to protect themselves. To err in needlessly dispatching an officer is less serious than to err in failing to send an officer when one truly is needed. Reported crimes increased about 20 percent in the absence of sergeant-supervisors.

A second city studied by McCleary and his colleagues experienced a 20 percent increase in burglaries over a six-month period. The authors attribute the increase to a change in chiefs of the city's policy department and the effects of that change on the administrative hierarchy. The retirement of the incumbent chief resulted in as many as three dozen personnel changes at or above the rank of captain and other changes below the rank. One change involved the commander and sergeant in charge of the statistics bureau of the department. As the commander, anticipating the administrative changes, distanced himself from the bureau, the sergeant began making all decisions concerning classification of cases as crimes. When the sergeant departed, clerks in the bureau exercised discretion in classifying crimes—a new freedom for them. Each person making classification decisions employed the definitional criteria for coding crimes slightly differently. The difference meant an increase of two or three burglaries per day which, taken together over six months, pushed the city's volume of burglaries up 20 percent.

McCleary et al. (1982) suggest that a researcher unfamiliar with the organizational changes in the departments studied would encounter problems in making sense of the sudden peaks and valleys in the departments' crime figures. In the present instance, all statistical changes apparently were attributable to organizational factors, not to changes in the behavior of criminals. This finding recalls our earlier warning that the first hypothesis offered to explain changes in a community's crime picture must focus attention on the activity of the criminal justice system and citizen reporting behavior.

PROBLEMS WITH CRIME STATISTICS

The organizational problems noted in the above example are only part of the influences on crime statistics. More general problems revolve around the degree of competence of policy agencies collecting crime statistics, the crime classification choices available to police, and unreported crimes.

NEWSPRINT AND COMMENT

Drug Arrests Up 78% in 4 Months

By Pearl Stewart

Drug arrests in Oakland during the first four months of 1983 increased 78 percent over the same period last year, due to a change of emphasis away from major dealers and toward small-time sellers and users.

A report issued yesterday by Police Chief George Hart said police have made 1686 drug-related arrests so far this year, 636 of them in key "target areas" identified by police as high trafficking locations. During the month of April, 358 drug arrests were made.

He said the increase in arrests is largely due to "new strategies" in tackling Oakland's drug problem.

"We're adjusting our resources and priorities away from the major dealers and more toward the street-level dealers and users who are polluting the parks and neighborhoods," Hart said.

Hart added that undercover officers are still concentrating on top-level traffickers, but that the "major thrust" of the department is to "clean up the streets." Three narcotics officers have been added to the previous six, and more will be added in coming weeks, Hart said. A "street enforcement task force" has been formed within the vice section to work daily on making on-the-street drug arrests.

The City Council in April asked Hart to begin making monthly reports on drug arrests in the city. His report yesterday was the first in response to their request.

Hart acknowledged that the new strategy is partly in response to demands from community groups that police crack down on blatant drug dealing in parks, housing projects and street corners.

One group in particular, Oakland Community Organizations, has held public meetings during the past few months to call attention to public drug-dealing areas.

One of the biggest increases has been in the arrests of addicts under the influence of drugs. So far this year, 415 addicts have been taken into custody, compared with 120 last year to date—an increase of 246 percent.

Hart said the drug problem in Oakland has become more noticeable, but not necessarily more prevalent.

The target areas for the drug arrests are in much of West Oakland, the San Antonio Park area of East Oakland, the Lockwood Gardens housing project, Arroyo Viejo Park and several areas along East 14th Street and 98th Avenue.

Source: © San Francisco Chronicle, 1983. Reprinted by permission.

The Crackdown *(Chief's Statistics)*

	This month	1983 to date	1982 to date	% change
Heroin and Cocaine				
Possession	48	180	133	+35
Possession for sale	51	154	97	+59
Sale	4	17	27	−37
Total	103	351	257	+37
Marijuana				
Possession	56	422	181	+133
Possession for sale	32	147	134	+10
Sale	24	54	40	+35
Cultivation	0	1	3	−67
Total	112	624	358	+74
Other Dangerous Drugs				
Possession	22	77	46	+67
Possession for sale	11	49	33	+48
Sale	0	6	12	−50
Total	33	132	91	+45
Addict (under influence)	78	415	120	+246
Miscellaneous Drugs	32	164	121	+36
Overall Total	358	1686	947	+78

Comment: What Do Crime Statistics Mean?

In this chapter, and later in Chapter 10, we view crime statistics more as a product of police work than as a reflection of actual crime levels. This is not the case across the board, of course. Some statistics better reflect the "reality" of crime than do others. We assume a fairly high level of validity in homicide statistics. But vice-crime statistics are our least valid. As the above article indicates, radical changes in arrest rates (the primary indicator of drug "problems" in most cities) can occur easily with changes in police arrest policy.

In the present instance, the police have concentrated their efforts on "street traffic" rather than on apprehending major dealers. "Street traffic" supposedly refers to both sale and possession of drugs. However, note that the largest increases in arrests pertain to possession of marijuana and being "under the influence" of drugs. In short, under pressure from various community groups to rid neighborhoods of drug activty, the police have turned their attention to the easiest to apprehend of persons involved in drugs—users. In so doing, they present a picture of police activity that satisfies the complaining interest groups. It is assumed, however, that the users will move on to other sites and that, soon, the police will have to respond to the complaints of residents of those sites. Arrest statistics will reflect this response.

Competence

The reliability of a set of statistics rests on the competence of the agency compiling it. Unsophisticated data-collection methods will produce unsophisticated estimates of the incidence of crime. Police departments vary in the expertise with which they collect and assemble crime information. The "mark on the wall" method of the small department and the complex computerized methods of larger urban departments both carry liabilities. Changes in crime statistics personnel or in procedures within police department statistics units will affect crime rates in the communities they serve. It is not unusual to find a new police chief, brought in from outside the department, in trouble after crime apparently has risen during his first year of command. The problem often reflects progressive changes the new chief has instituted in both the dispatching and statistics bureaus. Better dispatching and data collection mean more reported crime. Thus, the chief's competence creates the illusion of incompetence.

Classification Choices

Though legal definitions of crime might seem quite precise, police departments actually have considerable latitude in crime classification. For example, in a physical encounter between two citizens, any number of possible charges might materialize—attempted murder, assault, disturbing the peace. An attempted rape may be labeled assault. A burglary may be called trespassing. A purse snatching may be a robbery, an assault, or a theft. Crime classification often is made with the anticipated response of the district attorney's office in mind. Thus, it is clear that a police department's inclinations in classifying crimes will affect a community's crime rates.

It must be remembered also that crime statistics represent *political statements*. They may reflect on a political administration's promises to reduce crime, and crimes thus may be classified as of a less serious nature. For example, Seidman and Couzens (1974), reviewing the results of a Nixon administration "law and order" campaign against crime in the District of Columbia in the early 1970s, argue that though crime reductions appeared to reflect crime-control innovations, they actually reflected the police department's classification of offenses at less serious levels in order to protect the jobs of police officials. Similar charges were leveled against the Philadelphia police department under the Rizzo administration in the 1970s when that city's crime statistics appeared far out of line with those of comparably large cities (Guinther, 1975). Though obviously rarer, the possibility also exists that a police department's request for more funds, personnel, or equipment may be given credence by the establishment of a "crime problem" in the community—in part a matter of classifying crimes as highly serious.

Unreported Crimes

Official statistics do not account for the "dark area" of crime—offenses that are unreported or undetected by police, observers, or victims. Much of the "dark area" is attributable to police departmental policy. It is obvious that departmental decisions about deployment of resources to combat crime (use of patrol cars and officers on foot; placement and hours of patrol) will influence the number of crimes detected by police. Further, police campaigns against crime, especially vice crime, may dictate a nonreporting or nonarrest policy. All such policies always are unwritten. By law, police cannot purposely ignore crimes, but it is clear that choices must be and are made. An attempt to break an organized crime operation or a narcotics ring might be hindered, for example, by arrests of lower-level operatives. It is common for police departments to trade arrests for information about more highly-placed criminals. This practice, of course, means that the public never receives the complete picture of crime (Goldstein, 1960). Decisions to ignore certain crimes also can be influenced by members of other criminal justice agencies. For example, district attorneys and judges, by virtue of their ability to embarrass a police department in the news media, can demand that police ignore many vice crimes, such as drug sales, which tend to overburden the courts. Similarly, the courts may direct the police department not to file official reports in assault cases involving spouses. These cases increase the assault rate but rarely result in official indictments, thus making the criminal justice system appear inefficient.

Again, we recall the political nature of crime statistics. At times, political pressures result in a suppression of crime reports. While generally free of day-to-day political interference from outside the criminal justice system, police departments are susceptible, over time, to the pressures of the more powerful leaders of a community who choose the police chief and control the police budget (Wilson, 1968). Thus, it is not uncommon for business leaders to force police to devote attention to driving prostitution from a major commercial zone, thus inflating the officially reported prostitution rate. Of course, political pressure also may dictate ignoring certain types of offenses. Hotel and bar owners may pressure police to ease surveillance of unauthorized gambling or the sale of alcohol to minors. Political leaders may press for a softer approach to investigations of misuse of political office. Garage owners and car dealers may persuade the police to overlook the illegal parking of automobiles in restricted zones.

Police on Patrol

Officers in the field shape crime statistics as much as or more than does departmental policy. On the one hand it is clear that much of police work is structured by the department in the sense that directives are given, arrest records are monitored, and supervisors' wishes are made known. Promotions are based in large part on evaluations of an officer's performance in the field. Studies indicate that regardless of general departmental policy, a police officer's immediate superior, usually a sergeant, exerts the major influence on his or her work since it is that superior who evaluates that officer's work in the field (Rubinstein, 1973).

On the other hand, it is important to realize that police retain considerable autonomy in the field. They are not directly supervised throughout the majority of their watch and, for this reason, enjoy much discretion in dealing with crime situations. Much of their use of discretion is determined by their perceptions of what their jobs are designed to accomplish. Police officers in urban areas, for example, tend to view their jobs as "maintaining order" within specific neighborhoods or territories. Thus, "street justice" is often dispensed, with officers harassing or punishing individuals and sending them on their way (Bittner, 1967; Rubinstein, 1973). The same notion of "maintaining order" informs officers' decisions to settle disputes without arresting the parties involved, to escort home rather than to jail an intoxicated person, or to bring a juvenile offender to his parents rather than to the police station (LaFave, 1965). Finally, the police officers' views of their mission determine their attitudes toward procedural law. Officers vary in the extent to which they are willing to circumvent (and to lie about circumventing) procedural rules. It is nearly impossible to control this situation since there generally are no witnesses to encounters between police and citizens involving abuses of procedural law (Skolnick, 1975). Official statistics do not reflect accurately these various uses of discretion.

Both the seriousness of the crime investigated and various situational factors in an investigation shape the officer's decision concerning the reporting of a crime. Clearly, there are some offenses that an officer cannot ignore— homicide or armed robbery, for example. In general, reporting and arrest discretion occur more frequently regarding lesser offenses and vice crimes. A police officer's decision to file an official report for a crime incident or to make an arrest for a given crime depends on the physical setting in which the police-citizen interaction occurs, the number of witnesses present and their involvement in the interaction, the demeanor of the citizen making the complaint and the demeanor of any alleged offenders present, and the relational distance between the complainant and the suspect (a report is less likely if both are from the same family, for example) (Black, 1970). Finally, it is clear that an officer's personal biases easily can enter the potential reporting and arrest situation. Officers develop stereotypes of criminals and crime situations that may facilitate police work at times but may also result in discriminatory treatment of persons in the field (Piliavin and Briar, 1964; Rubinstein, 1973).

One last determinant of police decisions in the field must be considered: police corruption. Nonenforcement of laws may occur because police accept payoffs to "look the other way." Corruption represents more than a few "bad apples" on a police force. Most graft is related to vice crimes, and most police officers receive some form of encouragment to accept payoffs. A number of factors provide the encouragement: lack of a community consensus regarding the morality of the vices; relative community apathy regarding the enforcement of vice laws; a demand for vice services; lack of control over the police by honest, powerful citizens; low visibility of police graft; greater monetary rewards for graft than for its avoidance; lack of sanctioning from the police hierarchy; explicit encouragement by fellow officers; the occasional usefulness of graft to gain order within a given police territory; and constant offers of payoffs from every form of business (Gardiner, 1970; Rubinstein, 1973). As officers are constantly exposed to offers of money and favors, lower forms of corruption lead to greater forms (Sherman, 1974).

Citizen Nonreporting

Victimization survey results indicate that 55 percent of crimes of violence, 76 percent of thefts from individuals, and 64 percent of household burglaries, larcenies, and motor vehicle thefts are not reported to the police (U.S. Department of Justice, 1981:76). Even if these figures represent exaggerated estimates, clearly much crime is unreported by victims and considerably more goes unreported by observers not directly touched by the crimes they see.

There are many reasons why citizens do not report crimes. First, observers may not realize they are witnessing an illegal act. Second, they may know it to be illegal but may feel the matter is of a private nature, such as a family fight. Third, they may believe reporting a crime may result in inconvenience, harassment, or even reprisals. Fourth, they may fear their insurance policies may be cancelled or premiums increased if a victimization is reported. Fifth, they may place a negative value on cooperation with the police or may view them as incompetent or uninterested in the crime question. Sixth, they may simply be ignorant of the procedures for reporting a crime. Finally, they may be involved in other crimes that might be discovered if they reported the offense in question—for example, a person would probably be reluctant to report his car stolen if the backseat contained stolen goods.

Any rise in crime, it may be theorized, may simply represent increased citizen willingness to report crimes, and this problem makes interpretation of crime statistics particularly difficult. Thus, do currently increasing rape rates, for example, reflect more attacks on women, changes in women's attitudes about reporting rapes, or both? Perhaps the recent proliferation of rape crisis centers and the development of new police techniques for dealing compassionately with rape victims mean that rape rate increases represent, at least in part, changes in the reporting of rape. Similarly, are thefts on the rise? Or are theft reports on the rise because more people now carry theft insurance and insurance companies require that property thefts be reported to the police before claims can be settled?

The Uniform Crime Reports

Our present concern is with the FBI's *Uniform Crime Reports* (1982), which contains the most frequently cited crime figures. *The Uniform Crime Reports* is a yearly FBI publication that presents the number of crimes committed in the U.S. during the previous year. Individual law enforcement agencies compile crime statistics based on definitions of crimes supplied by the FBI and report their figures to the FBI every month. Agencies currently reporting such statistics serve 95 percent of the U.S. population. "Crimes," in the *Uniform Crime Reports* context, refer to *the complaints or reports of crimes made to the police and determined through investigation to be legitimate.*

The *Uniform Crime Reports* distinguishes between Part I (or Index) offenses and Part II offenses. Part I crimes are considered more serious. As we have stated, they include crimes of violence (homicide, forcible rape, aggravated assault, and robbery) and property offenses (burglary, larceny, motor vehicle theft, and arson). Statistics for these offenses generally are detailed, providing volume, rates, characteristics of arrestees, and comparisons of national regions and cities. Part II offenses generally are considered less serious (though this is debatable) and receive very little statistical attention in the *Uniform Crime Reports*. They include such crimes as forgery, fraud, embezzlement, vandalism, prostitution, gambling, possession of weapons, and buying, receiving, or possessing stolen goods. Most assessments of crime are based on analysis of Part I offenses. Hence, the problems with official crime figures pertain primarily to these crimes.

Critiques of the *Uniform Crime Reports* are abundant (Beattie, 1960; Chilton, 1980; Hindelang, 1974). One of the more thorough and recent is offered by Leonard Savitz (1982). Among the more prominent problems are:

1. The statistics reflect state cases only and ignore federal cases—a high number of offenses.
2. Not all police departments report their crime statistics to the FBI. Therefore, the FBI inflates police-reported figures to gain an estimate of total crime. This presents problems for states with low reporting levels. Savitz notes, for example, that only one-half of Mississippi's rural departments reported to the FBI in 1978. Since one-half of the state's population was rural, the FBI doubled the number of rural crimes (from 5,000 to 10,000). Thus, the state gained 5,000 new crimes which were not empirically validated.
3. Multiple offenses occurring in one crime incident (for example, a murder, a rape, and a robbery) result in only one crime appearing in the *Uniform Crime Reports*—always the more serious offense.
4. The *Uniform Crime Reports'* concentration on the Index crimes and relative lack of attention to other offenses tends to give the public a distorted view of crime and tends to force police to concentrate only on Index offenses.
5. The inclusion of motor vehicle theft among Index property crimes is attributed to insurance company demands for official crime reports before reimbursements for lost vehicles are allowed. Yet, 80 percent of stolen automobiles are recovered. Thus, the *Uniform Crime Reports* tends to inflate somewhat artificially the volume of property crime reflected in the reports.
6. In this same vein, thefts of any amount are included in the *Uniform Crime Reports*. This is done to counter inflated reports of an item's worth by owners, but also tends to inflate the volume of property offenses with relatively minor offenses.
7. Attempted as well as completed crimes are reported together for five of the Index offenses: rape, robbery, assault, burglary, and motor vehicle theft.
8. There is debate concerning the inclusion of robbery among personal as opposed to property crimes. Were robbery treated as the latter, the picture of personal crimes would alter drastically.
9. Local and FBI classification criteria for crimes are not always parallel. Thus, it must be assumed that local police departments take the time to translate their crime statistics so that they are in concert with *Uniform Crime Reports* definitional criteria.

In sum, official crime statistics are highly dependent on citizen and police decisions to report, and these decisions help shape public views of how much and what types of crimes are committed and by whom. In order to use official statistics for important inferences about crime, then, we must accept either of two questionable assumptions: (1) that the "dark area" of unreported crime is rather small and remains fairly stable over time, or (2) that known crime constitutes a representative sample of "real crime." Some are more willing than others to grant such assumptions. Skogan (1974, 1977) argues that the *Uniform Crime Reports* are less flawed than often is thought, and that the "dark area" is composed primarily of lesser crimes. Similarly, after comparing other data sets with the *Uniform Crime Reports,* Hindelang (1974) argues that the latter are fairly accurate indicators of the relative incidence of Index offenses known to police. This position is contradicted by more recent research which indicates that the *Uniform Crime Reports* are not accurately assessing crime, at least in terms of comparisons with other measures of criminal activity (Booth et al., 1977; Cohen and Lichback, 1982).

Overall, a few critics reject official statistics totally (Quinney, 1979). Others argue that they are useful only in studying police organizational activity and have no value as indicators of crime levels (Kitsuse and Cicourel, 1963; McCleary et al., 1982). Nearly all agree that city-by-city, state-by-state, and region-by-region comparisons of crime rates are extremely problematic. Most criminologists realize that the *Uniform Crime Reports* are probably the best practical measure of the amount of crime in this society (Savitz, 1982). They can and must be used cautiously, and it seems that considerable use is necessary before one gains a sense of the extent to which they can be applied legitimately toward an understanding of current criminological issues.

TWO ALTERNATIVE WAYS OF ESTIMATING CRIME RATES

Given the problems with official crime statistics, many criminolgists sometimes turn to other sources for estimating the amount of crime, both nationally and locally. These sources are self-reported crime and victimization surveys. Like official police reports, both data sets reveal something about crime, but both also have their own problems.

Self-Reported Criminal Behavior

One way to gain a sense of how many crimes are being committed is, simply, to *ask* people whether or not they have committed crimes. Obviously, this procedure creates problems since the honest answerer risks embarrassment and even legal penalties. To avoid this problem, most self-report studies employ self-administered questionnaires and guarantee anonymity to their respondents. No attempt is made to identify the persons reporting the crimes, and hence it is assumed that respondents will not over- or underreport their offenses.

But are respondents honest when they complete self-report question-naires? Actually, probably more so than we at first might suspect. Using po-lygraph (lie detector) tests, Clark and Tifft (1966) found that most responses to standard self-report items were truthful (see also Akers et al., 1983). Re-searchers (Elliott and Voss, 1974; Hirschi, 1969) also have found that few respondents who report no offenses have police records. Other researchers (Gold, 1966) have established that self-report data generally are free of dis-honesty by questioning the respondents' peers and teachers about the verac-ity of their statements. Some criminologists report a reasonable degree of consistency in responses when respondents are asked again at a later date to complete a self-report questionnaire (Dentler and Monroe, 1961). Farring-ton (1973) reports that 75 percent of self-reported delinquency in one study was re-reported in a second study two years later. In short, it is doubtful that respondents who were dishonest in completing a questionnaire the first time would make an effort at consistency the second time. Finally, Farrington (1973) also added support to self-report research through his ability to pre-dict future delinquency through self-reported delinquency. Forty-seven per-cent of the self-reported delinquents whom Farrington identified as "future" official delinquents, in fact, developed police records within two years.

Despite the surprising degree of honesty in self-reports of delinquent be-havior, we should not be lulled into accepting them as a true measure of the extent of crime in this society. We cannot ignore the self-report technique's reliance on memory—and, honest or not, respondents certainly will have dif-ficulty recalling offenses and the frequency with which they committed them. Beyond this, Savitz et al. (1971) and Elliott and Ageton (1980) point up a number of other problems with self-report research:

1. Self-report studies often include many trivial, nonserious offense items (e.g., truancy, disobedience) and exclude more serious offense items (e.g., rape). Some dwell only on theft offenses. In short, self-re-port studies often focus on nonrepresentative offenses.
2. Frequency of offense behavior often is inflated in self-report studies because offense items overlap. For example, three items—shoplifting an item worth approximately $5, theft of an item worth approxi-mately $5.00, and theft of an item worth between $5 and $10—may receive three admissions though all three may reflect only one act.
3. Response categories in self-report studies often are ambiguous. Some studies simply ask respondents whether they have committed a certain offense "often," "sometimes," or "occasionally." Others provide "never," "once," and "two or more" as categories—thus lumping to-gether those who have committed two illegal acts and those who have committed many more. Yet, simply asking for a full numerical esti-mate raises problems of memory.

4. Self-report studies vary in temporal referent. Some limit respondents to recall within three or six months. Others ask about offenses committed during the past year. Some ask respondents if they *ever* have committed a given offense.
5. Self-report research results are not easily generalized since they so often rely on small, unrepresentative samples.

Only one of these criticisms really is open to argument: that concerning trivial offenses. Jensen and Rojek (1980:95) counter this criticism by noting that much self-report research simply utilizes FBI Index offenses for offense items. Further, many researchers weigh the offense items by seriousness when analyzing their data. Finally, they note that most of "real-life" crime is trivial and that the bulk of *Uniform Crime Reports* offenses are petty larcenies.

The other criticisms of self-reported criminal behavior measurement recently have been addressed in research by Elliott and Ageton (1980). They interviewed a national probability sample of 1726 adolescents aged eleven to seventeen in 1977 concerning their involvement in delinquencies in 1976. Their list of offenses included all FBI Part I offenses except homicide, 60 percent of Part II offenses, and a number of other offenses pertaining specifically to juveniles. Offense items were unambiguous. Respondents were asked the number of times they committed an offense or were pressed for more specific estimates if they reported a frequency of ten or more. Finally, a one-year recall period was used, anchored by reference to Christmas ("From Christmas a year ago to the Christmas just past, how many times. . .?").

Elliott and Ageton's sample reported a total of 84,000 offenses. The average number of offenses per respondent was fifty-two. A total of nearly 14,000 personal crimes (sexual assault, aggravated assault, simple assault, and robbery) were reported—an average of nine per respondent. About 17,500 property offenses (vandalism, burglary, auto theft, larceny, stolen goods, fraud, and joyriding) also were admitted—an average of eleven per respondent. Most of the youths in the sample were "low-level" offenders. Eighty-six percent committed fewer than five personal crimes in 1976, the vast majority of which were simple assaults (hitting or threatening to hit someone without intent to do serious harm). Seventy-one percent committed fewer than five property offenses, the great majority of which were vandalism crimes (destroying property).

Clearly, if we assume that each youth in the U.S. between the ages of eleven and seventeen (about 27,000,000) commits nine personal and eleven property crimes, the number of such crimes is astounding. Even if we reduce these numbers to five personal and property offenses, the number of crimes committed by this age group still exceeds the number of crimes by persons of all ages reported in the *Uniform Crime Reports.* The "dark area" of crime is large indeed. Exactly how large is the "dark area" we cannot say by examining these self-report studies, for their major weakness lies in their attention only to adolescents. It has been assumed that adults risk greater losses in admitting to criminal behavior and are therefore unlikely to respond candidly to a self-reported criminality survey. Thus, we have little data concerning adult criminal behavior (see Chapter 6).

Until we are able to develop techniques to obtain self-reported criminality estimates for adults, it is only with serious reservations that we can use self-report data to estimate the amounts and types of crime in this society. Based on available self-report research findings, it *appears* that;

1. Most people violate the law at least occasionally.
2. Most of the violations people commit are of relatively minor seriousness.
3. The "dark area" of Index crime is at least two or three times the amount of crime now officially recognized. The "dark area" of lesser, Part II offenses is much larger.

Victimization Surveys

Rather than ask individuals what crimes they have committed, some researchers prefer to ask their respondents about crimes committed against them. In this so-called "victimization survey," members of a large sample of the population are systematically interviewed to determine how many crimes have been committed against them. There are three advantages to the victimization survey, which make it superior to self-report studies and to the *Uniform Crime Reports*. First, it is assumed that people are less willing to discuss the crimes they have committed and more willing to discuss the crimes committed against them. Second, unlike the *Uniform Crime Reports,* victimization surveys actively seek out information about crime rather than wait for victims to report crimes. Finally, victimization surveys have utilized more representative samples than either the *Uniform Crime Reports* or self-report studies. In these three ways, the "dark area" of crime seems more accessible through the victimization survey.

The first major victimization surveys were conducted in 1966. One survey by the Bureau of Social Science Research (Biderman et al., 1967) interviewed residents of Washington, D.C. Another, conducted by the National Opinion Research Center (NORC), interviewed a sample of 10,000 drawn from the entire nation (Ennis, 1967). Both studies suggested that *Uniform Crime Reports* estimates of the amount of crime in the nation should be doubled—and for some types of offenses, more than doubled.

Table 4–1 displays a comparison of the crime rates for 1965 as reported by the *Uniform Crime Reports* with the rates as estimated from the NORC victimization data for 1965–66. The NORC study indicates that forcible rapes are nearly four times more prevalent than the *Uniform Crime Reports* suggest. Aggravated assault is twice as prevalent. The *Uniform Crime Re-*

ports seem to report only two-thirds of the robberies and burglaries that actually occur, and also vastly underreport larcenies. It should be noted that the NORC sample does not include crimes against businesses and other nonresidential establishments, while the *Uniform Crime Reports* does; thus, the differences between the two estimates are even more alarming. The only crimes that the *Uniform Crime Reports* may be relied upon to report somewhat accurately are homicide and motor vehicle theft.

Since 1970, the U.S. Department of Justice, through the Census Bureau, has conducted victimization surveys for the nation and several major U.S. cities (see U.S. Department of Justice, 1981). These surveys generally bear out the findings of the original studies with respect to the "dark area" of crime. Yet, some caution must be exercised in attempts to compare *Uniform Crime Reports* and victimization statistics. While the original NORC survey was designed to assess differences between the two measures of crime, ensuing victimization surveys are not strictly comparable to the *Uniform Crime Reports*. Victimization surveys focus on victims twelve years of age and older. The *Uniform Crime Reports* makes no age distinction in reporting crimes. Victimization surveys employ a somewhat different crime classification scheme than does the Uniform Crime Reports. Most *Uniform Crime Reports* classifications (e.g., robbery, larceny) are subdivided and combined with other elements in the victimization scheme (e.g., armed robbery, serious assault with theft with weapon; robbery, no assault with weapon; attempted robbery, no assault with weapon).

TABLE 4–1

Comparison of Uniform Crime Reports (UCR) and National Opinion Research Center (NORC) Victimization Survey Estimates of Crime in the United States, 1965–1966

	Rates per 100,000 population		
Crimes	UCR for individuals (1965)*	UCR for individuals and organizations (1965)†	NORC for individuals (1965-66)
Homicide	5.1	5.1	3.0
Forcible rape	11.6	11.6	42.5
Robbery	61.4	61.4	94.0
Aggravated assault	106.6	106.6	218.3
Burglary	296.6	605.3	949.1
Larceny	267.4	393.3	606.5
Automobile theft	226.0	251.0	206.2

*Does not include commercial establishments.
†Includes commercial establishments.
Source: Philip H. Ennis, *Criminal Victimization in the United States* (Washington, D.C.: U. S. Government Printing Office, 1967), p. 8.

The timeframe of the victimization survey also differs from that of the *Uniform Crime Reports*. The latter refer strictly to the calendar year. But because victimization surveys do not occur until two or three months after a calender year and respondents' memories may not be accurate, it is possible that the victimization surveys cover a period of roughly fifteen months. More serious is the fact that the victimization survey and *Uniform Crime Reports* crime counting techniques differ. The former focuses on victims. Thus, if one robber robs two people (a husband and wife, for example), two robberies appear in victimization tallies. The *Uniform Crime Reports* counts incidents. In its scheme, only one robbery (incident) has occurred in the example just cited. Both the *Uniform Crime Reports* and victimization surveys count only the most serious of the crimes committed against a given individual in one crime incident. Thus, the rape and robbery of an individual would result in only one crime counted in the *Uniform Crime Reports* and victimization statistics—rape, the more serious crime. The possibility for vast differences between the two types of crime estimates occurs when we encounter multiple offenses and multiple victims in one incident. For instance, if a man stops a group of seven women, rapes one, and robs all of them, only one crime (rape) is recorded in the *Uniform Crime Reports* while seven (one rape and six robberies) are counted by victimization surveyors—assuming all seven women are interviewed (for reviews of these problems see Lehnen and Skogan, 1981). Finally, Levine (1976) argues that by the time vague incidents thought to be crimes by victimization survey respondents are abstracted and recorded by interviewers and, later, classified as offenses by coders processing the interview data, the potential for non-crimes to be classified as crimes is great. Levine probably underestimates the care taken by survey researchers in classifying events as crimes or non-crimes. Countering this charge, Schneider (1981) reports that in 91 percent of the cases reported in one victimization survey that could be matched with police records, the police and researchers had classified the crimes in the same manner. More generally, however, Levine's point is well taken; victimization surveys are more liberal in counting crimes than are the *Uniform Crime Reports*.

The problems described above are compounded by the same problems encountered in self-reported criminality research: under and overreporting due to memory error or deception. That is, respondents may forget victimizations or specifics about them, may manufacture victimizations to "please the interviewer" or gain attention, or may deny victimizations for any number of personal reasons. The victimization survey technique also is limited to estimations of offenses with specific, unwilling victims. Information on "victimless" crime, such as prostitution, is not gathered; nor is information on such offenses as embezzlement and shoplifting, both of which do not have as specific a victim as do the crimes studied by victimization surveyors.

We noted at the onset of this discussion that victimization surveys were superior to self-reported criminality surveys and to the *Uniform Crime Re-*

ports in one other important respect. Most of the problems discussed above are constant in victimization surveys. That is, they are built into the survey design and will appear yearly in much the same manner. Thus, annual changes in crime rates, as calculated from victimization survey results, can be treated as "real." If victimization rates appear to increase or decrease 15 percent, the change probably is not due to survey error (which remains constant year-to-year). The *Uniform Crime Reports,* however, cannot inspire the same confidence. Since they are reactive (dependent upon citizens to report crimes), yearly crime rate changes can be assumed to reflect changes in citizen willingness to report crimes. Since police patroling and crime-reporting techniques easily can change year-to-year, annual crime-rate changes also can be assumed to be artifacts of police organizational decisions. Only after these possibilities are negated systematically can *Uniform Crime Reports* yearly crime rate changes be treated as "real." Yet, we noted earlier that the *Uniform Crime Reports* are the best practical method of crime rate knowledge. This choice in the final analysis is a matter of cost. The cost of compiling *Uniform Crime Reports* data pales in comparison to the cost of a victimization survey (about $35 per interview). Thus, we see yearly national victimization surveys and occasional victimization surveys of some major cities, but we do not see victimization surveys in the majority of local areas in the U.S. Only the *Uniform Crime Reports* provide information—however flawed—on these areas.

HOW MUCH CRIME?

Given the problems with both official and victimization statistics, it is clear that we must look to both measures for a sense of the amounts and types of crime committed in our society. It is also clear that this sense is, at best, *very general.* More precise inferences are unreliable. Keeping this in mind, we may examine the estimates of crime taken from the 1981 *Uniform Crime Reports* and the 1982 Department of Justice report, *Criminal Victimization in the United States—1980.* These are the most recent statistics available at the time of this writing.

Table 4–2 displays *Uniform Crime Reports* estimates of the volume and rates (per 100,000 population) for the FBI Index offenses in 1981. Table 4–3 presents the victimization survey estimates of the volume and rates for relatively the same offenses in 1980. Although the offense classification systems of the two estimates vary somewhat, and victimization surveys ignore victims under twelve years of age and seek no information about homicides and crimes against businesses, comparisons of the tables indicate again that the *Uniform Crime Reports* grossly underestimate the amount of crime in our society. Even so, both sets of statistics tell much the same story. The great majority of our crimes are property offenses. Rapes, robberies, and assaults

TABLE 4–2

Estimates of Crime in the United States: 1981 *Uniform Crime Reports**

Crimes	Volume	Rate per 100,000 population
Homicide	22,520	9.8
Forcible rape	81,540	35.6†
Robbery	574,130	250.6
Aggravated assault	643,720	280.9
Burglary	3,739,800	1,632.1
Larceny-theft	7,154,500	3,122.3
Motor vehicle theft	1,074,000	468.7
Total	13,290,300	5,799.9
Violent crimes	1,321,900	576.9
Property crimes	11,968,400	5,223.0

*National arson data unavailable.
†Approximately 69 for females.
Source: FBI, *Uniform Crime Reports—1981* (Washington, D.C.: U.S. Government Printing Office, 1982), p. 36.

constitute less than 15 percent of the crimes reported in either table. In general, ranking by frequency of occurrence of the offenses reflects the reverse of society's view of their seriousness (less serious crimes occur more often): larceny, burglary, motor vehicle theft, aggravated assault, robbery, rape, and murder.

TABLE 4–3

Estimates of Crime in the United States: 1980 Victimization Survey Results

Crimes	Volume	Rate per 100,000 population
Personal victimizations		*Per 100,000 persons*
Rape	182,000	90*
Robbery	1,210,000	650
Assault	5,027,000	2,570
Theft	15,223,000	8,280
Household victimizations		*Per 100,000 households*
Larceny	10,617,700	12,650
Burglary	7,037,900	8,420
Motor Vehicle Theft	1,372,900	1,670

*Approximately 160 for females.
Source: Paez, A. K., and R. W. Dodge, *Criminal Victimization in the United States* (Washington, D.C.: U.S. Government Printing Office, 1982) p. 2.

TRENDS IN INDEX CRIMES

Much is made of the fact that crime rose tremendously during the 1960s and 1970s. Some of the increase undoubtedly stems from changes in crime-reporting practices of police departments and, perhaps, to a greater willingness by citizens to report crimes. As noted above, for example, there is certainly a change in women's attitudes toward reporting rape, so much so that it is difficult to determine how much of the 22 percent rise in rapes since 1977 reported by the FBI is a reporting increase and how much an actual increase. (Victimization survey results indicate a 5.7 percent increase since 1977). Overall, however, we deceive ourselves if we attribute rising crime rates wholly to altered reporting procedures. Crime, in fact, has increased since 1960.

Between 1960 and 1975, rates for violent crimes increased 199 percent and those for property offenses rose 178 percent. Yet, most of this increase occurred in the 1960s. As the data displayed in Table 4–4 indicate, crime "slowed-down" in the 1970s. Rate changes have decreased steadily. Indeed, 1981 figures show a decline in rates for all offenses over 1980 figures.

The story of crime in the 1970s is much the same according to the victimization survey results displayed in Table 4–5. Rates for only one form of offense, household larceny, rose greatly between 1973 and 1980. Rates for assault rose slightly. Rates for other offenses declined; in the cases of personal theft, burglary, and motor vehicle theft, the decline was quite large. Ignoring momentarily the differences between 1973 and 1980 figures, a year-

TABLE 4–4

Uniform Crime Reports Estimates of Crime Rate Changes—1981 Over Previous Years*

Crimes	1981 rates	Rate changes (in percent) over previous years		
		1980	1977	1972
Homicide	9.9	−3.9	11.4	8.9
Forcible rape	35.6	−2.2	22.3	58.2
Robbery	250.6	2.9	33.9	38.7
Aggravated assault	280.9	−3.3	16.3	48.8
Burglary	1,632.1	−2.2	15.7	43.1
Larceny-theft	3,122.3	−1.1	14.4	56.6
Motor vehicle theft	468.7	−5.2	4.7	10.0
Total	5,799.9	−1.7	14.7	46.7
Violent crimes	576.9	−0.7	23.6	43.9
Property crimes	5,223.0	−1.8	13.8	46.7

*National arson data unavailable.

Source: FBI, *Uniform Crime Reports—1981* (Washington, D.C.: U.S. Government Printing Office, 1982), p. 36.

TABLE 4–5
Victimization Rate Comparisons, 1973–80

Crimes	Yearly rates (per 100,000 population)								% rate change
	1973	1974	1975	1976	1977	1978	1979	1980	
Personal victimizations									
Rape	100	100	90	80	90	100	110	90	−1.1
Robbery	670	720	680	650	620	690	630	650	−3.0
Assault	2,490	2,480	2,520	2,530	3,680	2,690	2,720	2,570	+3.1
Theft	9,110	9,510	9,600	9,610	9,730	9,680	9,190	8,280	−9.1
Household victimizations									
Larceny	10,700	12,380	12,540	12,410	12,330	11,990	12,270	12,650	+18.3
Burglary	9,170	9,310	9,170	8,890	8,850	8,600	8,410	8,420	−8.2
Motor vehicle theft	1,910	1,880	1,950	1,650	1,700	1,750	1,750	1,670	−12.3

Source: Paez, A. L., and R. W. Dodge, Criminal Victimization in the United States (technical report) (Washington, D.C.: U.S. Department of Justice, 1982), p. 2.

by-year comparison of victimization rates during the 1970s indicates few startling annual changes. As the *Uniform Crime Reports* suggested, there was little major growth in crime during the 1970s.

CRIME STATISTICS: TAKING A CRITICAL APPROACH

Three major points have surfaced in the preceding pages:

1. Crime statistics suffer from problems of representativeness and accuracy.
2. Despite these problems, we cannot ignore the fact that Index crimes increased during the 1960s and early-1970s.
3. Crime rates seem to have stabilized as we move through the early 1980s.

In the previous chapter, we noted that public fears of crime have prompted drastic changes in the personal habits of citizens, increased government anticrime spending, and a greater societal willingness to surrender individual rights to combat crime. Are these sensible responses to our crime situation? Rather than answer this question directly, let us note that if they represent correct responses, it is quite by accident. We stated in Chapter 1 that solutions to any problem necessitate as thorough an understanding of the nature and scope of the problem as possible. Few people move beyond hearsay in assessing the "crime problem." Those who do tend to rely on official statistics concerning the volume, rate, and rate changes for particular crimes.

Statistics, even accurate ones, can be misleading. Examples of reporting insufficiencies are numerous. Percentages often are cited without base figures. (A 50 percent increase in crime may mean little if the base figure is small. For example, three thefts in 1975 as opposed to two the previous year constitute a 50 percent rise in theft.) Crime statistics usually are reported for the nation or, at best, for a community. In either case, averages can be deceiving. One should consider whether a national high crime rate is due to nationally pervasive crime or simply to a great deal of crime in certain areas or cities. Similarly, high crime rates in a city may be confined to a few neighborhoods, while the remainder of the city may be relatively safe.

Too little attention is given by the public, government, and some criminologists to the characteristics of crimes beyond the broad categories used to define and distinguish them. To say that property offenses are increasing is to say very little. Are they minor or major thefts? Do they occur at night or during the day? Who is victimized? To note that robberies are on the rise is to leave much to the imagination. Before we can prevent robberies or protect ourselves, we must know what forms the robberies take: bank holdups, muggings, households robberies, and so forth. It is important to understand when and where the robberies occur and against whom; the kind of weapon used also is important. Similarly, assaults committed by strangers in the streets carry different governmental and personal policy meanings from assaults committed during domestic or barroom quarrels among non-strangers.

In sum, the public must become more critical of the crime statistics it receives. In essence, every statistic should be challenged with the question, "How are these figures distorted or misleading?" In terms of personal adaptations to crime, individuals should also ask, "How does this affect me?" That is, what are the individual's chances of being the victim of a particular form of crime, given his or her sphere of social interaction—the home, neighborhood, and areas of work, shopping, and entertainment? In terms of support for government anticrime programs, people must ask if the solution is based on a misleading interpretation of crime statistics.

The consequences of uncritical acceptance of crime statistics easily are seen in two examples.

Example 1: Lifetime Murder Victimization Chances

Crime statistics can be frightening—especially when they suggest that an individual's likelihood of becoming the victim of a violent crime is high. The *Uniform Crime Reports* of 1981 (FBI, 1982:339–40) provides just such chilling statistics: estimates of the probability of being murdered during one's lifetime. Table 4–6 presents the estimated probability of eventually being murdered for all persons alive in 1980. The FBI estimates that one of every 153 people ultimately will be murdered. Males are considerably more likely to be killed than are females, and nonwhites seem vastly more likely than do whites to be homicide victims. The most dramatic statistic is that

TABLE 4–6

FBI Estimates of the Probability of Lifetime Murder Victimizations in the U.S.

Population	Victimization probability
Males	1 of 100
Females	1 of 323
Whites	1 of 240
Nonwhites	1 of 47
White males	1 of 164
Nonwhite males	1 of 28
White females	1 of 450
Nonwhite females	1 of 117
Total	1 of 153

Source: FBI, *Uniform Crime Reports—1981* (Washington, D.C.: U.S. Government Printing Office, 1982), p. 339.

which indicates that one of every 28 nonwhite (presumably black) males alive in 1980 eventually will become a murder victim.

Let us examine more closely the victimization probability for black males. Theoretically, the statistic could mean that one of every 28 black males will be murdered at random. Yet, we know that some black males have a much greater chance than do others of being killed—by virtue of social environment, lifestyle, and cultural attributes. The youth living in the ghetto and involved in gang activity runs a greater risk than does the youth living in the college dormitory and involved in academic activity. If the gang member has, for example, a one-in-five chance of being murdered in his lifetime, and the black population contains a large number of gang members, the victimization probability for the remainder of black males ("average" blacks) obviously is much lower than one in 28. Similarly, the already low probability that a white female will be murdered in her lifetime actually is much lower for the truly "average" white female.

Finally, the FBI report itself offers the major reason to distrust these statistics in terms of meaning for the "average" person's safety: [The] lifetime probability of murder victimization represents the probability of being murdered in one's lifetime, *assuming the current age-specific murder victimization rates and current life expectancy levels hold in the future*" (p. 339; italics added). Murder rates and life expectancies have not held and cannot be expected to hold constant. The former may increase or decrease and the latter likely will expand. The FBI lifetime murder victimization probabilities assume constancy for as long as 99 years, as if time and culture will stand still. Given this and the other problems we have raised, we cannot help but wonder why these probabilities were computed. What do they tell us that we do not already know simply from viewing traditional homicide statistics? We have learned long ago that males are murdered more often than females and that blacks have higher murder rates than whites.

Though nothing is gained from these probability calculations, the public unlikely will view the statistics critically. Rather than defining them as little more than the product of a statistical exercise, most people will become frightened by the "high likelihood" of being murdered. Their fears will have no empirical bases.

Example 2: Indecent Assault in Toronto

If the public were told that indecent or sexual assaults on females were becoming a problem, we could easily imagine proposed solutions to deal with it. On the less radical side, there would be demands for increased street lighting and police patrols. Judges would be asked to deal more harshly with convicted offenders. Public-awareness programs, some including courses in self-defense techniques, would be tried. On the more radical side, curfews might be suggested. Preventive detention of all known sex offenders might be encouraged.

These proposed solutions would indicate a public stereotype of indecent assault as a violent attack on a woman, probably at night. If the stereotype approximated reality, the public would indeed have cause for worry. Yet few citizens would stop to question the accuracy of the public view. Were they to do so, both their fears and their proposed solutions for the indecent assault problem might change drastically.

To illustrate this point, J. W. Mohr (1973) studied official cases of indecent assault in the city of Toronto. His report noted, first, the broadness of the legal definition of indecent or sexual assault. (Canadian and American laws on this point are pretty much the same.) The term applies not only to actual injurious attacks but also to unauthorized touches and even to threats and gestures. Reviewing Toronto's indecent assault cases, Mohr then observed that most involved female children as victims. Of these, only a few involved violence, none particularly serious. As the age of victims increased, so did the seriousness of the offenses, yet truly violent attacks were rare.

A rather larger number of indecent assaults, Mohr found, occurred in August and September during the Canadian National Exhibition. In most of these cases, the victims did not complain. Instead, arrests followed police observation of assaults. The "indecent assaults" that inspired these arrests were cases in which men took advantage of crowded situations to move close to and rub against females, a familiar occurrence on the subways of large cities. Mohr referred to a "crime wave" of indecent assaults that appeared when fifty-three extra cases were reported as the result of increased police activity along a crowded parade route.

The purpose of this illustration is not to minimize the seriousness of child molesting nor to condone the liberties taken by some men in crowds. Rather, we wish to demonstrate the importance of a critical approach to crime statistics. We often are given statistics for a form of crime without being told exactly what behaviors the legal definition of the act encompasses. Nor are we told the proportions of the total violations of a statute represented by each type of act covered by the statute. The dangers in these forms of ignorance are clear in the Toronto indecent-assault example. The solutions proposed if the assaults were assumed to be rapes would be both costly and, perhaps, drastic. They would also be needless if investigation of the Toronto statistics indicated that most cases of indecent assault were of a less serious variety. In sum, personal and government policy decisions should not be made without a critical review of all aspects of the problems they address.

SUMMARY

In this chapter we tried to accomplish two tasks: first, to provide an overview of the extent of crime in our society and, second, and more important, to raise a number of red flags concerning crime statistics.

Crime statistics may not be representative of actual crime. Even if they are, the statistics still do not meaningfully convey to the average citizen his or her actual chances of being victimized. Knowledge of what a definition of a criminal act actually includes and what a "rise" in crime actually means is mandatory if we are to make sound personal and governmental anticrime decisions. As we suggested earlier, incautious decisions regarding crime are often more costly than crime itself.

REFERENCES

Akers, R. L., J. Massey, W. Clarke, et al. 1983. Are self-reports of adolescent deviance valid? Biochemical measures, randomized response, and the bogus pipeline in smoking behavior. *Soc. Forces* 62:234–51.

Beattie, R. H. 1960. Criminal statistics in the United States–1960. *J. Crim. Law Criminol. & Pol. Sci.* 51:49–65.

Biderman, A. D., L. A. Johnson, J. McIntrye, et al. 1967. Report on a Pilot Study in the District of Columbia on Victimization and Attitudes toward Law Enforcement. Field Survey I: President's Commission on Law Enforcement and Administration of Justice. Washington, D.C.: U.S. Government Printing Office.

Bittner, E. 1967. The police on skid row: A study of peace keeping. *Am. Sociol. Rev.* 32:699–715.

Black, D. J. 1970. Production of crime rates. *Am. Sociol. Rev.* 35:733–48.

Booth, A., D. R. Johnson, and H. M. Choldin. 1977. Correlates of city crime rates: Victimization survey versus official statistics. *Soc. Prob.* 25:187–97.

Chilton, R. 1980. Criminal statistics in the United States. *J. Crim. Law & Criminol.* 71:56–67.

Cicourel, A. V. 1968. *The Social Organization of Juvenile Justice.* New York: John Wiley & Sons.

Clark, J. P., and L. L. Tifft. 1966. Polygraph and interview validation of self-reported deviant behavior. *Am. Sociol. Rev.* 31:516–23.

Cohen, L. J., and M. I. Lichback. 1982. Alternative measures of crime: A statistical evaluation. *Sociol. Q.* 23:253–66.

Dentler, R. A., and L. J. Monroe. 1961. Social correlates of early adolescent theft. *Am. Sociol. Rev.* 26:733–43.

Elliott, D. S., and S. S. Ageton. 1980. Reconciling differences in estimates of delinquency. *Am. Sociol. Rev.* 45:95–110.

Elliott, D., and H. Voss. 1974. *Delinquency and Dropout.* Lexington, Mass.: Lexington Books.

Ennis, P. 1967. Criminal Victimization in the United States: A Report of a National Survey. Field Survey II of the President's Commission on Law Enforcement and Administration of Justice. Washington, D.C.: U.S. Government Printing Office.

Farrington, D. P. 1973. Self-reports of deviant behavior: Predictive and stable? *J. Crim. Law & Criminol.* 64:99–110.

Federal Bureau of Investigation. 1982. *Uniform Crime Reports—1981.* Washington, D.C.: U.S. Government Printing Office.

Gardiner, J. 1970. *The Politics of Corruption: Organized Crime in an American City.* New York: Russell Sage.

Gold, M. 1966. Undetected delinquent behavior. *J. Res. Crime & Delinq.* 13:27–46.

Goldstein, J. 1960. Police discretion not to invoke the criminal process: Low visibility decisions in the administration of justice. *The Yale Law J.* 69:543–94.

Guinther, J. 1975. How to hide a crime wave. *Philadelphia Magazine* August 66–82.

Hindelang, M. 1974. The *Uniform Crime Reports* revisited. *J. Crim. Just.* 2:1–17.

Hirschi, T. 1969. *Causes of Delinquency*. Berkeley, Calif.: University of California Press.

Jensen, G. F., and D. G. Rojek. 1980. *Delinquency: A Sociological View*. Lexington, Mass.: D.C. Heath & Company.

Kitsuse, J., and A. Cicourel. 1963. A note on the use of official statistics. *Soc. Prob.* 12:131–39.

LaFave, W. 1965. *Arrest: The Decision to Take a Suspect into Custody*. Boston: Little, Brown and Company.

Lehnen, R. G., and W. G. Skogan, eds. 1981. *The National Crime Survey: Working Papers*, Vol. 1. Washington, D.C.: U.S. Government Printing Office.

Levine, J. P. 1976. The potential for overreporting in criminal victimization surveys. *Criminology* 14:307–30.

McCleary, R., B. C. Nienstedt, and J. M. Erven. 1982. *Uniform Crime Reports* as organizational outcomes: Three-time series experiments. *Soc. Prob.* 29:361–72.

Mohr, J. W. 1973. Facts, figures, perceptions and myths—ways of describing and understanding crime. *Can. J. Criminol. Corr.* 15:39–49.

Piliavin, I., and S. Briar. 1964. Police encounters with juveniles. *Am. J. Sociol.* 70:206–14.

Quinney, R. 1979. *Criminology*. 2nd ed. Boston: Little, Brown and Company.

Rubinstein, J. 1973. *City Police*. New York: Random House.

Savitz, L. D. 1982. Official statistics. In *Contemporary Criminology*. Edited by L. D. Savitz and N. Johnston. New York: John Wiley & Sons.

Savitz, L. D., M. Lalli, and L. Rosen. 1977. *City Life and Delinquency—Victimization, Fear of Crime and Gang Membership*. Washington, D.C.: U.S. Government Printing Office.

Schneider, A. L. 1981. Differences between survey and police information about crime. In *The National Crime Survey: Working Papers*, Vol. 1. Edited by R. G. Lehnen and W. G. Skogan. Washington, D.C.: U.S. Government Printing Office.

Seidman, D., and M. Couzens. 1974. Getting the crime rate down: Political pressure and crime reporting. *Law & Society Rev.* 8:457–93.

Sheley, J., and J. Hanlon. 1978. Unintended effects of police decisions to actively enforce laws: Implications for analysis of crime trends. *Comtemp. Crises* 2:265–75.

Sherman, L. W. 1974. Becoming bent: Moral careers of corrupt policeman. In *Police Corruption*. Edited by L. W. Sherman. Garden City, N.Y.: Anchor Books.

Skogan, W. G. 1974. The validity of official crime statistics: An empirical investigation. *Soc. Sci. Q.* 55:25–38.

———. 1977. Dimensions of the dark figure of unreported crime. *Crime & Delinq.* 23:41–50.

Skolnick, J. H. 1975. *Justice Without Trial*. 2nd ed. New York: John Wiley & Sons.

U.S. Department of Justice. 1982. *Criminal Victimization in the United States—1980*. Washington, D.C.: U.S. Government Printing Office.

Wilson, J. W. 1968. *Varieties of Police Behavior: The Management of Law and Order in Eight Communities*. Cambridge: Harvard University Press.

SUGGESTED READINGS

As this chapter has indicated, the primary sources of our knowledge about crime trends in the U.S. are the FBI *Uniform Crime Reports* and various Justice Department victimization surveys. Readers are encouraged to examine these documents since they are written in a language the public can understand easily.

Critiques of official police statistics are numerous, of course. Among the better known are Sophia Robinson's "A Critical Review of the Uniform Crime Reports," *Michigan Law Review,* April 1966, pp. 1031–54, and J. Kitsuse and A. Cicourel's "A Note on the Uses of Official Statistics," *Social Problems,* 1963, pp. 131–39. More recently, see R. Chilton's "Criminal Statistics in the United States," *Journal of Criminal Law and Criminology,* 1980, pp. 56–67. An effective review of the problems in victimization surveys is found in Wesley G. Skogan's *Issues in the Measurement of Victimization* (Washington, D.C.: U.S. Government Printing Office, 1981).

5

SELECTED OFFENSES

In the previous chapter we examined Index offenses more or less in the aggregate. Presently, to gain a better sense of Index offense trends, we will review each type separately. In addition, we examine a number of other offenses in some detail: "lesser" property crimes, "vice" offenses, organized crime, and "respectable," or white-collar, crime. The purpose of this review is to gain a better sense of all the offenses that seem to make up our "crime problem," to challenge some of our stereotypes about certain forms of crime, and to encourage some thought about our crime-fighting priorities.

HOMICIDE

Homicide is the willful taking of a person's life with malice. In the eyes of the law, the seriousness of the crime is determined by the degree to which it is deliberate and premeditated. First-degree murder, for example, represents a homicide that was planned and carried out with a purpose. Second-degree murder involves malice but is less deliberate and premeditated. Most murders of passion—relatively spontaneous attacks in moments of anger—are second-degree murders. Finally, nonnegligent, or voluntary, manslaughter represents deaths that result from an attempt to harm but not to kill another person. Often these are crimes of passion in which a blow was struck with more force than was intended by the striker. First- and second-degree murder and voluntary manslaughter are counted among *Uniform Crime Reports* statistics.

In 1981, 22,516 murders occurred in the U.S.—a rate of 9.8 per 100,000 population. This rate represents a 3.9 percent drop over that of the previous year. This decline is the first since 1960 when homicide rates began to climb steadily. Previously, homicide rates had risen dramatically from 1900 to the late 1930s, reaching levels comparable to those experienced during the 1970s. Rates dropped during the years of World War II, rose again in the late 1940s, and declined once more until 1960.

Murder victims tend to be male (77 percent), under forty years of age (60 percent), and white (54 percent). Offenders also are likely to be male (87 percent) and young (43 percent under twenty-five years of age). Blacks and whites are represented equally among offenders (each 49 percent). Though blacks have a much higher victim and offender rate than their 11 percent representation in the general population would suggest, it is important to note that homicide is intraracial. In all but 10 percent of homicides, the killer and victim are of the same race. Apparently they also are of the same social class—most often, members of lower socioeconomic groups killing each other. Homicides are not distributed equally throughout the states and across cities and local residential areas. The Southern region of the U.S. has the highest rate, followed by the Pacific region. Larger urban areas possess higher homicide rates within regions.

People who kill others most often use a handgun. Such weapons are used in half of all murders; rifles and shotguns are used in 13 percent. Knives and other cutting instruments are employed in about 19 percent of homicides. The remainder of killings are accomplished through more exotic (bombings, poisons) or more basic (beatings) means (FBI, 1982:12). Kleck (1979) reports a strong relationship between gun availability (ownership) and homicide rate. It is clear that guns are more deadly than are most other weapons. They cannot be outrun, and they produce wounds that are more likely to be deadly.

Despite public fears about being murdered on the street by a stranger, most homicides involve persons who already know one another. Only about 13 percent of the murders in which the police can determine the victim-offender relationship are committed by strangers to the victim. (The police cannot determine the victim-offender relationship in 32 percent of all homicides; presumably a large portion of these homicides involve strangers.) Thirty percent of all homicides are intrafamilial or result from romantic triangles and lovers' quarrels. Another 40 percent involve unspecified disputes—most often between people who know each other. Murders committed during robberies represent about 16 percent of total homicides. Known and suspected felony-related killings (linked to drug traffic, organized crime, and so on) constitute the remaining 14 percent.

A number of researchers have paid special attention to the circumstances surrounding homicide—victim-offender relationship, felony circumstances, dispute situations (Boudouris, 1974; Hepburn, 1973; Luckenbill, 1977; Wolfgang, 1958)—but few have applied the typologies derived from this special attention to broader homicide-related issues such as urban-rural rate differences, regional rate variations, and cultural and structural influences on rates. The importance of distinguishing types of homicide is indicated in recent work by Smith and Parker (1980; see also Parker and Smith, 1979). The authors distinguish two fairly rudimentary types of homicide: primary and nonprimary. The former type refers to more common murders; those involving people who know each other and occurring relatively spontaneously in dispute situations. The latter refers to less common homicides that occur more often between strangers and are felony-related. Smith and Parker argue that this distribution makes clearer the regional homicide differences noted above. The South, known as a high homicide region, is high in primary homicides but low in nonprimary homicides. Structural poverty (poor economic conditions) is related to primary but not to nonprimary homicides. Urban environment is linked to nonprimary but not to primary homicides.

Thus, the type of homicide seems crucial to any analysis of the determinants of murder rates. Similarly, the distinction between homicide types is important to an understanding of possibilities in preventing homicides. Given that most homicides are of the primary type—explosive, passionate, dispute-oriented, family-related—it is difficult to conceive of a government program that effectively could reduce murders. Most experts concede that the police are relatively powerless to combat the crime. Nor is capital punishment likely to reduce dispute-related murders.

AGGRAVATED ASSAULT

Aggravated assault represents an unlawful attack by one person upon another for the purpose of inflicting severe bodily injury. It is distinguished from simple assault in that simple assault lacks the intent to do severe or aggravated harm. The *Uniform Crime Reports* offers detailed statistics only for aggravated assault, an Index offense. National victimization surveys collect data concerning both aggravated and simple assault. Both sources of knowledge about assault are somewhat suspect: the former so because many assaults, occurring during disputes involving acquaintances, likely go unreported; the latter because they may overreport assaults, or at least, may classify too many simple assaults as aggravated.

The 1981 *Uniform Crime Reports* indicates a total of 643,720 aggravated assaults in the U.S.—a rate of 281 per 100,000 population (FBI, 1982:19). The national Department of Justice victimization survey for 1980 reports 1,661,000 aggravated assaults—a rate of 90 per 100,000 population

(Paez or Dodge, 1982:2). Both sources report recent downturns in aggravated assault rates after mild yearly increases during the 1970s. Victimization survey respondents indicate that only 54 percent of aggravated assaults are reported to the police (and therefore appear in *Uniform Crime Reports*).

Aggravated assault rates decline as city size decreases. The Pacific and Southern regions have the highest rates in the U.S. Both FBI and victimization reports indicate that assault is intraracial. Blacks comprise a larger-than-expected portion of both offenders and victims, though the average victim and offender likely are white. Victims and offenders are predominantly male, under twenty-five years of age, unmarried, and of lower socioeconomic background. According to victimization data, the majority (64 percent) of aggravated assaults occur between strangers, an unusual finding given the high nonstranger levels found in homicide. Injury to the victim is as likely to accompany aggravated assaults by strangers as by acquaintances.

Theoretically, assault differs from homicide by virtue of the absence of intent to kill. In reality, the difference simply may be a matter of success for a person bent on killing another or bad luck for someone only trying to hurt another. This point is borne out by both FBI and victimization data concerning the use of weapons in assaults. In only approximately a quarter of aggravated assaults is a firearm used. In the majority of cases, a knife, sharp object, or blunt object is employed. We noted earlier that firearms are the most frequent weapons in homicides. To the extent that firearm use in assaults increases, we can expect homicides to increase.

RAPE

The *Uniform Crime Reports* define forcible rape as carnal knowledge of a female forcibly and against her will. The FBI includes attempted rapes among the rapes it reports. The notion of force includes threat of force. In most states rape is constituted in terms of vaginal penetration (no matter to what degree or for what length of time) by the offender's penis. Critics of this view of rape have influenced some states to alter their rape statutes, making rape (or "criminal sexual conduct," as some states, like Michigan, have chosen to call the offense) a gender-neutral crime. Thus, any forcible intrusion of any part of a person's body (hand, mouth, penis, and so forth) or of any object into the genital or anal openings of another person's body constitutes rape or its equivalent in some states. Within these bounds, offenders may be of either gender and rapes may be homosexual as well as heterosexual.

Uniform Crime Reports has held to the more traditional view of rape in an effort to maintain uniform comparisons among states and over time. The Department of Justice victimization surveys lean toward the newer, more liberal view in terms of including heterosexual and homosexual forcible carnal knowledge among the offenses it counts as rape (U.S. Department of Justice,

1981:108). The notion of "carnal knowledge" in the victim survey refers to penetration of the vagina or anus by the offender's penis. Thus, victims may be male or female but offenders are male only. The small number of attacks on men relative to attacks on women, however, makes the victimization survey and *Uniform Crime Reports* findings practically if not technically comparable. That is, the victimization surveys do not uncover larger numbers of rapes than do the *Uniform Crime Reports* simply because the former employ a more liberal definition of rape.

According to *Uniform Crime Reports,* 81,536 rapes and attempted rapes occurred in the U.S. in 1981—about 69 per 100,000 females in the population. The 1981 rate reflects a 2 percent decline over that of the previous year. To this point, rape rates had been increasing steadily during the late 1970s (38 percent between 1976 and 1980, for example). 1980 victimization survey data (Paez and Dodge, 1982) indicate 169,000 rapes and attempted rapes—about 160 per 100,000 females. Unlike the *Uniform Crime Reports* data, however, the victimization survey data indicate little change in rape rates since 1973. Assuming that the victimization survey data are somewhat more reliable, it appears that victims have been less reluctant to report rapes to the police in the 1970s than in previous years, but that there are still twice the number of rapes committed as is known through police records (U.S. Department of Justice, 1981:76).

Victimization survey results from 1979 (Department of Justice, 1981) show only modest differences in rape rates by city size (though FBI statistics indicate much greater rates for larger metropolitan areas). Victims tend to be women of lower socioeconomic background, not working or working in the service sector. Black women have a rape rate of 260 per 100,000; white women have a rate of 180 per 100,000. In general, victims are between sixteen and twenty-four years old, though for blacks the higher risk age range is sixteen to thirty-four years of age. Rapes most often occur after 6:00 P.M. and away from the victim's home even when nonstrangers are involved. Sixty percent of rapes of white women involve strangers; 80 percent of black rape victims are attacked by strangers. A weapon (usually a knife or gun) is used in 37 percent of rapes involving strangers and 31 percent involving nonstrangers.

Three-fourths of rape offenders are perceived by their victims as beyond twenty-one years of age; *Uniform Crime Reports—1981* notes that 55 percent of rape arrestees are under twenty-five. Sixty-two percent are perceived to be white, 30 percent black, and the remainder as "other" or "unknown" (the *Uniform Crime Reports* notes an even black/white split among arrestees for rape). The extent to which rape is intraracial is problematic. Victimization survey results from 1979 indicate that 71 percent of white victims are raped by whites and 73 percent of black victims are assaulted by blacks. The white victim/white offender figure is in line with recent trends, but the black victim/black offender figure is not. Most studies show considerably higher levels of black victim/black offender rapes and lower levels of black victim/white offender rapes.

Aside from, but clearly related to, the underreporting of rape in official statistics, the most important issue regarding rape is prosecution of offenders and the treatment of victims. Though legal penalties for rape are fairly severe, arrests, prosecutions, and guilty verdicts are rarer than should be the case. Part of the problem lies in the difficulty of legally proving a rape has occurred within our legal system, which assumes innocence on the part of the accused. Most rapes are not committed in the presence of witnesses. Penetration and force are not easily proven unless the victim is badly battered. Cases reduce to a matter of the victim's word against that of the accused. The problem becomes more complicated if the parties involved were acquainted prior to the alleged offense.

But legal difficulties are not really at the heart of this society's failure to punish rapists. Unless the victim is a child, a relative, or a close friend, she arouses little sympathy from the average citizen. Traditionally, this society has viewed women who are raped as somehow deserving of their fate: "She asked for it." "She is loose." " 'Decent' women aren't raped, and no woman can be raped if she doesn't want to be." (See the discussion of victim-precipitated rape in Chapter 7.) These notions have carried over into humiliating interrogations of victims by police investigators, reluctant prosecutions by district attorneys, degrading courtroom cross-examinations by defense attorneys, and fewer convictions by juries than is the norm for other types of criminal cases. In a study of the American jury system, Kalven and Zeisel (1966) note that jurors demand stronger evidence than is usual in rape cases, and seem more willing to accept defense attorneys' definitions of "contributing behavior" on the part of the victim. In short, the victim becomes the person on trial. It is little wonder, then, that so many victims choose not to initiate this process of public scrutiny by reporting their rapes to the police.

The situation does appear to be changing gradually. Spurred by feminist criticism of their case-handling, many police departments have sought to bring more sensitive personnel, especially female police officers, into rape investigations. The same attempt at increased awareness is said now to be characteristic of hospital emergency service and coroner's office staffs who examine rape victims. Some states have passed laws limiting the extent to which defense attorneys may delve into a victim's past sexual history in an effort to degrade her before a jury. Some of these changes undoubtedly account for the apparent increase in reported rapes seen recently in police statistics. Women now may feel less stigmatized as rape victims. Yet, the extent to which cultural attitudes toward rape actually have changed remains to be seen.

ROBBERY

Robbery represents the stealing or taking of anything of value from the care, custody, or control of a person by force or violence, or by putting the person in fear. It includes such acts as strong-arm robbery, stickups, armed robbery, assault with intent to rob, and robbery attempts. Essentially the same definition of robbery is employed by both the *Uniform Crime Reports* and Department of Justice victimization surveys.

Robbery constitutes slightly less than half of the total violent offenses reported in *Uniform Crime Reports. Uniform Crime Reports* indicates that 574,134 robberies were known to have been committed in the U.S. in 1981. This number represents a rate of 251 per 100,000 population. FBI statistics suggest that robbery rates increased steadily from the early 1960s into the 1970s, declined in 1976 and 1977, and rose again to a historic high in 1981. It should be noted, however, that the 1981 rate is only 3 percent above that of the previous year, an indication of some decline in the speed of the increasing rates.

Recalling the tendency of FBI statistics to underreport offenses, we are able to learn something about robbery through examining the 1980 Department of Justice national victimization survey data (Paez and Dodge, 1982). By this study's estimate, 1,179,000 robberies occurred in 1980. This reflects about 650 robberies per 100,000 individuals in the population. Since victimization surveys do not count robberies of commercial establishments such as banks and retail stores, as does *Uniform Crime Reports, Uniform Crime Reports* seems substantially to underreport robberies. (Victimization survey results indicate that the percentage of robberies reported to the police is increasing.) Differing also from the *Uniform Crime Reports,* the victimization survey results indicate not an increase in robberies during the 1970s but a general decrease. The robbery victimization rate declined 18 percent from 1974 to 1978 and held constant during 1979 and 1980.

Robbery appears to be an urban (especially center-city) crime. According to *Uniform Crime Reports—1981,* 52 percent of the robberies reported in 1981 were committed in the streets, 11 percent in private residences, 25 percent in banks, stores, gas stations, and other commercial establishments, and 12 percent in miscellaneous locations. Victimization survey results are essentially the same: 53 percent of the robberies occurred in the streets and other outdoor places and 11 percent happened in the victim's home. Sixty percent of robberies happen at night. Robberies by a lone offender roughly equal the number of multiple offenders. The *Uniform Crime Reports* estimate of the percentage of robberies involving weapons differs from that of the victimization surveys. The former reports firearms used in 40 percent of robberies and knives used in 13 percent. Victimization survey results indicate the use of firearms in 33 percent of robberies and knives in 35 percent. The difference may be due to the fact that victimization surveyors locate more young victims likely to be robbed at school by other young persons but unlikely to report the incident to the police. The presence of a gun or knife tends to reduce the chance of injury to the victim; that is, the victim likely will not resist and, therefore, be beaten. Beyond this, firearms greatly enhance the success rate of robbers. In general, the more professional the robber, the more likely the preference for a firearm over a knife. The firearm facilitates the robbery by intimidating the victim more surely (it can also be used as a club), by keeping the victim at a safe distance, and by aiding in the escape (Conklin, 1972:108–12).

According to the 1979 U.S. Department of Justice (1981) victimization survey results, robber and victim are strangers in the vast majority of cases. As noted earlier, most robbery victims are city dwellers. In cities, black males have the highest victimization rate (2,850 per 100,000), followed by white males (1,350 per 100,000), black females (900 per 100,000), and white females (700 per 100,000). Overall, males are victimized twice as often as females. Regarding age, the higher rates are for people under twenty-five. Males over sixty-five and females over fifty have the lowest rates.

For both whites and blacks, the income group most victimized by robbers is that under $7500 per year. Those in the highest income groups in both races have considerably lower robbery rates than do members of other income groups. Blacks have higher rates than do whites in all income categories except the highest ($25,000 +).

Most robberies (66 percent) do not result in injury to the victim. Few victims (7 percent) incur expenditures for medical services or receive hospital treatment. However, most robbery victims (70 percent) do lose money either through the theft or through damage to their belongings (broken glasses, for example). Overall, losses are not great; most are between $10 and $50. Only 16 percent exceed $250. In most cases, losses are not recovered, even through insurance reimbursement. Interestingly, only slightly more than half of all robberies are reported to the police. Even when serious injury is involved, only 62 percent of the robberies are reported.

Robbery is committed almost exclusively by males. Sixty percent of those arrested for robbery in 1981 were black (FBI, 1982). Victimization survey data indicate that 40 percent of robberies of whites are committed by nonwhite, primarily black, offenders. Sixty-two percent of the robberies against whites by multiple offenders are committed by nonwhites. In contrast, blacks are robbed almost exclusively by members of their own race. Most of those arrested for robbery in 1981 were under twenty-five years of age. Victimization research indicates that in 1979, victims under twenty years old were more likely to be robbed by persons of their own age. Those over sixty-five were robbed more often by persons under twenty-one.

In a major study of robbery, John E. Conklin (1972:29–78; see also Letkemann, 1973; MacDonald, 1975) classified robbers into four categories. *Professional robbers* tend to be white and strongly committed to robbery as an occupation designed to support pleasurable life styles. Their robberies are well planned and the take is larger. The professional usually operates with accomplices, though seldom with a well-organized gang. Most often a firearm is used in the offense. The *opportunist robber,* the most common type in Conklin's opinion, is not committed to robbery as a way of life but will rob if in need of money and an opportunity occurs. Opportunists choose targets who are easy prey, and their robberies are generally done for a little spending money. The crimes usually are committed with the help of other robbers and do not involve weapons. The *addict robber* commits drug-related robberies. Robbery is viewed as the least preferable of a number of methods of obtaining money for drugs. Addict robbers plan their crimes somewhat, though they are often careless in the robberies. The crimes are designed to produce enough money for their next drug fix. Weapons vary; however, the addict prefers not to use loaded firearms. The *alcoholic robber* steals to buy alcohol or sometimes robs while under the influence of alcohol. Robberies by alcoholics often occur on the spur of the moment. They rarely are planned and are sometimes simply the conclusion to a fight or assault. Weapons rarely are employed by alcoholic robbers.

BURGLARY

According to the *Uniform Crime Reports,* burglary is the unlawful entry of a structure to commit a felony or theft. Forcible entry (breaking into the structure) is not necessary to constitute burglary, nor is the offense tied to theft. FBI statistics cover burglaries of businesses, public buildings, and other nonresidential structures, as well as homes. Victimization survey statistics pertain to a somewhat narrower picture of burglary. They refer to unlawful entry of a residence or of structures on the premises in which a person is staying temporarily (e.g., hotel room, vacation home). Thus, the two sources of knowledge about burglary are not entirely compatible.

Burglary represents the second most frequent crime (after larceny) reported in the *Uniform Crime Reports;* one-quarter of all crimes reflected in these reports are burglaries. Burglary is also the second most prevalent crime appearing in victimization reports—after personal thefts and household larcenies are combined. The FBI reports 3,793,821 burglaries in 1981; this represents a rate of 1632 per 100,000 population, a two percent rate decline over the previous year. Sixty-seven percent of the burglaries involved residences, while the remainder were nonresidential. Most burglaries resulted from forced entry into the structure in question. Though burglaries declined in 1981, the burglary rate had been increasing moderately throughout the late 1970s. Victimization survey information indicates that 6,817,000 households were burglarized in 1980—a rate of 8,400 per 100,000 households, the same rate as in 1979. Burglary victimizations declined 10 percent between 1974 and 1980 according to these survey data. Forced or attempted forced burglaries constituted slightly more than half of the cases. Only about 48 percent of burglary victims report their losses to the police. Most lose more than $250; many lose more than $1000. About half have insurance coverage.

Burglary is primarily an urban phenomenon. Black households (11,400 per 100,000) have the higher victimization rate than do white households (8,000 per 100,000). Highest burglary rates occur at either end of the income spectrum: 10,500 per 100,000 households with incomes below $3,000 and 9,200 per 100,000 households with incomes above $25,000. Burglary rates increase as number of persons in the household increase. Rental units have higher rates than do owner-occupied dwellings.

Little is known about burglars since the police clear only about 14 percent of the nation's burglaries. Ninety-four percent of those arrested are males and 68 percent are white. The majority (79 percent) are under 25 years of age. It is thought that most burglars are amateurs (Reppetto, 1974), but a substantial number of professional burglars exists. Various researchers (Inciardi, 1975; Letkemann, 1973; Scarr, 1973; Shover, 1972) have studied those who view themselves as professionals. Competent burglars steal successfully and avoid prison because they are tied to networks that support their profession: persons who tip them about potential targets, bondsmen and good attorneys for protection, and fences who buy stolen property for resale. Depending on the type of burglar in question, professional expertise varies. Highly respected within their "field" are those professionals who are able to break elaborate security systems. Most respected are professional "boxmen" who are able to open safes and vaults and, therefore, reap enormous rewards.

LARCENY

Larceny, according to the *Uniform Crime Reports,* is the unlawful taking, carrying, leading, or riding away of property from the possession or constructive possession of another. FBI larceny statistics reference such crimes as pocketpicking, purse snatching, shoplifting, and stealing items or parts from motor vehicles. But they do not refer to motor vehicle theft itself, or to fraud, forgery, con games, and writing bad checks. Department of Justice victimization surveys count two general forms of larceny: personal larceny and household larceny. The former refers to thefts of property or cash from a person with or without contact between the offender and victim and without threat of force (i.e., personal theft is not robbery). Thefts of wallets, purses, and bicycles would be classified as personal larcenies, for example. Household larceny refers to thefts from a residence or its immediate vicinity. Burglary is not involved. Thefts of potted plants from the front porch of a

home or of silverware by a dinner guest would be classified as household larcenies, for example. The major difference between FBI and victimization survey reports is that the former include thefts from commercial establishments
(e.g., shoplifting), which the latter do not include.

In 1981, 7,154,541 larcenies were reported in the *Uniform Crime Reports,* 3,122 per every 100,000 persons. Larcenies represent more than half
of all Index crimes reported. Most larcenies reported to the FBI involve shoplifting, thefts from motor vehicles (including automobile accessories), bike
thefts, and thefts from buildings (presumably commercial and public places).
Purse snatching and pocketpicking constitute less than 3 percent of reported
larcenies.

Victimization surveyors found nearly 15 million victims of personal theft
(8,300 per 100,000) and just over 10 million households victimized by larceny (12,650 per 100,000 households) in 1980. Personal larceny rates declined 9 percent between 1973 and 1980. Household larceny rates climbed
18 percent in that same period, though they decreased 5 percent between
1979 and 1980. Taken together, the two forms of larceny rose 2 percent in
the eight-year period.

Personal thefts occur more often in cities. Victims tend to be young, unmarried males of higher income backgrounds. Whites have a slightly higher
rate than do blacks. Purse snatching and pocket picking comprise only about
2 percent of all personal thefts reported to victimization surveyors. Given the
profile of the common victim and the survey finding that persons currently
in school have higher theft rates, it is assumed that much of personal theft
involves schoolboys stealing from each other. Household larcenies are also
higher in cities. Whites and blacks are equally victimized. Higher income
groups exhibit higher rates. The younger the head of the household and the
greater the number of people living in the household, the more likely will the
household experience a larceny. Renters display higher larceny rates than do
homeowners. Most personal and household larcenies occur after 6:00 P.M.,
and most losses from these crimes are in the $10–$250 range.

Only about 25 percent of persons and households victimized by theft report the crime to the police. In turn, the police clear only about 19 percent of
the cases reported to them. Therefore, we know little about persons committing thefts. Arrestees tend to be white males under twenty-one years of
age. Self-reported delinquency studies also indicate that youths commit large
numbers of thefts. These findings suggest that most thieves are amateurs. Beyond this, we have reasonable information only concerning professional
thieves and, here, more about modus operandi than social characteristics.

Like the professional burglars described above, certain people have
professional expertise in larceny. For these people, crime is a full-time occupation and generally involves contact with a network of other thieves and
fences. Most professional pickpockets, for example, acquire their skills from
other professionals, a process often taking years. Pickpockets know how to
"work a crowd" intently watching an event. Teams of pickpockets can lift a

wallet on a bus and pass it through three confederates before the owner discovers it missing. Professional shoplifters, often working in teams, wear coats specially designed to conceal stolen merchandise, carry bags and boxes with secret compartments in which to hide loot, and employ any number of tools to alter the labels of merchandise within stores.

Apparently, fewer professional thieves operate today than was once the case. Inciardi (1975) argues that law enforcement agencies now are more technologically sophisticated and better organized to cope with thieves. Elaborate, centralized information systems make thieves easier to track. Inciardi believes that these changes have made professional thievery more difficult, causing fewer persons to enter the field and collapsing time-honored networks. The result is a less professional, less skilled thief who tends to work alone and to engage in a variety of illegal offenses rather than to specialize.

MOTOR VEHICLE THEFT

A fairly uncomplicated crime, motor vehicle theft involves the stealing of automobiles, trucks, motorcycles, and any other motorized vehicle allowed on public roads. Both the *Uniform Crime Reports* and national victimization surveys count such vehicle thefts. The former, however, exceeds the latter in counting thefts from commercial as well as private owners of vehicles and in including snowmobiles and golf carts among the list of vehicles open to theft.

The FBI reports that 1,073,988 vehicles were stolen in the U.S., in 1981, a rate of 469 per 100,000 population. National victimization survey results indicate 1,354,600 households experienced a vehicle theft in 1980, a rate of 1,670 per 100,000 households. Both sources show recent drops in vehicle theft rates. Victimization survey data indicate higher theft rates in cities, for blacks, and for higher-income persons of both races. Most stolen vehicles eventually are recovered and losses from thefts normally are compensated, at least partially, through insurance policies. While it is popularly believed that most auto thefts are facilitated by keys left in ignitions, recent research indicates that this is the case in only 15 to 20 percent of such thefts (Karmen, 1979).

Though nearly nine of ten auto thefts are reported to the police and stolen cars often are found, thieves are not. The police clear only 14 percent of the crimes through arrest of the thief. Arrestees most often are young white males. Beyond this, we know little about them. Offenders generally may be classified as (1) joyriders who borrow cars for short-term kicks, (2) short-termers who "borrow" cars for transportation from one place to another, (3) long-termers who steal cars and alter their identifying features for their own use, (4) felony-motivated thieves who steal cars for use in the commission of some other crime, such as a robbery, and (5) profit-motivated thieves who steal cars to sell (whole or in part) to others (McCaghy et al., 1977).

ARSON

Arson represents any willful or malicious burning or attempt to burn, with or without intent to defraud, a dwelling house, public building, motor vehicle or aircraft, or personal property of another. The offense is new to the Index crime list, added as recently as 1979. Thus, little is known about it generally, and even less can be said about trends during the past decade.

Arson reached the Index list because of an increasing awareness that its losses exceed a billion dollars yearly and that it is not a subtle crime—it destroys buildings, homes, and, in some instances, lives. On the subtle side, its costs are distributed to everyone as insurance companies pass on their losses to consumers.

The *Uniform Crime Reports* indicates 122,610 arsons in 1981, a 7 percent decrease over the previous year. Most arsons known to the police involve residences (33 percent) or motor vehicles (20 percent). Seventeen percent involve industrial, commercial, or public property. Police clear only about 15 percent of the crimes and arson arrestees comprise less than 1 percent of all persons arrested. The vast majority of those arrested are white males under 25 years of age. The age factor, especially, causes speculation that police apprehend only the most amateur or reckless of arsonists—probably persons captured at the scene of a crime of passion or revenge. Much arson undoubtedly is of this nature or the product of vandals. Some arsons are related to attempts to hide other crimes. A very small percentage of fires is set by pyromaniacs—psychologically disturbed persons fascinated with fires. Recently, however, the form of arson gaining most attention is arson for profit. This form of arson generally involves insurance fraud. Fires are started by business owners who need the insurance money to cover financial problems. They are also started by persons who purchase old buildings cheaply but insure them at great value, thus reaping a profit when they burn. Exactly how much arson is done for profit is unknown and in many ways unknowable since so many fires are thought to be started by professional arsonists who sell their services and cover their tracks well (Boudreau et al., 1977, Inciardi, 1970).

"LESSER" PROPERTY OFFENSES

There are a number of property offenses that are not included among the Part I Index crimes. For this reason, they often are referred to as "lesser" offenses. The *Uniform Crime Reports* calls them Part II offenses. These include forgery, counterfeiting, fraud, embezzlement, and buying and receiving stolen property. On the one hand, the fact that they receive less attention than Part I offenses seems reasonable. They do not intrude directly into people's lives as do burglary and robbery and, often, victims are organizations rather than individuals. On the other hand, bad checks, confidence games, and swin-

Investigator Testifies Man Set Fire to Collect Insurance

By Nan Perales

An arson investigator for the New Orleans Police Department testified Tuesday that one of the owners of a school supplies company last year set fire to his insured building to pay off more than $100,000 in bills.

John Nuckley said he arrested Milton E. Burdine Jr., 40, of 3725 Napoleon Ave. for arson after the investigator found evidence a flammable liquid was used to start the fire at Burdine's School and Teacher's Supplies at 1410 N. Broad St.

During his investigation, Nuckley said he found a can of duplicating fluid in the middle of the floor. The state contends the fluid was used to start the fire.

Nuckley said he also found three trails on the building's floor indicating a flammable liquid had been poured there and then ignited.

The investigator testified he suspected Burdine set the fire after learning the owner lied when he said he left the building around 5 p.m. with one of his employees.

Nuckley said a witness later told him Burdine actually left later than that. "He locked the door behind her (the employee) and stayed in the building and five minutes later (after Burdine left) the place was completely involved in fire," he testified.

Nuckley said he also suspected Burdine after a check of the man's financial records showed his business was failing. "Burdine had properties and personal possessions backing the business. He had an outstanding loan of $90,000 coming up," Nuckley said.

"No bank would loan him any money. He had to go to a loan company which charges exorbitant rates. His back was against the wall.

"The opportunity and the means were there. I couldn't see no other recourse than to arrest Mr. Burdine for arson."

Earlier in the day, an insurance agent for Home Insurance Co. testified the building and contents were insured for $215,000.

Burdine was arrested after a four-month investigation lead by police Detective Donald O'Rourke and Nuckley. The company, a wholesale outlet for schoolbooks, paper products and duplicating fluids, was housed in a two-story stucco and wood building that burned to the ground during a five-alarm fire May 14, shortly after closing for the day.

Source: ©Times-Picayune Publishing Corp., 1982. Reprinted by permission.

Comment: What Is a Serious Crime?

It is only in recent years that arson has joined our list of "serious" offenses—Part I crimes like robbery and theft that command special attention from crime statisticians. There is good reason for arson's reclassification, of course. The damage caused by arsonists is staggering. It takes many personal thefts to achieve the financial loss incurred in even a small business fire. Occasionally arson also results in lost lives.

Yet even with its high-loss profile, arson stands apart from other Part I crimes. This is due in large part to the fact that much arson can be called white-collar crime. Like the fire described in the news story above, arson often is committed by respectable business persons who find themselves in serious financial binds. Perhaps this white-collar quality accounts for arson having so long been ignored as a "serious" crime, though its costs always have been substantial.

The reclassification of arson as "serious" raises the possibility that we may rethink our notions of crime seriousness. Over the years we have been conditioned to view seriousness in terms of overt attacks upon person and property. But less overt forms of theft—white-collar crimes like business fraud, insurance swindles, and price-fixing—harm most of us financially, at a level that surpasses the harm done by overt thefts. Are these crimes the Part I offenses of the future?

dles—fraud—often deprive individuals (usually elderly) of far greater amounts of money than does the common theft. And, again, organizations falling victim to these offenses pass their losses on to consumers. In all, these offenses result in considerably greater losses to the public than do the combined Part I property offenses. The average citizen pays from $200–$600 per year in extra costs at the checkout counter to cover embezzlement and other forms of employee theft. Some swindles are immense. A major insurance swindle in 1973, for example, resulted in a $2 billion fraud perpetrated on investors in the Equity Funding Corporation of America through the invention of 60,000 fake customers on the company's books.

Because they receive so little attention, these offenses basically are unknown statistically. So few arrests are made (few embezzlements are reported to the police, for example) that attempts at inference from arrest statistics are pointless. However, sufficient research (apart from knowledge gleaned from criminal justice statistics) has been conducted regarding check forgers and embezzlers that something can be written about the process by which people enter into these crimes.

Check forgery takes several forms. The most common is simply writing a check for which the writer has no funds. Less common forms are cashing phoney checks for which there is no account and using stolen checks. According to Edwin Lemert (1972; see also Gibbons, 1977), most check forgers are amateurs who are responding to some form of financial crisis—the need to cover gambling losses, for example (Lesieur, 1977). Most are socially isolated, without personal relationships or financial resources to turn for help. Often, they do not see their actions as seriously wrong and plan, however vaguely, to make good the check at some point. Professional or systematic check forgers, on the other hand, write bad checks for a living. They are imprisoned relatively frequently and, therefore, live anxiously and tend toward gambling, drinking, and check-writing sprees. For obvious reasons they assume many identities and move often. They are caught most often when they become careless in their use of these identities.

Embezzlement is the misappropriation or misapplication of money or property entrusted to one's care, custody, or control. It generally is conceded that official statistics for embezzlement reflect only the tip of the iceberg. Only 9032 cases were reported in the *Uniform Crime Reports* for 1981. Rather than estimate cases or numbers of people committing embezzlement, most experts tend to estimate economic losses caused by embezzlement. By relatively conservative estimates, employee thefts and embezzlement total at least $15 billion per year (Gibbons, 1977:337). Victimization research is unable to aid in assessing the extent of embezzlement. Overall, the crime is said to cost companies more money than all other forms of theft put together.

Embezzlement may occur in any situation in which an individual is given control of another party's money. Stock investment agents may use an investor's money illegally for personal gain. Sales representatives may systematically pocket portions of a store's income. Research into compulsive gambling provides examples of bowling alley managers using weekly business receipts to pay gambling debts and treasurers of bowling leagues using trophy and prize money for gambling (Lesieur, 1977:191). The major limitation on the crime is the extent to which the owner of the money takes precautionary measures to discourage embezzlement. Banks, for example, conduct regular audits to determine whether such offenses are committed. City governments, on the other hand, are notoriously lax in this regard.

Since few lower-class persons are given positions involving financial trust, it is not surprising that embezzlement is more often committed by "respectable" people—working or middle class, and better educated. Cressey (1953) has noted that embezzlers are often people who have become involved in problems that have no conventional solutions and cannot be shared with conventional persons. Cressey also argues that few embezzlers view themselves as "criminals" in the sense that they are morally evil or dangerous to society. In fact, in order to embezzle, the offender must be able to rationalize the theft as "borrowing." He is further encouraged by the fact that he is stealing from an organization rather than from an individual. As Smigel (1956) has noted, it is more difficult to commit a crime against an identifiable individual victim than it is to victimize a nonperson, an organization.

Few embezzlers go to prison. Those who do receive rather lenient sentences, in part because they are not viewed as being in need of rehabilitation, and because this society traditionally has not shown a condemnatory interest in this offense. Employers of embezzlers often do not report the offense, to avoid potential company embarrassment or insurance problems. Many times embezzlers simply are dismissed from their jobs; occasionally they agree to make partial restitution for the offense.

As noted earlier, little is known about "lesser" property offenses beyond what has been reported about check forging and embezzlement. And the situation grows more complicated to study as newer forms of thefts are invented. Computer crime—the use of access to computers in banks and businesses to shift funds from one account to another, to loot accounts, to create false accounts—has become a problem of monumental proportions. Illegal credit card use has become more problematic than is the use of bad checks. And thefts from government programs—welfare and social security fraud and illegal Medicare charges and claims by physicians and patients, for example—have increased far beyond the current ability of the government to combat them.

VICE CRIMES

The offenses we have reviewed up to this point reflect laws designed to protect us from those who would harm us. There is another set of laws aimed only in part at our protection from others. In part they also aim to "protect us from ourselves." These laws govern behaviors known as vices. *Vices* are activities thought by many to be immoral and liable to bring spiritual and even bodily harm to those engaging in them. These offenses also are known as crimes against public morals (because they disturb the community), and victimless crimes (because they are without unwilling victims). Vice crimes include crimes of sexual conduct (prostitution, obscenity, pornography, adultery, fornication, sodomy, and other "unnatural acts" such as oral-genital contact), illegal gambling, and illegal substance possession (for example, possession of heroin or marijuana).

Those who support laws governing these activities do so for both moral and pragmatic reasons. They argue that these activities corrupt the moral fabric of our society, preying especially on the moral values of youth. Society is viewed as in need of protection from corrupting influences because societies tend to "disintegrate from within." Individuals are viewed as morally weak and likely to fall victim to vices without legal vigilance. Persons already "morally corrupted" must be forced away from vice activities. Beyond the moral corruption, it is argued often that some vices, especially drug use, carry physical dangers from which current and potential users must be protected.

Utilitarian concerns also enter into the case for outlawing vices. Anti-vice laws are seen as efficient means of controlling certain "undesirable elements." Homosexuals can be controlled through selective enforcement of laws governing sexual conduct, for example. Most important, most persons supporting anti-vice laws argue that they are a necessary tool by which to harass members of organized crime who depend, in large part, upon vice activities for revenues.

Opponents of anti-vice laws counter the morality argument by noting that unlike the situation with predatory crimes such as rape and robbery, there is little consensus in this society regarding the morality of vice activities. Thus, anti-vice laws simply reflect the governmental imposition of the moral views of some people upon others who hold differing views. Further, opponents argue that the government should not interfere with activities carried out between consenting adults and lacking any individual, unwilling victims.

The utilization aspect of anti-vice legislation also is attacked by opponents of these laws. They argue that the laws are applied selectively and often discriminatorily (especially when the vices of higher-income individuals are overlooked). The laws are enforced selectively in part because they are so difficult to enforce. There is no complaining victim. Thus police must spend considerable time and money locating offense situations and catching offenders in a manner that does not constitute *entrapment,* whereby the police officer commits or initiates a crime which otherwise would not have occurred and then arrests the other party involved in the offense. The outlawing of vice activities also creates the potential for governmental corruption whereby police and other officials accept bribes to "look the other way." Finally, opponents argue that anti-vice laws create secondary crime—crimes committed to obtain money to pay for vices whose costs are inflated due to black market prices. In other words, the outlawing of goods and services for which there is a demand does not eliminate the demand; rather it seems to increase it. For this reason, organized crime is given a market in which to flourish. Indeed, there seems a blatant illogic in creating a market for organized crime by outlawing vices and then arguing that the laws are necessary tools to combat organized crime. Beyond this, Gilbert Geis (1978) argues, the problems which anti-vice legislation seeks to address—the spiritual collapse of America, the control of organized crime, the difficulty of monitoring legalized vice (gambling, for example)—must be dealt with in some other fashion. Currently, we are using the law to fight social problems rather than crimes (in the sense of predatory victimization).

Crimes against Nature

In most states, there is little that homosexuals can do in the way of legal sexual activity. Anal intercourse and oral-genital contact are outlawed. Most people do not realize, however, that the laws governing such "crimes against nature" do not pertain solely to homosexuals. *Any* persons, married or not, who practice such "unnatural acts" violate the law. These practices seem fairly common among heterosexuals, but the laws governing them rarely are enforced against this group. When they are enforced (and enforcement is relatively infrequent), it is usually against members of the homosexual community. The prescribed penalties for "crimes against nature" represent more than a "slap on the wrist." The average maximum length of imprisonment prescribed by the laws of most states is about ten years, though a life sentence (for oral-sexual activity, for example) is possible in some states.

The symbolic content of the laws governing "crimes against nature" is obvious (see the earlier discussion of symbolism in Chapter 3). Though the laws are difficult to enforce and are enforced infrequently and selectively, the fact that they exist gives solace to those who feel that society's moral structure is threatened by sexual overindulgence. Some argue that the sexual conduct laws deter homosexuals and other "sexual deviates" from public sexual activity and from attempts to recruit impressionable youth to their lifestyle. Yet, there is no evidence that homosexuals and others with sexual orientations different from those of the majority are more prone to public sexual displays or to recruiting youth than are heterosexuals. Thus, sexual conduct laws represent the prime example of the imposition of the moral standards of one powerful sector upon a smaller, less powerful sector in an arena involving consenting adults otherwise free to pursue life as they please. The fact that the behaviors proscribed by these laws (oral-sexual relations, anal intercourse, and so forth) are practiced by many of the people who champion the laws introduces an element of hypocrisy as well as power into the issue (see MacNamara and Sagarin, 1977).

Prostitution

Related legally to the "crimes against nature" is the solicitation of sexual activity for a fee—that is, prostitution. Prostitution may be committed either by females or by males, though the former appear the more frequent offenders (certainly the more frequent arrestees). The crime takes many forms. Some prostitutes walk the streets selling their favors to passersby, committing their crimes most often in clients' cars on in cheap hotel rooms. Many prostitutes still work in what was once the most common setting for their trade—the brothel. A *brothel* is a house containing several prostitutes under the charge of a *madam* who handles all negotiations with clients who enter the house. While prostitutes also operate out of bars and massage parlors, currently the most notorious, lucrative, and perhaps even respected type of prostitute is the call girl. *Call girls* are women (assumedly there is also a male counterpart) who develop lists of fairly "well-to-do" clients who pay handsomely for sexual favors. Call girls generally operate alone in well-furnished apartments or go "on call" to hotel rooms or clients' homes. Because they are well paid, they service only a small number of clients.

Numbers of researchers have attempted to describe how women enter prostitution (Bryan, 1965; James, 1976; Winick and Kinsie, 1971). There seems no evidence that many are forced by other persons into prostitution, that many are psychologically disturbed or "oversexed," or that drugs force many to sell their bodies. There is evidence that most enter the profession quite rationally for economic gain because they are poor or because prostitution appears more lucrative than do their current occupations. Many align or are recruited by "pimps," men who sometimes procure customers for the prostitute, sometimes protect her from aggressive clients, sometimes abuse her, often provide her with shelter and clothing, usually bail her out of jail, and always claim the major percentage of her take.

Essentially the same issues characterize prostitution laws as mark those governing other vices. Some argue that sex-for-sale is immoral and should be outlawed though the trade's persistence through the ages raises questions about moral consensus regarding prostitution. But most anti-prostitution arguments are utilitarian. Those favoring criminal sanctions argue that too many dangers accompany prostitution to consider decriminalizing it: venereal disease, associated robberies and thefts, organized crime involvement, and, occasionally, blackmail.

Again, opponents of criminal sanction argue that the law should not interfere in the conduct of adults willingly engaging in behaviors involving no one but themselves. As to the utility of anti-prostitution laws, opponents note that very little of this society's venereal disease problem stems from prostitution and that related crimes and organized crime involvement in prostitution exist because the trade is illegal. Blackmarket possibilities (prostitution is highly lucrative) always attract organized crime. Underground prostitution is unregulated and unsupervised, therefore creating the possibility of related crimes. Were prostitution treated as a regulated business, most of the tangential problems would be considerably more easily controlled. At present, prostitution is legal in privately owned, governmentally regulated brothels in thirteen of seventeen Nevada counties. There is no evidence of serious crime problems accompanying legalized prostitution in that state.

We also face two major legal dilemmas as long as prostitution is outlawed: entrapment and discriminatory legislation and enforcement of anti-prostitution laws. Since customers willingly visit prostitutes and are not "complaining victims," police must pose as customers in order to trap prostitutes. Thus, they walk a thin line between legal arrests and entrapment. Arrests that do not involve police decoys nearly always are arrests of the prostitute only, even in the few jurisdictions that have laws applicable to the prostitute's clients. Clients rarely are arrested because the police need them to file a complaint and pressure them to do so by threatening to arrest them for disturbing the peace. Beyond this, legislators in most states refuse to include the client in anti-prostitution statutes because they view clients as the "weak" victim of vice preyed upon by the prostitute.

Pornography

Of all outlawed vices, pornography creates the most confusion. At base, it refers to materials (books, magazines, films) depicting explicit sexual acts aimed to sexually arouse the reader or viewer of the materials. As with other sexual conduct laws, the first issue debated by those for and against anti-pornography laws is the state's right to censor what can and cannot be seen by the public. Proponents wish to protect society in general from immoral influences. Opponents wish to decide for themselves whether or not materials are immoral and whether or not they wish to expose themselves to those materials. The second issue involves the protection of youth from immoral influences. Proponents of censorship argue that without restraints, sexually explicit materials will find their way into the hands of impressionable youth. Opponents claim that the sale of pornography must be better regulated in order to protect youth from exposure to it, but that an adult's right to choose reading and viewing materials should not be sacrificed to attain this goal.

Related to the above is the important and more general issue of defining pornography legally. Pornography more than any other sexual conduct crime highlights the lack of societal consensus regarding sexual morality. Federal, state, and local laws refer to "obscene material," that is, to lustful material that offends prevailing senses of decency and morality. However, determining what is and is not obscene becomes problematic. Attempts have been made by moral zealots to ban as obscene such literary classics as James Joyce's *Ulysses* and J. D. Salinger's *Catcher in the Rye*. Unable to define obscenity exactly, the U.S. Supreme Court has ruled that obscenity is primarily a matter of contemporary community standards. The result, then, is that anti-obscenity legislation becomes an expression of the moral standards of the more powerful groups in a state or community, even if membership of these groups is small in relation to the remainder of the community. Obscenity trials also reduce to a single decision by a judge or a jury concerning what is or is not obscene.

Many persons seek to outlaw pornographic magazines and films because they allegedly exploit those whose bodies are photographed or filmed—especially women and children. To the extent that adults voluntarily choose to be the subjects of pornographic materials, exploitation (whether psychological or economic) is rather difficult to define legally—as difficult, for example, as would be defining exploitation of the public through television commercials. To the extent that children are involved, pornography is exploitative and most opponents of anti-pornography laws are quite willing to outlaw the use of children in pornographic materials.

Finally, an alleged justification for the banning of pornography is that pornographic materials produce sexual aggression and sexually assaultive crimes in men. Most research fails to find a link between pornography and aggressive behavior (Davis and Braucht, 1973; Goldstein, 1973). In a comprehensive review of the literature, Gray (1982: 393, 395) reports that hardcore pornography does not produce aggressive behavior but may increase levels of aggression in men already angered toward women. Thus, she concludes:

> ... [A]nger is a greater social problem than pornography, especially when anger is directed toward those less powerful. Anger is most dangerous in men who are unable to effectively distinguish between aggression, the control of women, and sexual arousal. The goals of social change might be better served by focusing on the source of anger in men, and by helping men to deal with that anger, than by focusing on pornography.
>
> ... If the relationship between pornography and the degree of violence against women is the key issue in the debate over pornography, it must be recognized that themes of violence have become an integral part of most of our media. A disturbed mind will find exciting stimuli wherever it looks. The amount of violence depicted in pornography is less than the amount of violence shown on television in the United States.

Gambling

Like prostitution, gambling is an ancient "vice." Its criminalization has religious roots. But general moral rationales for criminalization no longer suffice since many states now have lotteries and off-track betting, and most cities permit bingo games. Casino gambling is allowed in New Jersey and Nevada. And, in another context, millions are "wagered" daily on the stock market. Gambling is big business; it produces tremendous tax and direct revenues for the jurisdictions that permit it.

Gambling laws now are justified as necessary to combat organized crime. It is clear that if so many people are willing to participate in legal forms of gambling, they probably are as willing to engage in forms that are illegal. Where there is a demand, organized crime can become the supplier. Smaller, illegal gambling operations extend credit more easily than do legal operations, give better odds, are generally more convenient, and do not necessitate reporting winnings as taxable income.

Is it sensible to outlaw gambling? Legalization would increase tax revenues as participants emerged from gambling in the shadows. To the extent states desired, they could enter the gambling market for direct revenues, though the state's ability to compete with smaller, private, legal gambling operations is questionable. Decriminalization would decrease the market for organized crime and would curb the waste of police resources now directed at enforcing laws that so many people are so willing to disobey.

Substance Control Laws

Private, nonmedically prescribed use of many types of drugs is outlawed in the U.S. There is no particular logic to the criminalization of various drugs. Some laws seem accidentally to have been created; others clearly result from the skillful manipulation of political machinery (Graham, 1972). Presently, opiates (morphine, heroin), cocaine, marijuana, hallucinogens (LSD, mescaline), barbiturates, amphetamines, and tranquilizers are illegal or, at least, severely restricted in use. Alcohol, caffeine, nicotine, and various "remedies," such as diet and sleeping pills, are not.

The greatest era of drug concern—reflected in legislation and law enforcement—occurred in the 1960s when many types of drugs gained widespread use among middle-class youth. This same group also opposed the Vietnam War and many social values and conventions of the era. The passage and enforcement of drug laws in the 1960s and 1970s became entangled with the symbolic moral and political contests of those years. Today, the ideological content of those earlier drug laws largely is gone. Drug laws are justified today—as are all of the vice laws we have reviewed in this chapter—in the name of preventing physical and psychological harm to current and potential users and in the name of combatting organized crime. Beyond this, and more importantly, drug laws are justified in the name of preventing crimes by drug users—both crimes (usually violence) compelled by drug use and crimes (usually theft) committed to support drug use.

Even though the harm may at times be exaggerated by drug opponents, it cannot be denied that most of the drugs that now are outlawed can have fairly serious organic and psychological effects upon users. Evidence suggests that this is true of most drugs, legal and illegal, including caffeine. A few drugs appear harmful even if used occasionally; PCP or "angel dust" apparently is so harmful. Some drugs can be used occasionally without harm, though the possibility of addiction and ensuing harm presents a problem; cocaine and heroin apparently are such drugs. Most other drugs can be used occasionally without harm and without addiction, though frequent and prolonged use may carry the risk of serious organic harm. There is increasing but as yet inconclusive evidence that marijuana represents such a drug. But the issue of concern here is not the harm done to the user of drugs but the means by which the state seeks to "protect" that user. Educational programs and regulations aimed at restricting drug use to consenting adults seem reasonable. Laws preventing consenting adults from using drugs seem unreasonable. Assuming unimpaired mental processes (and drastic impairment is rare), adults should be free to make decisions concerning the experiences to which they wish to expose their minds and bodies. In this regard, drugs merit criminalization no more than do alcohol consumption, cigarette smoking, football playing, and auto racing. All involve risks of harm; all but drugs are considered matters of free choice. The law should not be used to dictate standards of personal morality.

There is no doubt that organized crime profits considerably from involvement in drug trafficking. However, as with laws governing other "vices," it is ironic that we seek to combat organized crime through enforcement of laws whose passage created the blackmarket potential for organized crime. Drug laws have resulted in considerable political and police corruption, primarily in the form of payoffs to ignore drug traffic. They have created as well a climate of disrespect for procedural law. Since drug use is a crime without a complainant, drug law enforcement is difficult. Pressured to make arrests, police often resort to entrapment and to illegal search and seizure tactics. Finally, undercover officers often violate the law themselves in engaging in drug deals and in using drugs to gain access to drug rings and eventually to make arrests.

With the possible exception of PCP's apparent occasional influence on violent behavior, there is no evidence that any form of drug use, however frequent, causes physical or psychological changes which compel the user to commit crimes (McBride, 1981). Much of the popularly supposed link between drug use and compulsive crime may be dismissed as propaganda fostered by persons behind anti-drug legislation. The link between drug use and crimes committed to support drug habits is more complex. Logically, the connection is to be expected. Outlawing of drugs creates a black market with inflated prices. Drug habits become expensive and property offenses offer a means to obtain money. Schur (1969:117) has argued effectively that the outlawing of "vices" may produce such "secondary crime" and that society may be inflating its own crime rate by outlawing drugs and fostering a black market.

Before accepting the "secondary crime" thesis, it must be remembered that not all drug users are addicts nor are all addicts classic street junkies.

Large numbers of addicts are able to live their lives without finding themselves in the streets. Most nonaddicts find drug use costly but affordable. There is no evidence of a connection between crime and the use of most forms of drugs. However, there does seem to be a rather strong association between heroin addiction (of the street junkie variety) and crimes committed to support that addiction (Gandossy et al., 1980). Inciardi (1979) reports that the 356 addicts he studied reported a total of 27,464 Index crimes in a one-year period. Male addicts tend to engage in burglaries, robberies, and drug sales to support their habits. Females are likely to turn to prostitution, shoplifting, and drug sales (Datesman, 1981). Crime drops markedly during periods of abstinence or nonaddiction (Ball et al., 1981). Poly-drug use (the use of many types of drug) also seems connected with criminal behavior though the extent to which the crimes are committed to support drug habits is unclear (Inciardi, 1974). Indeed, the temporal sequencing of drug use and criminal behavior generally is not well established. Most drug addicts seem to have had criminal records prior to drug use, but it seems as well that drug addiction fosters theft behavior (Gandossy et al., 1980).

Laws prohibiting drug sales and drug use have done little to stop the spread of drugs. Police wars on drug sales have accomplished little beyond short-term disruption of the trade. Heavy sentences for drug dealers have had little deterrent effect. The government concedes that it is powerless to halt all but a small percentage of drugs smuggled into this country.

Should anti-drug laws be struck? At least *some* crimes committed by addicts would be eliminated were drugs decriminalized and the black market short-circuited. Decriminalization would not eliminate the problems associated with drugs. They would still be used by youth too immature to determine responsibly the drugs' effects. But the law has done little to prevent this thus far and probably should not have been asked to do so in the first place. We cannot continue to look for legal remedies to address every form of social problem we encounter, whether drugs or any of the "vices" discussed in this chapter. This is especially true when the legal remedies themselves present problems (e.g., police corruption and entrapment) and when they dictate the private conduct of one's life (Geis, 1978).

ORGANIZED CRIME

Throughout the discussion of vice crimes, we made reference to *organized crime*. Most readers undoubtedly gave little pause to the fact that nowhere in that discussion was "organized crime" defined. The notions of organized crime and the Mafia are taken for granted in this society. Such has been the situation since 1891 when eleven Italians were lynched in New Orleans in an outburst of public hostility toward alleged Mafia activities. America's concern—and fascination—with organized crime increased during the prohibition era when gangsters like Al Capone made news headlines. And in 1950 the U.S. Congress Special Committee to Investigate Organized Crime in Interstate Commerce (the Kefauver Committee) raised the level of concern to near hysteria. Since that date the organized crime issue has ebbed and flowed intermittently in the American crime consciousness.

The legal notion of organized crime is fairly imprecise; definitions vary across states with laws governing organized crime. The following are offered as characteristics of organized crime by a national task force on organized crime (National Advisory Committee on Criminal Justice Standards and Goals, 1976:708):

> Organized crime is a type of conspiratorial crime, sometimes involving the hierarchical coordination of a number of persons in the planning and execution of illegal acts, or in the pursuit of a legitimate objective by unlawful means. Organized crime involves continuous commitment by key members, although some individuals with specialized skills may participate only briefly in the ongoing conspiracies.
>
> . . . Organized crime has economic gain as its primary goal, though some of its participants in the conspiracy may have achievement of power or status as their objective.
>
> . . . [I]t is not limited to patently illegal enterprises or unlawful services such as gambling, prostitution, drugs, loan-sharking, or racketeering. It also includes such sophisticated activities as laundering of illegal money through a legitimate business, land fraud, and computer manipulation.
>
> . . . [I]t employs predatory tactics such as intimidation, violence, and corruption, and it appeals to greed to accomplish its objectives and preserve its gains.
>
> By experience, custom, and practice, organized crime's conspiratorial groups are usually very quick and effective in controlling and disciplining their members, associates, and victims. Therefore, organized crime participants are unlikely to disassociate themselves from the conspiracies and are in the main incorrigible.

Major figures in organized crime rarely are caught committing the offenses usually associated with their enterprise (selling drugs, for example). Instead, they are arrested and prosecuted for offenses which normally would not receive the same degree of attention when committed by others: carrying a concealed weapon and income tax evasion. But the offenses for which they are tried most often as violators of organized crime or racketeering statutes are solicitation and conspiracy.

Solicitation involves requesting of another person the commission of a crime. It is difficult to prove because it is unclear how precise the words of solicitation must be and because it usually involves the testimony of one person (solicitee) against another (solicitor) without other witnesses. The use of undercover officers or informants to draw out a solicitation from another person raises further problems, not the least of which is entrapment.

It is the crime of conspiracy, however, that prompts the greater debate. This offense involves an agreement between two or more persons to commit a crime (including the solicitation of a crime). Again, the precision of the words or acts representing the agreement almost always is at issue. What exactly constitutes an agreement? What constitutes an affirmative answer to a suggestion or a request? To what extent does knowledge about a planned criminal enterprise represent the state of being a party to it? Does a later agreement not to commit the crime in question void the original conspiracy?

Beyond these problems, critics contend that conspiracy charges are filed selectively and often are utilized merely to harass persons when other charges cannot be made to stand. Technically, in states prohibiting fornication, an unmarried couple who agree to meet later to engage in sexual intercourse are guilty of conspiracy to commit a crime. For the most part, anytime two people violate the law, conspiracy may be assumed. But the conspiracy laws have been used against alleged members of organized crime and against persons who conspire to commit acts of civil disobedience. As noted in the discussion in Chapter 2 concerning the Organized Crime Control Act of 1970, political activists did not criticize the notion of conspiracy charges when they were applied to "crooks"—members of organized crime—but protested loudly when the same vague charges were brought against them.

It is clear that much crime in America is organized to some degree. But there is considerable debate about the structure and extent of organized crime in this country. On the one hand, we are offered the picture of a national—perhaps international—Mafia "family." The family is militarily organized, with bosses, underbosses, lieutenants, and soldiers. The national family is allegedly divided into twenty-four groups in various major American cities. A "commission" composed of the more powerful syndicate figures in the U.S. oversees the activities of the twenty-four subgroups. The commission settles disputes and enforces treaties within the family. The organization is protected from external government threats by a strict code of loyalty to and silence regarding the activities of family members (President's Commission, 1967).

Countering the picture of a national Mafia is the view that organized crime is less formally structured and more local in nature (Ianni and Reuss-Ianni, 1972; Smith, 1975). The key to this view is the notion that any supply-and-demand organization, whether legal or illegal, can survive only if it is flexible enough to withstand pressures and changes in its environment. The situation in Seattle, for example, may differ greatly from that of Miami or Detroit; political processes, historical acceptance of syndicate activity, demand for illegal services, and opportunities to enter illegal enterprises all may vary. The rigidity that characterizes the alleged national Mafia would prohibit the flexibility necessary for an organization to meet these dynamic situations. As Joseph Albini (1971) points out, persons who are patrons in one area may be clients in other areas. Those in power in one place are powerless in other places. Patron-client relationships are often symbiotic, each participant holding some measure of power over the other. In sum, organized crime is integrated into local social structures and cultures.

There is little disagreement about the activities of organized crime. The syndicate has interests in gambling, narcotics, prostitution, pornography, loan sharking, labor racketeering, and stolen securities. In addition, through investment of illegally earned profits or by "muscling in," organized crime has developed interests in vending machines, restaurants and taverns, real estate, the garment industry, trucking, food processing, and other legitimate businesses. Gambling activities alone are said to net at least $7 billion yearly. Narcotics worth over $350 million dollars on the street net tremendous sums for organized crime annually (President's Commission, 1967:1–15).

Organized crime is best understood when placed in a historical and social context. Organized crime has always been tied economically to the community. It traditionally has been linked to the immigration and social mobility of various ethnic groups into the U.S. As Irish, Jews, and Italians moved into American cities and, in succession, faced relatively blocked socioeconomic mobility, they moved into illegal endeavors. As each group, in succession, found more legitimate opportunities, its involvement in organized crime decreased. Presently, organized crime is increasingly being controlled by blacks and Puerto Ricans, current inhabitants of our society's socioeconomic cellar (Ianni, 1974).

It must also be realized that organized crime requires a demand for its services and alliances with government and law-enforcement groups in order to operate relatively freely. Most observers currently view organized crime as a moderate-sized business. As such, it is concerned with limiting the supply of vice services. Like any business, it thus attempts to eliminate competition. In the case of illegal services, this is accomplished by society when it outlaws "vices." While many forms of organized-crime interests can be thwarted (for example, labor racketeering), organized crime will exist as long as a demand for illegal services exists. The resistance to legalization of vices is more than moral; organized crime is so pervasive that economic involvement in it stretches to nearly every socioeconomic corner of the society. Put simply, benefits from organized crime are not limited to members of gangs. Large and small businesses, politicians, labor leaders, and other respectable citizens share in its profits and therefore resist decriminalization of its services.

It is difficult to know whether organized crime grows stronger or weaker or if the public's concern about it rises or falls. Either way, interest in it enlarges the scope of the "crime problem."

"RESPECTABLE" CRIME

The 1970s brought an increase in awareness of consumerism issues and, following the Watergate scandal, a high level of mistrust of government officials (Geis, 1981). Although most people remain fearful of personal and property crimes, they now are concerned as well with *white-collar crime*. This term is somewhat ambiguous since it is in no way a legal term. Depending upon context and speaker, white-collar crime may refer to corporate crime such as price fixing, to occupationally-related illegal personal gain through such crimes as embezzlement or physician Medicare swindles, to illegal activity by public officeholders, or simply to any crime committed by persons generally considered members of the middle and upper classes. Given these possibilities, it is clear why white-collar crime is often referred to as "respectable crime."

Respectable or not, white-collar crime is costly for our society. Unlike standard property offenses, which harm specific individuals, white-collar crime penalizes the entire society economically. The costs of Medicare fraud by patients and physicians is covered by tax increases. Corporate price fixing eliminates the industrial competition that keeps prices down for consumers. Income-tax evasion results in yearly government financial losses of more than $27 billion. Further, as Watergate demonstrated, the costs of white-collar crime are not only economic. Official corruption, when discovered, demoralizes the American public as much as the rise in traditional personal and property offenses.

Corporate Crime

Corporate crime is a special form of white-collar crime. The term refers to a number of business-related activities: defrauding stockholders (as with misreporting profits), defrauding the public (as with price fixing and product misrepresentation), defrauding the government (as with tax evasion), endangering the public welfare (as with industrial pollution), endangering employees (as with unsafe working conditions), and illegal intervention in the political process (as with making unlawful campaign contributions). Occasionally, corporate crime refers to misuse of a corporate position for personal gain. More often, it refers to practices performed for the financial benefit of a corporation.

A classic example of the latter form of corporate crime is the heavy electrical equipment case of 1961 (Geis, 1967; Smith, 1961). The case involved a number of antitrust violations by officials of twenty-nine corporations that produced and marketed electrical equipment. Representatives of the companies conspired to rig bids and set prices for their equipment. Meeting in secret, they sought to ensure that all the companies involved maintained their "fair" share of the market (that is, the share they held at the time the conspiracy was initiated). Nearly all the participants were "company men." Few sought personal gain from their actions; most were acting "in the company's best interests." That these interests countered consumer interests by limiting competition was, in the eyes of the conspirators, of lesser consequence.

The electrical equipment case is typical of corporate crime cases in that the offenders did not view themselves as criminals. Geis (1967:144–47) notes that the conspirators stated that they had not sought personal gain, had not harmed any individuals, and had violated only government "regulations" rather than important laws. In short, the offenders saw themselves as "respectable." Clinard and Quinney (1973:191) elaborate on this point:

> A major characteristic of occupational crime is the way in which the offender conceives of himself. Since the offenses take place in connection with a legitimate occupation and the offender generally regards himself as a respectable citizen, he does not regard himself as a criminal. At most, he regards himself as a "law-breaker." . . . The maintenance of a noncriminal self concept by the offender is one of the essential elements in the process leading to occupational crime.

The electrical equipment conspiracy is typical of corporate crime in yet another way. Such crimes often are seen as "good business," and good business often requires "cutting corners." Corporate legal violations are viewed by many as being part of our business system, much like industrial spying or psychologically suggestive marketing techniques. Basically, these activities are merely extensions of a capitalist ethic that stresses profit and a grudging semiadherence to the letter, rather than the spirit, of the law. That this is a pervasive view is in great part seen in the lack of both public outcry and governmental sanctions against offenders. Fines levied against the corporations involved in the electrical equipment case were negligible (though civil suits stemming from the case were more costly). Of the forty-five company officials charged in the case, almost all of whom pleaded guilty, most received fines or were given probation. Seven drew jail terms of thirty days, though none actually served more than twenty-five days.

How much corporate crime actually exists? A pioneering study of violations by seventy large corporations in the earlier part of this century (Sutherland, 1949:20–25) found that all of the corporations had encountered adverse court decisions concerning such activities as restraint of trade, infringement, unfair labor practices, and misrepresentation in advertising; 60 per cent of the corporations had been convicted in criminal court. Recent research indicates that during a twenty-four-month period, 60 percent of the 582 largest corporations in this country had to contend with federal legal actions for violations of criminal statutes. The average number of violations per corporation was four. The automobile, oil refining, and drug industries accounted for nearly half of the violations (Clinard and Yeager, 1978; Clinard et al., 1979).

Surely we see only the tip of the iceberg. Corporate crime takes so many forms, is committed in such secrecy, and has victims so generally unaware of their losses, that sound estimates of the extent and costs of corporate crime are impossible. Yet, even from the little we know, the costs seem staggering. An illegal restraint of trade agreement—price fixing—among the four major breakfast cereal makers in the U.S., for example, cost the public $128 million annually (*Newsweek*, 1976). False advertising induces the public to spend billions on products that do not supply the desired effect. Unsafe products injure thousands yearly. Unsafe drugs, pesticides, and food additives cause untold numbers of cancer cases bound to occur in future years. Exposure of workers to hazards in industry—unsafe equipment, deadly materials, and emissions—injures and kills thousands every year. We are only now beginning to understand the effects of environmental pollution as river fishing industries close due to polluted waters, as acid rain begins to plague the Northeast, and as entire communities are relocated from areas ruined through the dumping of toxic wastes.

A number of factors place the possibility of control of corporate crime in doubt (Kadish, 1963; Geis, 1973). First, legal definition of specific corporate offenses is problematic. That is, it is difficult to define exactly what constitutes such offenses as "illegal monopolies" and "manufacture of unsafe products." Second, even were these crimes well specified, it is difficult to determine whom to charge with an offense—a corporation or the individuals within it? How, for instance, does the state prosecute a corporation? Third, intent to commit a crime generally is difficult to prove in corporate crime cases.

Fourth, and probably most important, while the public grow increasingly aware of corporate crime, it remains relatively unperturbed about the situation and places little pressure on the government to solve the problem. Concern with corporate offenses rests primarily with a few consumer-protection groups. Policing corporations adequately would require a massive bureaucracy. As it is now constituted, law enforcement in this country cannot assume the task. A public that is not outraged by corporate crime would seem unwilling to finance fully adequate government surveillance of big business. This and the ability of corporations to lobby Congress regarding the means by which they will be monitored and controlled has meant that corporate wrongdoing more often represents violations of federal and state regulations (punishable most often by fines) than of criminal statutes (punishable by prison terms) (Sheldon and Zweibel, 1978).

The last of the above problems—corporate input into the process that regulates corporations—deserves special attention. Corporate crime is controlled far less by criminal statutes than by government regulatory agencies. These agencies essentially regulate and correct "problems" as opposed to apprehending and punishing offenders. Agencies are given their powers by commissions sanctioned by the legislative branch and appointed by the executive branch. They construct and apply their own rules; that is, regulations are not introduced to the legislature for enactment into law. This presents a major problem. Regulatory agencies are subject to industry pressure in creating and enforcing regulations. Industry participates in the rule creation process and, through political pressure (most often exerted through the executive branch), is able to shape much of the enforcement process.

Enforcement of regulations is a matter of agency investigation of potential violations and referral of findings to the appropriate commission. If it agrees that violations have occurred, the commission may handle the matter administratively or through criminal or civil court prosecution. The latter two avenues are used less frequently. Most often, a case is prosecuted before an administrative hearing officer by agency attorneys while the corporation in question is represented by its attorneys. The hearing officer's finding can be appealed to the appropriate commission and, afterwards, to the federal or state court of appeals. The vast majority of cases result in consent decrees— agreements between agency and industry whereby, without admitting to previous wrongdoing, the industry promises not to engage in future violations. Most of the remainder of agency cases are resolved through the imposition of a fine on the offending party. Fines rarely are large.

Enforcement of regulations and monitoring of conformity to consent decrees are difficult due to small agency staffs and budgets. In general, however, control of corporations is difficult through regulatory agencies because the key feature of the regulatory process is negotiation rather than prosecution. In fairness, however, it should be noted that most prosecuted cases in our criminal and civil courts involve negotiated resolutions (such as plea bargaining). Also, the rigorous proof necessary for prosecution in criminal court may be difficult to produce in corporate crime cases. Some observers argue that more loosely applied administrative sanctions provide better control over corporations than does the use of criminal law. Clearly, this is true only to the extent that agencies are independent of the industries they regulate.

Attention to corporate crime should not cause us to lose sight of another form of "respectable" crime: small business offenses. It is not only big business which takes serious advantage of the consumer but the neighborhood corner store as well. Sociological studies have documented offenses by retail pharmacists, landlords, and automobile dealers (Quinney, 1963; Ball, 1960; Leonard and Weber, 1970). Local "home improvement" companies cheat millions of people daily on poor-quality and overpriced paving, painting, air conditioning, roofing, and siding. Fraudulent real estate development schemes bilk thousands of persons out of millions of dollars. False weighing of meats and produce costs each consumer pennies daily but consumers as a group millions yearly. Illegal contracts, mortgages, loans, and credit-interest schemes cheat the poor and elderly out of millions of dollars. Physicians and nursing home operators chisel millions from Medicare and, since Medicare does not cover all expenses, from their patients. Used car dealers hide serious defects in the autos they sell. Automobile and appliance repair services take advantage of the mechanical and electrical ignorance of most of the public and net as much as 1000 percent on minor repairs passed off as major repairs.

The same problems are encountered in trying to control these abuses as are met in attempts to fight corporate crime. Unaware or embarrassed victims often do not complain to authorities. Local police and prosecuting attorneys are geared toward combatting Index offenses rather than commercial crime. And a change in priorities would result in fantastic public expenditures since the monitoring of local businesses and the successful investigation and prosecution of offenders would require far more governmental bureaucracy and crime-control costs than are now experienced in fighting street crime.

Political Crime

A similar analysis applies to political crime. Traditionally, we have thought of political crime in terms of corrupt politicians embezzling government funds or accepting bribes (Gardiner, 1967). Or we have envisioned political crime as treason or spying. However, recent events have caused us to expand our definitions (Heidenheimer, 1970). Our view of political crime now includes such acts as misuse of public office for political or personal ends; misuse of government agencies to cover up unethical or criminal acts; unauthorized, secret, and relatively indiscriminate gathering of intelligence information on U.S. citizens; misrepresentation of a government agency's activities to higher authorities such as the Congress; and government violation of both substantive and procedural laws during the investigation of suspected law violators or "threats to national security." Watergate and other recent political embarrassments suggest that far more political crime and unethical conduct occur than is generally imagined by the public (Simon and Eitzen, 1982).

Variants of political graft are so prevalent as to be nearly uncountable. Officials at the local, state, and federal levels often accept payoffs to use their influence to promote legislation favorable to the persons paying them. Such influence peddling often occurs under the guise of campaign contributions. Officials also are known to participate in decisions that benefit their own financial interests; legislators may support laws protecting their real estate holdings, for example. More direct forms of bribery occur when government officials accept payment to award government contracts to persons offering such bribes. Changes in zoning regulations often can be bought. Public lands that are rich in petroleum, water, timber, and so forth, sometimes are sold or leased to persons willing to pay government officials for the favor.

The abuse of political power to accomplish political ends has gained considerable attention since Watergate. Again, the forms such abuse may take are numerous. Government officals withhold information from the public in order to further some policy interest such as the placement of American troops on foreign soil. Officials refuse to surrender documents to congressional or judicial bodies investigating possible wrongdoings. Domestic surveillance rights are abused in efforts to discredit political opponents. Government agencies such as the FBI or local police fabricate stories to humiliate political opponents. Political activists have been harassed and tied up with legal problems as the government creates false charges in efforts to stifle their dissent.

Political crime differs somewhat from corporate crime, however, in that control of political crime is hampered by the direct or indirect involvement of the offenders in the control process. That is, we expect violators to police and prosecute themselves. This problem became most clear in President Nixon's attempt to suppress the Watergate scandal through his control of the Justice Department. It became apparent as well in revelations that the FBI has been virtually free to violate laws during investigations because no agency actively investigates the FBI.

Wilson and Rachal (1977) suggest that government regulation of government agencies is far more complicated than government regulation of private business. Government agencies now have many more laws by which to abide (for example, laws governing affirmative action and access to files on citizens), and therefore regulatory agencies face a more complex task. Further, most regulatory agencies are at best semipowerful. That is, control of other agencies and their personnel is primarily a matter of reporting offenses to a higher command rather than of initiating criminal proceedings. Since the higher command (such as a mayor, a governor, a president) cannot afford the scandal that often accompanies disclosure of governmental improprieties and, for that matter, cannot risk alienating large numbers of government personnel, he or she likely will handle the matter privately and informally (for example, through the forced resignation or reassignment of the major offenders). This structure of command obviously makes control of the higher command nearly impossible.

In the final analysis, however, two problems are the most crucial in the failure to prevent political deviance. First, regulation of political agencies and officers requires massive bureaucracy and financing—far more than that required to control street crime. Second, and related, is the problem of public resignation to political crime. While public outrage over political crime exceeds public anger over corporate crime—especially when high-level political leaders are involved—political crime generally is seen as "expected," occasionally expedient, and sometimes necessary. As if paraphrasing Merton's (1957:72–82), classic analysis of the functions of the political machine, the average citizen undoubtedly finds some positive features in political violations. This is evidenced by the frequent assessment of Justice Department "excesses" in investigating political radicals as the lesser of two evils (the greater evil being the success of the radical politics). Until the public becomes as indignant about political crime as about street crime, little will be done to control violations by politicians and government agencies.

White-Collar Crime Wave?

In sum, white-collar crime encompasses a multitude of offenses in the private, business, and political sectors. It is difficult to know whether the white-collar crime problem represents a crime wave or an "awareness wave." That is, we do not know whether various forms of white-collar crime have increased significantly or public knowledge and concern about such offenses have grown. Perhaps both possibilities have prevailed.

Whether or not grounded in real offenses, the general increase in the reporting of "respectable crime" has resulted in greater (though still relatively limited) government action against white-collar offenders. As governmental activity increases, the perception of white-collar crime as a social problem will increase and spur further government activity (Douglas, 1977). If the above analyses of corporate and political crime are correct, those concerned about these offenses can look forward to frustrating times. White-collar crime is rational and calculated and some offenders have much to lose if caught; therefore, white-collar crime *should* be deterrable through increased criminal sanctions. However, there is no evidence that penalties and apprehension rates for white-collar offenders will increase dramatically in the future. General public apathy and the enormity of the bureaucracy needed to control white-collar crime ensure its continued existence.

QUESTIONING PRIORITIES

However flawed the statistics presented throughout this chapter, one conclusion seems clear: A survey of the various forms of crime to which we give attention in this society raises questions about our priorities. We concentrate our resources on street crime almost to the exclusion of white-collar crime, though the latter is more costly to us in the final analysis. We squander valuable resources combatting (futilely) various "vice" crimes, and then complain about insufficient resources for the fight against street and white-collar crime. We worry over petty larcenies and virtually ignore far more costly "lesser" property offenses such as employee theft, embezzlement, and receipt of stolen goods. The last of these provides an excellent example of the consequences of rethinking priorities.

An Example: Theft Decreases through
Reductions in Stolen Goods Activity

Theft seems to be a problem for this society. Burglaries and larcenies are the most prevalent of Index offenses. Yet, there is another offense integrally tied to theft which receives little attention and is considered a "lesser" property offense. That offense is the purchase of stolen property. Those who engage in this offense offer numerous rationales for their behavior, the most frequent being that they did not steal the merchandise in question and that, since the property likely will never be returned to its owner, there is no harm in purchasing it. The counterargument, of course, is that the property might never have been stolen if no one were willing to purchase it on the black market. Thus, the person buying the stolen goods is as implicated in the theft as is the person stealing the goods.

Viewing theft (or at least a large portion of it) as a consumer market-oriented offense, presents a very interesting problem. How much could theft be reduced if the market for stolen goods were reduced, that is, if the pool of potential buyers decreased? Available data may be used to produce estimates that (1) there are about 17,500,000 thefts in the U.S. yearly, (2) that two salable items worth about $300 are stolen in each theft, and (3) that one of every eight persons purchases one stolen item yearly. Assuming that each item represents one-half of a theft, thefts will be reduced by one-half the amount of a reduction in buyers of stolen goods. Therefore, even a moderate reduction of purchases from one in eight to one in nine would accomplish a decrease of greater than 6 percent in thefts and a substantial savings to U.S. citizens of between $139,850,000 and $279,695,000 (Sheley and Bailey, 1983).

It is possible to stop people from buying stolen goods. Identifying purchasers and apprehending them committing the crime seems highly difficult. (At present, arrests for possession of stolen goods most often are incidental to arrests for other crimes, such as possession of drugs, which necessitate searches of homes.) Prosecution possibilities are low since the state must show that the possessor of stolen goods was aware that the merchandise was stolen at the time of the sale. It is possible that a criminal justice arrest and prosecution campaign against stolen goods purchasers would have short-term deterrent effects. High-level publicity and an inability to gauge criminal justice expertise in stolen property cases would force at least a degree of caution upon potential black market buyers. Over time, however, rates of stolen goods activity should begin to creep back to original levels as violators become aware of the general inability of the criminal justice system to apprehend and try them.

Given the probable failure of a "crack-down" approach, perhaps the better route is moral appeal to the public. In general, the public does not view the purchase of stolen goods particularly negatively (Rossi et al., 1974; Sheley, 1980). And those who purchase stolen goods seem not to view themselves as criminals in any serious sense. Perhaps if the public could be made angrier about the offense and offenders made less able to rationalize their behavior as noncriminal, some reduction in stolen goods activity and, therefore, in theft might appear. The key to a change in public sentiment seems to lie in convincing the public that buying stolen goods is not a victimless crime but one that implicates the buyer in theft through representing the demand for stolen products.

In sum, the point of this discussion is less to solve the theft-stolen goods riddle than to suggest that we give some thought to the crime-concern priorities we now seem to take for granted. Views do change; we have noted the possibility with reference to arson, now an Index offense. Whether or not our priorities change after review, the review itself forces us to confront issues like the implications of buying stolen goods and, therefore, permits more rational analysis of our "crime problem."

SUMMARY

In this chapter, we have examined data and speculation about numerous crimes, some of which we fear greatly, some not, and all of which make up our general "crime problem." We note that we could say much more about the Index offenses than about other crimes though some of the Index crimes seem less harmful to society than do some of the other crimes. The discussion of "vice" crimes raised a number of questions about the state's right to dictate the behaviors of adults engaging in behaviors which "harm" only themselves and about the wisdom of devoting so much of our resources to combatting these crimes. Organized crime was shown clearly to exist, but whether or not it is as organized as is publicly supposed is debatable. White-collar crime was portrayed as an enormous collection of offense-types about which we know and, apparently, care little. The points addressed in the chapter lead to a questioning of our crime-concern priorities. The questioning may or may not bring change but certainly will increase understanding of the dynamics of crime and concern about it in this society. This understanding is enhanced further in the coming two chapters that examine the characteristics of criminals and their victims.

REFERENCES

Albini, J. L. 1971. *The American Mafia: Genesis of a Legend.* New York: Appleton-Century-Crofts.

Ball, H. V. 1960. Social structure and rent-control violations. *A. J. Sociol.* 65:598–604.

Ball, J. C., L. Rosen, J. A. Fluek, et al. 1981. The criminality of heroin addicts: When addicted and when off opiates. In *The Drug-Crime Connection.* Edited by J. Inciardi. Beverly Hills: Sage Publications.

Boudouris J. 1974. A classification of homicide. *Criminology* 11:525–40.

Boudreau, J. F., Q. F. Kwan, W. E. Faragher, et al. 1977. *Arson and Arson Investigation: Survey and Assessment.* Washington, D.C.: U.S. Department of Justice.

Bryan, J. H. 1965. Apprenticeships in prostitution. *Soc. Prob.* 12:287–97.

Clinard M. B., and R. Quinney. 1973. *Criminal Behavior Systems: A Typology.* 2nd ed. New York: Holt, Rinehart & Winston.

Clinard, M. B., and P. C. Yeager. 1978. Corporate crime: Issues in research. *Criminology* 16:255–72.

Clinard, M. B., P. C. Yeager, J. Brissette, et al. 1979. *Illegal Corporate Behavior.* Washington D.C.: U.S. Department of Justice.

Conklin, J. E. 1972. *Robbery and the Criminal Justice System.* Philadelphia: J. B. Lippincott Co.

Cressey, D. R. 1953. *Other People's Money.* New York: Free Press.

Datesman, S. K. 1981. Women, crime, and drugs. In *The Drug-Crime Collection.* Edited by J. Inciardi. Beverly Hills: Sage Publications.

Davis, K., and G. N. Braucht. 1973. Exposure to pornography, character and sexual deviance: A retrospective survey. *J. Soc. Iss.* 29: 183–96.

Douglas, J. D. 1977. A sociological theory of official deviance and public concerns with official deviance. In *Official Deviance*. Edited by J. J. Douglas and J. M. Johnson. Philadelphia: J. B. Lippincott Co.

Federal Bureau of Investigation. 1982. *Uniform Crime Reports—1981*. Washington, D.C.: U.S. Government Printing Office.

Gandossy, R. P., J. R. Williams, J. Cohen, et al. 1980. *Drugs and Crime: A Survey and Analysis of the Literature*. Washington, D.C.: National Institute of Justice.

Gardiner, J. A. 1967. Wincanton: The politics of corruption. In *President's Commission on Law Enforcement and Administration of Justice, Task Force Report: Organized Crime*. Washington, D.C.: U.S. Government Printing Office.

Geis, G. 1967. White collar crime: The heavy electrical conspiracy case of 1961. In *Criminal Behavior Systems, A Typology*. 1st ed. Edited by M. B. Clinard and R. Quinney. New York: Holt, Rinehart & Winston.

———. 1973. Deterring corporate crime. In *Corporate Power in America*. Edited by R. Nader and M. J. Green. New York: Viking Press.

———. 1978. The criminal justice system without victimless crimes. In *Readings in Criminology*. Edited by P. Wickman and P. Whitten. Lexington, Mass.: D. C. Heath & Company.

———. 1981. Upperworld crime. In *Current Perspectives on Criminal Behavior*. Edited by A. S. Blumberg. New York: Alfred A. Knopf.

Gibbons, D. C. 1977. *Society, Crime and Criminal Careers*. 3rd ed. Englewood Cliffs, N.J.: Prentice-Hall.

Goldstein, M. J. 1973. Exposure to erotic stimuli and sexual deviance. *J. Soc. Iss.* 29:197–219.

Graham, J. M. 1972. Amphetamine politics on Capital Hill. *Society* 9:14–23.

Gray, S. 1982. Exposure to pornography and aggression toward women: The case of the angry male. *Soc. Prob.* 29:387–98.

Heidenheimer, A. J. 1970. *Political Corruption: Readings in Comparative Analysis*. New York: Holt, Rinehart & Winston.

Hepburn, J. R. 1973. Violent behavior in interpersonal relationships. *Sociol. Q.* 14:419–29.

Ianni, F. A. J. 1974. *Black Mafia: Ethnic Succession in Organized Crime*. New York: Simon and Schuster.

Ianni, F. A. J. and E. Reuss-Ianni. 1972. *A Family Business: Kinship and Social Control in Organized Crime*. New York: Russell Sage.

Inciardi, J. 1970. The adult firesetter: A typology. *Criminology* 8: 145–55.

———. 1975. *Careers in Crime*. Chicago: Rand McNally & Co.

———. 1974. Drugs, drug-taking, and drug-seeking. In *Drugs and the Criminal Justice System*. Edited by J. A. Inciardi and C. D. Chambers. Beverly Hills: Sage Publications.

———. 1979. Heroin use and street crime. *Crime & Delinq.* 25:335–46.

James, J. 1976. Motivation for entering into prostitution. In *The Female Offender*. Edited by L. Crites. Lexington, Mass.: Lexington Books.

Kadish, S. H. 1963. Some observations on the use of criminal sanctions in enforcing economic regulations. *Univ. Chicago Law Rev.* 30:423–49.

Kalven, J., and Zeisel, H. 1966. *The American Jury*. Boston: Little, Brown and Company.

Karmen, A. 1979. Victim facilitation: The case of automobile theft. *Victimology* 4:361–70.

Kleck, G. 1979. Capital punishment, gun ownership, and homicide. *Am. J. Sociol.* 84:783–804.

Lemert, E. M. 1972. *Human Deviance, Social Problems, and Social Control.* 2nd ed. Englewood Cliffs, N.J.: Prentice-Hall.

Leonard, W. N., and M. G. Weber. 1970. Automakers and dealers: A study of criminogenic market forces. *Law & Society Rev.* 4:407–24.

Lesieur H. R. 1977. *The Chase.* New York: Anchor Books.

Letkemann, P. 1973. *Crime as Work.* Englewood Cliffs, N. J.: Prentice-Hall.

Luckenbill, D. 1977. Criminal homicide as situated transaction. *Soc. Prob.* 25:176–86.

McBride, D. C. 1981. Drugs and violence. In *The Drugs-Crime Connection.* Edited by J. A. Inciardi. Beverly Hills: Sage Publications.

McCaghy, C. H., P. C. Giordano, and T. K. Henson. 1977. Auto theft: Offender and offense characteristics. *Criminology* 15:367–85.

MacDonald, J. M. 1975. *Armed Robbery: Offenders and Their Victims.* Springfield, Ill.: Charles C. Thomas, Publishers.

MacNamara D. E. J., and E. Sagarin. 1977. *Sex, Crime, and the Law.* New York: Free Press.

Merton, R. K. 1957. *Social Theory and Social Structure.* New York: Free Press.

National Advisory Committee on Criminal Justice Standards and Goals. 1976. *Organized Crime.* Washington , D.C.: U.S. Department of Justice.

Newsweek. 1976. Antitrust: Snap, crackle and pop. June 14, 79–80.

Paez, A. L., and R. W. Dodge. 1982. *Criminal Victimization in the U.S.* Bureau of Justice Statistics: Technical Report. Washington, D.C.: U.S. Department of Justice.

Parker, R. N., and M. D. Smith. 1979. Deterrence, poverty, and type of homicide. *Amer. J. Sociol.* 85:614–24.

President's Commission on Law Enforcement and Administration of Justice. 1967. *Task Force Report: Organized Crime.* Washington, D.C.: U.S. Government Printing Office.

Quinney, R. 1963. Occupational structure and criminal behavior: Prescription violations by retail pharmacists. *Soc. Prob.* 11:179–85.

Reppetto, T. A. 1974. *Residential Crime.* Cambridge, Mass.: Ballinger Publishing Co.

Rossi, P., E. Waite, C. Bose, et al. 1974. The seriousness of crimes: Normative structure and individual differences. *Am. Sociol. Rev.* 39:224–37.

Scarr, H. A. 1973. *Patterns of Burglary.* 2nd ed. Washington, D.C.: U.S. Government Printing Office.

Schur, E. 1969. *Our Criminal Society.* Englewood Cliffs, N.J.: Prentice-Hall.

Sheldon, J. A., and G. J. Zweibel. 1978. *Survey of Consumer Fraud Law.* Washington, D.C.: U.S. Government Printing Office.

Sheley, J. F. 1980. Is neutralization necessary for criminal behavior? *Deviant Behav.* 2:49–72.

Sheley, J. F., and K. Bailey. 1983. Theft reductions through decreases in stolen goods recipients. Manuscript, Tulane University.

Shover, N. 1972. The social organization of burglary. *Soc. Prob.* 20:499–514.

Simon, D. R. and D. S. Eitzen. 1982. *Elite Deviance.* Boston: Allyn & Bacon.

Smigel, E. O. 1956. Public attitudes toward stealing as related to size of victim organizations. *Am. Sociol. Rev.* 21:320–27.

Smith, D. 1975. *The Mafia Mystique.* New York: Basic Books.

Smith, M. D. and R. N. Parker. 1980. Types of homicide and variation in regional rates. *Soc. Forces* 59:136–47.

Smith, R. A. 1961. The incredible electrical conspiracy. *Fortune* April; 132–80; May; 161–224.

Sutherland, E. H. 1949. *White Collar Crime.* New York: Holt, Rinehart & Winston.
U.S. Department of Justice. 1981. *Criminal Victimization in the United States, 1979.* Washington, D.C.: U.S. Government Printing Office.
Wilson, J. Q., and P. Rachal. 1977. Can the government regulate itself? *Pub. Interest* 46:3–14.
Winick, C., and P. M. Kinsie. 1971. *The Lively Commerce: Prostitution in the United States.* Chicago: Quandrangle Books.
Wolfgang, M. 1958. *Patterns in Criminal Homicide.* Philadelphia: University of Pennsylvania Press.

SUGGESTED READINGS

As in the previous chapter, examination of the FBI *Uniform Crime Reports* and various Justice Department victimization surveys is recommended to gain a sense of Index offense patterns. Also valuable are Swigert and Farrell's *Murder, Inequality, and the Law* (Lexington, Mass. D. C. Heath & Company, 1976) and Inciardi's *Careers in Crime* (Chicago: Rand McNally & Co., 1975). See Schur and Bedau's *Victimless Crimes: Two Sides to a Controversy* (Englewood Cliffs, N.J.: Prentice-Hall, 1974) for a discussion of vice crimes. Ianni and Reuss-Ianni offer a well-rounded collection of readings concerning organized crime in *The Crime Society* (New York: New American Library, 1976), and Simon and Eitzen provide a critical view of "respectable" crime in *Elite Deviance* (Boston: Allyn & Bacon, 1982).

PART III

CRIMINALS AND THEIR VICTIMS

Most citizens possess ideas about who commits crimes and who are victims of crime. A review of available research on this issue may produce some surprises regarding stereotypes of criminals and their victims. Chapters 6 and 7 present such a review.

6

CORRELATES OF CRIMINAL BEHAVIOR

Though self-reported criminality research indicates that most people violate laws, there are different patterns in this society in the types of laws violated and the frequency of violation. For example, those who commit the offenses we seem to fear most—"serious" personal and property crimes—are predominantly young, lower-class males. This high-crime group also contains a greater proportion of blacks than chance alone would suggest. Crimes about which this society is showing increasing concern—white-collar offenses—are more often committed by middle- and upper-middle-class, white males over the age of twenty-five.

Delineating such correlates of criminality is very important for the formulation of crime-prevention programs. This is true whether we are seeking target groups for implementation of immediate preventive measures or engaged in long-term causal analysis aimed at more permanent answers to crime questions. Research that seeks out patterns of crime and criminal behavior is called *epidemiology,* and it is essential, since little else can be said about crime until its dimensions are accurately assessed.

It is important to stress that epidemiological analysis, although the starting point of the search for causes of crime, does not itself represent causal analysis. Throughout the history of both criminological and public thought on crime, *patterns* of criminality have been confused with *causes* of crime. For example, high crime rates among blacks have led many to assume that being black causes criminal behavior. However, it is not race itself that determines behavior patterns, but the social factors that accompany race—for example, economic deprivation. To interpret the situation otherwise is to fall victim to the type of muddled thinking that argues that fire engines must cause fires because they are so often found at fire scenes. The goal of epidemiological analysis, then, is not to find causes of crime but to point the way for the search for causes.

In this chapter, we will present an overview of the factors influencing differences in criminal involvement among various groups in society and will discuss four basic correlates of criminality: gender, age, socioeconomic status, and race.

The discussion of correlates relies primarily on inferences drawn from official arrest statistics and secondarily on those drawn from self-reported criminality and victimization survey results. Each of these data sets has its own problems, as we have noted in previous chapters. Also, each tends to focus predominantly on Index offenses. For this reason, our review of correlates of criminality is necessarily a review of possible correlates of the commission of Index offenses. Given our discussion of respectable crime in the previous chapter, for example, we know that the addition of such offenses as embezzlement, commercial fraud, corporate price-fixing, and false advertising to the list of Index offenses would greatly alter the profile of the average offender. He (male more likely than female) would become older, whiter, and wealthier.

OVERVIEW OF CRIMINALITY PATTERNS

Official statistics that indicate that some groups or categories of people are more criminal than others reflect combinations of three important differences among these populations. First, there are differences in the manner in which members of various groups are treated when caught committing crimes. That is, members of two groups may commit the same number of crimes, but members of one of the groups, owing to discrimination in the administration of justice, may be more apt to be arrested and processed by criminal justice agencies. Thus, the apparent differences in criminal behavior are, in fact, unreal. Second, members of various groups may commit crimes but differ in the types of crimes committed. Some types of crime are more easily detected than others and thus may lead to greater arrest rates for groups committing such crimes. Finally, the official statistics may be signaling real differences in criminal behavior among groups; some may actually commit more crimes than others.

Differential Processing of Suspects by the Criminal Justice System

Discretionary arrest, prosecution, and sentencing practices are built into our criminal justice system. Chapter 10 explores this theme in detail, but it is worth noting here that apparent differences among groups in officially tabulated crime rates may as easily reflect biases in the criminal justice system as actual behavioral patterns. Once detected, crimes are more likely to result in criminal justice actions if the suspect is lower-class, black, and young rather than middle-class, white, and older. Thus, the former may appear to be more criminal than the latter. When faced with official statistics indicating that one group is more criminal than another, we must assume first that the differences are manufactured, the product of criminal justice system bias. Only after we have tested this hypothesis can we proceed to others.

Differential Likelihood of Detection

Some groups are watched more closely than others: blacks are watched more than whites, youths more than older persons, males more than females. It is possible, then, that apparent criminal-behavior differences between these various groups actually reflect only greater detection rates. Thus, it may not be that males commit more crimes than females but that males more often are caught.

Similarly, some offenses are less visible than others. Child abuse is a case in point. The victim is unlikely to complain; any visible bruises can be falsely attributed to accidents. Other "hidden" crimes include embezzlement, blackmail, and various vice offenses—gambling, narcotics, prostitution. These crimes will likely go undetected. The victim may be reticent or even a willing party to the offense; or perhaps the victim is an organization that cannot afford the publicity accompanying a crime report. Robbery, theft, rape, and assault, on the other hand, are less likely to go undetected. Here, the victim can be more vocal in calling attention to the offense. Observers of the crime are also more likely to report its occurrence.

It stands to reason that if various groups engage in different forms of offenses, those committing "hidden" crimes will appear less criminal than those engaging in more visible crimes. It is theoretically possible, for example, that corporate executives violate the law as often as slum dwellers. Yet, corporate crimes (such as price fixing) are so much more difficult to detect than cruder offenses (such as burglary) that slum dwellers will always appear to be more criminal. We must always test this hypothesis before we examine the hypothesis that general crime-rate differences among groups are real.

Differential Criminal Involvement

If we are unable to account for apparent differences in criminal involvement among various groups solely as a function of criminal justice system biases or commission of hidden versus visible offenses, we must assume that the criminal-involvement differences are real. Since groups within this society differ in their economic situations and cultural views of what is right and wrong, we may expect differences in the extent to which members of these groups are pushed toward or encouraged to commit crimes. All else being equal, for instance, the poor person would seem to have greater motivation to rob a bank than would the rich person. Similarly, all else being equal, members of segments of society that encourage tax evasion would seem more likely to evade taxes than would members of segments that condemn the practice.

Groups in this society also differ in the extent to which they are faced with social constraints on criminal behavior. Assuming equal impetus, we may expect groups with fewer constraints to have higher crime rates. Low crime and delinquency rates among Asian-Americans traditionally have been attributed to strong familial ties within that subculture (for critical comments see Light and Wong, 1975). Higher crime rates among the lower classes may reflect, among other things, the fact that the lower classes have less to lose in terms of status and wealth and are therefore freer to engage in crime. There are, as well, differences among the classes and subcultures of this society in the degree to which members are socialized into "conventional" moral values. The South's consistently higher homicide rates often are attributed to its different view of violence as an appropriate response to certain dispute situations (Gastril, 1971). Accounts of youth gangs suggest their value systems eliminate conventional moral values as constraints against criminal behavior.

People also vary in the opportunity and skill necessary to commit a crime. This fact seems relatively obvious on the face of it, but opportunity and skill are variables that often are overlooked in discussions of differential crime rates among various groups. For instance, the fact that embezzlement is more a middle-class than a lower-class crime is in great part connected to the fact that lower-class persons rarely are placed in situations of financial trust in which embezzlement is a possibility. Nor is everyone who has the opportunity to embezzle able to capitalize on it. Not everyone possesses the knowledge necessary to "juggle the books" successfully (Cressey, 1953). Even the seemingly most basic of crimes—mugging, robbery, theft—require opportunity and expertise that not everyone has. Undoubtedly, few people reading this book could successfully commit a mugging without practice or the advice of a competent mugger.

In sum, we have seen that reported differences in crime rates among various groups in society may be due to a number of factors. They may represent criminal justice biases or the involvement of some groups in more "hidden" offenses. The differences may also be real. With these factors in mind, we may examine four variables often correlated with criminal behavior: gender, age, socioeconomic status, and race.

GENDER AND CRIMINALITY

Of all the variables that appear related to crime, the sex or gender variable displays the most consistent, uncontaminated relationship. In this and most other cultures, males have higher rates of involvement in most forms of criminal behavior than do females. This is the case whether official or self-reported criminal acts are considered. Table 6–1 displays 1981 *Uniform Crime Reports* arrest figures for males and females. For most crimes, male arrests outnumber female arrests about four to one. Even the crimes we might call "female offenses"—larceny, forgery and counterfeiting, fraud, and embezzlement—are still primarily committed by males. The only offense that is truly characteristically female is prostitution, and male participation in this offense seems to be growing.

Since these are official arrest statistics, we cannot know for certain the extent to which they reflect actual male-female criminal behavior patterns. Undoubtedly, women often receive preferential treatment from the criminal justice system, yet it is difficult to believe that this occurs frequently with regard to more serious offenses. It is also possible that women's crime rates for property offenses are underestimated because women engage in crimes that are harder to detect. For example, Cameron (1964) reports that amateur shoplifters are more often females and that female shoplifters steal more items than do males. This aside, self-report studies of criminal behavior suggest that official arrest statistics do mirror reality somewhat. Canter (1982), Cernkovich and Giordano (1979), and Smith and Visher (1980) report smaller, though still obvious, gender differences in self-reported delinquency

TABLE 6–1

1981 U.S. Arrests by Gender of Arrestee

Offense	Total arrests	Percent male	Percent female
Murder and nonnegligent manslaughter	20,432	87.3	12.7
Forcible rape	30,050	99.1	0.9
Robbery	147,396	92.8	7.2
Aggravated assault	266,948	87.4	12.6
Burglary	489,533	93.7	6.3
Larceny—theft	1,197,845	70.9	29.1
Motor vehicle theft	122,188	91.1	8.9
Arson	19,362	88.5	11.5
Other assaults	466,359	85.9	14.1
Forgery and counterfeiting	81,429	67.9	32.1
Fraud	272,900	58.8	41.2
Embezzlement	8,170	71.5	28.5
Stolen property—buying, receiving, etc.	122,452	89.2	10.8
Weapons—carrying, possession, etc.	170,660	92.5	7.5
Prostitution and commercialized vice	103,134	26.6	73.4
Drug abuse violations	586,646	86.8	13.2
Gambling	40,949	90.5	9.5
Disorderly conduct	748,603	84.4	15.6
Vagrancy	31,706	84.1	15.9

Source: FBI, *Uniform Crime Reports—1981* (Washington, D.C.: U.S. Government Printing Office, 1982), p. 178.

and criminality than we find in official statistics. Hindelang (1979, 1981) also reports that victimization survey data regarding offender characteristics point to male-female criminality differences similar to those found in official arrest statistics.

Despite its obvious relationship to criminal behavior, the gender variable until recently has attracted little attention among criminologists. At the root of the lack of interest are some basic assumptions about the "nature" of females and about sex roles in our culture. For the most part, women have been viewed as passive creatures who are relatively incapable of aggressive (criminal) acts and whose natural role is that of homemaker (Wilson and Rigsley, 1975; Steffensmeier and Cook, 1980). Further, from a policy point of view, there has seemed no reason for a concern with female crime; most crime has been committed by males.

Older crime theories clearly reflect this position. At the turn of the century, Caesare Lombroso (1903), a biology-oriented criminologist (see also Chapter 8), argued that women naturally lack the initiative to break laws, and that men possess this initiative. Female crime was therefore seen as a deviation from the basic female nature. This theme was also present in the writings of Freud. Noncriminal women were viewed as being naturally passive, and criminal women supposedly deviated from the norm as a result of an inability to repress a natural envy of males (Simon, 1975:2–9; Klein, 1973). Such views of female crime portrayed the female offender as "sick," a notion that still forms the basis of most female corrections programs (Smart, 1977).

One earlier theory of female crime stood apart from the rest. Rather than viewing female offenders as deviating from basic natural female inclinations, Otto Pollak (1950) argued that women are naturally inclined toward crime. He viewed women as being far more devious and cunning than men. Women are, he argued, biologically and socially better equipped for certain forms of crime. In fact, he felt women commit as many crimes as men but that they simply commit offenses that are more difficult to detect, offenses in keeping with their supposedly deceitful nature. Further, he stated, they receive preferential treatment from the criminal justice system.

Through the 1950s and 1960s, criminologists showed almost no interest in female crime. Anthony Harris's (1977) review of the major criminological theories of crime causation indicates that most of them would have to be severely altered in order to explain female crime rates. Yet, the 1970s fostered a new interest in the gender difference. Discussions of female crime are appearing with greater frequency in journals and textbooks, due in part to the growth of the women's movement and its focus of attention on all aspects of female behavior and, in part, to some recent apparent changes in female crime patterns. From 1960 to 1975, the percentage of females arrested for most types of crime increased an average of 100 percent, as opposed to an average of 23 percent for males. For adult females, the major increases occurred in rape (as accessories to that crime), robbery, and property offenses;

murder and assault rates increased less dramatically. Adolescent females displayed significant increases in violent and property offenses, including murder and assault (FBI, 1976:183).

Changes in the crime patterns of females do appear to have followed the birth of the modern women's movement, about 1966 (Austin, 1982). Some observers have been quick to conclude from these patterns that the criminality gap between males and females has begun to narrow as a result of changing sex roles and self-concepts and, more generally, the women's movement (Adler, 1975). Sex-role changes for adult women, it is argued, have resulted in a partial drift from the traditional female role into which they were socialized. No longer are adult women totally homebound. They have entered the work world and, thus, have greater opportunity to commit occupationally related crimes such as embezzlement (Klein and Kress, 1976; Simon, 1975). More importantly, adult women may have undergone a partial change in view of self (Harris, 1977:11–14). In addition to viewing themselves as workers, they may also now view themselves as capable of committing *some* acts traditionally thought to be performed only by males— more serious offenses such as robbery (Bruck, 1975).

The changes in traditional female sex roles, it is argued further, may have affected female adolescents to a greater degree. They have not been faced with a new set of values and expectations that conflict with those stressed in their earlier socialization. Rather, they have inherited from the youth-movement days of the 1960s a view of women able to work, to use drugs, and to protest politically. Further, a major socialization institution, the school, is no longer stressing the traditional feminine role. Female adolescents are given role values and expectations that do not differ greatly from those given males. We can, therefore, expect young females to view themselves as capable of engaging in most of the behaviors performed by young males—both violent and property crimes (Datesman et al., 1975; Noblit and Burcart, 1976).

This view of changes in female crime patterns has received considerable criticism. To begin, the apparent changes between 1960 and 1975 are less evident when data from 1972 and 1981 are examined. *Uniform Crime Reports* (FBI, 1982) data for these years are displayed in Table 6–2. Overall, arrest rates have increased for women during the past decade, but not radically more so than for men. The major gains for women are in the traditional "female" offenses—fraud, forgery, and prostitution. Homicides have increased only 2 percent for women overall and decreased 61 percent for women under eighteen (those supposedly now capable of violent, serious crimes).

Steffensmeier (1978; 1980; Steffensmeier and Cobb, 1981) has scrutinized official crime statistics from 1934 to 1979 and suggests that the sex differential has decreased somewhat in most types of offenses, the largest decrease having occurred in the 1960s and 1970s. Yet, women appear to

TABLE 6–2

U.S. Arrest Trends by Gender, 1972–1981

Offense	Total males	Total females	Males under 18	Females under 18
Murder and nonnegligent manslaughter	+36.2	+2.3	−7.8	+60.6
Forcible rape	+58.5		+16.8	
Robbery	+37.3	+51.5	+27.7	+9.9
Aggravated assault	+75.6	+71.0	+43.2	+41.8
Burglary	+59.1	+31.7	+96.3	+73.9
Larceny—theft	+79.0	+25.9	+75.1	+17.6
Motor vehicle theft	+2.4	+72.4	−23.0	+46.8
Arson	+82.2	+107.3	+36.6	+29.4
Other assaults	+54.5	+60.4	+35.4	+25.7
Forgery and counterfeiting	+70.7	+157.8	+92.7	+115.0
Fraud	+149.2	+317.7	+306.3	350.1
Embezzlement	+17.2	+22.9	+99.6	+203.2
Stolen property—buying, receiving, etc.	+70.6	+31.0	+49.9	+71.0
Weapons—carrying, possession, etc.	+39.8	+38.8	+33.5	+55.3
Prostitution and commercialized vice	+174.1	+110.1	+208.1	+145.3
Drug abuse violations	+46.2	+23.1	+4.9	−17.9
Gambling	−39.4	−35.3	−19.9	+7.3
Disorderly conduct	+27.7	+39.0	−4.1	−11.3
Vagrancy	−43.6	−83.8	−41.1	−48.9

Source: FBI, *Uniform Crime Reports—1981* (Washington, D.C.: U.S. Government Printing Office, 1982), p. 166.

have made little gain in arrest rates for violent, traditionally male, and white-collar crimes, despite inferences drawn from the earlier 1960s–1970s data. They always have and continue to be involved in traditional "female" crimes: fraud, forgery, and the prostitution-related crimes of vagrancy and disorderly conduct (Hoffman-Bustamante, 1973). Petty larceny arrests (not white-collar-related larceny) account for major proportions of apparent female crime increases. Smith and Visher (1980), analyzing numerous studies of sex differences in deviant and criminal behavior, also argue that female gains in this behavior have been predominantly in lesser types of offenses.

Steffensmeier joins Joseph Weis (1976) in labeling the "new female criminal" a fiction, more illusory than real and, to whatever extent real, having little to do with the women's movement. The status of women, they argue, has not changed sufficiently in this society to affect the types of role changes necessary for major crime pattern alterations. More women are working than ever before, but women still are blocked from all but lower-level jobs. In fact, their participation in professional and managerial occupations barely has changed in more than twenty years. Working women still are expected to maintain the home in traditional fashion (Coverman, 1983). Female incomes remain much lower than those of males. There is no evidence that sex-role socialization in the school has altered radically. It is clear that women have not gained access to structured criminal opportunity—professional criminal and underworld subcultures. Finally, rather than being influenced by women's movement ideology, female crime appears to be committed by women least conscious of oppression.

In line with our earlier stated mandate that changes in criminal justice policy and activity (including records-keeping) be examined before accepting apparent criminal behavior trends as real, Steffensmeier and Cobb (1981) offer reasonable alternative hypotheses to account for the illusion of the "new female criminal":

1. Citizens now are more likely to report crimes committed by females.
2. Police and prosecutors now are more inclined to process females alleged to have violated the law. Arrest and prosecution decisions now are less likely determined by extralegal factors. This especially is the case for women who depart from the stereotypical feminine role (Visher, 1983).
3. Police records-keeping and, therefore, *Uniform Crime Reports* arrest statistics now are more accurate. It is possible that female arrests were underestimated in earlier years.

To summarize, it appears that males are more involved in most forms of criminal activity than are females. Female criminality has increased over the past fifteen years, but so has male criminality. Whether or not the increase in female unlawful behavior is real or simply a statistical artifact is unknown. If it is real, it appears that the increase has occurred in more traditional "female" offenses. It is not known exactly how much the women's movement and changing sex role patterns have influenced female crime rates, but it does appear that their influence has been exaggerated by some observers.

AGE AND CRIMINALITY

Figure 6–1 indicates the age distribution of people arrested for Index crimes in the U.S. in 1981 according to the FBI (1982) *Uniform Crime Reports*. Examining the graphic trends for all offenses, we see that most arrestees are under thirty years of age. In fact, 12 percent are under fifteen, 33 percent under eighteen, 51 percent under twenty-one, and 62 percent under twenty-five years of age.

Crime (or, at least, arrest) seems to be a phenomenon of the young—persons under thirty. Those between eighteen and twenty-four account for twice the percentage of arrests for violent crimes as those under eighteen. Involvement in property crime is roughly the same for both of these groups. This was not always the case. In 1975, for example, an age correlation for property and violent offenses was much clearer. Those older than eighteen accounted

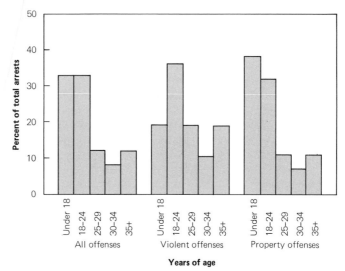

FIGURE 6–1

Percentage of Total Arrests for all Offenses, Violent Offenses, and Property Offenses by Age Group, 1981. *(Source:* FBI, *Uniform Crime Reports—1981.* (Washington, D.C.: U.S. Government Printing Office, 1982), pp. 171—72).

for the majority of violent offenses (as is still the case); those younger than eighteen accounted for the majority of property crimes. In recent years, however, the distribution of arrests for property offenses has changed. Between 1977 and 1981, property crime arrests of those younger than eighteen decreased 11 percent overall, and arrests of persons older than eighteen rose 29 percent. Violent crime arrests rose for both groups, but the greater increase was for those older than eighteen: 22 percent versus only 4 percent for those younger than eighteen (FBI, 1982:167). While once it was believed that crime rates began to decline after age eighteen, this no longer seems to be the case. It will be some years before we know for certain, but arrest statistics now suggest that the group between eighteen and twenty-four may be a high-crime cohort whose criminal activity could remain high even after age thirty.

Self-reported delinquency studies have found for years that younger adolescents commit less serious offenses than do older adolescents (Hirschi, 1969; Williams and Gold, 1972). The differential in violent offenses is confirmed further by analysis of victimization survey results. Studying those cases in which victims were able to hazard a guess as to the age of the offender (primarily rape, robbery, and assault), Hindelang (1981) argues that males between eighteen and twenty years of age have higher offense rates than those twelve to seventeen years of age. The reverse is true for females, although the number of cases in which the offender is perceived to be female is quite small compared to cases involving males. Those in the eighteen-to-twenty-year age group in Hindelang's study (1973—1977) would have been approximately twenty-two to twenty-four in 1981, the year of reference in the above discussion of arrests.

A number of factors may account for the fact that predatory crime appears to be an activity of youth. It is possible that crimes are committed equally by all ages but that youth are more likely to be arrested for their offenses. Perhaps the difference lies in the types of crimes committed by various age groups. Older persons may commit more "hidden" offenses, younger persons more visible crimes. It is also possible that since youth tend to associate more with peers, the number of youths arrested for a given crime may be larger than that for older persons, who are more likely to be arrested alone.

While these explanations suggest that the age differences in criminal behavior are apparent, not real, one recent article argues that older persons are indeed less criminal than younger persons. Rowe and Tittle (1977) studied "criminal propensity," an individual's estimate of the likelihood of his or her engaging in criminal behavior. They found that for four types of crime (theft of approximately $50, illegal gambling, physical assault, and cheating on income taxes), criminal propensity declined steadily with age.

Though Rowe and Tittle were unable to account for the age differences in criminal propensity, they did suggest a number of possible explanations. Youth are not only traditionally more adventurous but also freer than older persons to engage in deviant activities. Younger people have developed fewer stakes in conventional behavior; that is, they have not yet been burdened with the time-consuming responsibilities of work and family. They have less to lose in risking apprehension for a crime. They lack the maturity to comprehend fully the potential consequences of their crimes.

Opportunity is one possible factor governing "youth crimes"—property offenses and violent crimes such as robbery. Youth are seldom in a position to commit any other than standard offenses. Physical prowess may also influence crime-rate differences among age groups. The absence of older persons in the population committing the seven Index crimes may reflect the fact that many of these offenses require the strength, agility, and stamina of youth. We find few sixty-year-old burglars, for instance, because burglary often demands physical agility.

Some observers link the relationship between youth and high crime rates to urban industrialization. Friday and Hage (1976) argue that industrialization in urban societies has decreased the need for unskilled labor, emphasized skilled jobs requiring training, and thus increased the time period between childhood and the first major job. In essence, industrialization has lengthened adolescence. In the past, persons approximately fifteen years old were exposed to the diversity of the adult world through employment. Employment also served to build in the youth a commitment to conventional goals and values. Today this process has not simply been postponed, it has been replaced by longer exposure to the undiversified world of the youth peer group. Although youths have been delayed from joining the work force, they have not become less interested in the material rewards that are thought to result from work. For those who see these rewards as unattainable, especially those in the lower classes, frustration is likely to occur. Increased exposure to the youth peer group in this deprived setting will likely cause violent crimes of frustration and predatory crimes in the pursuit of the "good life."

Greenberg (1977) also attributes crime among youths to the changing structural position of juveniles in American society. In a Marxian vein, he argues that in the early nineteenth century, working-class children held jobs at an early age, and middle- and upper-class children were supervised closely. In modern capitalist societies, children of all classes do not take on the occupational roles that tie them to conforming behavior. Indeed, the position of juveniles in today's labor market is especially bleak. Jobs are scarce, according to Greenberg, due to the inclusion of juveniles under minimum wage laws, a changing economy with scarce farm employment, teenage preference for part-time employment, and competition among teenagers and women newly entering the job market. The job situation is coupled with increased years in school, which delay entrance into adulthood responsibilities and earnings, and put many youths in a prolonged situation of school failure and frustration (Mann, 1981). The lengthy period of school and unemployment exposes children longer to peer status expectations regarding material rewards that grow more complicated and even further from parents' abilities to provide them to their offspring—cars, cosmetics, drugs, stereo equipment. The result is a greater incentive and more free time to commit crimes (especially property crimes) and fewer constraints on the commission of crime; for example, less worry about the effects of a criminal record upon future job possibilities.

The above theory is supported by the fact that crime rates for most offenses drop dramatically after age twenty-five. Although most adult felons were juvenile delinquents, the majority of juvenile delinquents—including some rather serious offenders—do not become adult felons. Criminologists refer to this phenomenon as *maturational reform,* the decrease of illegal activity after adolescence (Matza, 1964:22). Reckless (1973:81–82) attributes the change in behavior to a "settling-down" process fostered by the acquisition of adult responsibilities. A clear example is the process by which some college students decrease marijuana use after graduation. Brown et al. (1974) studied various marijuana-use patterns among college graduates. They found that decreases in or cessation of marijuana use are tied not so much to changes in attitudes regarding the drug but to the constraints imposed by family and job situations and changes in friendship patterns after graduation. In short, the former users were experiencing the "settling-down" process implied in the concept of maturational reform.

Hirschi and Gottfredson (1983) recently have noted that no one has produced an explanation of the age factor in criminality that accounts for its invariability across all types of demographic and social conditions. Whether or not adequately explained, the age of persons committing crimes is highly important in policy-planning for the future. Although we are concerned that crime has increased in volume faster than our population during the past fifteen years, we generally fail to consider the role of the age composition of the population in the crime rise. If crime is, in fact, an activity of youth, we can expect more crime when we have a younger population. A review of population trends over the past century indicates that never before have we had so many people between the ages of twenty and thirty. The 1946–57 "baby-boom" that followed World War II ensured an unusually high number of youthful offenders in the 1960s through the mid-1970s (Chilton and Spielberger, 1971). Indeed, crime became a national problem in 1967 as the bulk of the post-war babies reached the "crime-prone" years. As the last of this population moves into its thirties, crime should decrease, for the trend toward population control will have resulted in fewer babies and therefore fewer young offenders during the early 1980s. As we noted in Chapter 4, crime trends have stabilized in recent years.

However, our optimism about declining crime rates in the future is best tempered with caution. We assume that general socioeconomic conditions will not worsen. Changes in these conditions can alter the age-crime pattern. If the economic woes of the early 1980s were to continue, for example, members of the baby-boom population might be expected to continue their criminal activity well into their thirties. This possibility is given some credence in the previously noted fact that arrests of persons over eighteen have been increasing recently rather than decreasing as expected.

In the final analysis, we must wait several years before the baby-boom crime-rate theory can be fully evaluated. Interestingly, many population experts predict a new, though smaller, increase in the birth rate in the 1980s as many people who have thus far postponed having babies begin to have them. Thus, we may be faced with increased crime rates around the turn of the century.

SOCIOECONOMIC STATUS AND CRIMINALITY

Despite the importance of socioeconomic status (SES) as a major variable in criminological theory and research (see Chapter 9), the link between SES and criminality is hotly contested among criminologists. At the source of the disagreement is the fact that most criminological conclusions about SES and criminal behavior have been based on problematic data and have concentrated on juvenile delinquency. Official crime statistics (police, courts, corrections) consistently show the lower classes to be more criminally involved.

Yet official crime statistics so often reflect biases by the criminal justice system toward the lower classes that they cannot readily be trusted. Self-report studies have not shed much light on the problem. They have produced contradictory results and have had problems of generalizability.

Victimization studies (U.S. Department of Justice, 1981) indicate that the poor, especially the black poor, have high victimization rates for both personal and property offenses. They report also that central-city residents—predominantly lower class—have consistently higher victimization rates (see Chapter 7). It is unlikely that members of higher-SES groups enter lower-SES areas and victimize lower-SES individuals. Rather, we assume that lower-class victimizations are perpetuated by lower-class criminals.

Since the late 1970s, a number of criminologists have attempted systematically to settle the SES-crime issue. Tittle and co-researchers (1977, 1978) report that their extensive review of thirty-five self-report studies pertinent to the issue produced no evidence of a link between criminality and SES. They call for abandonment of an espoused link as a major feature of criminological theories. Hindelang et al. (1979) argue that the self-report evidence is inconclusive in every sense, since samples most often are small and nongeneralizable, offense indices contain too many minor offenses, and the timeframe of self-report studies (usually one year) is impractical. They therefore cannot agree with the conclusion of Tittle et al. Elliott and Ageton's (1980) more recent and more sophisticated self-report study of delinquent involvement produces evidence that the lower classes are substantially more involved than other classes in serious crimes against persons and property, though there are no class differences in involvement in "lesser" offenses (vice crimes, for example) (see also Elliott and Huizinga, 1983).

Braithwaite (1981) offers the most comprehensive review of previous research, though he covers studies that Tittle et al. (1978) and Hindelang et al. (1979) might reject as methodologically unsound. He notes that even though self-report studies generally do not find links between crime and SES, more of these studies find links than chance alone would indicate. He refuses to dismiss official statistics as being so biased that all inferences based upon them must be considered invalid. Braithwaite concludes that only twenty-one of ninety studies of both official records and self-reported criminality which he reviews fail to provide outright support that SES is linked to crime. Further, his research omits ecological studies of crime (comparisons of crime rates by geographic sector), though these studies consistently report an SES crime association (see also Kleck, 1982).

Finally, Thornberry and Farnworth (1982) offer the results of their study of law violations committed through the years by a cohort of males born in 1945 who resided in Philadelphia from the ages of ten to eighteen. Their research includes examination of arrest data for the members of the cohort and of data gathered from personal interviews of many of those members. Looking at both types of data for crime generally and for Index offenses and violent offenses particularly, they report that for juveniles only a very weak relationship exists between SES and delinquent activity; lower SES youth seem only slightly more involved in delinquency than do higher SES youth. For adults, however, the relationship is considerably stronger. Lower SES adults clearly are more actively criminal than are higher SES adults.

In sum, the debate about the SES-crime relationship is far from settled. However, it has spurred some technically better research on the subject. The results of the newer research seem to point toward SES differences in criminality, at least for adults and for Index offenses.

To the extent they exist, SES-related patterns of criminal behavior appear linked to three factors: opportunity, moral validity granted the law, and conditions conducive to crime. Clearly, lower-SES groups do not have access to situations of white-collar crime. One indicator of the upward mobility of lower-SES groups is increasing involvement in such offenses. We find few lower-SES persons engaged in illegal rebates, violations of import laws, or copyright violations, for example.

Opportunity alone, however, cannot account for class differences in crime patterns. Although the lower classes are blocked from white-collar crime, the middle and upper classes are not blocked from traditional Index offenses. Yet the middle- and upper-class commission rates for these crimes are lower than those of the lower classes. The difference *may* be, in part, a matter of definitions of right and wrong and the extent to which the law is viewed as being sacred. Perhaps the lower classes do not place the severe moral connotations on theft and receipt of stolen goods, for example, that the middle and upper classes place on these acts. This theme, in one way or another, has characterized much of criminological theory and is much taken for granted by the American public. It should be noted, however, that there is little empirical evidence to support the theme. While individuals may vary in their beliefs about what is right and wrong (Sheley, 1980), no reliable research has found this variation linked to class, racial, or ethnic differences (Kornhauser, 1978).

More traditionally, we look to crime-conducive conditions as the source of higher crime rates for lower-SES groups. Low economic status and little opportunity to alter that status in a consumption-oriented society is thought to foster property crime. A low stake in the economic structure of society provides the freedom ("nothing to lose") to commit such crimes. Living conditions that are both relatively and actually substandard create an atmosphere of despair and frustration, leading to the violent offenses that characterize inner cities.

RACE AND CRIMINALITY

The 1981 *Uniform Crime Reports* (FBI, 1982) concerning characteristics of arrestees show blacks to be disproportionately involved in most offenses. Although they comprise about 12 percent of the general population (though about 50 percent of some large cities), blacks represent 25 percent of our arrest population. Table 6–3 indicates the proportion of blacks among arrestees for various crimes. "Black crimes," those for which blacks are arrested more often, appear to be robbery and gambling. Homicide, rape, and prostitution arrests are essentially equal in number for whites and blacks. Crimes displaying a very low percentage of black arrests (less than 20 percent) are vandalism and drinking violations.

In the past, official crime statistics seemed discrepant with the findings of self-reported delinquency studies regarding race and criminal behavior. The latter suggest much smaller differences in crime commission rates than do the former (Chambliss and Nagasawa, 1969; Hirschi, 1969; Gould, 1969).

TABLE 6–3

1981 U.S. Arrests by Race of Arrestee

Offense	Total arrests	Percentage white	Percentage black	Percentage other*
Murder and nonnegligent manslaughter	20,404	49.6	49.0	1.4
Forcible rape	30,032	50.2	48.2	1.6
Robbery	147,519	38.9	60.0	1.1
Aggravated assault	266,764	61.3	37.3	1.4
Burglary	488,868	68.5	30.3	1.2
Larceny—theft	1,196,247	66.3	31.8	1.9
Motor vehicle theft	122,027	68.1	30.2	1.7
Arson	19,319	78.4	20.5	1.1
Other assaults	465,618	66.1	32.3	1.5
Forgery and counterfeiting	81,283	63.2	35.9	.8
Fraud	276,721	68.4	30.8	.8
Embezzlement	8,163	74.4	24.5	1.1
Stolen property—buying, receiving, etc.	122,266	65.3	33.8	.9
Weapons—carrying, possession, etc.	170,451	62.3	36.6	1.1
Vandalism	228,509	81.3	17.4	1.2
Prostitution and commercial vice	103,103	49.4	49.3	1.3
Sex offenses (except forcible rape and prostitution)	68,240	78.2	20.3	1.6
Drug abuse violations	584,776	74.0	25.1	.9
Gambling	40,973	32.1	65.1	2.8
Offenses against family and children	51,766	62.9	36.0	1.2
Driving under the influence	1,405,471	87.6	10.8	1.6
Liquor laws	453,184	90.5	7.5	2.0
Drunkenness	1,085,296	82.2	15.3	2.5
Disorderly conduct	747,109	64.5	34.1	1.4

*Other—American Indian, Alaskan Native, Asian, or Pacific Islander.

Source: FBI, *Uniform Crime Reports—1981* (Washington, D.C.: U.S. Government Printing Office, 1982), p. 179.

However, as noted in Chapter 4, much of the racial-behavioral similarity found in self-reported studies may be a function of the use of low seriousness offenses, ungeneralizable samples, and juvenile (as opposed to adult) populations in these studies (Hindelang et al., 1979). Attempting to compensate for some of these problems in a self-report study, Elliott and Ageton (1980) report racial differences in delinquent behavior. Black youths are particularly more involved in predatory crimes against persons and property (as opposed to vice and lower-level delinquent offenses), though the magnitude of the racial difference is smaller than that suggested through study of official arrest statistics.

Hindelang (1978, 1981) analyzed victimization survey results in an attempt to shed further some light on black-white differences in criminal behavior. Reviewing incidents in which victims of crime thought they could identify the race of the offender, he reports that the percentages of whites and blacks involved in robbery and simple assault are nearly identical to those indicated by official arrest statistics. The percentages for rape and aggravated assault differ by about 10 points from those indicated by the arrest data; percentage of white arrests increases by ten points while that for blacks decreases by about the same amount. Looking more directly at rates of offending for rape, robbery, assault, and thefts from persons, Hindelang reports tremendous differences between whites and blacks. The latter have much higher offense rates—for example, 35,000 robberies per 100,000 black males eighteen to twenty years old, as opposed to 2,245 per 100,000 for the comparable white groups. Thus, Hindelang argues, arrest rate differences between races reported in the *Uniform Crime Reports* should not be dismissed simply as resulting from criminal justice system bias.

The findings reviewed here seem to suggest that whites and blacks commit minor offenses in roughly the same proportions, but that blacks have rates of Index offense commission far beyond those to be expected, based on the proportion of the general population they represent. It is important to note, however, that these findings do not point to a causal relationship between race and criminal behavior. Rather, it seems that black crime is high because blacks are overly represented among the lower classes that, as we learned earlier in this chapter, have higher Index crime rates than do other socioeconomic groups. This point was articulated years ago by the President's Commission on Law Enforcement and Administration of Justice (1967:44–45):

> Many studies have been made seeking to account for these differences in arrest rates for Negroes and whites. They have found that the differences become very small when comparisons are made between the rates for whites and Negroes living under similar conditions. However, it has proved difficult to make such comparisons, since Negroes generally encounter more barriers to economic and social advancement than whites do. Even when Negroes and whites live in the same area the Negroes are likely to have poorer housing,

lower incomes, and fewer job prospects. . . . If conditions of equal opportunity prevailed, the differences now found between the Negro and white arrest rates would disappear.

Thus, the social environment in which blacks are found is seen as the cause of their higher crime rates. Economic pressures encourage property offenses. Frustration, disorder, and weak social ties foster crimes of violence (Curtis, 1975; Gibbons, 1977:203). Urban life magnifies these conditions and provides greater opportunities for criminal behavior. In rural and suburban areas, black crime rates closely resemble black population rates. In urban areas, black crime rates far exceed black population rates.

But urban environment and poverty alone do not account fully for our high black crime rate. Other minority groups—immigrant ethnic groups entering this country at the turn of the century—worked their way through these conditions without a perpetually high crime rate. The difference, according to Charles Silberman (1978), is that other groups could move into the middle classes over time. They were not subjected to three centuries of slavery, segregation, and continued institutionalized discrimination. The result is a *culture* of frustration, anger, and violence often directed at blacks (historically the only target group available), sometimes exploding into riots, recently and more frequently directed at whites. This culture will live beyond changes made to the social environment and the economic opportunity structure. Silberman (1978:223–24) argues:

> . . . The connection between poverty and criminal violence is far too complex to expect a drop in violence to follow automatically, and without delay, from every reduction in poverty. . . . The "Great Society" programs [of the 1960s], a strong civil rights movement, and a booming economy combined to produce dramatic improvements in the condition of [black people]. The crime rate skyrocketed—not because of perversity on the part of those who benefitted—but because of increased anger and alienation on the part of those who did not share in the gain.
>
> . . . If black Americans were to improve their status at the rate achieved during the 1960s, it would take two generations before they achieved economic parity with whites.
>
> We cannot afford to wait that long.

The crime-rate gap between whites and blacks may or may not decrease in the near future. In viewing the difference in rates, however, we should not overlook two important facts:

1. On the average, crime is *not* a black phenomenon in this society. Although the black crime *rate* is higher, the vast majority of crimes, including all Index offenses except homicide and robbery, are committed by whites.
2. The fact that blacks are ensconced among the lower classes means that they are not involved in the "respectable" political and business

crimes that, as the previous chapter suggested, result in greater economic losses to the public than all robberies and property crimes combined. White involvement in these less conspicuous crimes and black involvement in more visible, more "dangerous" offenses (also more easily cleared by the police) creates a never-ending cycle. Black crime patterns draw attention to black crime and, in turn, lead to increased police surveillance of blacks. Increased surveillance produces higher levels of detection and, again, higher levels of surveillance. Whites, on the other hand, are watched less closely and, due to lack of surveillance, are encouraged in many ways to enter into and continue traditional white crimes.

Needed: Self-reported Adult Criminality Data

Our discussion of the correlates of criminal behavior has been hampered by a glaring gap in our information concerning criminals. We know almost nothing about adult criminality—only what we have learned from the criminal justice records of those who "got caught." Victimization survey data have added a bit to our knowledge of the gender-age-race features of adult offenders. But we cannot say about adults what we have come to know about juveniles: that a given percentage commits one type of crime and a given percentage another type; that one form of criminal behavior is or is not related to another; that racial and class characteristics influence criminal behavior.

What do the average man and woman do in the way of illegal behavior in this society? Only a few researchers can even begin to supply an answer. Wallerstein and Wyle (1947) surveyed 1698 adults (predominantly upper class) in metropolitan New York City concerning commission of forty-nine types of offenses. Ninety-nine percent admitted to at least one offense. Sixty-four percent of the men and 29 percent of the women admitted committing felonies. These findings are somewhat startling. But they are tempered by the fact that the wording of the questionnaire items did not permit us to distinguish well between "real" and "purely technical" offenses. For example, when asked if the respondent had driven a car without the owner's permission, sixty-one percent answered "yes." Technically, of course, this act violates the law. Yet, the car could have belonged to a friend who would not have objected to the act. The act could have been done for legitimate reasons, for example, as in an emergency. Thus, we are unable to draw real meaning from answers to such offense items.

Studies of college student offense behavior offer a look at non-juvenile crime, that is, crimes by persons beyond the age covered by most juvenile court statutes. Silberman (1976) reports that of the 174 undergraduates he questioned, 8 percent admitted assaults; 10 percent hard drug use; 12 percent petty theft; 20 percent vandalism; and 30 percent shoplifting. Only one admitted to theft of an item valued at over $50 and only one reported an auto

NEWSPRINT AND COMMENT

Summit on Crime is Recommended to Black Leaders

By Lovell Beaulieu

Self-esteem, restraint and more voluntary and social service support groups could help reduce crime in black communities, said psychiatrist Alan Poussaint.

A summit meeting of black leaders to deal with crime would be a start, said Lee Brown, chief of police in Houston.

Poussaint and Brown were guest speakers at a National Urban League seminar entitled "Crime in Black Communities." The 73rd convention ends Wednesday.

Poussaint, author of "Why Blacks Kill Blacks," said that racial self-hatred and low self-esteem contribute to high crime rates in black communities.

He said the problem is especially noticeable in young black males.

Self-esteem and self-worth often have a lot to do with blacks murdering blacks after an argument, the psychiatrist said.

"It's an attempt to say in a macho kind of way we were not messed over," he said. "But it is also testimony to how fragile our self-esteem might be when it's very little that we'll do to protect it."

Poussaint said a major step blacks can take toward crime in black communities is to meet it face to face.

He said that, when he was a member of the special commission investigating the killings of 29 Atlanta children, there were times when the panelists would "pray" it wasn't a black person.

"We internally didn't want to face this kind of thing," he said, "that blacks weren't really doing this to black people," he said.

Brown, who was Atlanta police commissioner during the time of the killings, said violent crime is the most critical problem confronting American society.

"The quality of life in black communities has become the biggest victim of crime and violence," he said. He said there has to be greater emphasis on economic remedies to address it.

He criticized get-tough measures when they are offered as the only solutions.

"The solutions calling for more prison space and manda-tory sentences have not reduced crime," he said. "We have accommodated ourselves to the problems instead of confronting them."

In 1980, 6,165 blacks in the United States were killed by other blacks, Brown said.

He said that, as the crime problem is addressed in black communities, there's a number of "ready-made solutions sprouting up."

"It is clear that idleness and inability to find employment creates conditions which contribute to high crime rates," he said. "If there is not a sincere commitment to address this problem, then the unemployment rate and especially high black youth unemployment will continue to impact significantly on the crime problems in our communities."

Brown said he knows there are people who say the crime problem is happening now, while the economic solutions to it are long-range. But that shouldn't prevent blacks from tackling it themselves, he said.

Source: Times-Picayune Publishing Corp., 1983. Reprinted by permission.

Comment: Facing Up to Black Crime

The subject of race and crime always has generated tension in this country. For years, a large portion of white America has viewed our "crime problem" as a black phenomenon. Official crime statistics in many ways supported this view; while the average arrestee is white, black arrest rates are disproportionately high. Blacks have responded that arrest statistics do not reflect differences in crime rates but differences in arrest rates that reflect criminal justice bias. Criminologists, fearful of adding fuel to racist fires, generally have espoused this same view. They have argued traditionally that given biases in criminal justice statistics, no conclusive evidence exists to indicate that blacks are any more criminal than are whites.

This view has been altered somewhat by victimization survey results regarding offenders that indicate that blacks, especially black youth, have very high robbery rates. This finding, and a maturing social climate that has seen blacks gain respectable work and political positions, has caused a revision in thinking about race and crime. As the above news item indicates, black leaders are asking blacks (and society in general) not to deny the link between race and crime but to address and remedy it. Some of the material presented in this chapter indicates that criminologists too are publicly facing up to something they undoubtedly have suspected for years. But they remain cautious in *how* they address the issue of crime among blacks. It is too easy to return to racist distortions of the crime picture. We cannot and should not deny black involvement in street crime. However, we must not forget that the average offender for most offenses remains white and that the notion of "white collar crime" refers to more than the color of the collar.

theft. These findings roughly parallel others that indicate that over the course of a year, about one in four college students engage in low-seriousness property offenses (Sheley, 1980, 1983).

Do students (and other adults) fail to admit to more serious offenses in self-report studies? It is possible but doubtful. More likely, truly serious offenses are committed by a small number of people whose chances of becoming respondents in a self-reported criminality study are slim. Are students really adults? Some observers would answer "no." But, if the students were removed from the college setting, there would be little argument about their membership in the adult world. The problem with self-report studies of college students is not questionable adult status but the special circumstances of the lives of these young adults. They exist in the college environment, which is part of but still differs from that of the larger world. Whether or not this makes a difference in self-report research will not be known until we gather information from the larger adult population.

A few studies have been able to gather some information about adult criminality through self-reported criminality studies of general and selected adult populations. These have concerned relatively low-seriousness offenses (Grasmick and Bryjak, 1980; Hollinger and Clark, 1983; Tittle, 1977; Tittle and Villemez, 1977). The findings from these studies are similar to those found in studies of college student populations. In research by Tittle and Villemez (1977), for example, randomly selected persons fifteen years and older living in three states were asked if they had committed any of six offenses: thefts of items worth approximately $5, thefts of items worth approximately $50, gambling, income tax cheating, assault, and smoking marijuana. Overall, the percentage of respondents involved in these offenses ranged from a high of 32 percent (gambling) to a low of 7 percent (thefts of items worth approximately $50; 23 percent reported thefts of approximately $5). Involvement in all offenses declined with age, but by no means disappeared. As with the college students, one in four adults in the outside world appears to engage in minor property offenses.

Studies like these offer some hope for adult criminality research, though their list of offenses is too limited to tell us much. Adult self-report research is indeed a hard nut to crack and, until we find a way to crack that nut—an accurate and confident way to ask adults about crimes they commit—our knowledge about adult crime is severely limited. So then are the tests of our theories of criminal behavior and our attempts at anticrime policy formulation.

SUMMARY

In this chapter we reviewed some basic correlates of criminal behavior. Groups in this society appear to vary in involvement in crime. Some of the differences are real and are due in large part to group differences in freedom from various social constraints on criminal behavior, and in the opportunity and skill necessary for the commission of crimes. However, some of the differences in crime rates are only apparent, the result of differential detection and processing by the criminal justice system.

The inventory of crime correlates demonstrates both how little and how much we know about criminals. That is, though a considerable amount of information has been gathered, its usefulness in policy-planning and causal analysis is limited. At the moment, we tend to use the information we have to formulate short-term policy decisions and to initiate the search for the more basic causes of the offenses. Chapters 8 and 9 comment on the present state of the search for causes of crime.

Finally, we return to a major theme in this book: What is the impact of knowledge about patterns of criminal behavior on the average citizen's everyday life? The patterns discussed in this chapter are as crucial to our making sound anticrime decisions as was the information on crime trends discussed in Chapter 4. Again, a critical approach to stereotypes about criminals and their behavior patterns is needed if we are to avoid unnecessarily restrictive personal responses to crime and ill-conceived government anticrime policies. For example, knowing that youths are increasingly becoming involved in crime may suggest a number of harsh policies to reduce their involvement. A more critical look at the statistics suggests that the effects of the baby boom are fading; hence, the need for harsh policies seems less pressing. In this chapter, we hope to have shown that crime patterns are complicated and dynamic. Our responses to crime must be equally sophisticated and flexible.

REFERENCES

Adler, F. 1975. *Sisters in Crime*. New York: McGraw-Hill Book Company.

Austin, R. L. 1982. Women's liberation and increases in minor, major, and occupational offenses. *Criminology* 20:407–30.

Braithwaite, J. 1981. The myth of social class and criminality reconsidered. *Am. Sociol. Rev.* 46:36–57.

Brown, J. W., D. Glaser, E. Waxer, et al. 1974. Turning off: Cessation of marijuana use after college. *Soc. Prob.* 21:527–38.

Bruck, C. 1975. Women against the law. *Hum. Behav.* 12:24–33.

Cameron, M. O. 1964. *The Booster and the Snitch: Department Store Shoplifting*. New York: Free press.

Canter, R. J. 1982. Sex differences in self-report delinquency. *Criminology* 20:373–93.

Cernkovich, S., and P. Giordano. 1979. A comparative analysis of male and female delinquency. *Sociol. Q.* 20:131–45.

Chambliss, W. J., and R. H. Nagasawa. 1969. On the validity of official statistics: A comparative study of white, black and Japanese high school boys. *J. Res. Crime & Delinq.* 6:71–7.

Chilton, R., and A Spielberger. 1971. Is delinquency increasing? Age structure and the crime rate. *Soc. Forces* 49:487–93.

Coverman, S. W. 1983. Gender, domestic labor time, and wage inequality. *Am. Sociol. Rev.* 48:623–37.

Cressey, D. R. 1953. *Other People's Money*. New York: Free Press.

Curtis, L. 1975. *Violence, Race, and Culture*. Lexington, Mass.: Lexington Books.

Datesman, S., F. Scarpitti, and R. Stephensen. 1975. Female delinquency: An application of self and opportunity theories. *J. Res. Crime & Delinq.* 12:107–23.

Elliott, D. S., and S. S. Ageton. 1980. Reconciling differences in estimates of delinquency. *Am. Sociol. Rev.* 45:95–110.

Elliott, D. S. and D. Huizinga. 1983. Social class and delinquent behavior in a national youth panel: 1976–1980. *Criminology* 21:149–77.

Federal Bureau of Investigation. 1976. *Uniform Crime Reports–1975*. Washington, D.C.: U.S. Government Printing Office.

———. 1982. *Uniform Crime Reports—1981*. Washington, D.C.: U.S. Government Printing Office.

Friday, P. C., and J. Hage. 1976. Youth crime in post-industrial societies. *Criminology* 14:347–68.

Gastril, R. D. 1971. Homicide and a regional culture of violence. *Am. Sociol. Rev.* 36:412–27.

Gibbons, D. C. 1977. *Society, Crime, and Criminal Careers*. 3rd ed. Englewood Cliffs, N.J.: Prentice-Hall.

Gould, L. 1969. Who defines delinquency: A comparison of self-reported and officially-reported indices of delinquency for three racial groups. *Soc. Prob.* 16:325–36.

Grasmick. H., and G. Bryjak. 1980. The deterrent effect of perceived severity of punishment. *Soc. Forces* 59:471–91.

Greenberg, D. F. 1977. Delinquency and the age structure of society. *Contemp. Crises* 1:189–223.

Harris, A. R. 1977. Sex and theories of deviance: Toward a functional theory of deviant type-scripts. *Am. Sociol. Rev.* 42:3–16.

Hindelang, M. J. 1978. Race and involvement in common law personal crimes. *Am. Sociol. Rev.* 43:93–109.

———. 1979. Sex differences in criminal activity. *Soc. Prob.* 27:143–56.

————. 1981. Variations in sex-race-age-specific incidence rates of offending. *Am. Sociol. Rev.* 46:461–74.

Hindelang, M., T. Hirschi, and J. Weis. l979. Correlates of delinquency: The illusion of discrepancy between self-report and official measures. *Am. Sociol. Rev.* 44:995–1014.

Hirschi, T. 1969. *Causes of Delinquency.* Berkeley, Calif.: University of California Press.

Hirschi, T., and M. Gottfredson. 1983. Age and the explanation of crime. *Am. J. Sociol.* 89:552–84.

Hoffman-Bustamante, D. 1973. The nature of female criminality. *Iss. Crim.* 8:117–36.

Hollinger, R. C., and J. P. Clark. 1983. Deviance in the workplace: Perceived certainty, perceived severity, and employee theft. *Soc. Forces* 62:398–418.

Kleck, G. 1982. On the use of self-report data to determine the class distribution of criminal and delinquent behavior. *Am. Sociol. Rev.* 47:427–33.

Klein, D. 1973. The etiology of female crime: A review of the literature. *Iss. Crim.* 8:3–30.

Klein, D., and J. Kress. 1976. Any woman's blues: A critical overview of women, crime and the criminal justice system. *Crime So. Just.* 5:34–49.

Kornhauser, R. R. 1978. *Social Sources of Delinquency: An Appraisal of Analytic Methods.* Chicago: University of Chicago Press.

Light, I., and C. Wong. 1975. Protest or work: Dilemmas of the tourist industry in American Chinatown. *Am. J. Socio.* 80:1342–68.

Lombroso, C. 1903. *The Female Offender.* New York: Appleton-Century-Crofts.

Mann, D. W. 1981. Age and differential predictability of delinquent behavior. *Soc. Forces* 60:97–113.

Matza, D. 1964. *Delinquency and Drift.* New York: John Wiley & Sons.

Noblit, G. W., and J. M. Burcart. 1976. Women and crime: 1960–1970. *Soc. Sci. Q.* 56:651–57.

Pollak. O. 1950. *The Criminality of Women.* Philadelphia: University of Pennsylvania Press.

President's Commission on Law Enforcement and Administration of Justice. 1967. *The Challenge of Crime in a Free Society.* Washington, D.C.: U.S. Government Printing Office.

Reckless, W. C. 1973. *The Crime Problem.* 5th ed. Englewood Cliffs, N.J.: Prentice-Hall.

Rowe, A. R., and C. R. Tittle. 1977. Life cycle changes and criminal propensity. *Sociol. Q.* 18:223–36.

Sheley, J. F. 1980. Is neutralization necessary for criminal behavior? *Deviant Behav.* 2:49–72.

————. 1983. Critical elements of criminal behavior explanation. *Sociol. Q.* 24:509–25.

Silberman, C. E. 1978. *Criminal Violence, Criminal Justice.* New York: Random House.

Silberman, M. 1976. Toward a theory of criminal deterrence. *Am. Sociol. Rev.* 41:442–61.

Simon, R. J. 1975. *Women and Crime.* Lexington, Mass.: D. C. Heath & Company.

Smart, C. 1977. Criminological theory: Its ideology and implications concerning women. *Br. J. Sociol.* 28:89–100.

Smith, D. H., and C. Visher. 1980. Sex and deviance/criminality: An empirical review of the quantitative literature. *Am. Sociol. Rev.* 45:691–701.

Steffensmeier, D. J. 1978. Crime and the contemporary woman: An analysis of changing levels of female property crime, 1960–1975. *Soc. Forces* 57:566–83.

———. 1980. Sex differences in patterns of adult crime, 1967–1977: A review and assessment. *Soc. Forces* 58:1080–08.

Steffensmeier, D., and M. J. Cobb. 1981. Sex differences in urban arrest patterns, 1934–1979. *Soc. Prob.* 29:37–50.

Steffensmeier, D., and R. Cook. 1980. Sociocultural vs. biological/sexist explanations of sex differences in crime: A survey of American criminology textbooks, 1918–1965. *Am. Sociol.* 15:246–55.

Thornberry, T., and M. Farnworth. 1982. Social correlates of criminal involvement: Further evidence on the relationship between social status and criminal behavior. *Am. Sociol. Rev.* 47:505–18.

Tittle, C. 1977. Sanction fear and the maintenance of social order. *Soc. Forces* 55:474–503.

Tittle, C., and W. Villemez. 1977. Social class and criminality. *Soc. Forces* 56:475–502.

Tittle, C., W. Villemez, and D. Smith. 1978. The myth of social class and criminality: An empirical assessment of the empirical evidence. *Am. Sociol. Rev.* 43:643–56.

U.S. Department of Justice. 1981. *Criminal Victimization in the United States—1979*. Washington, D.C.: U.S. Government Printing Office.

Visher, C. 1983. Gender, police arrest decisions, and notions of chivalry. *Criminology* 21:5–28.

Wallerstein, J. S., and C. Wyle. 1947. Our law-abiding lawbreakers. *Probation* 25:107–12.

Weis, J. 1976. Liberation and crime: The invention of the new female criminal. *Crime Soc. Jus.* 6:17–27.

Williams, J. R., and M. Gold. 1972. From delinquent behavior to official delinquency. *Soc. Prob.* 20:209–29.

Wilson, N., and C. Rigsley. 1975. Is crime a man's world? Issues in the exploration of criminality. *J. Crim. Just.* 3:131–40.

SUGGESTED READINGS

Material on various correlates and patterns of criminal behavior is relatively scattered throughout the criminological literature. The reader who wishes to pursue the topics raised in Chapter 6 would do well to examine the data on characteristics of arrestees presented in the FBI *Uniform Crime Reports*. However, these reports should be read with all the biases of official crime data firmly in mind. Among the better summaries of the sociological literature concerning correlates of criminal behavior are "Correlates of delinquency: The illusion of discrepancy between self-report and official measures," by Hindelang, Hirschi, and Weis (*American Sociological Review*, December 1979:995–1014), and Hindelang's "Variations in sex-race-age-specific incidence of offending" (*American Sociological Review*, August 1981: 461–74).

7

VICTIMS OF CRIME

The American system of justice often is accused of ignoring the victims of crime—a criticism that can also be directed at criminologists, who traditionally have concentrated their research on the relationship between society and the individual as it affects criminal behavior. A few voices in the wilderness have argued that criminologists also must direct attention to the role of the victim in the criminal act. Hans von Hentig (1948) first stirred interest in this theme when he suggested that we cannot have crimes unless we have victims; that many victims actively are involved in their victimizations (as in con games); and that some victims, through personality factors, actually invite or even encourage criminal acts.

Despite a criticial receptivity to von Hentig's speculations and an occasionally provocative study of victim-precipitated crime (Amir, 1971; Wolfgang, 1958), criminologists have only recently begun systematically to devote attention to patterns of crime victimization. *Victimology,* the study of victims—not only of crime but of accidents as well—is fast gaining acceptance as a social science subfield. This chapter explores two victimology themes—patterns of victimization and victim-offender relationships—and then examines the theoretical and policy implications of these themes.

PATTERNS OF VICTIMIZATION

In American society, criminal victimizations do not occur randomly. Surveys of victims during the past several years consistently demonstrate that some groups and categories of people represent higher-risk victim populations.

New Conclusion On Gay Victims

Gays and lesbians are reluctant to report crimes to the police, making it difficult to determine whether they are more likely to be victimized than heterosexuals, said a survey of crime victims released yesterday by Mayor Dianne Feinstein's office.

This conclusion differs from one drawn last year in an initial draft of the same survey. Based on the earlier report, Feinstein had labeled a "myth" the belief that gays are more likely to be victims of violent attacks.

This statement was criticized by many gays, and Feinstein agreed to withdraw the report and have its conclusions independently reviewed by a panel made up of a cross section of gays.

"Many people know being gay is a very good way to get beaten up on the streets," said Randy Stallings, president of the gay Alice B. Toklas Democratic Club. Stallings, who served on the review panel that went over the report, said the revised version of the survey was "fair" and "accurate."

The final report also cites data culled from community agencies that provide emergency services to gays. These data suggest that 82 percent of anti-gay attacks are not reported to the police.

In other respects the report, based on a survey of 700 crime victims, remains basically unchanged from the draft version released last November.

"Now that the report has been reviewed and clarified, we can concentrate on implementing the recommendations that will address the needs of victims," Feinstein said in a statement released by her office. "Two of the key recommendations—establishing a 24-hour clearinghouse to serve victims of violent crimes and an emergency fund to help them—will receive immediate attention."

Source: ©San Francisco Chronicle, 1983. Reprinted by permission.

Comment: The Value of the Victimization Survey

The ability to survey the public about their experiences as crime victims has added new dimensions to our knowledge of crime in general. Through victimization surveys we have learned more about the uneven distribution of crime throughout our populace. We have discovered some major ironies—that poor people are more likely burglary victims, for example. We have exposed some myths—that the elderly have higher victimization rates, for instance. We have learned also that large segments of the public do not report their victimizations to the police. This is the theme in the above newspaper item. Though some apparent methodological errors (probably involving sampling) may raise doubts about the validity of the victimization report in question, the point of the report retains validity: Some segments of the populace suffer greater losses from crime than do others, but we cannot know this through standard assessments of crime levels.

Gays more often may be victimized by violent attacks. They may not be free to report the incident, however, because they cannot risk exposure to a public unsympathetic to their sexual orientation. Or they may feel that the police do not treat their cases as important. Only the victimization survey can uncover these patterns. Until they are uncovered, we cannot formulate reasonable anticrime policies nor direct resources to victims most in need of them.

The variables thus far examined in victimization research are basic demographic characteristics: gender, age, race, income, marital status, and residence. Any patterns discovered in these investigations undoubtedly mask more complex relationships involving other variables. The following discussion of victim characteristics is based on data collected for a U.S. Department of Justice (1981) national survey of 1979 crime victims.

Gender

Except in the crime of rape, males more often than females are the victims of most crimes. As Figure 7–1, indicates, males suffer twice the rate of crimes of violence as females do: 46 per 1000 males versus 25 per 1000 females. Males also are more likely to be victims of theft: 99 per 1000 as opposed to 85 per 1000 for females.

Age

Figure 7–2 indicates that crimes of violence are committed most often against persons sixteen to nineteen years of age (70 per 1000). For theft, people twenty to twenty-four years of age are more likely to be victims (149 per 1000). For both violent and theft offenses, the rates decline steadily with age after twenty. Age-victimization patterns are similar for both genders, though the victimization rate for sixteen- to nineteen-year-old females is higher than

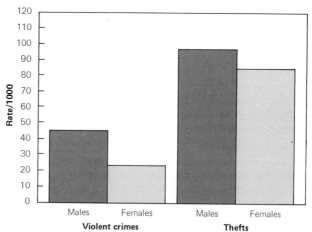

FIGURE 7–1

Victimization Rates by Gender (*Source:* U.S. Department of Justice. Criminal Victimization in the United States—1970 (Washington D.C.: U.S. Government Printing Office, 1981), p. 24.)

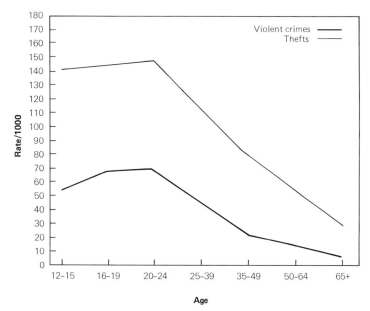

FIGURE 7–2

Victimization Rates by Age (*Source:* U.S. Department of Justice.
Criminal Victimization in the United States—1979 (Washington,
D.C.: U.S. Government Printing Office, 1981), p. 25.)

that for females twenty to twenty-four years old—a pattern opposite that of
males.

Why higher victimization rates among younger people? One possible explanation is that younger victims are more likely to be in more frequent contact with a high-offense rate group: younger persons. Also, given physical
differences between age groups in the teen years, younger teenagers are more
vulnerable to coercive acts by older youth (Skogan, 1976:138).

Despite public belief that the elderly are a highly victimized group, some
researchers believe that fear of crime is not the greatest concern of the aged
(Yin, 1982). As the data displayed in Figure 7–2 indicate, persons over sixty-
five are crime victims much less often than are persons under sixty-five. The
only exception is found in purse snatching and pocket picking rates, which
are higher for the elderly than for those under sixty-five. These relationships
have held throughout the 1970s. In fact, the end of the decade showed general declines in violent and property crimes against the elderly, though 1980
victimization data indicate renewed but minor increases in victimizations of
this group (U.S. Department of Justice, 1981). It must be remembered, however, that lower rates for the elderly may be due in part to the fact that age
and a fear of crime keep them indoors so that they present themselves as po-

tential crime victims less often. Further, we cannot overlook the fact that the elderly often suffer considerably more trauma when victimized than do younger persons. Physical injuries take a greater toll, and fixed incomes of the elderly mean that property crimes have a more severe impact on their life-styles.

Race

Figure 7–3 shows victimization rates according to race. Blacks are victimized much more by violent crime (42 per 1000) than are whites (34 per 1000)—that is, they are more likely to be robbed, assaulted, or raped. They are also more likely to be victims of homicide, according to the FBI *Uniform Crime Reports* (1982). Black males are more apt to be victimized by violence (53 per 1000) than are their white counterparts (44 per 1000), and black females (32 per 1000) exceed white females (24 per 1000) in violent victimizations.

But whites are victimized more often by theft (93 per 1000) than are blacks (87 per 1000). This is to be expected, since the white population has a higher income level and greater wealth. Yet, given white/black economic differences, it is surprising that the theft victimization rates are not more disparate. The rate for blacks is greater than expected probably because blacks are more vulnerable to theft, owing to the fact that they live in poorer neighborhoods and have poorer home security. Thus, though the "take" from blacks is less, it is nonetheless often more easily taken. This notion is supported by the finding that the homes of blacks are burglarized more often than are those of whites: 114 per 1000 for blacks versus 80 per 1000 for whites.

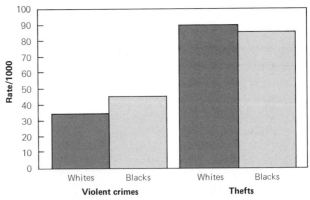

FIGURE 7–3
Victimization Rates by Race (*Source:* U.S. Department of Justice, Criminal Victimization in the United States—1979 (Washington, D.C.: U.S. Government Printing Office, 1981), p. 31.)

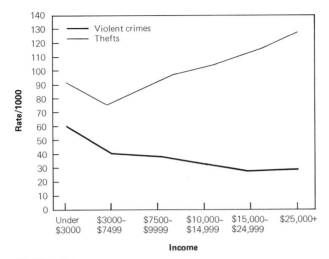

FIGURE 7–4
Victimization Rates by Income (*Source:* U.S. Department of
Justice, Criminal Victimization in the United States, 1979
(Washington, D.C.: U.S. Government Printing Office,
1981), p. 31.)

Income

As Figure 7–4 indicates, lower economic groups tend to have higher rates of
victimization for violent crimes than do upper economic groups. But for theft
offenses the opposite generally is true: The higher the income, the higher the
victimization rate. Note, however, that the lowest income group also is high
in theft rate. These patterns are roughly the same for both races.

We can only speculate as to why violent-crime victimization patterns differ so, but whether prompted by gain or frustration, violent crime seems to
be a lower-class phenomenon. The victimization survey findings further the
view that most violent crime is intracommunity, intraracial, intrasubcul-
tural, and intrafamilial. The fact that theft victimizations correlate with income is not surprising, for upper-income persons obviously have more to
steal. Still, it is noteworthy that lower-income homes are burglarized more
often than are upper-income homes, which, as noted above, are usually better protected.

Marital Status

As Figure 7–5 suggests, for both violent and theft offenses, those who have
never married or are separated or divorced have much higher rates than married or widowed persons. Although males generally have higher rates than
females, the overall victimization patterns according to marital status are rel-

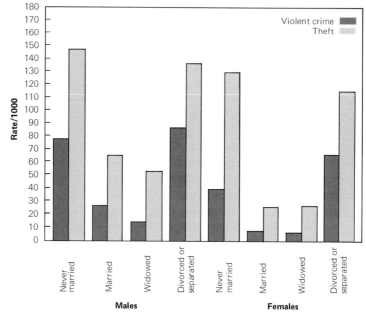

FIGURE 7–5

Victimization Rates by Marital Status and Sex (*Source:* U.S. Department of Justice Criminal Victimization in the United States— 1979 (Washington, D.C.: U.S. Government Printing Office, 1981), p. 29.)

atively the same for both sexes. The key to explaining marital-status differences in victimization rates undoubtedly rests with a link between marital status and age. The "never married" category contains the greatest number of younger victims, followed by those "separated or divorced," "married," and "widowed," respectively. Thus, we suggest that it is not marital status per se that influences victimization rates but factors related to marital status, such as age and lifestyle.

Residency

Figure 7–6 indicates that nonmetropolitan areas have lower victimization rates than metropolitan areas. Within metropolitan areas, central city and noncentral city settings differ somewhat in violent-offense victimization rates but show almost no differences in rates for theft. The size of the metropolitan area does not seem to determine victimization rates; rates neither rise nor fall consistently as the metropolitan areas increase in size.

In sum, victimization surveys have found that some segments of society represent greater target populations for crime than other segments. The sin-

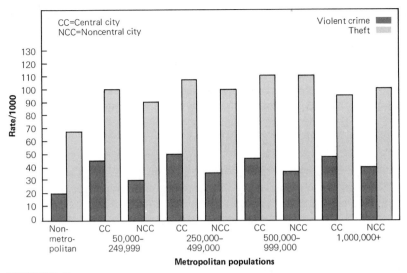

FIGURE 7–6

Victimization Rate by Area of Residence (*Source:* U.S. Department of Justice, Criminal Victimization in the United States—1979 (Washington, D.C.: U.S. Government Printing Office, 1981), pp. 36, 43.)

gle most likely victim of Index offenses is the young black male—the member of the population segment that also, as we noted in Chapter 6, is more likely to commit such offenses. The higher crime and victimization rates for this group testify to the consequences of socioeconomic inequality.

The victimization patterns described above, basic though they may be, should aid in crime-prevention strategies. Higher burglary rates for the poor, for example, should prompt some thought concerning preventive patrols. Equally important, however, the victimization patterns should cause the average citizen to give serious consideration to his or her own chances of victimization. As we noted in previous chapters, an increasing public fear of crime has prompted changes in people's personal habits and resulted in increased pressure being brought to bear on government agencies. However, the average citizen must recognize that victimizations are not random occurrences and that for many, such changes in personal habits are needless.

VICTIM-OFFENDER RELATIONSHIPS

Von Hentig's (1948) thesis that crime victims bring about their victimizations and Wolfgang's (1957) report that at least 20 percent of homicides are "victim precipitated" (see Chapter 5) have slowly focused criminological attention on the relationship of victim to offender. An examination of crimes reported in the newspapers of any major city reveals that many are committed by persons known by the victims. Here are two examples from the *New Orleans Times–Picayune* (1978a, 1978b):

> A 15-year-old girl was raped Friday night while babysitting. Police arrested [a 19-year-old] after the girl reportedly identified him as the attacker. According to the police reports, the girl invited the man, who was a friend, to visit her while she babysat. [After] she asked him to leave, he forced her into a bedroom and allegedly committed the rape.

> The young men were playing pool in the back room of a First Street bar . . . when 19-year-old Willie Moran criticized a shot his half-brother, 25-year-old Vernon Pittman, had just made.
> "When I want advice from boys, I call 'em by name," sneered Pittman. . . .
> That stung Moran. "Don't call me boy," he retorted. . . . [T]he two exchanged words. Everyone who talks about it now calls it a minor incident, no big thing. No one thought it was serious until the young Moran pulled out a small, chrome, .32 caliber snub nose revolver.
> "Put that away before you hurt someone," said Pittman.
> "You don't think I'll shoot you, do you?" asked Moran, who then fired once, hitting his half-brother in the stomach.

The 1981 FBI *Uniform Crime Reports* indicates that 25 percent of the nation's homicides were committed by persons who knew the victim well or were related to the victim. At least another 30 percent involved "acquaintances," most in the course of "arguments." A U.S. Department of Justice national victimization survey (1981:54) reports that 37 percent of violent offenses involved nonstrangers. Of these, assault and rape are most likely to occur between nonstrangers (41 and 40 percent, respectively). Robbery (20 percent) by nonstrangers occurs less often. Findings such as these clearly point to a need for an examination of victim-offender relationships for various types of crime. They also suggest that we should revise our stereotype of the criminal, that it is not always the stranger we should fear.

Victim-precipitated Crimes

Victim precipitation has become a popular term in discussions of victim-offender relationships. Wolfgang (1957) seems to be the first to have used the term when he argued that as many as 20 percent of homicides result from violence initiated by the person who is the eventual victim of the altercation; that is, it is the eventual victim who strikes the first blow.

Amir (1971) further popularized the victim-precipitation theme through his study of forcible rape. Using police records, Amir analyzed 646 rapes that occurred in Philadelphia in 1958 and 1960. He found that in 58 percent of the rapes, the victim had at least some knowledge of the rapist's identity. In

47 percent of the cases, the rapist was at least an acquaintance of the victim. Spurred by these findings, he examined the role of the victim in the Philadelphia rape cases. In Amir's (1971:259) opinion, some rapes represent the victim's

> . . . acting out, initiating the interaction between her and the offender, and by her behavior she generates the potentiality for criminal behavior of the offender or triggers this potentiality, if it existed before in him. Her behavior transforms him into a doer by directing his criminal intentions which not only lead to offense but also may shape its form.

Included within Amir's possibilities of victim-precipitated rape is the woman who supposedly gives sexual cues—wittingly or unwittingly—and somehow leads an offender to believe she desires sexual relations with him. Amir (1971:266) is unclear about what constitutes such cues but does note that they might include "indecency in language and gestures, or . . . what could be taken as an invitation to sexual relations." By Amir's estimate, 19 percent of the Philadelphia rapes were victim precipitated.

Criticism of the Concept of Victim Precipitation

The concept of victim precipitation, especially Amir's use of it, has drawn criticism. Not the least of the problems with the concept is that it has been overemphasized in subsequent summaries of Amir's work. The result is that victim-precipitated rape has come to be pictured as the norm rather than as the exception, and this misinterpretation has been used to bolster sexist views of rape. Beyond this, the term implies a passive offender, one who would not have committed his crime were it not for the victim's provocation, and an active victim, one who intended the offense to occur. "Proof" of this claim is often noted in the fact that some women do not physically resist the rapist. Such "evidence" takes little note of the fact the victim may be paralyzed with fear or certain that resistance will only increase her injuries (Weis and Borges, 1976:241).

The active victim-passive offender view of victimization has stressed the offender's interpretation of the victim's actions. Amir (1971:261) writes:

> the [precipitative] behavior can be of an outright and overt seduction, or covert and suggestive. Whether it is really so is not as important as the offender's interpretation of her actions within the then current situation. Because *even if erroneous,* it leads to action. . . . [The] offender may see the victim's behavior as being contrary to the expectation about appropriate female behavior as well as conflicting with the whole image of a woman's propriety. [Emphasis added.]

Whether or not the offender's definition of the situation is erroneous is more important than Amir would have us believe. If the offender's definition is correct, then the victim-precipitation concept is viable, and we should devote study as to why some females give such sexual cues. If the offender is misinterpreting the situation, however, then our research should be directed more toward his interpretative processes and less toward the victim's actions. It is certainly not unusual for rapists to claim that the victim's behavior was precipitative (Landau, 1973). Yet only one study has made any attempt to assess the accuracy of that claim, and it underscores the hazards in relying on the offender's definition of the situation as the criterion for determining the degree of victim precipitation. The research (Gehbard et al., 1965:177–206) examined the sexual case histories of 146 persons convicted of sexual aggression against adult females. The investigators found that it is not unusual for such offenders to claim that the female encouraged the rape even though official records indicate that she required "five stitches taken in her lip" after the attack. Further, the rapists are often surprised at their arrests, claiming that the victims wanted it "since they did not fight the attacker or protest his actions." In other words, victim precipitation is defined rather liberally by offenders.

A final criticism of the victim-precipitation concept is offered by Franklin and Franklin (1976). They argue that causation and facilitation are often confused. That is, not every key left in an ignition results in a car theft. Nor can we speak of victim-precipitated (as opposed to victim-facilitated) car theft if the thief was actively looking for a car to steal—the keys in the ignition did not cause the theft. Beyond this, the authors argue that at no time has victim precipitation been proven independent of the victimization itself. One cannot use the outcome of an act as an explanation of that act. Some other measure of victim precipitation must be devised.

In sum, we see that the victim-precipitation concept has numerous problems. It is logically flawed in the sense that it implies that a victim's provocation is necessary and sufficient for an offense to occur. It treats the offender as overly passive in the victimization situation. It suffers from measurement problems. And it carries questionable moral and legal implications (who is the guilty party?). Somehow, we must find an analytical framework that salvages the positive contribution of the victim-precipitation concept (that is, the demonstration of the fact that not all offenses reflect an active offender victimizing a passive victim) while avoiding its flaws.

Victim-Offender Interaction

In an effort to avoid the pitfalls of the victim-precipitation concept, we suggest that offenses be understood in terms of the extent that they involve interaction between victims and offenders and the extent of activity or passivity of both parties. In so doing, we need not become involved in problematic issues of cause and unconscious intent on the part of the victim. Instead, we may develop a continuum of various victim-offender patterns of interaction and describe their implications for anticrime policy.

With the exception of some victimless crimes, every crime involves at least two parties, an offender and a victim. We must assume that a crime is the product of the interaction of two social-action systems: the offender's and the victim's. As the continuum in Figure 7–7 indicates, the activity and passivity of either of these parties may vary greatly and produce very different types of offenses. A victim may be passive and, simply by fate, become the target of an offender (situation A in Figure 7–7). The shopper whose purse is snatched and the man who is robbed while leaving his office building are victims of this type. The activity level of the victim increases when, for example, keys are left in the automobile or one walks through New York's Central Park at two o'clock in the morning (situation B). An assault by one person upon another when both are ready to come to blows represents yet another increase in victim activity, this time roughly equal to that of the offender (situation C). Some crimes involve victims who are more active than the offender—for instance, a homicide in which the victim strikes the first blow (situation D). Finally, there is the rare case of the active victim and the passive offender (situation E). The best example available is the crime of passion occurring when, for instance, an individual discovers his or her spouse in bed with another and impulsively assaults either or both of the lovers.

The continuum illustrated in Figure 7–7 may eliminate some of the problems with the traditional victim-precipitation concept. Although it leaves open the possibility of offenses intended or caused by the victim, it does not assume either intention or causation in cases deviating from situation A. To

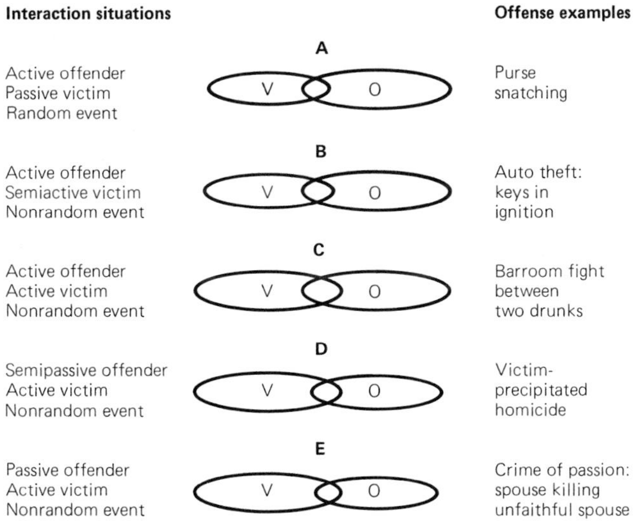

Interaction situations   **Offense examples**

                                        A
Active offender   Purse
Passive victim   V   O   snatching
Random event

                                        B
Active offender   Auto theft:
Semiactive victim   V   O   keys in
Nonrandom event   ignition

                                        C
Active offender   Barroom fight
Active victim   V   O   between
Nonrandom event   two drunks

                                        D
Semipassive offender   Victim-
Active victim   V   O   precipitated
Nonrandom event   homicide

                                        E
Passive offender   Crime of passion:
Active victim   V   O   spouse killing
Nonrandom event   unfaithful spouse

FIGURE 7–7
Victim-Offender Interaction Situations

point to a victim's more than passive role in an offense neither suggests that the victim desired or caused it nor absolves the offender of guilt. Thus, while we may argue that the person who enters Central Park at night more actively facilitates a mugging than one who enters the park during the day, we do not argue that either wishes to be mugged. Nor is the mugger any less a criminal at night than during the day.

Immediate Environment

To complicate the notion of victim-offender interaction somewhat, we must also recognize that a third element in an offense situation also helps form its outcome—namely, the immediate social environment. The environment in which the interaction occurs is probably as important as the predispositions and actions of the interactants in determining whether or not a crime results. In fact, it undoubtedly partly shapes the extent to which the victim takes an active or a passive role in the offense. The immediate social environment includes all aspects of the arena in which the interaction occurs: physical characteristics (a room, outdoors, and so on) and other persons and the degree to which they participate in the event. For example, the result of a marital dispute may be violence or simple yelling, depending on where the disagreement occurs, how many people are present, and whether or not those present encourage, discourage, or ignore the dispute.

Pertinent Research

The importance of viewing offenses in terms of victim-offender interaction patterns and immediate social environment is demonstrated by detailed analysis of homicide cases. Luckenbill (1977) conducted such an analysis of eighty nonfelony-related homicides committed in one California county between 1963 and 1972. The usual pattern characterizing these homicides began with an action taken or a statement made by one person and perceived as offensive by another. The "offended" person thus viewed himself or herself as being in a position necessitating some face-saving action. This most often was accomplished through a verbal or physical challenge to the person committing the "insult." The challenge served to place the person whose actions or words initiated the confrontation on the defensive, needing to save face. If that person chose to stand his or her ground or perhaps even retaliated physically or verbally, Luckenbill argues, an agreement to settle the problem by violent means was forged between the potential combatants. One person, more often the originally "offensive" person, became a murder victim.

Luckenbill's research (see also Felson and Steadman, 1983) suggests that most homicides fall within situation C of Figure 7–7—more-or-less equally active offender and victim, both with the option to avoid the violent outcome, neither choosing the option. Luckenbill also notes that the outcome of the confrontation is determined in part by the immediate social environment in which the encounter occurs. In the cases he studies, the key factor was the degree of neutrality of the onlookers of the dispute. To the extent that they became involved in the problem—encouraging either party, supplying a weapon—a homicide was more likely to occur.

THEORETICAL AND POLICY IMPLICATIONS

Taking a victim-offender interaction approach to the study of crime carries implications for a number of policy areas.

Crime Prevention

Greater knowledge of victim-offender relationships for specific forms of crime would aid greatly in crime-prevention strategies. What is especially needed is a description of various crimes in terms of degree of victim-offender interaction. Homicide and robbery represent contrasting examples. We noted in Chapter 5 that between 66 and 75 percent of homicides occur between relatives or acquaintances. It appears that most of these cases would fall within situations C, D, and E of Figure 7–7. The police are relatively powerless to prevent such murders. Thus, it would be foolish to allocate police resources as if the majority of murders were street crimes, falling within situations A and B of Figure 7–7 and theoretically preventable by police patrols. However, our discussion of robbery in Chapter 5 suggests that most robberies occur between strangers. Thus, we would expect them to fall within situations A and B of Figure 7–7 and therefore to be more preventable. Depending upon which situation—A or B—best reflects robberies, increased police patrols and decoy work (responding to situation A) or increased public education about potential robbery situations (responding to situation B) might effect a change in robbery rates.

Correction of Offenders

Current knowledge of victim-offender interactions indicates that there are degrees of predatoriness among offenders. Corrections programs traditionally design their rehabilitation programs around the classification of offenders by type of offense for which they have been convicted. Perhaps their success rates could be improved if prisoners were also classified according to patterns of interaction with victims in their offenses, if such patterns can be found. Offenders who habitually commit crimes falling within situations A and B of Figure 7–7 are clearly more social and predatory than those committing crimes of the situation C, D, or E variety and would require evaluation and treatment aimed at making the offender more responsive to social norms and the rights of others. Offenders who continually are involved in offense situations of types C, D, and E seem to be displaying an inability to sustain interactions with others within conventional bounds. Evaluation and treatment of these persons would be directed toward making the individual better able to interact with others.

Restitution to the Victim

Many consider the victim the forgotten person in legal and criminological interest in crimes. Criminal law treats offenses as acts against the state, not against its individual members. Violations generally are punished by and on behalf of the state, not the victim. Occasionally, a court sentence will require some form of restitution to the victim of a crime. Embezzlers often are required to make at least partial repayment of the money they misappropriate, for example. This occasional practice has led to consideration in many quarters of more structured programs of restitution to victims by offenders.

Restitution by an offender refers to payment to victims who have experienced financial losses through the offender's actions (Chesney et al., 1978). Repayment may take the form of cash or of service. It may be directed at replacing stolen or damaged property or at compensating losses due to fraud. It also may be used to compensate the victim for medical expenses, lost wages, or legal services stemming from the crime in question. We note that restitution is determined in criminal court; it does not involve damages in return for pain and suffering, which may be sought in civil court.

Historically, restitution has occurred in the form of informal settlements as part of the plea bargaining process. It rarely has been employed in systematic fashion. A few programs appeared in the U.S. during the 1970s, funded in large part by federal grants. Many model sentencing proposals now encourage the practice. Advocates argue that not only do victims recoup some losses, but offenders are made to see some direct link between their actions and real consequences to individuals, as opposed to society at large (Eglash, 1975).

Whether or not restitution programs can accomplish their goals remains to be seen. One research project (Harland, 1981) attempted to assess the feasibility of restitution by offenders to victims of property offenses: larceny, burglary, vehicle theft, purse snatching and pocket picking, and unarmed robbery. Analysis of national victimization survey data indicates that victims of theft rarely are compensated through return of their stolen property or through insurance coverage. Thus, restitution could provide some aid to victims who now receive none. Further, the project report notes that most property offenses involve relatively small losses to victims, which could be repaid by offenders of even the lowest financial status. But, the report also notes, too many thefts go unreported (perhaps because victims see no hope of redress) and arrest and conviction rates for these offenses are low. More importantly, we confront the very real practical problem of how restitution will occur. Incarcerated offenders generally cannot earn enough in prison to repay victims. Community-based corrections programs, whereby offenders live and work in the community as part of their sentence (see Chapter 11), may hold at least a partial answer to this dilemma.

Compensation to the Victim

While restitution programs seek compensation from offenders themselves, another recent response to the plight of victims considered by state legislatures is the victim compensation program (Geis, 1976; Meiners, 1978). These programs provide some form of monetary compensation from public funds to crime victims. At present, about half of the states have such programs, though more are expected if the U.S. Congress approves federal subsidies for state compensation programs.

States with victim-compensation programs vary somewhat in underlying philosophies regarding aid to victims. Many seem to justify aid by claiming that the government has failed its responsibility and should compensate victimized citizens. Others point to the welfare principle held by most states: People in need through no fault of their own should be helped by the government. Finally, some argue that at the present time, potential criminal victimization should be considered as much a fact of everyday life as health and employment problems and natural disasters. If federal and state governments can administer various insurance and compensation programs for the latter ills, they can widen the scope of the programs to offset losses from crime (expenses resulting from injury or death, loss of earning power, losses by dependents, and pain and suffering).

States with victim-compensation programs also vary in organization and administration of the programs. Some favor an autonomous quasi-judicial body to handle claims, others favor expansion of current court systems to deal with claims, and others argue for assignment of compensation programs to extant organizations such as the state welfare department. Whatever their differences in administration techniques, most of the programs offer compensation only to victims of violent crime that is not family-related. Most set a limit on the amount that can be awarded to a victim. In some jurisdictions, the victim must be able to show financial need before receiving state money. Finally, most consider the degree to which a crime was "victim precipitated" in arriving at a just compensation.

Critics of victim-compensation programs claim that they will encourage more crime by discouraging citizens' fear of crime's consequences and subsequent precautions to avoid victimization. It is also argued that compensation programs will eliminate feelings of guilt by criminals, who will feel free to steal or injure knowing that the losses or injuries will be "insured." Fi-

nally, some critics argue that victim-compensation programs represent a de-
moralizing statement as to the hoplessness of crime prevention, encouraging
society to "live with crime" and perhaps encouraging exaggerated claims of
injury to gain compensation funds.

In rebuttal, proponents of victim-compensation programs argue that it is
unlikely that many people purposely will place themselves in danger of serious physical harm for a limited monetary reward that they would have to
convince the state they deserve. Nor is it likely that criminals will make the
possibility of state compensation of their victims a major factor in decisions
about whether to commit a crime. Exaggerated injury claims could be offset
by effective management of compensation programs. Finally, proponents argue that if society becomes demoralized by the crime problem, victim-compensation programs will not be the primary cause of the demoralization.

Clearly, then, we see a shifting social concern for the victim, which in turn
fosters a similar criminological concern, for victim-compensation programs
require research into victim-offender relationships. At the most obvious
level, the research results can help form the basis for criteria concerning victim precipitation used in awarding compensation. At a more general level,
knowledge about victim-offender relationships can aid policymakers in making decisions concerning the types of victim-compensation programs necessary for various states and communities.

In sum, recent interest in victimization patterns and victim-offender relationships has raised a number of research problems that will occupy criminologists for some time. Most basic among these problems is the assessment
of the victimological implications of various forms of crime. While we know
much about some offenses (such as homicide), we know very little about others (such as arson). We conclude this chapter with an example that illustrates
that most offenses have at least some victimological implications, even commercial and corporate crimes.

AN EXAMPLE: VICTIMS OF COMMERCIAL
AND CORPORATE CRIME

Gilbert Geis (1973) and Simon and Eitzen (1982) have enumerated some of
the victimization patterns and implications of two forms of white-collar
crime: commercial and corporate crime (crime related to the furtherance of
business interests). They note that this crime category includes such offenses
as antitrust violations, deceptive advertising, commercial espionage, and
false weighing and measuring by retailers. Simon and Eitzen (1982:91–92)
argue convincingly that these are not "minor" offenses:

> Two problems that especially concern Americans are street crimes and infla-
> tion. . . . Street crimes, for example, are miniscule in their economic costs

when compared to the costs of illegal activities by corporations. To cite just one example, the two to three billion dollars lost in the Equity Insurance fraud [amounted to] more money [than is lost because of street crimes in an entire year].

. . . [T]he existence of shared monopolies increases prices by twenty-five percent. . . . [C]onsumers pay, in addition, all the costs of advertising, which amounted to thirty-billion dollars in 1978. . . . [C]onsumers pay inflated prices brought about by price fixing and other collusive arrangements by "competitors." Finally, . . . consumers spend billions on products sold under false pretenses, products that do not perform as claimed, products identical to cheaper ones but unavailable or unknown, and the like.

Victimization Patterns

According to Geis, patterns of victimization in commercial and corporate crime are more difficult to discern than are patterns for other offenses. Occasionally, we can point to a specific victim, as in the theft of trade secrets by a competitor or the overcharging of a customer by a mechanic. More often than not, however, it is the general consumer who is victimized, through unnecessary price increases for goods and services (the result of such offenses as corporate price fixing) or lost government revenue (the result of corporate tax evasion). Commercial and corporate victimization is not a matter of businesspeople searching out a weak prey, though an unorganized and unaware public is weak. Instead, victims will be any person whose losses will help resolve an offender's financial difficulties. Thus, the strong (other businesses) and weak (the poor, the elderly) are both likely targets.

Victim Involvement

There is little evidence of victim precipitation or active victim involvement in commercial and corporate crimes. For many types of such offenses—for example, overpricing merchandise—victimizations are randomly distributed and victims enter into the offense passively. For other types—for instance, physician malpractice or overcharging—certain classes of people are more vulnerable: the uneducated, the poor, the elderly. Again, however, their involvement in the offense is highly passive.

Anticrime Policy

Victimization patterns for commercial and corporate offenses are linked to policies to combat them or, more precisely, to a lack of such policies. Elimination of such crimes is hindered by the lack of a complaining victim. Specific victims often are too embarrassed to complain. The more general victim, the public, is either unaware of the offenses or not disturbed by them. The lack of public indignation is due to the relatively small losses suffered by individual members of society, the fact that many of these acts have only recently been criminalized and therefore lack traditional moral weight, and the fact that perpetrators are powerful enough to control the mass media to the extent that public ire is not provoked. Geis and Simon and Eitzen make it abundantly clear that commercial and corporate crimes will continue until victimization patterns are deciphered and impressed upon the public.

SUMMARY

In this chapter, we introduced the victim into the "crime problem," with important implications for the average citizen's crime fears and for various types of anticrime policy. The discussion suggests that victimization is not a random occurrence. Some classes are more likely targets of crime than are others. The extent to which individuals must fear and take precautions against victimization therefore varies. It would seem appropriate that the average citizen attempt to calculate his or her apparent chances of being a victim before devising personal anticrime strategies.

Governmental anticrime policies should be grounded in knowledge about societal victimization patterns. Resources are easily wasted if the patterns are ignored. Further, this chapter's discussion of victim involvement in various types of crime indicates the need for research into victim-offender interaction patterns for most forms of crime. Such research holds great promise for crime-prevention strategies, treatment of offenders, and compensation of victims.

REFERENCES

Amir, M. 1971. *Patterns in Forcible Rape.* Chicago: University of Chicago Press.

Chesney, S., J. Hudson, and J. McLagen. 1978. A new look at restitution: Recent legislation, programs, and research. *Judicature* 61:348–57.

Eglash, A. 1975. Beyond restitution—creative restitution. In *Restitution in Criminal Justice.* Edited by J. Hudson. Collection of papers presented at the First International Symposium on Restitution, Minneapolis, 10–11 May, 1975.

Federal Bureau of Investigation. 1982. *Uniform Crime Reports—1981.* Washington, D.C.: U.S. Government Printing Office.

Felson, R. B., and H. J. Steadman. 1983. Situational factors in disputes leading to criminal violence. *Criminology* 21:59–74.

Franklin, C., and A. Franklin. 1976. Victimology revisited. *Criminology* 14:125–36.

Gebhard, P. H., J. H. Gagnon, W. B. Pomeroy, et al. 1965. *Sex Offenders: An Analysis of Types.* New York: Harper & Row, Publishers.

Geis, G. 1973. Victimization patterns in white-collar crime. In *Victimology: A New Focus,* Vol. 5. Edited by I. Drapkin and E. Viano. Lexington, Mass.: Lexington Books.

———. 1976. Crime victims and victim compensation programs. In *Criminal Justice and the Victim.* Edited by W. F. McDonald. Beverly Hills, Calif.: Sage Publications.

Harland, A. T. 1981. *Restitution to Victims of Personal and Household Crimes.* Washington, D.C.: U.S. Department of Justice.

Landau, S. F. 1973. The offender's perception of the victim. In *Victimology: A New Focus,* Vol. 1. Edited by I. Drapkin and E. Viano. Lexington, Mass.: Lexington Books.

Luckenbill, D. 1977. Criminal homicide as a situated transaction. *Soc. Prob.* 25:176–86.

Meiners, R. E. 1978. *Victim Compensation: Economic, Legal, and Political Aspects.* Lexington, Mass.: D. C. Heath & Company.

New Orleans Times-Picayune. 1978a. Police reports. January 9, sect. 1, 6.

———. 1978b. Teen is convicted of killing brother. January 12, sect. 1, 9.

Simon, D. R., and D. S. Eitzen. 1982. *Elite Deviance.* Boston: Allyn and Bacon.

Skogan, W. G. 1976. The victims of crime: Some national survey findings. In *Criminal Behavior and Social Systems,* 2nd ed. Edited by A. L. Guenther. Chicago: Rand McNally & Co.

U.S. Department of Justice. 1981. *Criminal Victimization in the United States—1979.* Washington, D.C.: U.S. Government Printing Office.

von Hentig, H. 1948. *The Criminal and His Victim: Studies in the Sociobiology of Crime.* New Haven, Conn.: Yale University Press.

Weis, K., and S. S. Borges. 1976. Rape as a crime without victims and offenders? A methological critique. In *Victims and Society.* Edited by E. Viano. Arlington, Virg.: Visage Press.

Wolfgang, M. 1957. Victim-precipitated criminal homicide. *J. Crim. Law Criminol. & Pol. Sci.* 48:1–11.

———. 1958. *Patterns in Criminal Homicide.* Philadelphia: University of Pennsylvania Press.

Yin, P. 1982. Fear of crime as a problem for the elderly. *Soc. Prob.* 30:240–45.

SUGGESTED READINGS

As Chapter 7 has indicated, victimization is a relatively unexplored aspect of crime. The Department of Justice victimization surveys cited in this and other chapters provide the majority of our data concerning victims and crime situations. Drapkin and Viano have collected a large number of papers on various aspects of victimology. They appear in five volumes under the general title, *Victimology: A New Focus* (Lexington, Mass.: Lexington Books, 1973). Readers are urged to explore the journal *Victimology* as well. *Perspectives on Crime Victims,* edited by Galaway and Hudson (St. Louis: C. V. Mosby Co., 1981), also contains a number of important readings. Those interested in the technical side of victimization surveys will find two collections interesting: Lehnan and Skogan's *The National Crime Survey: Working Papers, Vol. 1* and Skogan's *Issues in the Measurement of Victimization* (both 1981, Washington, D.C.: U.S. Government Printing Office).

PART IV

SEARCHING FOR CAUSES

If crime really is a problem for our society, its solution must be grounded in reliable knowledge about it. We must learn under what circumstances criminal behavior occurs and what "causes" seem to underlie that behavior. Anticrime policies differ greatly, depending on our assumptions about crime causation. Chapters 8 and 9 summarize thoughts on these issues.

8

TYPES OF
CAUSAL VARIABLES

Why is there crime? Why are crime rates so high? Why do people break the law? These questions are popular variations of the criminologist's query: How can we discover scientifically the causes of criminal behavior? The criminologist's search for an answer to this question differs from the lay person's, and the difference is primarily a matter of method. Most people have ideas about crime, but the criminologist's ideas are supposed to be more logically formulated and scientifically scrutinized and tested. In this chapter we will examine some traditional thoughts on crime causation. Before doing this, however, we will devote some attention to the general assumptions, principles, procedures, and problems of causal analysis. Many attempts to explain criminal behavior fail not because their hypotheses are flawed but because basic principles and methods of causal analysis are violated in testing the hypotheses. As we shall see, causal analysis is no simple task.

STRUCTURING CAUSAL ANALYSIS

Two basic assumptions underlie a scientific approach to causal analysis of crime. First, we assume that every social phenomenon has a cause (if there is a B, there must be an A that caused it). Every social phonomenon is, therefore, an effect. Further, most phenomena are both causes and effects. That is, they exist in a causal chain, influenced by some phenomenon and, in turn, influencing others. This point is best understood if we imagine the commonly occurring "chain reaction" collisions on our highways. In these accidents, most cars are propelled forward by one car and, in turn, propel another car forward. The movement of any given car is, then, both the effect of one car's movement and the cause of yet another car's movement.

Second, we assume that if we can identify various social phenomena related to a form of crime and correctly establish the order in which these phenomena influence each other, we can predict the occurrence of crime. Figure 8–1 illustrates this basic process. In square I are a number of explanatory variables possibly linked to crime. Square II displays those identified as actually linked to crime and those not. Square III suggests a few possible orderings of the explanatory variables and the eventual successful ordering.

Needless to say, this "domino-theory" model is uncomplicated. However, few explanations of social phenomena fit this model. Instead, more complicated models attempt to capture some of the more intricate interrelationships among sociological variables—how a variable is both directly and indirectly influenced by other variables, for example. Figure 8–2 displays a more complicated causal model, in this instance, one that tries to explain a juvenile's involvement in theft (Smith, 1980). As the model suggests, theft involvement by juveniles is linked to the strength of the social bond between youth and society (the value the youth places on relationships with conventional persons and on conventional goals and objects—parents, school, future job plans, moral beliefs, and so forth). All are posited to influence theft activity. The model also suggests that the social bond is related to the juvenile's socioeconomic background (SES) and race (which themselves are correlated). SES and race influence theft involvement directly—primarily by virtue of pressures thought to be characteristic of lower-class life—and indirectly through their relationship to the elements of the social bond.

Although the social bond-delinquency model is more complicated than the domino-theory model in Figure 8–1, it is also undoubtedly only a rough

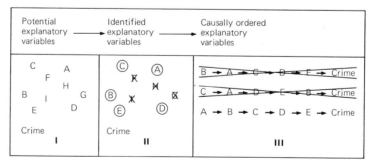

FIGURE 8–1

Causal Analysis of Explanatory Variables Linked to Crime: The "Domino-Theory" Model

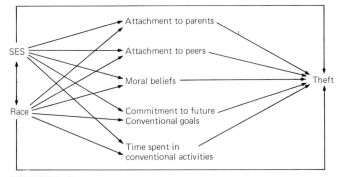

FIGURE 8-2

Causal Model Showing SES, Race, Social Bond, and Theft
Involvement by Juveniles (*Source:* Modified and adapted from:
M.D. Smith, A Longitudinal Analysis of Social Control Theory.
Ph.D. diss., Department of Sociology, Duke University, 1980, p.
70.) Used with permission.

approximation of reality. Surely other variables are implicated in a youth's
commission of delinquent act, both directly and indirectly. It will be a long
while before our models and measurement techniques allow us to incorporate them.

The immediate goal of causal analysis is understanding and prediction.
That is, criminologists hope to understand the interrelationships of a number
of variables to such an extent that they can predict the outcome of any given
arrangement of those variables. The ultimate goal of this venture is intervention in and control of particular social processes. Thus, criminological causal
analysis has traditionally attempted to locate the causes of crime (in general
or with reference to specific offenses) so that "something can be done about
it." Causal research has always been policy-oriented. It seeks to discover
ways by which a society—or, more specifically, governmental agencies—can
break the causal chain of crime.

A review of criminological literature on causes of crime indicates that the
search has not been particularly successful. Although we have often established what does not cause criminal behavior (for instance, criminal ances-
tors), we cannot say with any certainty what does cause it. Many factors
impede the search for causes. Our basic theories about crime remain relatively unsophisticated. We are also dealing with concepts and variables that
do not easily lend themselves to precise measurement. Our earlier discussion
of estimates of the amount of crime in this society (see Chapter 4) provides a
fine example of a measurement problem: How are we to begin to explain
crime when we have so much difficulty determining how much we have and
who commits it?

Aggregate Data

A persistent problem for criminological research is its frequent reliance on aggregate data—pieces of information about groups of people (such as a society, a city, a neighborhood, a racial or ethnic group) as opposed to information about specific individuals within those groups. Aggregate data are often secondary data; that is, information collected for one use and later adopted for criminological research. Such research generally involves the analyses of rates—that is, the number of persons for some unit of the population (10,000 or 100,000) who share a particular characteristic at a given time. Thus, we note, for example, that low-income areas have higher delinquency rates than high-income areas do. The low-income areas are also marked by higher rates of overcrowded and poor housing. Pending further research, it may be inferred from these findings that overcrowding and substandard living conditions influence delinquency rates (Chilton, 1964).

The criminologist must be very careful in drawing conclusions from correlations found in aggregate data. It is possible that correlations found in aggregate data will disappear when data collected from individuals within the aggregation are examined. Figure 8–3 provides a hypothetical example. Using census data and FBI statistics (both forms of aggregate data), a researcher may find that crime rates climb as the proportion of blacks in given areas grows. Should the researcher conclude that blacks are more crime-prone than whites? This conclusion may be unwarranted. If we were somehow to obtain self-reported criminality information and the race of all the individuals in the three areas (nonaggregate data), we could determine how much of the crime in each area is committed by whites and how much by blacks. As Figure 8–3 indicates, the results could seriously challenge our earlier con-

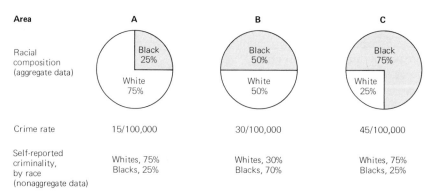

FIGURE 8–3

Problems in Interpreting Crime Correlations in Aggregate Data

clusions based on aggregate data. In area A, the percentage of crimes committed by both races is the same as the percentage of both in the population. In area B, blacks commit more of the crimes than do whites, though they are equal in the population. A look at area C tells us that the small number of whites in the area commit the majority of crimes. Thus, though we may say that the amount of crime in a given area is correlated with the size of its black population, we cannot say that blacks are more crime-prone. The hypothetical results in Figure 8–3 suggest that we study some other aspect of the geographic areas in question—economic conditions or transient criminals, for example—to explain their crime situations. Sociologists refer to the assumption that we may infer individual correlation on the basis of a group correlation as the *ecological fallacy* (Galtung, 1967; Robinson, 1950). It is a potential problem we cannot ignore.

Nonaggregate Data

Given the weaknesses encountered in the use of aggregate data, most criminologists prefer to use nonaggregate data whenever possible. More often than not, these data are collected by survey methods. The survey utilizes questionnaires or interviews to gather information about members of a population. Using this information, researchers attempt to explain variations among respondents with respect to a particular behavioral or attitudinal characteristic (such as amount of theft behavior) by linking this variation to differences regarding other behavioral, attitudinal, or biographical variables (such as socioeconomic status).

During the late 1970s, for instance, members of the Behavioral Research Institute conducted the National Youth Survey (Elliot et al., 1983). Employing a sophisticated sampling design, researchers interviewed 1725 youth, between the ages of eleven and seventeen, throughout the nation. The survey concerned involvement in an extensive list of illegal acts. The results of the survey allowed the researchers to estimate the prevalence and incidence (frequency) of delinquency in the U.S. Further, by asking questions about the sociodemographic characteristics of respondents (age, gender, race, SES, and so forth), the investigators were able to study variables seemingly related to delinquency. They found, for instance, that SES differences operate inversely for involvement in serious offenses; lower SES youth reported more serious offense activity (Elliott and Huizinga, 1983).

Criminologists also occasionally attempt controlled experiments to find answers about crime and criminals. Generally, a group of individuals is subdivided into two or more smaller groups. The researcher is careful to ensure that each of the subgroups is similar either by randomly assigning individuals to the subgroups or by carefully matching an individual in one group with a similar individual in the other group. This accomplished, the researcher applies a stimulus to the members of one group only. The extent to which this group now differs from the other may be attributed to the effects of the stimulus.

Experimental research is less common in criminology than is *survey* research because experimenters face many methodological and ethical problems when engaging in such research. Yet, there are a few examples of experimental studies in the criminological literature. One recent investigation, for example, sought to determine whether or not different types of treatment programs for persons arrested for driving while intoxicated influence rearrest rates (Holden, 1983). The study focused on 4126 persons arrested for driving while intoxicated in Memphis from 1976 to 1980. The subjects were classified as either social or problem drinkers (measured in terms of degree of intoxication) and randomly assigned to one of several treatment groups: control (unsupervised probation), supervised probation, education/therapy, or supervised probation and education/therapy. The treatment programs all were found ineffective in reducing arrests for driving while intoxicated and for other offenses.

Constraints on Criminological Research

Criminologists must constantly cope with their personal biases in choosing research topics and methods, interpreting research results, and publishing those results. As social beings, researchers themselves have inherited many of the attitudes and biases of their society. Graduate-school training also gives them a set of ideas by which to make sense of what they see. Sometimes researchers begin to take their views of the world for granted. Rather than challenge their ideas, they distort or "bend" their research findings to fit those ideas. Unquestioned assumptions about the "natural" inclinations of women, for instance, could heavily influence a criminologist's research on prostitution.

The base of operations of criminologists will also greatly affect their research. Generally, criminologists conduct research as members of an academic institution, as researchers in governmental or private research organizations, or as employees of business concerns. Within the academic setting, which is the most common base of operations, the criminologist is fairly autonomous regarding choice of research topics, research designs, and publication of research results. But as the academician turns to funding agencies for research support, some autonomy is sacrificed, particularly with respect to choice of topic and research design.

Nonacademic criminologists generally lack autonomy and are, in fact, under considerable pressure to produce certain kinds of results. Often the agency-affiliated criminologist's ability to publish research results rests on the extent to which the funding organization defines the results as threatening to its existence. At times, the business-affiliated criminologist's job is at stake if his or her research results do not bode well for the organization's financial future. Such pressures work to hamper sound criminological research.

More than most sociological subfields, criminology faces a number of ethical and legal research constraints. That is, certain forms of research may provide answers to key criminological questions but may also present ethical or legal dilemmas. Much as the police officer must work within a framework of rules protecting the rights of crime suspects, so also must the criminologist honor the rights of research subjects. For instance, to ascertain the effects on trial outcomes of the U.S. Supreme Court's *Miranda* ruling (stating that suspects must be informed of their legal rights upon arrest), the criminologist cannot legally or ethically conduct an experiment whereby some suspects are informed of their rights and others are not. Gaining information about the customers of prostitutes by spying on them also raises ethical questions. Determining the effectiveness of police patrols on crime rates by overpatrolling one area and underpatrolling another is to engage in legally and ethically problematic research.

A classic example of legal constraints on criminological research is what has come to be known as the Wichita Jury Study (Vaughn, 1967). In 1954, a group of social scientists interested in how juries arrive at verdicts proposed secret recording of jury deliberations. They were granted permission by a Wichita, Kansas judge to bug jury deliberations in his trials, provided that the judge maintain complete control of the research, that only civil cases be studied, and that counsel for each party consent to the research. Despite these precautions, members of Congress who learned of the research argued that it violated the safeguard of secrecy by which jurors could feel free to state their opinions without fear of public scrutiny. Were future jurors to suspect that their jury room conversations were being recorded, they might impose restraints upon their participation in deliberations to the extent that the fairness of the trial would be jeopardized. As a result, a law was passed that forbade jury recordings. For this reason, most jury studies today take the form of mock trial deliberations.

DIRECTIONS OF CAUSAL ANALYSIS

The search for the roots of crime traditionally has taken three forms. The first states that criminality is an inherent individual trait. Variations of this theme have stressed biological and genetic explanations of crime; supporters argue that criminal behavior is a symptom of a congenitally flawed individual. The second form, which also stresses the problematic individual, views criminality as the result of acquired individual predispositions toward crime. Many such explanations stress the role of personality development and glandular malfunctions in criminal behavior. The third form places the weight of explanation on sociological variables; supporters claim that crime originates in problems with the structural or cultural makeup of society.

Some of the more sociological explanations treat the individual criminal passively. That is, they make little attempt to explain the manner in which societal factors influence the individual to commit crimes. Instead, they deal simply with variations in societal crime rates as they relate to variations in other societal conditions. Others (a smaller number) attempt to establish the link between societal conditions and individual perceptions in trying to account for criminal behavior.

The approach to causal explanations chosen by the criminologists is, of course, a matter of training and personal preference. The approach which dominates the field of criminology will influence, at least to a small degree, public perceptions about the causes of crime and, to a greater extent, crime prevention and criminal-corrections policies.

BIOLOGICAL VARIABLES

Historically, much emphasis has been placed on the notion of a "born criminal" in attempts to account for criminal activity. Theories have varied in sophistication, but all have assumed that the difference between criminals and their conventional counterparts is a difference brought into this world. Some early biological theories assumed that criminals were throwbacks to more primitive species of man (Lombroso, 1911). Hence, researchers attempted to establish that criminals differed from noncriminals in such features as body type, skull shape, length of arms, hair texture, and facial characteristics— features felt to mirror primitive man.

Body-Type Theories

Body-type theories of criminal behavior were popular as late as the 1950s. Two of the better known theories were offered by Hooton and Sheldon. Hooton (1939) published the results of thousands of measurements of physical characteristics of criminals (in prisons) and noncriminals. He claimed to have found differences between criminals and noncriminals and differences among the various criminal types. He noted, for example, that criminals tended to have thicker, straighter, and more reddish hair. They tended as well to have low, sloping foreheads, thin lips, long necks, and sloping shoulders. First-degree murderers, Hooton further found, had an abundance of the characteristics described above, assaultists had an excess of olive skin color and broad noses, burglars had concave noses, and arsonists had protruding ears.

In a series of books in the 1940s, Sheldon (1942; see also Sheldon et al., 1940, 1949) attempted to attribute temperament to body type and body type to criminality. In essence, he believed that physical constitution shaped personality and that certain personality types were more crime-prone. Sheldon and, in later years, the Gluecks (1956) claimed to have discovered links between delinquency and, especially, a more athletic build, which they argued, signaled a more aggressive temperament. Body-type theories have diminished in popularity during the past two decades. Part of this decline is attributable to the strong methodological criticisms directed at the studies cited above. Generally, most have not taken care to define clearly delinquents and criminals. Hooton, for instance, relied on institutionalized prisoners as his "criminals." Prisoners are certainly not a representative sample of criminals—indeed, they may have been imprisoned because they fit judges' stereotypes as to what dangerous persons look like. Sampling in the studies was also generally poor. Overall, we may say that the purer the methods employed in these studies, the weaker the link found between physical characteristics and criminal behavior.

Beyond their methodological flaws, however, the body-type and "throwback" theories lacked substance; that is, the theories paid little attention to the question of how physical characteristics are linked to social acts. How, for instance, does a "primitive" man become inclined toward law violations rather than some other acts? How is it that some people who are inherently "aggressive" become football players or shrewd businesspeople rather than criminals?

Biogenetic Theories

While research like the above has lost favor, biogenetic research is still very much alive. This is especially true of attempts to explain violent crime. Some scholars approach criminality as an inherited trait, passed on from generation to generation. The more sophisticated of research attempts to test the "bad seed" hypothesis have centered on studies of identical and fraternal twins. If criminality is, in fact, inherited, it is assumed that identical twins, the product of a single fertilized egg, will be more alike in their criminal behavior than will fraternal twins, the product of two separately fertilized eggs. Again, it is generally argued that the more methodologically rigorous of studies into the matter have found few differences between the types of twins. Further, if differences existed, it would be impossible to determine the extent to which they were inherited and the extent to which they were environmentally transmitted. We need only to view the extent to which so many identical twins are treated alike to realize the difficulty of attributing like behavior purely, or even partially, to heredity.

The best known of recent biological research into criminality concerns the alleged relationship between the XYY chromosomal pattern and violent criminal acts. Briefly, scientists have observed that some males are genetically abnormal in the sense that they possess an extra Y sex chromosome

NEWSPRINT AND COMMENT

Criminal Behavior May Be Inherited and Treatable, Psychologist Says

By Warren Froelich

Washington—Criminal behavior may be an inherited disorder that eventually could be treated.

And, according to a psychologist at the University of Southern California, scientists—using biological and sociological testing—will one day be able to predict the likelihood that a child years later will commit a crime.

"I think these facts suggest that perhaps the time is ripe for a serious interdisciplinary program of research into early detection and prevention of chronic criminal behavior," said Dr. Sarnoff H. Mednick, who also is director of the Psychological Institute in Copenhagen, Denmark.

Sarnoff stopped short of saying there is a "crime gene"—a term popular nearly two decades ago to describe a chromosomal aberration that some thought at the time was responsible for abnormally aggressive or criminal behavior.

But he noted that alcoholism and low intelligence, both inherited to some degree, are also linked to criminal behavior.

"What we have," Sarnoff said, "is some genetically controlled physiological factors which in some way elevate an individual's probability to commit crimes, and this is transmitted from one generation to the next."

Sarnoff based his remarks on several years of biological and sociological studies conducted in Denmark, an ideal place for such work because of the lack of diversity among its people.

In one study involving 14,427 adopted children, he compared the criminal behavior of those whose biological parents had been convicted of crimes with those whose parents were non-criminals.

The results showed that those children whose parents had been criminals were two to three times more likely to commit crimes than those children whose parents never broke the law.

"Despite the fact that their adopted parents are typically orderly, middle-class people," Sarnoff said, "if the biological parents were criminal this greatly increased the likelihood that the adopted children will evidence criminal behavior."

In another study, Sarnoff found that 43.4 percent of all violent crime committed by a group of 32,000 native residents of Copenhagen was linked to less than four-tenths of one percent of those in the study sample—or about 109 persons.

Other series of studies analyzed such biological components as brain waves, heart rate, skin conductance and intellectual capacity. For example, he found that persons with a cer-

tain brain-wave pattern were more likely to engage in criminal behavior.

From this work, Sarnoff concluded that a small group of chronic offenders were "biologically quite different" from those who committed milder offenses.

"If this small, highly disturbing group of chronic offenders could be identified quite early in their careers," Sarnoff concluded, "even a partially successful preventive intervention with them could have a very powerful effect on overall crime rates and also would have a disproportionate effect on more serious crime."

Sarnoff suggested that further studies could help identify potential chronic offenders while they are still children. Biological, intelligence and sociological testing for first offenders could screen these potential problem cases, who then could be treated.

Therapy would not involve drugs or pills, because they might do more harm than good, Sarnoff said.

Instead, treatment would rely on training techniques that would help these children become responsible and productive citizens.

Source: Copley News Service, 1982. Reprinted by permission.

Comment: Easy Answers to the "Crime Problem"

Articles like the one reprinted above appeal to the public. People prefer to conceptualize social problems in terms of individual flaws. Thus, crime control becomes far simpler; all we must do is identify and treat "sick" individuals. But let us look briefly at the issue raised in the article, that criminal behavior may be inherited and treatable through preventive therapies. Perhaps we can stretch our imaginations sufficiently to accept the possibility that some genetically controlled physiological factors in some way elevate an individual's probability of a spontaneous violent outburst. But the article suggests that *crime in general* reflects inherited traits. It is difficult to conceive of theft behavior as in any sense genetically influenced. Nor can we imagine the forger's action as genetically inspired.

Beyond this, what is the key variable at work here? The article suggests that criminal "tendencies" may come to the fore under certain, presumably social, conditions. Yet, the treatment emphasis is not upon these social factors, without which genetically inherited traits mean little. (The opposite is not true, however; the social triggering mechanisms may influence behavior regardless of genetic factors.) Crime will not disappear until its social causes are addressed. To direct our treatment efforts to the individual (at least exclusively) gains us little.

One other issue requires attention. How do we treat children who *might someday* commit crimes? If we cannot predict perfectly accurately, do we proceed with treatment even if the target group includes children who mistakenly have been identified as potential chronic offenders? Is the treatment physiological, psychological, or social? Is it voluntary? What stigma accompanies the label of potential deviant? How does it affect the child's future?

(XY is the normal male sex chromosomal arrangement; XYY is an abnormal pattern). A rare occurrence, the extra Y pattern has appeared with slightly higher regularity in incarcerated populations of mentally retarded and criminal persons than it has in the greater population. Some persons have speculated that the extra Y chromosome is linked to antisocial, especially violent, behavior.

Although the news media have given considerable coverage to this hypothesis, there is, in fact, little evidence to support it. Quite the contrary, some argue, XYY individuals are less prone to aggression than chromosomally normal persons are. Most reviewers of XYY research conclude that the studies done so far are methodologically inadequate and ungeneralizable. More sophisticated research indicates no link between violence and the extra Y chromosome (Ellis, 1982; Fox, 1971; Mednick et al., 1982). Again, current theories involving the phenomenon lack content in terms of spelling out *how* the genetic condition influences social actions. And given the rarity of the pattern, it is felt that, at best, the XYY pattern could account for only a small amount of violent behavior.

The list of potential biological links to criminal behavior grows constantly. Biogenetic research now includes exploration of crime's relation to autonomic nervous system activity (often studied through monitoring of the sweat glands of the palm during emotional stress), central nervous system and neuropsychological functioning (often monitored through electroencephalographic (EEG) tests), and pharmacological and biochemical factors (focusing, for example, on testosterone levels, hypoglycemia, and the uses of various drugs such as alcohol and amphetamines).

Interestingly, social scientists recently have softened somewhat their traditional opposition to theories espousing biological links to criminal behavior. They now seem more willing to concede that some forms of aggression and crime may in some way be influenced biologically (Ellis, 1982; Kelly, 1979). Mednick et al. (1982:25–26), for example, argue that if alcohol addiction increases the probability of aggression and such addiction has some partial, genetically based predisposition, studies of the crime patterns of twins may yet yield positive results. But the support for biological variables clearly is not the equal of that given to psychological and social-environmental variables. Social scientists now argue generally that some rarer forms of crime (a sudden violent outburst, for example) may be explained by environmental stimuli acting in conjunction with individual biogenetic factors. Only when the correct environmental influences occur, they assert, will the genetic features bring their influence to bear (Shah and Roth, 1974). It is stressed that no one has yet proposed a reasonable theoretical link between biological factors and more common forms of crime—theft, for example.

PSYCHOLOGICAL VARIABLES

A second strain of causal analysis focuses on the psychological makeup of individuals as the source of criminal behavior, or, in popular jargon, "People who do such things must be crazy." In more scientific terms, crime is attributed to mental, emotional, or personality disturbances. The noncriminal is one who is psychologically sound enough to control impulses to commit crimes and to appreciate the moral and social implications of criminal behavior.

Intellectual and Mental Impairment Theories

Once a popular scientific notion, the claim that most criminals are somehow intellectually or mentally impaired is no longer generally accepted. While occasional offenses may be related to mental retardation, there is no evidence that criminals are any more or less intellectually endowed than noncriminals are. Indeed, many forms of crime require high levels of intelligence—embezzlement, for example, requires considerable mental skill. Although unpopular among criminologists, the question of mental and intellectual capacity remains open for now since the measurement of intelligence remains problematic. Only when the measurement problem is resolved and the measures applied to representative samples of criminals and noncriminals will the question be laid to rest.

A 1977 article by Hirschi and Hindelang argues that the problem cannot be ignored any longer. Their examination of recent research concerning delinquency and IQ indicates that intelligence is at least as strongly related to delinquency as are class and race. The link is not direct but indirect; they argue: IQ influences school performance; low IQ produces school failures; school failures produce delinquency. However, Hirschi and Hindelang have drawn heavy criticism, particularly for failing to stress that IQ is not inherited but rather environmentally formed, that standard IQ measurement cannot be trusted, and that other orderings of variables are possible (Simons, 1978; see also Hirschi and Hindelang, 1978). Regarding this last point, rather than IQ being directly or indirectly implicated in the causes of delinquency, low IQ scores and delinquency may both be the effects of the same cause: a negative attitude toward teachers and school and a resultant lack of motivation to excel in school or in conventional behavior. Whether or not correct, the Hirschi and Hindelang article performs a needed service. It forces criminologists to specify better the presence or absence of a relationship between intelligence and crime.

It should be noted that similar work is occurring with respect to espoused links between learning disabilities and juvenile delinquency (Holzman, 1979; Murray, 1976). Better known learning disabilities take the forms of dyslexia and aphasia. These involve the child's inability to process written and verbal vocabulary, thus ensuring problems in comprehension and expression in school. Exact causes of learning disability are unknown. But some observers argue that the problem indirectly may lead to delinquency. This may occur by virtue of poor school performance, which leads to school dropout and subsequent delinquency, or by virtue of the labeling and grouping together of learning-disabled children with other "problem" children who become alienated from and hostile toward school, thus drifting toward delinquency. Most of the "evidence" for this assertion relies on clinical observation. Though several, more systematic studies have addressed the issue of learning disability and delinquency (Jacobson, 1974; Poremba, 1975; Wacker, 1974), and many have claimed to find a link between the two problems, the evidence for such a link is very weak. It is not clear that learning disability, in fact, leads to delinquency, though it is quite clear that most delinquents are not learning-disabled. Yet, until better evidence is amassed, the question—like that of IQ—cannot be laid to rest.

Psychoanalytic Theories

Today, theories that emphasize emotional or personality disorders as causes of criminal behavior are in greater favor than mental-inferiority explanations. One variation of this theme is the psychoanalytic approach. Current versions of this approach are modifications of Freudian psychoanalytic theories, which posit that behaviors and feelings are overtly symbolic of unconscious conflicts between three supposed components of every human personality—the *id* (the biological drives component), the *superego* (the socially responsive component), and the *ego* (the component that attempts to subdue the id to minimize conflict with superego). According to psychoanalytic theory, most people are viewed as being able to keep these components somewhat in harmony (at least most of the time), usually through repression of the id. However, some are not able to produce this harmony, and the imbalance may create problematic or even antisocial behavior.

Thus, in the psychoanalytic framework, crime is viewed as antisocial behavior that is symptomatic of unconscious conflicts. A crime may be the result of a lack of repression of the id or symbolic of unfulfilled impulses. Since the superego is continually present, the ego may feel guilty. Further crimes may be committed in order to bring about punishment to eliminate the feelings of guilt. The only resolution to criminal-behavior syndromes such as this, these theorists suggest, is psychoanalysis, a highly individualistic, long-term therapy program in which a patient comes to recognize his or her unconscious conflicts under the guidance of a therapist or analyst.

The major criticism of the psychoanalytic approach is that it is scientifically untestable. Although all theories are essentially acts of faith, some hold more promise of verification than others. Psychoanalytic theory holds none. The various components of the personality are neither observable nor measurable. The result of psychoanalysis is an analyst's interpretation of a patient's interpretation of what is occurring in the subconscious. We are left with a small number of highly individualistic, nongeneralizable accounts of behaviors and events (Vold, 1958).

Personality-Disorder Theories

Less problematic than psychoanalytic ideas are theories that view personality or emotional problems as the source of crime but do not assume any unconscious motives or symbolism in criminal behavior. Basically, this viewpoint asserts that personality flaws contribute to criminal behavior. Some theories have stated this thesis in rather extreme terms, attributing crime to *psychopathic* or *sociopathic* personalities, terms that refer to chronic antisocial behavior. Psychopaths generally are seen as being callous persons with problematic social relationships who have few ties to society, and as relatively amoral and unafraid of sanctions against crime.

Most social scientists are distrustful of the psychopath concept, however, noting that its vagueness prevents any meaningful attempts to link it to criminal behavior. Some argue that there is no such thing as a psychopath, that the concept was created to deal with otherwise unclassifiable personality disorders, or that if psychopaths do exist, their numbers are so small that they could not account for much crime.

Less extreme versions of personality-disorder theories point to such problems as overaggression, insecurity, paranoia, emotional instability and immaturity, and egocentrism as possible causes of delinquent or criminal behavior. The social-science literature in this area is divided. On the one hand, there are reviews of most studies done through 1965 that fail to find a conclusive link between personality disorders and criminality (Waldo and Dinitz, 1967). On the other hand, some criminologists argue that there is promise in personality-disorder research (Gibbons, 1977:177). They view the problem of low correlations as a measurement problem and suggest that the relationship of crime to personality will appear stronger when we are better able to define and measure personality attributes.

The general position of most criminologists regarding personality-disorder research (and other psychological-variable research as well) seems to be one of cautious encouragement (Hindelang, 1972). This research may discover certain personality traits that when interacting with certain social and environmental stimuli may foster criminal behavior. At present, however, the major constructs of psychological theories face serious measurement problems (Megargee, 1982:160). Until these are corrected, links between crime and the psychological realm will remain obscured.

SOCIOLOGICAL VARIABLES

The biological and psychological causal explanations discussed above generally have viewed criminal behavior as the result of individual abnormalities or defects. However, the sociological approach to explaining crime tends to view criminal behavior as somewhat more "normal," an expected response to social and cultural events and situations. Some sociological explanations of criminal behavior are more formal than others. That is, some represent full-blown theories while others are essentially attempts to link a given variable—exposure to urban poverty, for example—to criminal behavior. We will review the more formal theories in Chapter 9. At present, we are concerned with the links between criminal behavior and several sociological variables (that is, variables that do not attempt to link criminal acts to characteristics inherent in the individual): urban poverty, criminal companions, weakened family ties, alcohol consumption, and exposure to mass media.

It is no accident that the variables we will examine are the same as those that characterize what might be termed "popular guesses" about the causes of crime. A survey of the American public concerning crime's causes undoubtedly would uncover a set of "evil causes evil" ideas. Some of the evils of society (such as poverty and family disruption) are thought to produce other evils (such as crime, mental illness, and drug use). To the extent that popular opinion considers any causal variable beyond the biological and psychological, it views the social environment—either past or present—of criminals as the cause of their illegal behavior. The fact that these ideas about crime causation are popular guesses does not render them invalid. Indeed, they have fostered a great deal of insightful criminological research.

Urban Poverty

Generally, urban areas experience higher crime rates than suburban and rural areas. Crime rates also vary by type of urban pattern: older versus newer cities; sprawling versus concentrated cities; ethnically and racially mixed cities versus homogenous cities; industrial versus frontier cities; and so on. Further, crime rates differ within cities; some areas—most often those closest to the central city—have higher crime rates. Yet we do not know with certainty exactly what aspects of urbanization are related to crime, causally or otherwise. Some argue that population density (urban overcrowding) is at fault. By itself, density cannot explain crime. In 1982, for example, Odessa, Texas (not New York or Detroit), had the highest homicide rate in the country, though it is not a high-density city. Simply crowding people together does not produce crime. For example, Tokyo, one of the world's largest and most crowded cities, has a low crime rate.

Cultural and class variation, so apparent within most cities, is apparently linked to crime. Crimes of violence and most property offenses are concentrated in the lower classes, especially in lower-class black and ethnic groups. Urbanization concentrates poverty into ghettos and makes class distinctions more apparent. Absolute and relative poverty certainly cause the kinds of frustration that can lead to violent outbursts. Yet rural areas also have high levels of poverty but lower crime rates.

Clearly, the reasons for higher crime rates in urban areas are complex. So are the differences between and within cities in physical deterioration, migration patterns, population density and composition, and historical and cultural features. No one can say which factors, individually or jointly, account for crime. In the final analysis, we may discover that urbanization does not *cause* crime so much as provide greater *opportunity* for it. Cities offer more targets for crime as well as greater degrees of anonymity for the criminal. Cities provide countless networks for the acquisition and sale of stolen goods.

Criminal Companions

"Getting in with the wrong crowd" often is viewed as a source of criminal behavior. This theme is most pronounced in theories of juvenile delinquency. It occurs infrequently in theories of adult crime. In one sense, it is clear that if one interacts only with persons who encourage law violations, one will probably favor such behavior. Yet few people are fed such a socialization diet. Instead, they receive a number of definitions of morality, conventional and unconventional. The key question is: What governs the choice of definitions by the individual? (This is discussed in greater detail in Chapter 9 in an examination of *differential association* theory.)

We really do not know at present whether bad companions cause delinquency or vice versa. That is, which comes first, the commission of a crime or the affiliation with evil people? Some argue that delinquents seek out and join other delinquents more often than innocent people are corrupted by evil ones. Others suggest that juveniles caught committing delinquencies are, by virtue of the structure of juvenile justice, forced into the company of other delinquents (Hirschi, 1969:135–161).

Whether or not they spawn or simply attract delinquents, bad companions often are associated with juvenile delinquency. Jensen and Erickson (1978) argue that the key to the relationship is not the fact of association with delinquent peers but the degree of commitment to those peers. They note that those who report a willingness to counter conventional authority (parents, law), when asked to do so by peers, are more likely to report delinquent activity. This finding, of course, leads to other questions: What promotes such a degree of commitment to delinquent peers? Is such commitment the product of poor parent-child relations or does it cause poor relations? If it is the product, is this a matter of poor parental supervision of children or of some more complicated "cause" (Jensen, 1972)?

We need to determine what effect, if any, the delinquent peer group has on the movement of delinquents into adult criminal activity. Further, we must find if adult offenders, whether or not they offend alone, are influenced in decisions to violate the law by criminal acquaintances.

Weakened Family Ties

Members of societies that are undergoing social change characteristically perceive social-control institutions to be failing. Thus, perceived changes in the status of the family as an informal mechanism of social control often are viewed as being causes of criminal behavior, especially among the young. The "broken home" often has been credited with placing a juvenile on the path to delinquency and, for some juveniles, to adult crime. However, evidence regarding this relationship, especially its causal aspects, has been contradictory. While many studies (Glueck and Glueck, 1950:122; Nye, 1958:43–48) have claimed that higher proportions of delinquents than nondelinquents come from broken homes, a smaller number have argued persuasively that there is little support for such a claim (Rosen, 1970). Toby (1957) stated that the broken home is not related to the delinquencies of older male juveniles but is associated with female and preadolescent male delinquency.

If home situation is related to delinquency, the question is: How? Among the possible answers is the socialization of the child by the family into criminal values. This seems among the least likely occurrences, however, since, as

Hirschi (1969:97, 108) points out, even criminal parents will not teach their child to be a criminal. A second possibility is that parents simply do not prepare the child to function conventionally in society. As we shall see later, the poor socialization theme is at the heart of many formal theories of delinquency. Yet if we are to believe the evidence cited in Chapter 4, that most juveniles at some time commit delinquencies, and we wish to attribute the acts to poor family socialization, then we must also accept the unlikely fact that poor family socialization is highly characteristic of most of this society. (This is not to deny the possibility that it is related to the commission of serious offenses by a smaller number of juveniles.)

Some argue that juvenile delinquency is an attention-getting device employed by the child in an unhappy home; others claim that delinquency is a means of punishing or hurting parents in the unhappy home. There is little evidence to support either claim. The most plausible of the possibilities relating home life to delinquency is that which concerns parental supervision of juveniles. This thesis reflects the popular sentiment that some parents "let their kids get away with anything." Indeed, there is evidence that poorer parental supervision is linked to delinquency (Hirschi, 1969:83–109). If the broken home also means weakened supervision of juveniles, then the higher delinquency rates among children from broken homes are somewhat understandable.

Strictly speaking, the parental supervision thesis is not causal. Instead, it speculates that causal factors are allowed to operate on an individual because he or she is free from parental control. To illustrate, we may imagine two boys who enter a store and see an item they wish to have but cannot afford. The owner of the store is not watching them, and the risk of being caught shoplifting is very low. Both boys know shoplifting is wrong. However, one chooses not to shoplift; the other shoplifts the item. How are we to explain the different behaviors of the two boys, whose desires and opportunities to steal were the same and whose beliefs about the morality of shoplifting were alike? One possible answer is that the boy who stole is not as closely tied to his parents as the boy who did not. That is, the "good" boy may be more fearful of what his parents' reaction would be if they learned that he shoplifted. He may also be more highly supervised by his parents and more likely made to explain how he obtained an item he could not afford. Thus, we may say that poor parental supervision did not cause the "bad" boy to shoplift; it permitted him to shoplift.

Gove and Crutchfield (1982) recently have added support to the parental supervision thesis. Their research indicates that boys from broken homes or homes with poor marital relations exhibit higher levels of delinquency. They find the strength of the bond between parents and the boys highly important. These results prompt them to conclude:

> [W]e can be fairly certain that characteristics of the family are integrally related to delinquency, and that these characteristics generally involve ineffectual family functioning which is experienced as problematic by children. It is

time that we start taking the relationship between family characteristics and delinquency very seriously and systematically determine the precise mechanisms of how family characteristics are related to delinquency.

If we assume that family supervision is a key to delinquency, we may also extend the control thesis to adult crime. It would seem that the more attached the adult is to the family—in the sense that he or she is responsive to family pressures, has little opportunity to be secretive, and fears losing the family's respect or hurting the family if caught in a criminal act—the less that person is free to commit a crime. Again, this thesis views family situations not as a causal but as an intervening variable. At this date, we lack a definitive test of this line of explanation.

Alcohol and Crime

The "evil causes evil" thesis is nowhere more obvious than in the popular belief that drinking and crime are related. This view is not without some basis. One review of twenty-eight studies of homicide reports that twenty-two found alcohol implicated in at least 30 percent of the offenses—in terms of alcohol use by either or both victim and offender (Greenberg, 1981). Convicted criminals are believed to have higher rates of alcoholism than the general population, though the majority of offenders do not have a drinking problem and the majority of alcoholics do not commit serious offenses (Roizen and Schneberk, 1977). Forty-three percent of approximately 10,400 state prison inmates in one study reported that they were drinking at the time of the offense for which they were currently incarcerated. Percentages were highest for arson, homicide, assault, and sex offenses (Roizen and Schneberk, 1977).

The extent to which these findings actually link alcohol causally to criminal behavior is open to question. Several observers point up a number of methodological problems in studies of this subject: poor and nonuniform definitions of both alcohol use and crime, biased samples, failure to control for relevant variables, inattention to the context in which drinking and crime interact, and failure to distinguish subgroups of alcohol users and offenders (Goodwin, 1973; Greenberg, 1981; Pernanen, 1976). We note, for example, that imprisoned persons may display higher rates of alcoholism than the general population, not because there is a link between alcohol and crime, but because of a link between alcohol and an inability to defend oneself in court.

Assuming momentarily that alcohol may be associated with criminal activity, the question becomes: In what way? Pernanen (1981) offers several possibilities. He suggests that alcohol may produce physiological effects that disinhibit aggressive behavior or that activate or combine with other physiological conditions to produce aggressive behavior. For example, alcohol use is postulated by some to cause or to join with temporal lobe dysfunctions and, thus, to produce violent acts. The same often is suggested of alcohol and hyperglycemia or sleep deprivation.

These explanations may be complicated by attempts to account for situational factors in the production of aggressive behavior. That is, it may be argued that no physiological change due to alcohol can produce aggression unless certain features of the immediate social environment are present (other persons or weapons, for example). The notion of psychological stress may further complicate the issue. Hence, aggression may result from the impact of alcohol upon one's psychological state (whether or not combined with special physiological effects or interacting with situational factors).

Sociologists, not surprisingly, focus on the social-situational environment in accounting for a possible association between alcohol and aggression. That is, they tend to assume that alcohol affects most people to relatively the same degree physiologically and psychologically. Thus, the production of violent behavior is attributed to the social situation in which the drinking occurs. Roman (1981) suggests a few elements of the drinking situation that might influence its behavioral outcomes:

1. The presence or absence of other persons during the drinking event
2. The relationship of the drinker to the others present (stranger, friend, relative, and so forth)
3. The number of persons at the event who are drinking
4. The normal social roles expected of the drinker vis-à-vis the others (dominant, submissive, and so forth)
5. The mobility of the drinking event (movement from one home or bar to another, for example)
6. The aim of the drinking event (escapism, recreation, ceremony)
7. The drinking environment (home, tavern, open space)
8. The presence or absence of phenomena that may facilitate violence (guns, knives, and so forth)
9. The presence or absence of social control agents (security guards, for example)

In sorting through these possible explanations, we must remember that alcohol and crime may be unrelated causally even though otherwise associated. That is, both may be reflecting some other cause; both may be symptoms of the same problem. Stress factors, for example, may lead to drinking and to violence independently though at one time. The point in raising this possibility is to suggest how very far we are from solving the drinking-crime riddle. So far, in fact, that we can spend considerable theory-building energy trying to reason out the correct causal path from alcohol to crime when, in the final analysis, there is no causal path.

Mass Media and Crime

Recently, there has been considerable popular concern that the mass media, particularly motion pictures and television crime dramas, have influenced juveniles to commit crimes. Most of the criticism is directed at the impact of mass media portrayals of violence, since, on the whole, property offenders are usually not glorified and are usually caught by "supercops" (Dominick, 1973). The argument concerning violence is stated thus:

1. Mass-media emphasis on violence—murder, rape, robbery, assault, arson—desensitizes the public, especially youth, to the reality of violence. In short, people are not shocked by it.
2. The mass media provide knowledge and techniques for violent crime to youth who are already in some way predisposed to violence. (A 1978 lawsuit against a major television network claimed that an explicit rape scene in a crime drama inspired a group of youths to imitate the rape with a young girl. The suit was dismissed by the courts.)

That the mass media dwell on violence is well documented. As a special committee report noted in 1972, not only crime dramas, but almost all children's cartoons and many situation comedies as well, contain violent episodes (Surgeon General's Scientific Advisory Committee, 1972a). Less documented is the effect of entertainment violence on viewers; that is, do television and motion pictures influence behaviorally those who watch them, especially children? Most of the research in this area has attempted to discern whether or not television encourages children to be violent either through teaching them methods of violence or through removing their inhibitions against violence (by portraying it as frequent and normal).

There is *some* evidence that television violence has a short-term impact on viewing youngsters. The Surgeon General's Scientific Advisory Committee (1972b, 1972c) argues that in controlled experiments in which some children viewed "aggressive" and others "nonaggressive" programs, those who viewed the former displayed higher levels of aggressive attitudes and play immediately following the viewing.

Most of the research reviewed by the committee and the majority of subsequent research has been experimental. In most instances, children have been exposed to varying degrees of film violence while related variables have been manipulated (for example, whether the aggression is rewarded or punished in the film and whether or not animate targets for violence were offered to the children after the film).

Berkowitz et al. (1974), for instance, conducted an experiment in which half of a group of institutionalized delinquent subjects were insulted by a peer and half received no insult. Two-thirds of the subjects in each group were then shown a movie in which a boxer was beaten severely. The remainder saw no movie. Viewers of the movie also were given a summary of events leading to the boxer's beating. Half were told he deserved his fate, half that he did not. In subsequent tests, those who viewed the film exhibited a greater willingness to administer pain to the boy who earlier had insulted some subjects. Those who had been insulted were most willing to do so. The portrayal of the boxer as deserving or undeserving of his fate had no effect on aggression levels of the youths.

Experimental studies have been faulted for the artificial context into which they place the media-violence question. Actual television shows rarely are shown to research subjects. Violence seems artificially stimulated by the research situation—measured, for example, by willingness of one subject to give an electric shock to another (Berkowitz et al., 1974). Experiments nearly always allow only a short time period after the exposure to the media stimulus before attempting to assess its effects (Kaplan, 1972; Hartnagel et al., 1975).

Two major field (nonexperimental) studies on media effects report contradictory findings. The first, by Eron et al. (1972), was a panel study in which 422 youths were interviewed as third-grade students and, again, ten years later, as teenagers. At both times the subjects reported their television-viewing preferences. Among the third-grade subjects, children who chose violent shows also exhibited higher levels of aggressiveness. Ten years later, the same relationship was discovered, but for males only. Eron and co-researchers claimed that these results indicated that exposure to violent television programs in the early formative years influences levels of aggression in later years. This conclusion was challenged for failing to account for the possibility that both viewing preferences and aggression were functions of some common cause experienced during early childhood—parental response to aggressive behavior, for example (Howitt, 1972; Kay, 1972). More generally, even assuming a causal relationship between viewing preference and aggression, we may ask which caused which?

A second study reports no relationship between viewing television violence and subsequent violent behavior. Hartnagel et al. (1975) sought to avoid the artificiality of the experimental setting. They questioned respondents—junior and senior high school students—about actual television program preferences. The students were asked whether or not they perceived violence to be a feature of their favorite show and whether or not such violence was rewarded.

Finally, instead of focusing on laboratory-type aggression, the researchers measured students' involvement in actual violent acts—fights with others. The study's findings indicated that television preferences did not influence levels of violent activity for the entire sample or for selected subgroups within it.

In sum, the question of media effects on violent behavior is far from settled. Experimental research provides a qualified "yes" to the question. Field research, supposedly better reflecting "real life," provides contradictory though generally negative answers. We note that little has been done to study the issue with respect to the television viewing behavior of adults. We note also the problem that will confront us if we find a relationship between media and violent behavior. What will be done about it? Is radical censorship of television and movies appropriate (Watts, 1976)? Worse, we note the more serious problem of censorship *before* the issue is settled definitively.

THE VALUE OF THE "SECOND LOOK"

It is clear from the preceding discussion of biological, psychological, and sociological variables central to many explanations of criminal behavior how little we know with certainty. We know only that what we *think* may or may not be related to crime later may be viewed quite differently. This was apparent in the discussion in Chapter 6 in the relation of social class to criminality. This situation frustrates a public that wants answers and grows cynical about a research process that never provides answers it can "trust." But the researcher's hesitancy to treat research findings as "true" and definitive represents the heart of the scientific process of seeking answers. It is assumed that errors of conceptualization and measurement plague every study and that constant reconceptualization and refined measurement will produce the purer finding. The need for replication and revision becomes apparent in the following example concerning the relation of church attendance to delinquency.

An Example: Religiosity and Delinquency

In 1969, Hirschi and Stark published the results of a study in which they sought a better understanding of the link (if any) between religiosity (church attendance) and delinquency. Traditionally, church attendance had been thought to inhibit delinquency through the promotion of moral values and respect for conventional authority and through the development of a fear of supernatural sanctions for wrongdoing. However, analyzing data collected from youths in California, Hirschi and Stark found religiosity unrelated to moral values and only slightly linked to the acceptance of conventional authority. They did find it related to a belief in the devil and an afterlife but, more importantly, found belief in supernatural sanctions, respect for conventional authority, and religiosity unrelated to delinquency. Only moral values were found related to delinquency. Hirschi and Stark argued that in terms of promoting moral values and adherence to the law, churches are failing their constituents.

Five years after Hirschi and Stark published their findings, Burkett and White (1974) released the results of a study of youth in the Pacific Northwest. They also found no relation between religiosity and delinquency. However, they argued that the reason for this is not that churches do not provide their members with moral values but that most delinquent behavior is condemned by churches and secular institutions (schools, for example) alike. Their findings indicated that involvement in activities condemned by the church but less so by secular institutions is negatively related to religiosity. Alcohol and marijuana use, for instance, were found inhibited by church attendance.

In 1977, another refinement of the religiosity-delinquency issue was offered by Higgins and Albrecht. Analyzing data collected from nearly 1400 tenth-grade students in Atlanta high schools, they reported a moderately strong relationship between religiosity and delinquency. They argued that the link between these variables is that in their Atlanta sample church attendance is related to respect for conventional authority, which in turn influences delinquency involvement. The authors argued that the difference between their results and those found with West Coast samples may rest on regional variation in commitment of church attenders to religious principles. They felt it possible that youth who attend church in the south are more religious and less secular than are those in the West.

Thus, Higgins and Albrecht have given us yet another hypothesis to pursue in trying to pin down the link between religiosity and delinquency. What began in 1969 as a denial of such a link became in 1974 and 1977 a qualified affirmation of the link. So also goes the march toward understanding the relation of most variables to delinquent and criminal behavior. Every finding deserves a "second look."

SUMMARY

In this chapter we reviewed criminological attempts to answer the well-worn but still unanswered question: What causes crime? The search for causes has centered, at different times, on the biological, psychological, and social characteristics of the criminal. Although it would seem we have developed a progressively sophisticated understanding of criminal behavior, if we review present knowledge we see that it is far from definitive.

We noted a recent softening among sociologists toward biological and psychological explanations of criminal behavior. It is now conceded that some physiological and psychological conditions may predispose some persons to certain forms of violent behavior. But these conditions are seen to be meaningless apart from the social-environmental factors influencing crime. Most offenders are not biologically or psychologically compelled to violate the law; but all are influenced in their violations by social factors. Those espousing biological and psychological explanations still must address exactly how nonsocial factors influence behavior.

Chapter 8 also reviewed evidence concerning the relation of a number of sociological variables to criminal behavior. Urban poverty, criminal companions, weakened family ties, alcohol consumption, and exposure to media violence all seem in some manner related to criminality. Whether or not the relation is causal remains to be seen. Before we can find the answers, we clearly must conceptualize better the supposed associations and develop better methods of testing for these associations.

To this point, we have not considered the relation to crime of one variable that characterizes many popular and sociological attempts to explain criminality: economic opportunity. This is remedied in the coming chapter, which evaluates a number of more detailed, formal sociological theories of crime causation.

REFERENCES

Berkowitz, L., R. D. Parke, J. P. Leyens, et al. 1974. Reactions of juvenile delinquents to "justified" and "less justified" movie violence. *J. Res. Crime & Delinq.* 11:16–24.

Burkett, S. R., and M. White. 1974. Hellfire and delinquency: Another look. *J. Sci. Study Rel.* 13:455–62.

Chilton, R. J. 1964. Continuity in delinquency area research: A comparison of studies for Baltimore, Detroit, and Indianapolis. *Am. Sociol. Rev.* 29:71–83.

Dominick, J. R. 1973. Crime and law enforcement on prime-time television. *Pub. Opinion Q.* 37:241–50.

Elliott, D. S., and D. Huizinga. 1983. Social class and delinquent behavior in a national youth panel: 1976–1980. *Criminology* 21:149–77.

Elliott, D. S., D. Huizinga, B. A. Knowles, et al. 1983. *The Incidence and Prevalence of Delinquent Behavior: 1976–1980.* Boulder, Colo.: Behavioral Research Institute.

Ellis, L. 1982. Genetics and criminal behavior. *Criminology* 20:43–66.

Eron, L. D., L. R. H. Mann, M. Lefkowitz, et al. 1972. Does television cause aggression? *Am. Psychol.* 27:253–63.

Fox, R. G. 1971. The XYY offender: A modern myth? *J. Crim. Law Criminol. & Pol. Sci.* 62:59–73.

Galtung, J. 1967. *Theory and Methods of Social Research.* New York: Columbia University Press.

Gibbons, D. C. 1977. *Society, Crime and Criminal Careers.* 3rd ed. Englewood Cliffs, N.J.: Prentice-Hall.

Glueck, S., and E. Glueck, 1950. *Unraveling Juvenile Delinquency.* New York: Commonwealth Fund.

———. 1956. *Physique and Delinquency.* New York: Harper & Row, Publishers.

Goodwin, D. W. 1973. Alcohol in suicide and homicide. *Q. J. Stud. Alcohol* 34:144–56.

Gove, W. R., and R. D. Crutchfield, 1982. The family and juvenile delinquency. *Sociol. Q.* 23:301–19.

Greenberg, S. W. 1981. Alcohol and crime: A methodological critique of the literature. In *Drinking and Crime.* Edited by J. J. Collins. New York: The Guilford Press.

Hartnagel, T. F., and J. J. Teevan, and J. J. McIntyre, 1975. Television violence and violent behavior. *Soc. Forces* 54:341–51.

Higgins, P. C., and G. L. Albrecht, 1977. Hellfire and delinquency revisited. *Soc. Forces* 55:952–58.

Hindelang, M. J. 1972. The relations of self-reported delinquency to scales of the CPI and MMPI. *J. Crim. Law & Criminol.* 63:75–81.

Hirschi, T. 1969. *Causes of Delinquency.* Berkeley: University of California Press.

Hirschi, T., and M. J. Hindelang, 1977. Intelligence and delinquency: A revisionist review. *Am. Sociol. Rev.* 42:571–87.

———, 1978. Reply to Ronald L. Simons. *Am. Sociol. Rev.* 43:610–13.

Hirschi, T., and R. Stark. 1969. Hellfire and delinquency. *Soc. Prob.* 17:202–13.

Holden. R. T. 1983. Rehabilitation sanctions for drunk driving: An experimental evaluation. *J. Crime & Delinq.* 20:55–72.

Holzman, H. R. 1979. Learning disabilities and juvenile delinquency: Biological and sociological theories. In *Biology and Crime*. Edited by C. R. Jeffrey, Beverly Hills: Sage Publications.

Hooton, E. A. 1939. *Crime and the Man*. Cambridge, Mass.: Harvard University Press.

Howitt, D. 1972. Television and aggression: A counter argument. *Am. Psychol.* 27:969–70.

Jacobson, F. N. 1974. Learning disabilities and juvenile delinquency: A demonstrated relationship. In *Handbook of Learning Disabilities*. Edited by R. E. Weber, Englewood Cliffs, N.J.: Prentice-Hall.

Jensen, G. F. 1972. Parents, peers, and delinquent action: A test of the differential association perspective. *Am. J. Sociol.* 78:562–75.

Jensen, G. F., and M. L. Erickson. 1978. Peer commitment and delinquent conduct. Manuscript.

Kaplan, R. M. 1972. On television as a cause of aggression. *Am. Psychol.* 27:968–69.

Kay, H. 1972. Weaknesses in the television-causes-aggression analysis by Eron et al. *Am. Psychol.* 27:970–73.

Kelly, H. E. 1979. Biology and crime. In *Biology and Crime*. Edited by C. R. Jeffrey. Beverly Hills: Sage Publications.

Lombroso, C. 1911. *Criminal Man*. New York: Putnam Publishing.

Mednick, S. A., V. Pollock. H. Volavka, et al. 1982. Biology and violence. In *Criminal Violence*. Edited by M. Wolfgang and N. Weiner. Beverly Hills: Sage Publications.

Megargee, E. I. 1982. Psychological determinants and correlates of criminal violence. In *Criminal Violence*. Edited by M. Wolfgang and N. Weiner. Beverly Hills: Sage Publications.

Murray, C. A. 1976. *The Link Between Learning Disabilities and Juvenile Delinquency*. Washington, D.C.: U.S. Government Printing Office.

Nye, F. I. 1958. *Family Relationships and Delinquent Behavior*. New York: John Wiley & Sons.

Pernanen, K. 1976. Alcohol and crimes of violence. In *The Biology of Alcoholism*. Vol. 4, *Social Aspects of Alcoholism*. Edited by B. Kissin and H. Begleiter. New York: Plenum Press.

———. 1981. Theoretical aspects of the relationship between alcohol use and crime. In *Drinking and Crime*. Edited by J. J. Collins. New York: The Guilford Press.

Poremba, C. D. 1975. Learning disabilities, youth and delinquency: Programs for intervention. In *Progress In Learning Disabilities*, Vol. 3. Edited by H. R. Myklebust. New York: Grune & Stratton.

Robinson, W.S. 1950. Ecological correlations and the behavior of individuals. *Am. Sociol. Rev.* 15:353–57.

Roizen, J., and D. Schnebeck. 1977. Alcohol and crime. In *Alcohol, Casualities, and Crime*. Edited by M. Aarens, T. Cameron, J. Roizen, R. Roizen, R. Room, D. Schnebeck, and D. Wingard. Berkeley: Social Research Group.

Roman, P. 1981. Situational factors in the relationship between alcohol and crime. In *Drinking and Crime*. Edited by J. J. Collins. New York: The Guilford Press.

Rosen, L. 1970. The "broken home" and male delinquency. In *Sociology of Crime and Delinquency*. 2nd. ed. Edited by M. E. Wolfgang, L. Savitz, and N. Johnson. New York: John Wiley & Sons.

Shah, S., and L. Roth. 1974. Biological and psychophysiological factors in criminality. In *Handbook and Criminology*. Edited by D. Glaser. Chicago: Rand McNally & Co.

Sheldon, W. H. 1942. *Varieties of Temperament*. New York: Harper & Row, Publishers.

Sheldon, W. H., E. M. Harth, and E. McDermott. 1949. *Varieties of Delinquent Youth*. New York: Harper & Row, Publishers.

Sheldon, W. H., S. S. Stevens, and W. B. Tucker. 1940. *Varieties of Human Physique*. New York: Harper & Row, Publishers.

Simons, R. L. 1978. The meaning of the IQ-delinquency relationship. *Am. Sociol. Rev.* 43:268–70.

Smith, M. D. 1980. A longitudinal analysis of social control theory. Ph.D. diss., Department of Sociology, Duke University.

Surgeon General's Scientific Advisory Committee on Television and Social Control. 1972a. *Television and Social Behavior: Volume 1—Media Content and Control*. Washington, D.C.: U.S. Government Printing Office.

———. 1972b. *Television and Social Behavior: Volume 3—Television and Adolescent Aggressiveness*. Washington, D.C.: U.S. Government Printing Office.

———. 1972c. *Television and Social Behavior: Volume 4—Television in Day-to-Day Life: Patterns of Use*. Washington, D.C.: U.S. Government Printing Office.

Toby, J. 1957. The differential impact of family disorganization. *Am. Sociol. Rev.* 22:505–12.

Vaughn, T. R. 1967. Governmental intervention in social research: Political and ethical dimensions in the Wichita jury recording. In *Ethics, Politics, and Social Research*. Edited by G. Sjoberg., Cambridge, Mass.: Schenkman Publishing Co.

Vold, G. 1958. *Theoretical Criminology*. New York: Oxford University Press.

Wacker, J. A. 1974. *The Reduction of Crime through the Prevention and Treatment of Learning Disabilities*. Report to the National Institute of Justice, Law Enforcement Assistance Administration.

Waldo, G. P., and S. Dinitz. 1967. Personality attributes of the criminal: An analysis of research studies, 1950–65. *J. Res. Crime & Delinq.* 4:185–201.

Watts, M. W. 1976. Television and socialization to violence: Policy implications of recent research. In *Civil Liberties*. Edited by S. L. Washby. Lexington, Mass.: D. C. Heath & Company.

SUGGESTED READINGS

C. R. Jeffrey has edited a collection of papers that provides one of the better assessments of potential links between biological and sociological theories of criminal behavior: *Biology and Crime* (Beverly Hills: Sage Publications, 1979). James J. Collins, Jr. offers a similarly effective anthology on the relation of drinking to crime: *Drinking and Crime* (New York: The Guilford Press, 1981). Traditional sociological attempts at causal theorizing are reviewed admirably by Hirschi and Selvin in *Delinquency Research: An Appraisal of Analytic Methods* (New York: Free Press, 1967). And for summaries of research trends in most types of causal analysis, see Sutherland and Cressey's *Criminology*, 10th ed. (Philadelphia: J. B. Lippincott Co., 1978).

9

FORMAL CAUSAL THEORIES

We continue in the present chapter our discussion of sociologists' attempts to explain criminal behavior. Unlike the previous chapter, however, Chapter 9 examines more formal causal theories. That is, rather than simply reviewing the evidence regarding a link between a given variable (the broken home, for example) and criminal behavior, we now explore more detailed theories that attempt to explain how certain structural and cultural characteristics of this society influence groups and individuals within them in a manner that increases their chances of criminal involvement. Five theoretical approaches to causal analysis are explored in Chapter 9: *structural-strain* theories, *cultural transmission* theories, *control* theories, the *labeling perspective,* and *Marxian* theories. Following this, some general critical comments are made concerning these approaches and directions for future analysis are suggested. The chapter closes with an examination of the link between causal analysis and anticrime policy.

STRUCTURAL-STRAIN THEORIES

Influenced primarily by Emile Durkheim's work at the turn of the century, many American sociologists came to view societies as social systems generally organized or structured to maximize their chances of continued existence. Thus, Durkheim's disciples have argued, societies develop structures (institutions such as religion, law, government, and family) to cope with system maintenance problems. The family, for example, is the major mechanism for population growth or control; religion serves to explain and allay fears about the unknown as well as to control individuals through moral codes. As social systems grow more complex, their institutions become more complex and distinct.

Societies that persist over time are assumed to possess high levels of consensus concerning social values and norms. That is, most members of persisting societies are thought to view the world in much the same fashion. To maintain this consensus, structural theorists argue, societies develop elaborate socialization patterns and supplement these with various informal and formal social control mechanisms (gossip and police, respectively, for example). All are aimed to control the self-interested side of the individual, to limit deviance and conflict within the society, and to direct individuals toward the playing of roles and the pursuit of goals that further the system's chances of persistence.

It comes as no surprise that the perfectly structured social system cannot be found. No society is so well structured that it is free of problems. That is, social institutions are imperfect. At times they fail to accomplish their designated tasks; religion, for example, may fail to obtain allegiance to traditional norms. At times, institutions may conflict with each other. For example, a consumption-oriented economic system will not be compatible with a religious system stressing thrift and moderation. Moreover, when a society is undergoing rapid social change, so that its institutions lag, break down, or conflict with other institutions, social problems such as racial strife, unemployment, and mental illness will likely arise. Thus, the sociologist who adheres to the above ideas (the *structuralist*) tries to understand social problems by examining social institutions for disruptions, conflicts, or weaknesses.

Traditionally, structuralists have looked to three institutions as the sources of criminal behavior: the family, religion, and the economic system. Crime, especially juvenile delinquency, has often been viewed as the result of a decline of both family and religion as strong mechanisms of social control. However, the best-known structuralist explanations of crime have emphasized the economic system as the key problematic institution. Changes in the economy, for example, have long been thought to be associated with homicide and suicide trends. Henry and Short (1954) suggest that suicide increases with economic depression and homicide rises during economic prosperity. They also believe that suicide is an upper-class phenomenon that will rise during depression times because the upper class then suffers more financial hardship, and that homicide is a lower-class phenomenon that is more likely to occur during economic good times when the lower class experiences intense frustration at standing still in prosperous times.

Merton's Structuralism

The structuralist formulation that inspired the majority of theory and research into the relation of the economic opportunity system and crime was that of Robert Merton (1938, 1957). Durkheim had argued that larger societies, given their sheer numbers of members and complexity of social institutions, encountered greater problems of social control—left members without the goals, values, and norms that tied them to the group. Merton modified and extended this theme. He posited that in our society criminal behavior is not simply a matter of casting people adrift without social control. Rather, he felt that this society, by virtue of a flawed economic system, placed individuals (particularly those of the lower classes) in a bind that could produce criminal behavior out of necessity. In Merton's view, therefore, crime is a normal response to *strain* placed upon the individual in a society with structural problems.

More specifically, Merton characterized our society as one whose culture strongly encourages all members of society to pursue relatively the same goal—material success—but the economic system does not provide equal access to the culturally prescribed means to attain success—sufficiently lucrative employment. In short, cultural values and structural opportunities are not in harmony. The greater the discrepancy between success goals and access to the means to attain them, Merton felt, the more problematic the life situation of, the greater the strain upon, those caught in the discrepancy.

Merton outlined a number of possible responses or adaptations to the means-ends discrepancy. The responses most relevant for a discussion of crime are innovation and retreatism. *Innovation* represents a creative response to the problem of blocked means to goal attainment. When legitimate means are not available, individuals will create or turn to illegitimate means. Organized crime is often viewed as an innovative avenue of socioeconomic mobility for newly arrived lower-class immigrant groups (Light, 1977). Merton argued that, overall, much of the lower-class high crime rates, especially for property crimes, represents illegitimate attempts to get ahead in a system that denies the lower classes legitimate avenues of success.

Retreatism involves a drop-out response to the means-ends discrepancy, with individuals rejecting both the goals and the means and searching for nonproblematic situations in drugs, alcohol, transiency, and the like. In addition to fostering drug violations, retreatism is also implicated in secondary offenses, such as robbery or theft, committed to support a drug habit.

Merton's notion of differential economic opportunity and responses to structural strain influenced a great deal of criminological theory and research during the 1950s and 1960s, especially regarding juvenile gang delinquency. Two works gained special attention: Cohen's *Delinquent Boys: The Culture of the Gang* (1955) and Cloward and Ohlin's *Delinquency and Opportunity* (1960). We review them briefly here.

Reaction Formation and Gang Delinquency

In 1955, Albert Cohen published *Delinquent Boys: The Culture of the Gang,* a highly provocative causal theory that attempted to tie together structural and cultural phenomena with individual motivations for delinquent acts. Cohen traces delinquency to status problems among lower-class youth. The status problems arise from the fact that the social institutions to which the youth are exposed (education, work, religion) emphasize middle-class values somewhat foreign to the lower-class youth. Middle-class values include deferment of gratification, ambition, responsibility, control of aggression, wholesome use of leisure time, and respect for property. Middle-class children have been well socialized into these values and are likely to succeed in institutions that emphasize them. Lower-class youth, on the other hand, are not well socialized into these values and will likely fail in institutional settings, such as school, that measure the youth's worth by such middle-class standards. The result is a low level of self-esteem for the lower-class child and withdrawal from the institutional setting.

Youths who fail and withdraw are drawn into each others' company. Together, they develop standards by which they can succeed and thereby raise their self-esteem. The resulting delinquent subculture represents what Cohen calls a "reaction formation." The lower-class juvenile develops a set of behaviors and values in direct opposition to middle-class values. Status and self-esteem are derived from violating middle-class rules. To buttress his stance, Cohen argues that the delinquency (even theft) of lower-class gangs is nonutilitarian—that is, done not for profit but for thrills or simply out of meanness. The lower-class gang is oriented toward immediate pleasure. Courage, shown through toughness and violence, is paid off in status in the eyes of peers. Delinquent youth have simply switched social systems, moving from one in which they were failures to one in which they are successes. The ultimate causes of delinquency, then, are structural failures of the system: the failure of the lower-class family to prepare the youth for success in institutional settings, and the failure of the institutional settings, primarily educational, to accommodate the lower-class youth.

Blocked Opportunity and Juvenile Delinquency

In 1960, Cloward and Ohlin presented a theory of lower-class gang delinquency primarily influenced by Merton's structuralist scheme. Like Merton, these authors begin with the premise that material-success goals are pervasive, though the legitimate means to attain them are not equally available to everyone. The response to the situation of blocked opportunity is governed by the amounts and types of illegitimate opportunities available to the potential delinquent. That is, it should not be assumed that the social structure provides equal access to illegitimate means of goal attainment any more than it does to legitimate means.

According to Cloward and Ohlin, there are three basic subcultural responses to blocked opportunity. The first is the *criminal subculture*. This response is primarily a neighborhood phenomenon, reflecting the presence of a stable, relatively organized adult crime pattern. Juveniles observe and are inducted into the neighborhood crime structure (mainly property crimes), learn the neighborhood criminal values, and work in apprenticeship fashion into the adult crime structure.

The second response pattern is the *conflict subculture*. This pattern arises in neighborhoods that have neither legitimate nor stable illegitimate opportunities for success. Because the community is devoid of the criminal subcultural values and structure, there is no apprenticeship in organized crime. The result is a more violent form of gang delinquency, perpetrated on members of the neighborhood as well as on strangers. Robberies, assaults, and gang fighting are the primary crimes in this subcultural setting.

The third form is the *retreatist* pattern. Juveniles who are blocked from or fail to capitalize on legitimate and illegitimate opportunities are prone to withdrawal from the community into drug usage. In essence, this response is the same as that postulated by Merton in his reference to retreatism—an abandonment of or withdrawal from both the goals and means of the society.

In sum, the major contributions of Cloward and Ohlin's blocked-opportunity theory are its emphasis on the failure of the economic system as the source of criminal behavior, its claim that illegitimate means to offset blocked opportunity are not open to all, and its notion that responses to blocked opportunity will reflect the structure and culture of the neighborhood.

Criticisms

Merton's work has been criticized for its assumption that this society displays goal, value, and normative consensus rather than the plurality of world views suggested by its class, racial, and ethnic differences. Some critics argue that the "consensus" about which Merton writes is anything but universal and is, rather, decidedly middle class. Beyond this, strain theory has been attacked for its apparent overemphasis on lower-class offenses, especially theft. Critics contend that his scheme fails to account for the offenses of those who are not denied access to the means of success attainment—for example, the bank president who embezzles. Merton has attempted to address this problem by suggesting that *most* people are *relatively* deprived—that is, blocked from attaining some desired end—and must adapt. Yet, this seems to make this theory too loose, too easily applied to any situation. Finally, the theory is not explicit concerning what governs the choice of adaptation to blocked means for those actually or relatively deprived. Why retreatism and

NEWSPRINT AND COMMENT

School Discipline: Problems More Likely with Poor Students, Educators Say

By Rhonda McKendall

A teen-ager pulls a gun on a classmate in the hallway at school. In a classroom nearby, a student is cursing her teacher, disrupting the entire math period.

Are these troubled children likely to come from poor families?

Most of those contacted in a random survey of New Orleans educators believe poor children are more likely to be discipline problems. A few, however, say blaming poverty for violence and (bad) behavior is unfair.

U.S. Education Secretary T.H. Bell last week said most discipline problems in America's schools are caused by children who grow up poor.

"There is a definite relationship between the economic status of children and their adjustment in school," said Daniel Thompson, a New Orleans sociologist who has been studying poverty among black families for 10 years.

"Our schools are the epitome of middle-class virtues and these children come from less than middle-class backgrounds," he said.

Thompson, director of research at Dillard University, said children who live in poverty are part of "the underclass." Generally, he said, these children go to school unprepared because they come from homes where the parents are illiterate and unemployed and have not taught them social skills.

These youngsters "become unhappy in school because they don't fit in with the culture," said Thompson. "So, they try to disrupt the culture and force their own patterns of behavior on the school."

"I see a definite relationship among poverty, education and crime," said Bobby Leonard, who works with New Orleans public school children who have been suspended from regular classes.

Ninety percent of children with behavior problems function below their grade levels in school, Leonard said. Most of these children come from poor neighborhoods, he said.

Statistics show that 80 percent of the people in jails and prisons come from low-income areas and 60 percent of those people have less than a sixth-grade education, Leonard said.

New Orleans has the sixth largest-jail population among U.S. cities, he said.

Twenty-two percent of Orleans' 84,300 public school children come from homes that receive Aid to Families of Dependent Children benefits and 60 percent qualify for free lunch.

Poverty should not be used as an excuse for not educating children from disadvantaged backgrounds, said Lee Gary of the Business Task Force on Education in New Orleans.

"Violence and student misbehavior are symptoms and we need to look for the causes," said Gary, a former teacher and college professor.

All children have learning potential and educational programs should be geared to that, he said.

"We can't say that because you're black and poor you're not going to succeed," he said.

Source: © Times-Picayune Publishing Corp., 1984. Reprinted by permission.

Comment: Economic Opportunity and Crime

During the 1960s we witnessed a great national effort to equalize economic opportunities. This effort was grounded in social-science theories linking deprivation to social problems. It failed in large measure, but the belief that poverty is the root of social ills lives on. It is not wholly unfounded. There *is* some connection between poverty and crime; the poor are overly represented among persons committing what this society calls "serious" personal and property crimes. However, the link is far from straightforward. The vast majority of poor persons are not criminal, and persons from more affluent backgrounds sometimes stray.

To the extent that poverty is responsible for crime, many theorists argue that criminal patterns among the poor begin in the school, wherein unprepared poor children cannot compete in what is essentially a middle-class institution. Some believe that it is in school that despair and frustration begin and that desperate and frustrated children find others like themselves. Others locate the source of crime and delinquency in a lack of parental control over children found among the poor.

The fact is that we are a long way from understanding the role poverty plays in crime and delinquency. By itself, poverty has little relation to crime. It is only in relation to other antecedent and intervening variables—as yet not well identified—that poverty becomes important in crime causation.

---

not innovation in certain cases? And what governs the movement from the initial criminal response to structural strain into the prolonged criminal career?

Although Cohen is credited with turning our attention to the possible role of the school in delinquency, his work is open to criticism (Bordua, 1961). For one thing, it focuses exclusively on subcultural or gang delinquency and is inapplicable to the offenses of individual delinquents. Further, it is limited to lower-class delinquency and so is unable to offer insight into the offenses of middle- and upper-class juveniles. In Cohen's defense, however, we must note that he has never claimed that his theory is directed to any other than lower-class gang delinquency; that is, he has not attempted to formulate a general theory of delinquency.

The more serious problem with Cohen's thesis lies with the reaction-formation concept. Miller (1958) argues that Cohen fails to recognize that lower-class values differ from those of other classes and that what Cohen sees as "reactive" gang values are, in reality, simply extensions of general lower-class values (see the following discussion on "Cultural Transmission Theories"). Beyond this, we find no evidence that lower-class delinquents directly reject middle-class values. In the final analysis, the reaction-formation concept is not able to be validated, since it refers to a social-psychological process about which, presumably, even the delinquent is unaware. We also cannot help but wonder why delinquents must gain status and self-esteem from negativistic acts. Why does their reaction to school failure not include an attempt to succeed through illegal *utilitarian* acts—that is, crimes committed for profit?

Cloward and Ohlin's theory may be criticized in much the same fashion as Cohen's was—that is, it is limited to lower-class gang delinquency and leaves us searching for answers concerning individual's offenses and those of middle- and upper-class youth (Bordua, 1961). However, like Cohen, Cloward and Ohlin were not attempting to construct a general theory of delinquency. Unlike Cohen, though, they picture lower-class gang delinquents as youths who have succeeded, not failed, in their preparation for life in the American economic system. The delinquency results not from limited preparation but from limited opportunities to which to apply it.

We must wonder, given current criticism of inner-city education, whether lower-class youth are indeed well prepared for conventional economic success. If they are not, perhaps "blocked opportunity" is not so much a cause of delinquency as an espoused justification for it. In sum, though Cloward and Ohlin have succeeded in focusing our attention on potential links between the lower-class opportunity structure and crime, they have left many important questions unanswered.

In sum, structural strain theory leaves us with a criminal who, at least initially, wished to succeed by legitimate means. Poor preparation in the use of these means or, simply, lack of availability of the means, has *forced* the individual into illegal activity. Some readers undoubtedly will have problems accepting this view of criminal motivation and, more importantly, research results do not square well with it (Hirschi, 1969; Kornhauser, 1978). On the one hand, research concerning strain theory indicates that lower-class youth do aspire to a better material life and that school failure seems associated with delinquency. On the other hand, research consistently fails to find lower-class youth having a sense of blocked opportunity or a reactive-malicious stance toward society. In short, while structural-strain theorists rightly have called attention to the potentially serious problems caused by differential economic opportunity, they apparently have not determined exactly what forms the problems may take, especially regarding crime and delinquency.

CULTURAL TRANSMISSION THEORIES

A second type of sociological theory of criminal behavior asserts that such behavior (indeed *all* behavior, criminal and noncriminal) is learned—that is, transmitted from one person to another, from a group to its individual members. Behavior is assumed to reflect values and beliefs that characterize groups and individuals and are learned primarily during the childhood socialization process. The central theme of cultural transmission theories is that larger societies are sufficiently heterogenous culturally and economically to produce *numbers* of groups whose values and beliefs (and therefore behaviors) differ. Sometimes the differences are not problematic (as with varying culinary practices, for example); other times the differences may be problematic (as with differing views of the morality of abortion, for instance). Some groups have greater power to determine which behaviors (and therefore values) are given legitimacy by the law. Once the issue has been legalized, some persons who act in accord with their values do so legally. Others acting in accord with their values do so illegally. Thus, criminality is the process of acting normally (that is, in accord with one's learned values) but, unfortunately, in a manner that conflicts with the learned values of a more powerful group.

Culture Conflict

Gabriel Tarde (1912) suggested in the late 1800s that many criminal ideas and techniques are learned through close contact with others. In the 1920s and 1930s, the notion of *cultural pluralism,* the idea that American society is composed of diverse subcultures, formed the basis of numerous theories of crime and other social problems. Ethnic subcultures introduced into this society during peak immigration periods were viewed as the transmitters of values that clashed with mainstream conventions. Thus, immigrants and their offspring, by learning and adhering to values stressed by their respective subcultures, often would find themselves at odds with American law.

This theme particularly characterizes the work of many socialists at the University of Chicago during the second and third decades of this century (see, for example, Shaw and McKay 1931). They conceived of large cities as ecologically zoned, possessing interdependent residential, commercial, industrial, transitional, and slum areas. The zones are dynamic—once wealthy, now poor; once rotting, now revitalized; and so forth. As such, the distribution of persons across these zones varies by social class and, as new immigrant groups arrive, by ethnic origin. In slower times, uniformity in beliefs and values characterizes these zones (neighborhoods). However, rapid social change (industrialization, immigration, and so forth) makes these zones less interdependent and less homogeneous. Values and behaviors begin to conflict.

The Chicago sociologists paid specific attention to rapidly developing slum communities, often composed of members of newly arrived ethnic groups. It was assumed that these communities developed values distinct from those of more affluent communities. Some values specifically encouraged criminal behavior while others (the majority) simply made it more likely.

The culture conflict theme reached its zenith in Walter Miller's theory (1958) of lower-class delinquent subcultural values as reflections of general lower-class values. Miller argues that there is a distinctive lower-class cultural system in this society that differs from middle- and upper-class cultures in its emphasis on imminent trouble (usually legal), toughness (masculinity, bravery), smartness (shrewdness, capitalizing on opportunities), excitement (pursuit of risk, danger, adventure), fate (favored or unfavored by fortune), and autonomy (independence). Miller claims that lower-class juvenile concern with peer-group status leads to behavior reflecting virtues implicit in the lower-class culture. Thus, lower-class boys pick fights to show toughness and steal to demonstrate shrewdness and daring. Often, simply living up to lower-class standards will place a juvenile in violation of the law; certainly, pursuit of these standards increases the likelihood of legal violations.

Techniques of Neutralization

Yet another variation of the cultural transmission thesis is Sykes and Matza's (1957) notion of techniques of neutralization. These authors suggest that American society is really not as culturally diverse as many observers believe. Instead, they argue that societal norms are more or less universally honored in spirit but that greater levels of violation exist for some groups than for others. Sykes and Matza feel that this is because some groups have developed "techniques of neutralization"—that is, rationalizations that allow an individual to violate a norm without denying its legitimacy (a concept discussed further in the next section, "Control Theories"). For example, a person may agree that theft is generally wrong yet feel that it is acceptable if the victim will never miss the loss (as in shoplifting from a large department store). Similarly, an individual may disavow attacks on others—unless the victim is not a "full-fledged" citizen (as in the case of youth gangs beating up homosexuals).

The rationalizations take many forms: denial of responsibility for an act, denial of injury to anyone, denial of an actual victim of an act, denial of the moral character of those who condemn the act, and appeal to higher loyalties. Sykes and Matza suspect that the use of techniques of neutralization is distributed unequally by age, sex, social class, ethnic affiliation, and so on. Also, they feel that these techniques are learned—passed on to individuals by family and peer groups. Whatever their source, the learning of such values would seem to increase the likelihood of criminal behavior.

Differential Association

While many theorists sought explanation of the development of structural and cultural influences on criminal behavior, others attempted more social-psychological explanations of the process by which values and behaviors are learned and enacted. E. H. Sutherland's work in this area has endured over time as *differential association* theory (Sutherland and Cressey, 1974:71–93). Basically, differential association theory suggests that we are all exposed to numerous definitions of acceptable and unacceptable behavior through exposure to many groups, subcultures, and persons that view the world differently. Some of the sources will favor law violations of certain types; others will not. A person who commits a criminal act is one who has received more positive definitions than negative definitions of that act. Thus, the key to understanding differential crime rates among groups is to understand their differing views about violating the law. And the key to understanding an individual's criminal acts is to understand the duration, frequency, and intensity of the associations by which he or she came to view the acts as acceptable.

Sutherland and Cressey (1974:75–76) offer a more systematic rendition of their theory:

1. Criminal behavior is learned.
2. Criminal behavior is learned in interaction with other persons in a process of communication.
3. The principal part of the learning of criminal behavior occurs within intimate personal groups.
4. When criminal behavior is learned, the learning includes (a) techniques of committing the crime, which are sometimes very complicated, sometimes very simple, and (b) the specific direction of motives, drives, rationalizations, and attitudes.
5. The specific direction of motives and drives is learned from definitions of the legal codes as favorable or unfavorable.
6. A person becomes delinquent because of an excess of definitions favorable to violation of law over definitions unfavorable to it.
7. Differential associations may vary in frequency, duration, priority, and intensity.
8. The process of learning criminal behavior by association with criminal and anticriminal patterns involves all of the mechanisms that are involved in any other learning.
9. While criminal behavior is an expression of general needs and values, it is not explained by them, since noncriminal behavior is an expression of the same needs and values.

This last statement suggests that it is not enough to argue that criminal behavior stems from general needs and values. For example, we all need and value money. But some attain it legally and some illegally. What are important are the values placed upon certain, specific types of behavior by which to obtain money. Some of us are given positive definitions of criminal behaviors and others negative definitions. This, Sutherland and Cressey argue, is the key to explanation of criminal activity.

Social Learning Theory

Burgess and Akers (1966) have criticized differential association theory for failing to state exactly how behaviors are learned, that is, the process by which positive and negative values come to be attached to behaviors by individuals. They offer in its place a social learning theory of criminal behavior. According to Akers (1977), learning is a matter of operant conditioning through which behavior is shaped by the stimuli that are consequences of the behavior. Conditioning may be direct or imitative. Behavior is strengthened by reward and avoidance of punishment and weakened by punishment or lack of reward. Behavior persists depending upon the combinations of re-ward and punishment attached to it. The learning process also involves the acquisition of evaluative definitions of types of behavior. The more individ-uals define a behavior as desirable (as opposed to undesirable), the more likely they are to engage in it. Overall, this process of conditioning and ac-quiring definitions of right and wrong occurs through the interaction of the individual with groups representing the major sources of positive and nega-tive behavioral and definitional reinforcement. In short, the greater the ex-posure to positive reinforcement for behaviors and definitions, and the greater the avoidance of negative reinforcement for the same behavior and definitions, the more likely the behavior will occur and continue.

Criticisms

Cultural transmission theory has not been spared the critic's pen. Research into the notion of cultural pluralism and culture conflict has failed to pro-duce evidence of class or ethnic basis of diverse views of right and wrong in this society (Hirschi, 1969; Kornhauser, 1978). That moral values differ from individual to individual seems probable (Sheley, 1980, 1983); that they differ in the manner suggested by cultural transmission theorists seems im-probable.

Differential association theory has been criticized as nearly, if not wholly, untestable: How is the researcher to trace the number and strength of various influences on an individual's beliefs? How also is the theory able to explain impulsive crimes (unless, of course, impulsiveness also is somehow learned)? Studies of some forms of crime have found an absence of positive reinforce-ment for the act in the criminal's social background and environment. Such is the case, Cressey found (1953:149–50), with embezzlers. Further, to say that all behavior is learned is similar to saying that all water is wet. Just as the more important questions concerning water are those that ask what gov-erns its chemical content, its temperature, and so on, so we must ask about learned behavior: What accounts for the particular positive definitions of law violation learned by the offender? In what situations do these definitions come into play? Finally, Sutherland and Cressey state that a person becomes criminal because of an excess of definitions favorable to law violations. Be-liefs do not *cause* behavior, strictly speaking. We must ask what causes an individual to act in accord with those beliefs.

Burgess and Akers' social learning theory has done much to counter some of the above criticisms. Initial entries into criminal behavior are accidental or are ordered by, encouraged by, or modeled after the behavior of others. En-try is encouraged by learned positive definitions of the behavior. Repetition of the behavior is a matter of the criminal's definition of the criminal act as intrinsically rewarding and without sufficient sanction to outweigh the re-ward after initial completion. Akers et al. (1979) consider this formulation of social learning theory particularly applicable to the explanation of marijuana and alcohol use and abuse by adolescents, though criticisms of their method of testing the theory raise some problems for it (Stafford and Ekland-Olsen, 1982; Strickland, 1982). The continuing problem faced by social learning theorists is demonstration of the sequence in which behavior, exposure to others' definitions of right and wrong, and positive and negative reinforcement occur (Hirschi and Gottfredson, 1980; Liska, 1978).

Whether or not ever empirically verified, differential association theory and social learning theory still leave us in a quandry. They may identify the mechanisms by which criminal behavior is learned, but they cannot account for the distribution of definitions and behaviors throughout society. In short, these social psychological theories ignore the major structural variables (economic opportunity, for example) that characterize society and are presumedly implicated in criminal activity.

However problematic they may be, cultural transmission theories can be credited with calling our attention to the fact that in a complex society we can expect some variation in world views. The typical city represents a large array of socioeconomic situations and cultural beliefs. It seems highly unlikely that the middle-class businessman and the ghetto dweller will view welfare fraud or shoplifting in exactly the same way. Although subcultural ideas that support crime and, perhaps, even teach crime techniques cannot be said to cause criminal behavior, they definitely make it more likely to occur.

CONTROL THEORIES

Control theorists differ from theorists discussed above in that they interest themselves, not in motivations to deviate, but in hindrances to the deviant act. Some control theorists simply dodge the issue of motivation. Others argue that motivation is universal—a constant—and therefore need not be studied as a predictor of criminal behavior. Still others claim that motivation is so situation-specific that we cannot possibly study it. More important, they argue, is the answer to the question: Why do we conform?

Control theorists hold in common, though with varying degrees of emphasis, the following assumptions:

1. People are more amoral than moral. Deviant tendencies are to be taken for granted; conformity must be explained.
2. Society and its members are engaged in a struggle that finds the former placing obstacles in the latter's path as they seek fulfillment of self-interests that may or may not be compatible with society's desires for them.
3. To the extent that social constraints on deviant behavior are removed

by or for individuals, they are free to pursue self-interests, free to violate society's norms.

Freedom and Constraint

Control theorists suggest that the elements that persuade the individual to conform or, by their absence, provide the freedom to deviate are: desired approval of loved ones, material rewards and possessions, threat of punishment, and level of self-esteem (Briar and Piliavin, 1965; Hirschi, 1969; Matza, 1964; Nye, 1958; Reckless, 1967; Reiss, 1951; Silberman, 1976; Toby, 1957; Wiatrowski et al., 1981). The notion of threat of punishment characterizes a well-known form of control theory: *deterrence theory.* The latter differs from the former in its almost exclusive focus upon the risk of formal punishment as a hindrance to crime. This theme particularly dominates discussions of the efficacy of capital punishment (Gibbs, 1975; Tittle and Logan, 1973; Zimring and Hawkins, 1973).

External Constraints

As suggested in Chapter 6, constraints on or hindrances to criminal behavior may take the form of anticipated losses of the liberty to do as we please, physical health and comfort, the respect of persons for whom we care, general social status, and certain material possessions. Briar and Piliavin (1965:39) suggest that in considering a criminal act, we are concerned about:

> . . . the material deprivations and punishments which might result from being discovered as an offender [and] . . . the deleterious consequences of such a discovery on one's attempts to maintain a consistent self image, to sustain valued relationships, and to preserve current and future statuses and activities.

Thus, the person with nothing to lose need not conform—even if there is nothing to be gained in deviating from conventional paths. Conversely, one who has much to lose likely will conform—even if much might be gained in deviating. To illustrate simply, all else equal, the minister stands to lose more, at least in terms of community respect, by visiting a prostitute than does the drifter passing through town.

Control theorists assume that few rule violations are carried out by individuals who do not perceive the odds against apprehension greatly in their favor. Commitment to the conventional world comes into play in decisions to deviate when it is realized that the calculating potential deviant possibly may miscalculate both the odds against apprehension and the gains and losses associated with the deviance (Becker, 1968:206). Few deviant acts are absolutely devoid of the possibility of discovery, and few people are unaware of this. Thus, the potential deviant asks: "Is the gain from this deviant act worth more than the loss I would incur if my calculation of the odds against apprehension is in error?" To the extent that an affirmative answer holds, the individual is free to deviate.

Control theorists suggest that relationships with other persons whose respect we value constrain us in considering criminal behavior; to the extent that parents will be disappointed in a youth's delinquent act, for example, that youth faces a hurdle in the path toward delinquency. Among youths whose parents would be disappointed in their delinquencies, constraint on delinquency takes the form of the extent to which they are supervised directly by their parents. At the adult level, the extent to which an individual is attached to family and friends and the degree to which these people are likely to learn of the individual's criminal behavior govern the likelihood that the individual will engage in that behavior.

In the same manner, control theorists argue that commitments to present or future goals and possessions also influence our behavioral choices. Indeed, the possibility that we weigh the potential goals of deviant behavior against the potential losses in terms of valued commodities, aspirations, and expectations is the central premise of deterrence theory. The deterrence theorist views individuals as rational in their decisions to pursue various behavioral paths. Before choosing to commit a deviant act, individuals are thought to weigh the degree to which investments in what they value may be jeopardized by the discovery of their rule violations.

Chief among the possessions we cherish seems to be freedom. This is the possession society threatens to withhold if we violate its more important laws. A high risk of physical punishment or deprivation of freedom seems to prevent most of us from violating serious laws. Beyond physical losses, many consider investments in future goals too important to risk through deviance. College students, for example, may see themselves as having devoted too much time and effort to their education and as having moved too close to a secure job future to risk these through criminal activity (Rogers, 1977). Persons already having entered the job world undoubtedly would fear losing what they have worked so hard to gain. They become fearful of job loss but also of the loss of property and community status already accrued through the job.

Internal Constraints

In addition to external constraints, some control theorists argue that individuals must contend with their own beliefs about right and wrong in order to deviate. In internalizing society's rules through socialization, persons come to grant moral validity to those rules. They *feel* it is wrong to commit a given criminal act and are constrained by that feeling. The key to the constraint is the self-esteem that individuals are said to draw from acting in accord with their perceptions of right and wrong (Reckless, 1967). Control theorists argue that both moral beliefs and self-esteem vary in this society and that these variations are linked to criminality. It is in this same sense that differential association theory may be considered a form of control theory. For differential association theory links moral beliefs (positive and negative definitions of behavior) to criminality. Rather than conceptualizing these beliefs as motivational, it can easily be argued that they provide freedom for (or place hurdles in the path to) deviation.

As noted earlier, there is little evidence that moral beliefs are distributed unevenly across classes, races, and sexes. Rossi et al. (1974) report that crime seriousness ratings are not influenced by these variables. Ball-Rokeach (1973) finds no evidence of subcultural support for violent behavior. Matza (1964) and Buffalo and Rogers (1971) report that institutionalized delinquents grant validity to conventional norms; and Short and Strodtbeck (1965) find lower-class gang and nongang boys and middle-class boys placing equally high importance on legitimate conventional values. Hirschi (1969) interprets findings like these to suggest that while we can conceive of a common, general belief system in this society, we also must conceive of differential individual socialization into that system. Some rare individuals grant absolutely no moral validity to many of society's rules and are, to that extent, perfectly free to violate those rules. The majority are less free; they are able to violate society's rules only under certain qualified conditions (for instance; "It is acceptable to steal food for your hungry children.").

Finally, it can be argued that persons with low self-esteem (for whatever reason) are free of internal constraint in that the object to which beliefs are anchored is absent. Beliefs only constrain individuals if they will "feel bad" about themselves if they violate those beliefs. Those who already "feel bad" about themselves have nothing to lose and are free to violate their beliefs.

Circumventing Constraints

External constraints are rendered relatively inoperative by the potential deviant's perception that he or she likely will not be discovered as a criminal. Secrecy, therefore, is the key to circumventing external constraints. But secrecy does not permit the circumvention of moral beliefs since we presumably cannot easily keep secrets from ourselves. Some control theorists assert that this moral bind is avoided through the process of *neutralization* whereby individuals extend or distort socially acceptable conditions for norm violation in order to deviate without forfeiting allegiance to the norm (Sykes and Matza, 1957; Matza, 1964:60–62). For example, persons engage in neutralization of a norm when they extend the ordinarily acceptable reasons for violating speeding laws (as in the case of an emergency trip to the hospital) to include such instances as being late for a social engagement, etc.

Chronologically, this form of "conscience gymnastics" apparently works in this fashion:

1. Individuals face moral dilemmas when they wish to commit acts they define generally as morally wrong.

2. In order to circumvent their moral dilemmas, the individuals neutralize the norms governing the contemplated deviant acts—rendering them inapplicable to the current situation.
3. Having neutralized the norms, the individuals commit the deviant acts without denying the legitimacy of the norms and without decreases in self-esteem.

In sum, it appears that some persons are free of constraints on deviant behavior by virtue of a lack of attachment to conventional persons, little commitment to conventional goals and possessions, low self-esteem, or the absence of conventional beliefs. Those who possess these constraints must find ways, such as secrecy and neutralization, to circumvent them. To the extent that they can do this, they are free to deviate.

Criticisms

The most basic criticism of control theory pertains to its focus on rationality in the commission of crimes. Though calculation of potential gains and losses probably characterizes most criminal acts, control theory nonetheless offers no explanation of the impulsive crime, the crime of passion. Beyond this, control theorists must address the issue of motivation more directly in their theories. As Cohen and Short (1958) suggest, criminal behavior does not occur "every time the lid is off." That is, freedom to deviate does not cause deviance to occur. Something motivates an individual to take advantage of that freedom. Gibbs (1975) seems to recognize this point in a critique of deterrence research when he notes that studies of the impact of threat of punishment on varying populations' (states' and cities') crime rates too often fail to account for differential generative factors, such as unemployment rate differences, which might influence those rates. Further, there is no reason to assume equally distributed motivation in a population when we examine specific types of offense behavior, such as armed robbery.

These problems aside, it is clear that control theory has fared better than have strain and cultural transmission theories when subjected to empirical testing (Hirschi, 1969; Kornhauser, 1978). Persons who are free of the various external and internal constraints display higher levels of involvement in criminal activity. And much deterrence research at the aggregate level suggests that certainty of formal punishment for offense behavior inhibits crime rates. Still, control theorists have yet to determine what types of conventional ties best inhibit criminality, and they have only begun to address the problem of interaction of ties to both conventional and unconventional persons (Linden and Hackler, 1973).

Finally, control theorists must reexamine the neutralization concept, now a "given" in most control theories. The concept never has been empirically grounded and likely will not be, since it refers to psychological processes which cannot be studied directly. Beyond this, however, users of the concept seem to be unclear about its chronological place in the process of the commission of a crime. Does it occur before, during or after commission? As suggested above, the original formulation of the concept points to neutralization as a process occurring between contemplation and commission of a crime (Sykes and Matza, 1957). Not all applications of the concept seem to view it in this manner.

Some argue also that neutralization is a necessary condition for the commission of most types of crime. Critics contend that this assumption suggests little variation in the population concerning right and wrong though existing evidence indicates that variation exists (Austin, 1977; Sheley, 1980). If variation exists and is linked to criminal behavior, why is neutralization necessary? People who grant no moral validity to a norm do not have to neutralize the norm in order to deviate. They already possess the freedom to violate the norm.

In sum, control theory has displayed the greatest promise of major theoretical attempts at causal explanation. Aside from the motivation issue, the problems raised above reflect the need for specification of control theory, which can only improve its explanatory ability. The motivation problem, in the final analysis, may be addressed best through integration of control theory with other types of theory (Elliott et al., 1979; Hirschi, 1979; Sheley, 1983).

THE LABELING PERSPECTIVE

In the mid-1960s, the interests of some students of crime and deviance began to shift. Frustrated with the inability of causal analysis to produce significant answers to traditional criminological questions, their concern with these questions began to fade. The discovery, through self-reported deviance studies, that most people violate the law but few are treated as criminals suggested a new line of inquiry. Rather than ask why people commit crimes, some criminologists began to ask why and how people come to be called "criminals." This approach developed into the *labeling perspective,* the study of the process by which an individual is defined as criminal by society and the effects of the definition on the individual's self-concept and behavior (Becker, 1963; Lemert, 1951).

It is important to note that the labeling perspective is not, strictly speaking, causal, though, as we shall see, it has some causal elements. Though the perspective has never fostered a systematic set of theoretical propositions, it does rest on some identifiable assumptions:

1. Before individuals can be labeled criminal, their behavior must be observed or thought to be observed by society.

2. Societal observation must be followed by societal reaction. Individuals cannot be labeled criminal unless society reacts to their alleged offenses—that is, an act is void of social meaning until society attempts to give it a meaning.
3. Society's attempt to label people criminal may succeed or fail. The attempt alone will not guarantee the successful imposition of a label.
4. The outcome of the negotiation of a label between society and individuals involves more than qualities of alleged criminal acts. Characteristics (such as race, sex, economic situation) of the alleged offenders and the social and political climate in which the negotiation occurs will also influence the outcome.
5. The eventful effects of labels for individuals are also negotiable, dependent on individuals' reactions to their labels, society's perception of those reactions, and society's willingness to negotiate.

The Process of Being Labeled Deviant

Figure 9–1 depicts the steps leading to the imposition of a deviant label on an individual. The process begins with the perception by society (or community or group) that an individual appears to have violated a societal norm. The violation—whether real or assumed—is referred to by labeling theorists as *primary deviation*. It is the stimulus that begins the labeling process. It

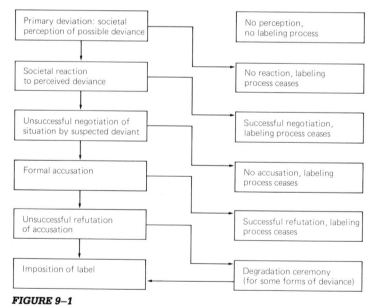

FIGURE 9–1
Stages in the Labeling Process

provides something to which society can react. Norm violations that are not observed by society are meaningless in terms of the eventual creation of a population of labeled deviants. Labeling theorists are not interested in the causes of primary deviation. They are concerned instead with what prompts societal reaction to it and the results that follow the reaction.

Perception or observation of primary deviation does not automatically lead to the imposition of a label. The average member of society often observes possible norm violations—some very serious—and does nothing by way of initiating a societal reaction. The decision to react, in the sense that the member of society makes verbal or nonverbal inquiries about the perceived deviance, highlights the fact that the deviant label is negotiable. For in making the decision to move toward reaction, the member of society takes into account various aspects of the situation and potential deviant. The potential deviant can influence the outcome of the decision-making process through his or her basic presentation of self. That is, age, sex, race, apparent socioeconomic status, dress, demeanor—all are factors with which the potential deviant influences the potential reactor. The potential reactor's biography and general attitudes about deviants, as well as the immediate environment in which the encounter occurs, will also influence the outcome (Steffensmeier and Terry, 1973).

The negotiation process may continue to another level of interaction and negotiation. The decision to react—either personally or by referral to the rest of the society—does not ensure the imposition of a label. Rather, it demands an account from the potential deviant. The potential deviant may stand mute or provide an explanation of the situation. Either posture represents a response to the observers' demand for an account. The posture, together with social-environmental facts and various characteristics of the potential deviant, will determine whether or not the labeling process stops or continues.

Not all accounts are sufficient to persuade the observer not to further the labeling process. Some accounts are socially more acceptable than others. That is, most acceptable accounts are merely extensions of societal beliefs that make certain forms of deviance acceptable, if not right (Mills, 1940; Matza, 1964). Delinquents may find a partially sympathetic ear, for example, when they account for beating a person by noting that the victim was some form of "second-class citizen," such as a homosexual (Hartung, 1965). Scott and Lyman (1968) argue that an account will be deemed illegitimate when the event it seeks to explain is more serious than the account allows. For example, a contractor can excuse a slight plumbing malfunction in a new house by pleading oversight. However, oversight is not a legitimate excuse for installing an entirely defective plumbing system in the house. Accounts are labeled unreasonable, Scott and Lyman further argue, when they exceed social expectations of normal behavior. To argue that one has shoplifted food because he or she is starving is to offer a far more reasonable account than if one claims he or she is driven by "inner voices." In sum, the labeling process will cease or continue depending on the social acceptability of the potential deviant's response to an observer's inquiries.

If the potential deviant is unsuccessful in accounting for his or her actions, the observer will generally bring the matter to the attention of the rest of the community or society. Again, negotiation occurs, centering on the seriousness of the alleged deviance of the potential deviant and the acceptability of his or her account. If the potential deviant again fails in negotiation, he or she is subjected to the imposition of a deviant label—that is, the person is no longer considered a potential deviant but is, in fact, considered a deviant.

Depending on the form of deviance in question, the social-political climate in which the labeling occurs, and various characteristics of the deviant, a status degradation process may also occur (Garfinkel, 1956). That is, the label of deviant may be extended beyond reference to the fact that the labeled individual violated a norm and, instead, convey the meaning that the individual is *inherently* deviant. In fact, the society may engage in building a deviant biography for the individual, that is, try to make sense of the individual's present deviant act by reinterpreting past events. Thus, the surprising discovery that a friend thought heterosexual is, instead, homosexual will be followed by attempts to go back and review past interactions with the person for missed clues as to his or her sexual deviance (Kitsuse, 1962). Hence, we hear statements such as, "Now that I think about it, he always was kind of weird." Or, "She was always kind of quiet, kept to herself; I just never thought about it much until now." Or, "Thinking back, he never did talk much about girls."

The Effects of Labeling

Whether totally or partially labeled, the stigmatized individual is now interacted with in terms of that label. The label is, in the words of Everett Hughes (1945), the individual's "master status," the primary attribute by which society identifies and refers to the deviant. For the nondeviant, the master status is based on such characteristics as age, sex, race, and occupation. For the deviant, the master status is based on the fact that the individual is or was deviant. Thus, we hear persons referred to as ex-convicts, mental patients, former alcoholics, and drug users, with only secondary reference to their other qualities.

Figure 9–2 depicts various consequences of a label for an individual. The figure also points out that the effects of a label are not predetermined but, like the label itself, emerge from an interaction with nondeviants and, sometimes, with other deviants. Although students of deviance have up to this point not studied and identified the various combinations of variables in the interaction process, so that we can predict the effects of labeling, we do know that the variables include the seriousness of the deviance that led to the label, socioeconomic-status characteristics of the deviant, the social-political cli-

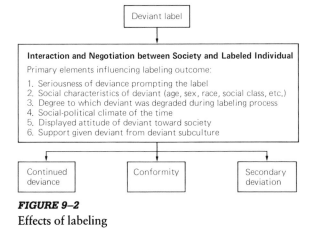

FIGURE 9–2
Effects of labeling

mate of the time, the posture adopted by the deviant regarding the label, and the extent of positive reinforcement from a deviant subculture.

The seriousness of deviance and the socioeconomic status characteristics of the deviants—what they did and who they are—are fairly obvious determinants of the effects of labeling. Whether or not people were fully degraded as deviant will affect the extent of society's willingness to interact with them and perhaps "give them another chance." The social-political climate with regard to deviance is also important; for example, the consequences of being labeled a sex offender will vary depending on whether or not society is currently upset about this form of deviance. The posture of deviants with respect to their labels is also of consequence; for example, we can expect society to react somewhat differently to the deviant who is repentant than to one who is defiant. In addition, the acceptability of any accounts deviants may offer are important. Finally, the effects of a label will be influenced by the extent to which the deviant is able to find support from others. Occasionally a deviant subculture (discussed further below) will act as a buffer for a labeled individual and thus remove some of the sting of societal rejection.

The variables above determine the consequences of being labeled. Again, as with the imposition of the label in the first place, the consequences of a label are determined by a two-party negotiation between society and the deviant. As Figure 9–2 indicates, there are three possible consequences of labeling: *conformity, continued deviance,* and *secondary deviance.* The latter two can occur simultaneously.

Conformity or Deviance

Labeling can have positive effects in terms of converting deviants to conforming behavior. This is often the consequence of a family's imposition of ᵗhe label of alcoholic or mentally ill on one of its members (Jackson, 1954). The label of alcoholic imposed by the family may force the individual to accept the fact that he or she is deviant and to attempt to conform. Sometimes the seriousness of the deviance that occasioned the label causes a form of societal reaction that makes conformity the only possible outcome. Ostracism or imprisonment, for instance, means that an individual will no longer violate social norms.

Labeling can also have minimal effects on the deviant's behavior. If the seriousness of the deviance is minor, or if the deviant refuses to accept society's label, it is possible he or she will simply continue the form of deviance that occasioned the label. Professional thieves, for example, are known to do their time in prison and return to theft immediately upon release (Letkemann, 1973). Or an alcoholic may accept society's definition of him or her as deviant and make no effort to reform, or may refuse to accept the label and continue drinking.

Secondary Deviance

The possible consequence of labeling that has gained the most attention is *secondary deviation*. According to Lemert (1951:76): "When a person begins to employ his deviant behavior or a role based upon it as a means of defense, attack, or adjustment to the overt and covert problems created by [his label], his deviation is secondary." Lemert thus argues that the label of deviant may force an individual into forms of deviance that would not have occurred had it not been for the labeling or into greater commitment to the deviance that occasioned the label than would otherwise have occurred.

The often-told story of the problems of ex-convicts relates a classic example of secondary deviation. Having paid their debt to society and returned to the outside world, former prisoners soon discover that the label "ex-con" has many negative consequences. Unable to obtain work or legitimately secure money, they soon commit new crimes or drift into the company of other criminals and subsequently increase their own commitment to crime (see Irwin, 1970).

Labeling theorists suggest that the deviant subculture may be important in explaining entrance into both primary and secondary deviance. First, an individual's drift into or decision to enter such a subculture may mark the primary deviation to which society reacts. Second, involvement in subcultural deviance may also cushion the society's reaction, thereby influencing the eventual outcome of the labeling process. Finally, and most important with respect to secondary deviation, labeling may place limits on an individual's social options resulting either in isolation or drift into a deviant subculture. The deviant subculture may provide support for the labeled deviant. It also may induce the person into further commitment to the deviance. In this sense, labeling may cause secondary deviation—a greater involvement in and commitment to deviance than would be expected were it not for the label.

Causation?

It was noted earlier than the labeling perspective does not represent causal theory. Yet, the strong emphasis of labeling theorists upon the notion of secondary deviation has earned them criticism as if they were attempting causal explanation. In other words, some have criticized labeling theory for apparently claiming that labeling *necessarily* causes secondary deviation (Schur, 1971:7–36). The picture of deviants thus brought to mind is that of individuals passively going about their own business until seized by society, labeled deviant, and forced into a deviant lifestyle. One need only review self-reported criminality studies to realize that much deviance occurs without societal reaction (Mankoff, 1971). The concept of "primary deviation" also suggests that not all rule violation is secondary. Thus, labeling theorists fail to account for crime's causes.

Still, however much labeling theorists brought these attacks upon their work through imprudent emphasis upon secondary deviation, the fact remains that the attacks are not accurately placed. A thorough reading of the labeling literature makes clear that labeling theorists did not intend their analysis as causal, at least in the traditional sense. Not all deviance is caused by labeling. Secondary deviation is but *one possible* outcome of labeling. Whether or not it occurs depends on the interaction of the variables depicted in Figure 9–2.

Criticisms

If we accept the labeling theorists' assertion that theirs is not a causal perspective, there are few criticisms we can levy against that perspective in the context of the present chapter. Rather than speaking of criticism, we may speak of preference. Those interested in causal explanations of criminal behavior undoubtedly will prefer other theoretical approaches. The labeling perspective disavows interest in primary deviation. Given its open-ended view of the effects of labeling, the perspective defies empirical testing in terms of behavior causation. Labeled individuals may or may not engage in further deviance; thus, research results that find conformity and those that find deviance following labeling both can be used to support labeling perspective assertions.

Preferred or not, the labeling perspective is open to two specific criticisms. First, it has not fostered definitive research that demonstrates that the espoused outcome of labeling (whether or not criminal behavior) would not have occurred despite the label. Second, the labeling perspective has not pursued what could become a major contribution to causal analysis. Assuming that labeling can lead, in some cases, to criminal behavior, labeling theorists could better research exactly what types of cases are susceptible to causal influence and under what specific conditions such influence is likely.

MARXIAN THEORIES

In recent years, some criminologists have developed a renewed interest in the writings of Karl Marx and their implications for the study of crime (Greenberg, 1977; Quinney, 1980; Taylor et al., 1973). Called by some the "new criminologists" or "radical criminologists," the Marxian criminologists have devoted most of their energies to exploring the economic interests behind legislation and criminal justice activities (see Chapter 3). Few have focused on the issue of crime causality. Young (1975) points out that the lack of attention to causation left earlier Marxian criminologists unable to account for the increases in crime that occurred in the 1960s. Nor could they adequately account for corporate and governmental crime. In response, some writers began to call for causal analysis within the Marxian theoretical framework (Gordon, 1971; Spitzer, 1975; Taylor et al., 1973). Such analysis, according to Spitzer (1975:639), "should neither beg the explanation of deviant behavior and characteristics by depicting the deviant as a helpless victim of oppression, nor fail to realize that his identification as deviant, the dimensions of his threat, and the priorities of the control system are part of a broader social conflict."

Before reviewing the recent causal theory attempts of Marxian criminologists, a brief review of Marxian theory, drawn from Chapter 3, may prove helpful. The theory argues that capitalist society possesses an inherent tension between its two primary economic classes: the owners (those who own the wealth and industry) and workers (those who supply the labor for industry). To maintain and increase their wealth, the owners must exploit the workers; that is, get the workers to accept less in wages than the full market value of the products they manufacture. The lower the workers' wages, the greater the profit realized by the owners. Capitalist-system history, Marxian theorists assert, is the history of the attempts by owners to structure the world view of the workers so that they readily accept their unequal economic position. These attempts are made through owner control of the major social institutions that shape ideas—law, education, government, religion—and the use of the criminal justice system to suppress attempts to alter the owners' favored position.

The Marxian analysis of capitalism suggests that problems within that system will eventually cause its destruction. In order to keep workers dependent on the owners and willing to work for low wages, the capitalist system generates a labor surplus—that is, more workers than available jobs—so that workers compete with each other for jobs and do not unite against the owners. Further, to increase profits, owners constantly seek to mechanize industry and cut production costs and to create monopolies and reduce competition. The result is an ever-growing population of unemployed or poorly paid workers who face a rising cost of living. This, in turn, leads to workers' disenchantment and discontent with the economic system. When the workers begin to examine the roots of their situation and understand how the system operates, they have begun to gain a class consciousness, Marxian theorists argue, an awareness of the fact that their interests as a unified group are opposed to those of the owners.

Against this backdrop, some Marxian theorists have attempted to specify the structural conditions that lead to crime (Colvin and Pauly, 1983). Spitzer (1975) argues that the capitalist mode of production contains contradictions that make capitalism dynamic—that is, constantly modifying its basic character and its influence on social and political relations within the capitalist society. Capitalism operates with a *relative surplus-population* (people who are not needed in the production sector). These people nonetheless are invaluable as a pool of potential laborers, in that current workers' wages can be kept low through the threat of replacement by members of the surplus pool. The contradiction in capitalism, however, is represented in the problems the relative surplus-population creates for the society. This population requires control, and control is accomplished primarily through religious, educational, charitable, and welfare institutions. To the extent that the population is not controlled, it threatens the social relations of production. For example, members of the relative surplus-population create disorder through criminal behavior. Revenues and energies must be diverted from capital investment to address the problems created by the problem population.

In some instances, the mechanisms designed to control problem populations cause further problems. The welfare system serves as an example in that it creates a population expensive to care for and does so in a fashion that negates its value as a threat to keep skilled workers from demanding higher wages. Spitzer suggests, as well, that mass compulsory education in the U.S. produces large numbers of trained workers and at the same time occupies the time of persons destined for problem populations. But education also raises the material aspirations of youth beyond the ability of the system to satisfy them. Further, it creates in many students a critical perspective regarding the socioeconomic system of which they are a part. In other words, it may foster frustration and dissent (see Greenberg, 1977).

According to Marxian theorists, members of problem populations regularly engage in behaviors that could be labeled criminal. Crime rates (levels of crime recognized by the state) vary according to the extent to which such behaviors are viewed as threatening to the economic order, the problem populations appear organized, other control systems (the church, for example) fail to address the problem, or the problem populations are useful (as evidence of the need for a strong state, for example) (Spitzer, 1975:644–45).

It is clear from the above discussion that Marxian criminologists are employing the notion of causality loosely. Better said, they seem to be referring to the structural origins of labels given to problem populations (Greenberg, 1981:59). But they do not attempt explicitly to account for the behaviors of the members of problem populations. Why crimes and not other behaviors? What governs entrance into crime?

We may infer from our examination of Marxian criminology several possible "causal hypotheses" to account for criminal behavior among the relative surplus-population:

1. Members of the relative surplus-population "bounce about" randomly from one form of behavior to another so that the commission of crime is spontaneous, unplanned, and relatively accidental.
2. Crimes by members of the relative surplus-population represent attempts to improve their economic situations or acts of frustration in response to thwarted economic aspirations.
3. The frequency of the predatory and frustrated acts referred to above is a direct function of the extent to which members of the relative surplus-population perceive themselves at risk of punishment for these acts (that is, crime is a "natural" and constant tendency of the problem population and occurs to the extent this population is free of social control).

The last two of these hypotheses reflect structural strain and control theory formulations respectively.

Quinney (1980:38–71) extends Marxian causal analysis beyond the explanation of criminal behavior by the relative surplus-population and includes in his theory of crime in capitalist societies the (implied) explanation of crimes by the ruling classes and by workers. Some crimes, he argues, are crimes of *domination* and *repression*. These are offenses committed by the owners and the state as they attempt to maintain the economic status quo (crimes such as corporate price-fixing and state use of illegal wiretaps to monitor political radicals). Some crimes are crimes of *accommodation*, offenses committed by the workers and the poor as they seek to deal with the deprivations stemming from their class position. These crimes include predatory acts (stealing from others) and personal violence stemming from anger and frustration. Quinney feels that even when these crimes are committed against other workers, they represent unconscious rebellion against the capitalist system. Finally, Quinney writes of *crimes of resistance* committed by workers and the poor who have gained a class consciousness and seek to disrupt and bring down the system. These are "political" crimes—illegal strikes, civil disobedience, sabotage, and terrorism.

We may assume that crimes of accommodation are addressed by the second and third hypotheses above. To these hypotheses, we may add two more inferred from Quinney's work:

4. Crimes by members of the ruling classes represent responses to perceived threats to their economic interests.
5. Crimes by workers and the poor who have gained a class consciousness are a function of this group's perception that crime can accomplish intended political ends.

In the view of most Marxian criminologists, crime can only increase in the capitalist system as it plunges further toward its own destruction. Increasingly, owners must commit crimes of dominance and repression as they try to hold the line against a growing worker-class consciousness. Crimes of accommodation and adaptation will increase as the plight of workers and the poor worsens. And crimes of resistance will increase as more workers gain a class consciousness. Quinney (1980:67–68) writes:

> Variations in the nature and amount of crime occur in the course of developing capitalism. Each stage in the development of capitalism is characterized by a particular pattern of crime. . . . The contradictions and related crises of capitalist political economy are now a permanent feature of advanced capitalism. . . . The dialectic between oppression by the capitalist class and the daily struggle by the oppressed will continue—and at an increasing pace. . . . The *essential* meaning of crime in the development of capitalism is the need for a socialist society.

Criticisms

Though only limited research has been conducted to ground Marxian theory empirically, Marxian theorists are to be credited with providing a testable theory of the conditions that produce crime in the capitalist system. The size of the relative surplus-population, for example, can be documented historically as a function of the dynamics and the inherent contradictions of capitalism. Marxian researchers face methodological difficulties, however, in empirically demonstrating the responses of capitalists to the contradictions within their economic system. For much of their theory focuses upon capitalists' perceived threats and instrumental responses to those threats. Neither perceptions nor intentions are examined easily, though in theory they are open to examination.

More serious problems occur with regard to the causal explanations of criminal behavior inferred from Marxian writings. That is, how well do Marxian theorists address the issue of individual behavioral responses to their life situations? In terms of crimes of accommodation, Quinney and others are faced with much the same problems as are encountered by strain theorists. Empirical research fails to demonstrate that lower-class persons who commit predatory property crimes are more aware of "blocked opportunity" than are other segments of the population. To the extent that Marxian and strain theorists attribute lower-class assaultive crimes to frustration with the economic situation or any crimes to "unconscious rebellion," they move beyond their means to test their theory.

Thus, at the individual-behavioral level, Marxian theories lack content. They are not specific about the manner in which offenders view the world and the reasons for their choice of criminal behavior from among potential responses to their situations. In terms of crimes of resistance, how explicitly do workers come to gain a class consciousness, and how do they interpret their own crimes? Why do they choose crime as their resistant response? Are those who have gained a class consciousness capable of crimes that are not resistant?

Marxian theorists have not dealt adequately with the vast stratification in this society and the types of crime ties to it. How, for instance, do they account for shoplifting by the economically comfortable middle-class person or embezzlement by the bank vice-president? While Quinney, for example, writes of crimes of domination and repression by the ruling classes, he does not address the possibility of other forms of crime by these people. Are other types of crime, both instrumental and assaultive, possible? If so, what is their cause? We cannot simply argue that they reflect the inherent wickedness of capitalists. Marxian theories have left no room for noneconomic behavior among capitalists and, thus, leave us with weak references to capitalists' behaviors as a sign of their evil natures.

Whether or not Marxian criminologists are correct in their theory of crime causation and their predictions of increasing crime, they must be credited with stimulating criminological theory and more rigorous investigation of the relationship between crime and our political and economic system.

SOCIOLOGICAL CRIME THEORIES APPRAISED

In this and in the previous chapter, we have discussed possible sources of criminal behavior. We have reviewed—and dismissed as sound explanations, at least standing alone—biological and psychological theories of criminality. But what of the sociological approach, with its emphasis on social structure, learned behavior, and social control? Does it fare any better? Yes, in many ways.

Sociological theories have turned our attention away from the traditional view that criminal behavior is abnormal and have suggested instead that it may be *quite* normal. Blocked opportunity theories basically ask: What are we to expect from people who are given a goal and then denied the opportunity to pursue it? In this light, criminal attempts to reach the goal seem a normal response to a problematic situation. Marxian theories view criminal behavior as a normal and unavoidable response to oppression. Cultural transmission theories similarly ask: What is abnormal about basing our behavior on beliefs that we have been taught? The normal response to a set of internalized beliefs favoring norm violation is—norm violation. Control theories depict norm violation as the expected outcome of the pursuit of self-interests to the extent that we are free of the burden of society's interests. Finally, the labeling perspective makes criminal behavior an understandable, even if not the only, response to being labeled deviant.

In short, sociological theories are to be credited with turning our attention away from the individual as a "bad apple" and focusing it on such important social facts as economic deprivation and cultural variation. Whether or not strictly causal, these factors undoubtedly are implicated in crime.

However, despite their saving virtues, sociological theories of crime causation hold only a slight edge over other approaches. Most sociological theories have overstressed the notion of subculture and have given too much attention to juvenile delinquency, especially gang delinquency. Moreover, as we noted in Chapter 6, the theories have concentrated almost totally on male criminal behavior. In addition, they have tended to focus on lower-class crime, generally ignoring the offenses of other classes. We currently have no systematic causal theory of adult criminal behavior, whether male or female, lower or upper class.

PRESCRIPTION FOR FUTURE CAUSAL THEORY

What will improve causal theory? One of the major problems that theorists face deals not with explanatory variables but the variable to be explained: criminal behavior. In Chapter 5, we raised the issue of distinguishing various types of homicides rather than speaking of homicide in general. We can ask as well whether robbery should be treated as a personal or a property crime. Is mail order fraud the same type of crime as shoplifting? Implicit in such questions is the understanding that, though these behaviors are all of the same legal species (i.e., violations of legal statutes), they may not be related as social actions. Thus, should we direct our theories to "crime" or to "types of crime"?

Some criminologists have tried to address this problem by constructing crime typologies. These vary in their focus. Roebuck (1967), for example, developed a scheme centered on race and number of arrests and used it to identify thirteen offender types (e.g., black armed robbers). Gibbons (1968) created twenty-four types based on role career, encompassing such elements as the offender's attitude toward society (e.g., the adult, naive check forger). Clinard and Quinney (1973) constructed nine types of offense behavior "systems" based upon legal aspects of the offense-type, the career of the offender, group support of the criminal behavior, overlap of the offense-type with legal behavior, and societal and legal reaction to the offense-type. The nine "criminal behavior systems" included: (1) violent personal criminal behavior, (2) occasional property criminal behavior, (3) public order criminal behavior, (4) conventional criminal behavior, (5) political criminal behavior, (6) occupational criminal behavior, (7) corporate criminal behavior, (8) organized criminal behavior, and (9) professional criminal behavior.

It is clear from viewing Clinard and Quinney's criminal types that their typology is not easily utilized. Classification of crimes from classifier to classifier could be expected to differ. Indeed, crime typologies have not fared well when put to the test. They are not easily validated. Categories are too few or too many. There is too much within-category variation and across-category overlap. For this reason, causal theorists continue to develop their theories with only the slightest regard for typing crimes, at best distinguishing between property and violent Index offenses. However, until the problem of specifying the variable that theorists seek to explain is addressed more directly, causal theories will progress little beyond their current state of development.

Yet, as the majority of this chapter has indicated, it is not simply the dependent variable that creates problems for causal theorists; conceptualizing the independent (causal) variables remains equally problematic. What should be the critical elements in an explanatory theory? A careful review of the work of theorists attempting to describe the elements of the criminal act (Becker, 1963; Lesieur, 1977; Lofland, 1969; Matza, 1964, 1969; Reckless, 1967; Sutherland and Cressey, 1974) indicates that each mentions at least two and sometimes three of the following four elements as crucial to criminal behavior: motivation (the push toward criminal behavior which translates into the will to deviate), freedom from social constraints (freedom from concern regarding material and emotional losses and self-deprecation as a result of criminal behavior), skill (technical ability to commit a crime), and opportunity (the chance to act upon the other elements). These same four variables were introduced earlier in Chapter 6 of this book as necessary to an understanding of differences in criminal involvement among various gender, age, social class, and racial groups.

Despite occasional reference to three of the above variables in the work of some theorists, most causal theory centers on only two variables: motivation and freedom from social constraints. We have reviewed most of these theories in this chapter. Most focus on either one *or* the other variable. In so doing, they assume that the element not given attention is a constant. Yet, neither should be equally distributed among us. We vary in the pressures that motivate us to deviate and in the constraints that inhibit deviance. To ignore this is to insure that our theories will fall short in explaining criminal behavior.

Beyond the inclusion of both motivation and freedom variables in causal theories, two other elements must be present to produce the "complete" causal theory. One of these is *skill*. Though a number of studies stress the importance of skill in professional criminal behavior (Bryan, 1965; Conklin, 1972; Klockars, 1974; Letkemann, 1973; Polsky, 1967), little thought is given to skill in other forms of crime. Skill is the ability to put thoughts and acts together in a manner conducive to attaining the goal of commission of a particular criminal act. Though it is ignored in most studies of law violation, Becker (1963) indicates fully its importance in becoming a marijuana user when he notes that continued use of the drug depends upon mastery of the smoking and perceptual techniques associated with it (see also Lesieur, 1977; Lofland, 1969). Common sense alone suggests similar import for skill in even more mundane deviance. We often refer, for example, to "skillful liars," "accomplished drinkers," "bullshit artists," and "champion womanizers." In short, there is little that people do that does not require some skill and much that people do that requires considerable skill. Taking this variable for granted as a constant in studies of criminal behavior would seem to insure a degree of failure in our attempts to explain criminal behavior.

Like skill, *opportunity* too often is ignored in most studies of criminal behavior. Only in the strain theory of Cloward and Ohlin (1960), wherein blocked access to legitimate means to culturally encouraged goals provides the motivation toward delinquency and open access to illegitimate means to these goals provides the opportunity for delinquency, have we seen the latter variable integrated with and assigned importance equal to that of the former. Even here, there are problems in distinguishing opportunity from skill and freedom from social constraints.

While a few earlier studies gave attention to criminal opportunity (Boggs, 1965; Gould, 1969), only recently, in studies of property crime rates, has opportunity (presence of susceptible victims or easily movable objects of theft) been given major attention as an explanatory variable (Cohen et al., 1979, 1980, 1981; Sparks, 1980). In this context, opportunity is defined as the presence of a physical environment conducive to the commission of a particular offense. In its simplest use, this means, for example, that bank robberies cannot occur unless there are banks, and people cannot be mugged if they remain indoors. This notion lies behind campaigns to discourage rapists through better street lighting, attempts to prevent crime through incapacitation of criminals, and analyses of victimization survey data in terms of the physical setting in which crimes occur (Dunn, 1976). Opportunity is not equally distributed for most forms of crime. This fact cannot be ignored in causal theories of crime.

In sum, it is argued that at some point in the future, theories that seek to explain a given type of criminal behavior (for example, purchase of stolen goods) must account for the coincidence of four variables: motivation, freedom from social constraints, skill, and opportunity (Sheley, 1983). The manner in which these pieces of the causal puzzle fit together undoubtedly varies by crime type and perhaps by group or individual. Some may possess motivation before freedom; others opportunity before motivation; and so forth.

All may occur at once. But, in the final analysis, all must be present. It will be some time before the "complete" model of criminal behavior is accomplished. Until that time, we must content ourselves with partial models. And, until that time, the impact of sociological theories on anticrime policy will be limited.

CAUSAL ANALYSIS AND ANTICRIME POLICY

A sound anticrime policy must lean on at least tacit assumptions about crime. Empey (1977:6–7) has noted:

> Any time a [juvenile-justice] program is set up, or any time one technique is chosen over another, someone has an idea in the back of his or her mind that it will make a difference—that it is somehow preferable to other programs and techniques. That person, in other words, does have a theory—however ill stated—as to what leads to delinquency and how it can best be dealt with.

Most certainly, different assumptions about the source of criminal behavior may lead to very different anticrime policies. Some theories target individuals for change; others focus on structural changes in society. Some direct attention toward treatment and rehabilitation of offenders; others emphasize preventing crime by eliminating the sources of crime. Still others encourage neither treatment of offenders nor elimination of crime sources but call instead for punishment of offenders to deter them from future crimes.

It is important to remember that anticrime policies rest on more than just knowledge about causes of crime. There are ethical and legal limits to consider. A plan to study from the time of birth all XYY chromosomal pattern babies born in a given city could be expected to be quashed because, though it might lead to invaluable knowledge, the project could also seriously influence, in a negative way, the children's lives by branding them as "different" or even as "potential criminals."

Policy issues are also political and economic issues. Legislators may base support for a policy program on its potential influence on voter behavior. None wishes to be "soft" on crime, and "overspending" on crime is also not popular with voters. Yet, policy implementation costs money; some programs call for billions of dollars and receive only millions. Relatively speaking, millions are too little and, if the program fails, it is difficult to determine if it was faulty or if it simply was not given a chance.

The American public seems to prefer theories of crime causation that stress the individual abnormality of criminals: If criminals are not born flawed, then they have been damaged by family or bad companions. Not only are such theories more "sensible" to most people, they are also somewhat easier to live with, for they do not implicate the *average citizen* in either the cause of or the cure for crime. Thus, anticrime policies constructed along this line of thought are less costly and can be attempted without disrupting the public: Basically what is required is the identification of the bad apples and their subsequent custody, whether to punish them or treat them. If treated, the treatment program may require some form of behavior modification—a few prisons, for instance, now conduct volunteer treatment programs for child molesters, which include the use of electric shocks to modify sexual desires. If the source of offenders' problems can be traced to something in their environment (a problem family, for example), then treatment may be extended there, too.

Today, sociological crime theories—especially those with a structural approach—are less popular with the public, for they implicate all of society in both the cause and cure of crime. Structural changes (such as redistribution of wealth and restructuring education) would be both costly and disruptive and the governmental programs based on such theories would likely encounter political turmoil. At the same time, structural changes are also most prone to failure, the result of a combination of problems with translating theory to policy, general public distrust of structural theories, and lack of financial support for their implementation. Thus, while sociological theories seem sounder than individual-abnormality theories, they are resisted more strenuously in the policy arena.

PROBLEMS WITH ATTEMPTED STRUCTURAL CHANGE: THE MFY EXAMPLE

The sociological structural approach to the solution of social problems reached its height during Lyndon Johnson's Great Society era of the 1960s. Poverty and blocked socioeconomic opportunities were viewed as being the causes of most problems. The strategy to combat these ills aimed not at changing individuals but at making large-scale changes in the opportunity structure of American society.

An important example of attempted structural change was the Mobilization For Youth (MFY) program, begun in New York City in the early 1960s (Helfgot, 1974; Mobilization For Youth, 1964). The program was based directly upon the structural-strain theory of Cloward and Ohlin (1960; see above), itself heavily influenced by Robert Merton's work. Alarmed by an increase in juvenile delinquency and convinced that lack of opportunity lay behind delinquency, several welfare, civic, and religious groups developed an action program and gained financial support from the city and federal governments and the Ford Foundation. Unlike traditional social-reform projects that sought to alter delinquents so that they responded more conventionally to their environment (however conducive to crime) or that were primarily charity-oriented, MFY mustered together several social services designed to incorporate the poor in systematic structural change—that is, in essence, to fight "the system," to politically effect needed changes that would create opportunities for the poor. Among its concerns were education, employment, legal services, community development, and family and group services. Once the barriers to opportunities for the poor were removed, social problems such as crime and delinquency were expected to diminish.

Was MFY successful? Few would argue it was. However, there is considerable disagreement as to why it failed. Liberals claim the program was but a drop in the bucket and could not be expected to alter the plight of the poor to any significant degree. Conservatives argue the project represented yet another avenue by which the "welfare element" could exploit the society; that is, rather than take the project seriously the poor allegedly sought only what immediate profit could be gained from it. Radical leftists assert that MFY was a cosmetic Band-Aid designed to co-opt the oppressed into thinking reform rather than revolution. If any of these analyses are correct, it is clear that MFY could not possibly succeed in combating crime.

But the most persuasive analysis of MFY's failure suggests that political and social pressures forced constant goal and organizational changes in the project and generally rendered it powerless. Helfgot (1974; see also Marris and Rein, 1973; Moynihan, 1969) argues that the political implications of any governmentally sponsored structural-change program render it doomed the moment it becomes effectual, that is, the moment it threatens status quo power relationships. He argues that as soon as the poor began to organize and demand participation in the MFY program, they were placated by MFY's hiring of professional middle-class minority workers. The poor themselves participated very little in MFY. Further, since MFY was so dependent on government and private foundation grants, it could hardly be expected to exist for long if it attacked the power structure that the funding agencies represented. In fact, Helfgot argues, increasing financial insecurity slowly forced MFY away from its structural-change goals to more traditional social reform aimed at changing individuals through such means as vocational training. In short, it became "just another program."

The MFY example illustrates a major point concerning the relationship of causal theory (especially structural theory) to anticrime policy. The ultimate test of a causal theory is the *implementation* of the social intervention it suggests. Yet, the intervention strategy is so tied to social and political concerns that it is most often doomed to failure. The result is twofold: (1) no impact on the social structure and consequently on the crime situation, and (2) neither confirmation nor negation of the causal theory.

SUMMARY

In this chapter we reviewed more formal criminological theories to answer the still unanswered question: What causes crime? Although it would seem we have developed a progressively sophisticated understanding of criminal behavior, if we review these theories we see that we have minimal knowledge about the causes of crime.

In fact, causal analysis seems to be the most frustrating of criminological endeavors. The frustrations encountered in trying to answer a question of such magnitude—together with the social, political, economic, and ethical problems of forming and testing causal theories—have caused many criminologists to shift their attention to other types of questions (see Chapter 3).

Regarding the average citizen's concerns about crime and personal safety, this chapter has tried to illuminate the complexity of the causes of crime and demonstrate that complex problems do not have simple answers. Criminal behavior is not caused *simply* by biological or psychological disorders. Nor is it *simply* the result of such factors as urban overcrowding, poverty, bad companions, and lax parents. "Better education" by itself will certainly not eliminate crime, and eliminating poverty, though it will undoubtedly rid us of many related problems that encourage crime, will not ensure which problems or how much crime.

The complexity of the problem should make us suspect of many recent government anticrime policies. We should be particularly suspect of simple, conservative anticrime proposals: incarcerating "habitual behaviors" will not necessarily lead to a sharp drop in crime rates. Complex problems rarely have such simple answers.

REFERENCES

Akers, R. L. 1977. *Deviant Behavior: A Social Learning Approach.* 2nd ed. Belmont, Calif.: Wadsworth Publishing Company.

Akers, R. L., M. D. Krohn, L. Lanza-Kaduce, et al., 1979. Social learning and deviant behavior: A specific test of a general theory. *Am. Sociol. Rev.* 44:636–55.

Austin, R. L. 1977. Commitment, neutralization and delinquency. In *Juvenile Delinquency: Little Brother Grows Up.* Edited by T. N. Ferdinand. Beverly Hills: Sage Publications.

Ball-Rokeach, S. 1973. Values and violence: A test of the subculture of violence thesis. *Am. Sociol. Rev.* 38:736–49.

Becker, H. S. 1963. *Outsiders.* New York: Free Press.

———. 1968. Conventional crime: Rationalization and punishment. In *Ortho-Psychiatry and the Law.* Edited by M. Levitt and B. Rubenstein. Detroit: Wayne State University Press.

Boggs, S. 1965. Urban crime patterns. *Am. Sociol. Rev.* 30:899–908.

Bordua, D. 1961. Delinquent subcultures: Sociological interpretations of gang delinquency. *Ann. Am. Acad. Pol. Soc. Sci.* 338:120–36.

Briar, S., and I. Piliavin. 1965. Delinquency, situational inducements, and commitments to conformity. *Soc. Prob.* 13:35–45.

Bryan, J. H. 1965. Apprenticeships in prostitution. *Soc. Prob.* 12:287–97.

Buffalo, M. D., and J. W. Rogers. 1971. Behavioral norms, moral norms and attachment: Problems of deviance and conformity. *Soc. Prob.* 19:101–13.

Burgess, R. L., and R. L. Akers. 1966. A differential association-reinforcement theory of criminal behavior. *Soc. Prob.* 14:128–47.

Clinard, M. B., and R. Quinney. 1973. *Criminal Behavior Systems: A Typology.* 2nd ed. New York: Holt, Rinehart & Winston.

Cloward, R., and L. Ohlin. 1960. *Delinquency and Opportunity.* New York: Free Press.

Cohen, A. K. 1955. *Delinquent Boys.* New York: Free Press.

Cohen, A. K., and J. F. Short. 1958. Research in delinquent subcultures. *J. Soc. Iss.* 14:20–37.

Cohen, L., and M. Felson. 1979. Social change and crime rate trends: A routine activity approach. *Am. Sociol. Rev.* 44:588–607.

Cohen, L., M. Felson, and K. Land. 1980. Property crime rates in the United States, 1947–1977; with ex ante forecasts for the mid-1980s. *Am. J. Sociol.* 86:90–118.

Cohen, L. E., J. R. Kluegel, and K. C. Land. 1981. Social inequality and predatory criminal victimization: An exposition and test of a formal theory. *Am. Sociol. Rev.* 46:505–24.

Colvin, M., and J. Pauly. 1983. A critique of criminology: Toward an integrated structural-Marxist theory of delinquency production. *Am. J. Sociol.* 89:513–51.

Conklin, J. E. 1972. *Robbery and the Criminal Justice System.* Philadelphia: J. B. Lippincott Co.

Cressey, D. R. 1953. *Other People's Money.* New York: Free Press.

Dunn, C. S. 1976. *Patterns of Robbery Characteristics and Their Occurrence Among Social Areas.* Washington, D.C.: U.S. Department of Justice, Law Enforcement Assistance Administration, National Criminal Justice Information and Statistics Service.

Elliott, D. S., S. S. Ageton, and R. J. Canter. 1979. An integrated theoretical perspective on delinquent behavior. *J. Res. Crime & Delinq.* 16:3–27.

Empey, L. T. 1977. *A Model for Evaluation of Programs in Juvenile Justice.* Washington, D.C.: U.S. Government Printing Office.

Garfinkel, H. 1956. Conditions of successful degradation ceremonies. *Am. J. Sociol.* 61:420–24.

Gibbons, D. C. 1968. *Society, Crime and Criminal Careers.* Englewood Cliffs, N.J.: Prentice-Hall.

Gibbs, J. 1975. *Crime, Punishment, and Deterrence.* New York: Elsevier Science Publishing Co.

Gordon, D. M. 1971. Class and the economics of crime. *Rev. Radical Pol. Econ.* 3:51–72.

Gould, L. 1969. Who defines delinquency: A comparison of self-reported and officially-reported indices of delinquency for three racial groups. *Soc. Prob.* 16:325–36.

Greenberg, D. F. 1977. Delinquency and the age structure of society. *Contemp. Crises* 1:189–223.

———. 1981. *Crime and Capitalism.* Palo Alto, Calif.: Mayfield Publishing Company.

Hartung, F. E. 1965. A vocabulary of motives for law violators. In *Delinquency, Crime, and Social Process.* Edited by D. Cressey and D. Ward. New York: Harper & Row, Publishers.

Helfgot, J. 1974. Professional reform organizations and the symbolic representation of the poor. *Am. Sociol. Rev.* 39:475–91.

Henry, A. F., and J. F. Short, Jr. 1954. *Suicide and Homicide.* Glencoe, Ill.: Free Press.

Hirschi, T. 1969. *Causes of Delinquency.* Berkeley: University of California Press.

———. Separate and unequal is better. *J. Res. Crime & Delinq.* 16:34–38.

Hirschi, T., and M. Gottfredson. 1980. The Sutherland tradition in criminology. In *Understanding Crime: Current Theory and Research*. Edited by T. Hirschi and M. Gottfredson. Beverly Hills: Sage Publications.

Hughes, E. C. 1945. Dilemmas and contradictions of status. *Am. J. Sociol.* 50:353–59.

Irwin, J. 1970. *The Felon*. Englewood Cliffs, N.J.: Prentice-Hall.

Jackson, J. K. 1954. The adjustment of the family to the crisis of alcoholism. *Q. J. Stud. Alcohol* 15:564–86.

Kitsuse, J. I. 1962. Societal reactions to deviant behavior: Problems of theory and method. *Soc. Prob.* 9:247–56.

Klockars, C. B. 1974. *The Professional Fence*. New York: Free Press.

Kornhauser, R. R. 1978. *Social Sources of Delinquency: An Appraisal of Analytic Methods*. Chicago: University of Chicago Press.

Lemert, Ed. 1951. *Social Pathology*. New York: McGraw-Hill Book Company.

Lesieur, H. R. 1977. *The Chase*. Garden City, New York: Anchor Books.

Letkemann, P. 1973. *Crime As Work*. Englewood Cliffs, N.J.: Prentice-Hall.

Light, I. 1977. The ethnic vice industry, 1880–1944. *Am. Sociol. Rev.* 42:464–79.

Linden, E., and J. C. Hackler. 1973. Affective ties and delinquency. *Pac. Sociol. Rev.* 16:27–46.

Liska, A. 1978. Deviant involvement, associations, and attitudes: Specifying the underlying causal structures. *Sociol. & Soc. Res.* 63:73–88.

Lofland, J. 1969. *Deviance and Identity*. Englewood Cliffs, N.J.: Prentice-Hall.

Mankoff, M. 1971. Societal reactions and career deviance: A critical analysis. *Sociol. Q.* 12:204–18.

Marris, P., and M. Rein. 1973. *Dilemmas of Social Reform*. 2nd ed. Chicago: Aldine Publishing Co.

Matza, D. 1964. *Delinquency and Drift*. New York: John Wiley & Sons.

———. 1969. *Becoming Deviant*. Englewood Cliffs, N.J.: Prentice-Hall.

Merton, R. K. 1938. Social structure and anomie. *Am. Sociol. Rev.* 3:672–82.

———. 1957. *Social Theory and Social Structure*. New York: Free Press.

Miller, W. B. 1958. Lower-class culture as a generating milieu of gang delinquency. *J. Soc. Iss.* 14:5–19.

Mills, C. 1940. Situated actions and vocabularies of motive. *Am. Sociol. Rev.* 5:904–13.

Mobilization For Youth. 1964. *Action on the Lower East Side, Program Report: July 1962–January 1964*. New York: Mobilization For Youth.

Moynihan, D. P. 1969. *Maximum Feasible Misunderstanding Community Action in the War on Poverty*. New York: Free Press.

Nye, F. I. 1958. *Family Relationships and Delinquent Behavior*. New York: John Wiley & Sons.

Polsky, N. 1967. *Hustlers, Beats and Others*. Chicago: Aldine Publishing Co.

Quinney, R. 1980. *Class, State and Crime*. 2nd ed. New York: Longman.

Reckless, W. C. 1967. *The Crime Problem*. 4th ed. New York: Appleton-Century-Crofts.

Reiss, A. J. 1951. Delinquency as the failure of personnel and social controls. *Am. Sociol. Rev.* 16:196–207.

Roebuck, J. B. 1967. *Criminal Typology*. Springfield, Ill.: Charles C. Thomas, Publishers.

Rogers, J. W. 1977. *Why Are You Not A Criminal?* Englewood Cliffs, N.J.: Prentice-Hall.

Rossi, P., E. Waite, C. Bose, and R. Berk. 1974. The seriousness of crimes' normative structure and individual differences. *Am. Sociol. Rev.* 39:224–37.

Schur, E. M. 1971. *Labeling Deviant Behavior*. New York: Harper & Row, Publishers.

Scott, M. B., and S. M. Lyman. 1968. Accounts. *Am. Sociol. Rev.* 33:46–62.

Shaw. C., and H. McKay. 1931. Social factors in juvenile delinquency. In *Report on the Causes of Crime*. Vol. 2. National Committee on Law Observance and Law Enforcement. Washington, D.C.: U.S. Government Printing Office.

Sheley, J. F. 1980. Is neutralization necessary for criminal behavior? *Deviant Behav.* 2:49–72.

———. 1983. Critical elements of criminal behavior explanation. *Sociol. Q.* 24:509–25.

Short, J., and F. Strodtbeck. 1965. *Group Process and Gang Delinquency*. Chicago: University of Chicago Press.

Silberman, M. 1976. Toward a theory of criminal deterrence. *Am. Sociol. Rev.* 41:442–61.

Sparks, R. F. 1980. Criminal opportunities and crime rates. In *Indicators of Crime and Criminal Justice: Quantitative Studies*. Edited by S. E. Fienberg and A. J. Reiss. Washington, D.C.: U.S. Government Printing Office.

Spitzer, S. 1975. Towards a Marxian theory of deviance. *Soc. Prob.* 22:638–51.

Stafford, M. C., and S. Ekland-Olson. 1982. On social learning and deviant behavior: A reappraisal of the findings. *Am. Sociol. Rev.* 47:167–69.

Steffensmeir, D. J., and R. M. Terry. 1973. Deviance and respectability: An observational study of reaction to shoplifting. *Soc. Forces* 51:417–26.

Strickland, D. E. 1982. Social learning and deviant behavior—a specific test of a general theory: A comment and critique. *Am. Sociol. Rev.* 47:162–67.

Sutherland, E. H., and D. R. Cressey. 1974. *Criminology:* 9th ed. Philadelphia: J. B. Lippincott Co.

Sykes, G., and D. Matza. 1957. Techniques of neutralization: A theory of delinquency. *Am. Sociol. Rev.* 22:664–70.

Tarde, G. 1912. *Penal Philosophy*. Boston: Little, Brown and Company.

Taylor, I., P. Walton, and J. Young. 1973. *The New Criminology*. New York: Harper & Row, Publishers.

Tittle, C., and C. Logan. 1973. Sanctions and deviance: Evidence and remaining questions. *Law & Society Rev.* 7:371–92.

Toby, J. 1957. The differential impact of family disorganization. *Am. Sociol. Rev.* 22:505–12.

Wiatrowski, M. D., D. B. Griswold, and M. K. Roberts. 1981. Social control theory and delinquency. *Am. Sociol. Rev.* 46:525–41.

Young, J. 1975. Working-class criminology. In *Critical Criminology*. Edited by I. Taylor, P. Walton, and J. Young. Boston: Routledge & Kegan Paul.

Zimring, F., and G. Hawkins. 1973. *Deterrence: The Legal Threat in Crime Control*. Chicago: University of Chicago Press.

SUGGESTED READINGS

Readers interested in further discussion of causal analysis of crime should first read the original works that were summarized in this chapter or at least a collection of pieces of these works. R. A. Farrell and V. L. Swigert have edited a well-rounded anthology, *Social Deviance* (Philadelphia: J. B. Lippincott, Co., 1975), as have S. H. Traub and C. B. Little, *Theories of Deviance* (Itasca, Ill.: F. E. Peacock, Publishers, 1975).

A look at some of the theory and research inspired by major criminological theories is also helpful. For example, R. L. Akers provides us with a clearer understanding of differential association theory through his efforts to refine it. See his book, *Deviant Behavior: A Social Learning Approach,* 2nd ed. (Belmont, Calif.: Wadsworth Publishing Company, 1977).

Causal theories are best understood when their theoretical assumptions are clearly stated and placed within a historical context. Two books do this very well: Travis Hirschi's, *Causes of Delinquency* (Berkeley: University of California Press, 1969) and Ruth Kornhauser's *Social Sources of Delinquency* (Chicago: University of Chicago Press, 1978). N. J. Davis offers a particularly critical analysis of sociological theories of deviance in *Sociological Constructions of Deviance* (Dubuque, Iowa: William C. Brown, Company 1975). An equally critical Marxist analysis of the same theories is found in I. Taylor, P. Walton, and J. Young's, *The New Criminology* (New York: Harper & Row, Publishers, 1973).

PART V

CREATING CRIME AND CRIMINALS

People tend to view American society and its criminal justice system as *reacting* to a "crime problem." In many ways, this is correct. Yet it is also correct to say that society and various criminal justice agencies *create* "crime problems." They do so in terms of their exercise of discretion in determining when, how, and against whom to make and enforce laws. Thus, our crime situation is not simply an occurrence. It is, at least in part, a product of organizational activity. This theme is pursued in Chapters 10 and 11.

THE CRIMINAL JUSTICE SYSTEM AND ITS PRODUCTS

When a society creates rules, it also creates the need for rule enforcers (Becker, 1963:155). In smaller societies, legislators and law enforcers may be the same persons. In larger societies, legal systems generally are more complex, and legislative, enforcement, and judicial duties become more distinct. Larger societies usually have highly developed criminal justice systems for preventing crime, apprehending suspects, determining legal innocence or guilt in criminal cases, and punishing or treating persons found guilty of crimes.

In this chapter we will analyze two elements of our criminal justice system: the police and the courts. (Analysis of the corrections system is reserved for Chapter 11.) The present discussion differs from most others on the subject in that it treats the criminal justice system as an organization that has two products: official crime rates and officially labeled criminals. In a very real sense, the ultimate product of the activity of the American criminal justice system is a *picture* of crime in this society. This picture is transmitted to the public and forms the basis of crime fears and demands for "law and order." As we shall see, whether or not this picture of crime and criminals reflects reality is open to question.

CRIMINAL JUSTICE AGENCIES

The criminal justice system in the U.S. is a collection of interrelated, semi-autonomous bureaucracies. Figure 10–1 displays the various stages through which persons are processed in the criminal-justice system and indicates the primary agencies that comprise the system: law enforcement, prosecution, courts, and corrections. Law enforcement involves a diverse number of agencies such as local police and sheriff's departments and state and federal police organizations (for example, state and federal narcotics bureaus). Prosecutorial agencies, whether state or federal, investigate cases, make decisions about charges against criminal suspects, present cases to grand juries, negotiate pleas, and try cases in criminal courts. The courts supervise the treatment of accused persons, decide bail arrangements and trial dates, conduct trials, and sentence offenders. Finally, the corrections system is composed of prisons and probation and parole agencies that serve various custody, rehabilitation, and punishment functions.

Figure 10–1 does, however, present a somewhat deceptive picture of the interrelationships among the various criminal justice agencies. It suggests a far more organized and compatible system than actually exists. Ideally, a case would proceed through the criminal justice system in the following manner:

1. Police observe a possible offense or answer a complaint and initiate an investigation.
2. If the investigation indicates that a crime has occurred, the suspected offender is located and arrested.
3. The suspect is informed of his or her rights, taken to police headquarters, and booked; that is, the arrest is entered into police records. The suspect is also taken before a magistrate so that the arrest is duly noted.
4. The process now moves into the prosecutorial stages. The district attorney investigates the case and determines whether it warrants prosecution. If it is decided that charges are deserved, after a hearing before a magistrate concerning the merits of the evidence and the legality of the manner in which it was obtained, the district attorney will take the case to the grand jury and seek an indictment.
5. The grand jury, a representative group of citizens, hears the evidence presented by the prosecutor. If it agrees with the prosecutor, the grand jury returns a true bill (an indictment) formally declaring that the suspect should be tried. (Some jurisdictions do not have a grand jury system. Instead the prosecutor files an "information" [a formal charge]. A preliminary hearing is used to evaluate its merits. Even in jurisdictions with grand juries, an information is the standard method of handling misdemeanor cases.)
6. The indicted suspect appears before a judge for arraignment. The formal charges are read and the suspect enters a plea: if guilty, the suspect is held for sentencing; if not guilty, he or she is given a choice of having the trial before either a judge or a jury.

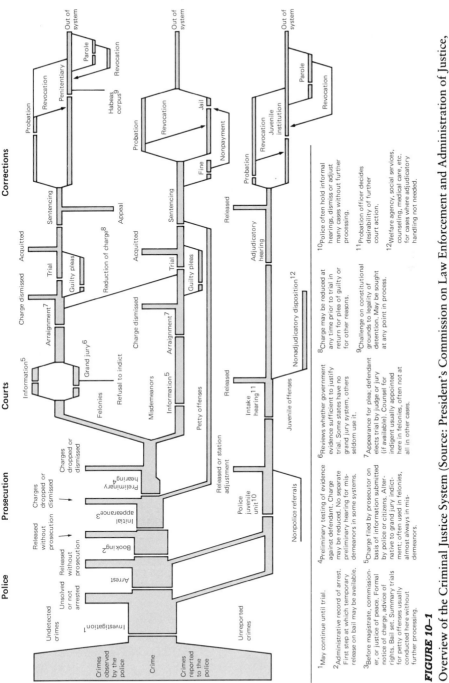

FIGURE 10-1

Overview of the Criminal Justice System (Source: President's Commission on Law Enforcement and Administration of Justice, *The Challenge of Crime in a Free Society* (Washington, D.C.: U.S. Government Printing Office, 1967), pp. 8–9.)

7. A trial is held and the judge or jury reaches a verdict based on the evidence presented by the prosecutor and criticized by the defense attorney. If found guilty, the convicted criminal is held for sentencing.
8. In some cases, specific penalties are legally prescribed for an offense. In other cases, a judge has discretion in sentencing. Usually, the judge relies on a presentence report from probation officers in determining the sentence. Following sentencing, the criminal is turned over to the corrections department.

In reality, the process by which the citizen-suspect moves through the criminal justice system is not as smooth and systematic as the above description implies. Nor is the interdependence and cooperation among criminal justice bureaucracies as strong as this description suggests. While the process is indeed governed by rules and formulas, criminal justice agencies possess considerable discretion and can circumvent the rules. The suspect-defendant can also do much to thwart the smooth operation of the system. For example, a capable defense attorney can, in many cases, delay a trial long enough for the prosecution's chief witness to move away, die, or become less cooperative.

Criminal justice agencies are themselves often at odds. Police departments often complain that district attorneys do not prosecute the cases brought to them. District attorneys counter that the police do not provide them with sound evidence or that judges are too restrictive in allowing evidence to be presented. Judges argue that police and prosecutors constantly present them with weak cases, try cases incompetently, or violate procedural rights in forming a case. Judges are criticized for turning too many felons back onto the streets. They in turn argue that they cannot in good conscience place individuals in such inhuman settings as overcrowded and understaffed prisons. In granting too many probations, the judge incurs the probation department's wrath. In sentencing too many persons to prison, the judge is criticized by prison officials.

In sum, the workings of the criminal justice system cannot be fully understood through a chart such as that presented in Figure 10–1. The system is not fully subject to a hierarchical chain of command. Interagency cooperation is often less the result of commitment to criminal justice goals than of the fact that each agency has the power (through the media) to discredit and embarrass the other agencies.

CRIMINAL JUSTICE SUBSYSTEMS

Discussions of the criminal justice system often overlook two of its peripheral yet important segments: the legislature and the citizenry. The legislature clearly influences the criminal justice system by passing laws and controlling criminal justice budgets. By enacting or rescinding laws, the legislature can increase or decrease the work load of other criminal justice agencies and can complicate or simplify the nature of that work load. The legislature can also greatly control the amounts and types of criminal justice activity by controlling the purse strings of funds for police and corrections programs. In general, the legislature's primary effect on the criminal justice system involves the structuring of its activities around the interests of the major power groups in this society (see Chapter 3).

Citizens influence the criminal justice system in at least three ways. First, as Chapter 3 suggested, the public applies pressure on the legislatures and on criminal justice agencies. Since most upper-level positions in the criminal justice system are political in nature, decisions made by persons in these positions can be swayed by public opinion. The passage of laws, the deployment of police patrols, decisions to plea bargain, sentencing of convicted criminals, and granting of parole are all examples of criminal justice decisions and acts that do not occur in a vacuum. Rather, they occur within a general social and political climate. To understand this point, we need only view the cutbacks in prison work furloughs when a prisoner on furlough is caught committing a crime. Similarly, we note the flurry of political-crime investigations following the Watergate scandal.

Citizen crime-reporting practices represent the second form of impact the citizenry has on the criminal justice system. As Chapter 4 noted, a rise or fall in crime rates may be caused by an actual increase or decrease in crime *or* may simply reflect a change in citizen willingness to report crimes observed by or committed against them.

A number of factors govern willingness to "get involved" in reporting crimes. As Chapter 4 indicated, witnesses or victims may be concerned about the inconvenience or economic hardship that involvement may entail (for example, loss of work time in order to appear as a witness) or about harassment or reprisal for involvement. Or the witness may even be a criminal who cannot afford police attention.

Results from the 1980 U.S. Department of Justice (1982) national victimization survey indicate that only 3 percent of victims of personal crimes who did not report the crimes to the police cited fear of reprisal or inconvenience as reasons for nonreporting. More importantly, 46 percent felt that the crime was not sufficiently important to be reported, that no proof of a crime existed, or that the police would not want to be bothered. Another 8 percent considered the crime a personal matter.

While these findings clearly point to a need for better relations between police and public, it is doubtful that the reasons offered by the survey sample fully account for nonreporting. The study did not consider various situational factors—sex, age, and demeanor of the parties involved; the presence of witnesses; and the victim's previous history of victimization—which could influence a citizen's decision to initiate the criminal justice process. Further, the study asked victims, in a sense, to provide reasons for avoiding their civic duty. The reasons given may have had little to do with what occurred at the time of the offense but may instead represent attempted "accounts" offered to an inquirer.

The third area in which the citizenry becomes involved in the criminal justice process is in the personal decision as to whether or not to be a prosecution witness. Prosecutors often complain that they cannot bring an alleged offender to trial because witnesses refuse to cooperate with the police or district attorney. A major study (National Institute of Law Enforcement and Criminal Justice, 1976) of 1973 felony and misdemeanor cases in Washington, D.C., attempted to identify the reasons for noncooperation by victims and witnesses. Twenty-four possible explanatory factors were examined. Surprisingly, demographic factors (age, sex, income, education, for example), attitudes toward the criminal justice system, and fears of reprisal were found to be unrelated to cooperation.

The study found three factors that were implicated in prosecutors' labeling of witnesses as uncooperative. First, if prosecutors had a large number of witnesses in a particular case, they would be less likely to pursue a witness they thought uncooperative and would more readily label the witnesses so. Second, if the relationship between the offender and the witness was close, witnesses would not cooperate or prosecutors would assume they would not and would label them uncooperative. Third, communication breakdowns between the police or prosecutor and the potential witnesses would cause many witnesses to be labeled uncooperative when, in fact, they were willing to cooperate. That is, potential witnesses were not contacted or given adequate information about their role as witnesses. The last factor was deemed most important by the researchers. It suggested that the blame for noncooperation lies not with the public but with the criminal justice system.

THE CRIMINAL JUSTICE FILTER

One approach to understanding the criminal justice system as a production organization is to view it as a giant filtering system. As Figure 10–2 indicates, the number of persons arrested in 1974 represents only one-fifth of the number of major crimes reported to the police. Only about 16 percent of those arrested are held for prosecution. Forty percent of those held for prosecution are eventually found or plead guilty and about 60 percent of that group are sent to prison. (More recent statistics are unavailable. It is assumed that the general distributions reflected in Figure 10–2 remain relatively accurate.)

What governs these reductions? The largest gap, occurring between crimes reported and arrests, reflects the expertise of and decisions made by police. The percentage of persons charged, found guilty, and sentenced reflects decisions made by prosecutors, jurors, and judges. The key to under-

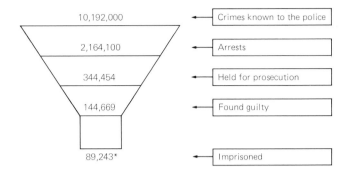

*Source did not define type of crime for which sentence was administered.
It is assumed that most were Index offenses.

FIGURE 10–2
The Criminal Justice Filter, 1974 (Source: M. J. Hindelang et
al., *Sourcebook of Criminal Justice Statistics—1976* (Washington, D.C.: U.S. Government Printing Office, 1977), pp.
443, 524, 587, 698. Note: These figures are for FBI Index
offenses only and for state jurisdictions only.)

standing the filtering effect of the criminal justice system is understanding the
discretion inherent in the system—the ability to choose one option from
among more than one in dealing with a situation or case. For example, police
officers have discretionary powers in dealing with family disputes, and may
try to calm the situation by talking or resolve it by making an arrest. District
attorneys have discretion in negotiating pleas. Judges exercise discretion in
sentencing offenders.

PROCESS VERSUS PRODUCTION

If we ignore the notion of discretion in the criminal justice system, we come
to view the system primarily as a passive processing organization or simply
as a number of steps through which a person passes on his or her way to receiving justice. However, if we take discretion into account, the criminal justice system may be viewed as a *production* organization. That is, it is a system
that provides two products: official crime rates and officially labeled criminals.

Figure 10–3 aids in clarifying the production aspects of the criminal-justice system. The figure displays three elements:

1. A pool of potential candidates for labeling as official criminals (A)
2. The criminal justice system (B)
3. A population of officially labeled criminals (C)

At any given time, the size and composition of the labeled criminal population (C) is a function of the interaction of activities from within the pool of

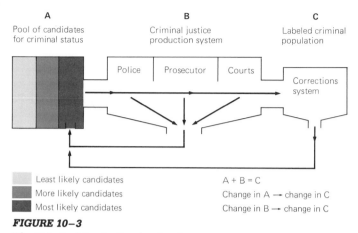

FIGURE 10–3

The Criminal Justice Production System

candidates for labeling (A) and decisions made within the criminal justice system (B) (Johnson et al., 1977).

In theory, every member of society is eligible for selection from the pool of potential labeled criminals by virtue of real or suspected criminal actions. In reality, however, selection from the pool of candidates is not random. Some persons are more likely than others to be drawn into the criminal justice system process by virtue of differential involvement in crime and social-status characteristics that insulate some persons from criminal justice labeling activities.

As Figure 10–3 demonstrates, selection from the pool of candidates for criminal status does not guarantee that status. From among the persons selected from the pool, the criminal justice system filters out or produces a select few for eventual inclusion in the official criminal population. The filtering or production process is, in large part, a matter of criminal justice discretion. Officially labeled criminals are produced through decisions made by police, prosecutors, and courts.

Figure 10–3 also indicates that if the size and composition of the officially labeled criminal population (C) is a function of candidate characteristics and actions (A) and criminal justice decisions (B), then changes in the size and composition of C are functions of changes in either or both A and B. The following sections discuss the effects of changes in either A or B.

Changes In the Criminal-Candidate Pool

One reason for a change in the size or composition of the official criminal population may be a change in the characteristics or behaviors of segments of the pool of candidates for criminal status (that is, a change in A may be reflected in C). If the pool were altered through immigration, for example, or if a major change in society's power structure occurred, we could expect a change in the type of person selected by the criminal justice system. Changes in the number of persons committing crimes within the pool could also influence the eventual size and composition of the official criminal population, provided that the criminal justice system could detect and handle the increased criminal activity. Thus, an increase or decrease in a community's marijuana supply could alter the usage patterns of marijuana smokers and therefore the number of smokers caught and processed for violating the law. Similarly, an influx of prostitutes into a community could result in an increase in the number of prostitutes in the community's official criminal population.

Changes in the Criminal Justice System

The criminal justice system is a production organization that can alter the size and composition of its product (labeled criminals) regardless of changes in the pool of candidates for official labeling (that is, a change in B may be reflected in C). For instance, a police department's decision to deploy patrols in one part of a city rather than in another may eventually result in different numbers and types of persons labeled criminal. A city's better business association may intermittently pressure the police department and the district attorney to rid commercial areas of prostitutes and drug dealers. The resultant crackdowns on these violators will be reflected in the characteristics of the labeled criminal population: it will contain more prostitutes and drug dealers. When pressures are eased, the criminal population will contain fewer of these offenders.

Further, within the criminal justice system, a change in district attorneys may alter plea-bargaining procedures and so influence the number and kinds of cases sent to trial. Public pressure may influence district attorneys to file more severe charges than customary. Judges may become more reluctant to grant bail to alleged offenders or may become more liberal or more conservative concerning questions of due process. More defense lawyers may opt for trial before a judge rather than a jury. Such changes ultimately will be reflected in the size and composition of the officially labeled criminal population.

It is wise at this point to return to a theme introduced in Chapter 4. In a discussion of suitable hypotheses by which to account for crime-rate changes, it was stressed that the ability of criminals to alter crime rates through changes in their behavior could not be denied. But it was argued also that attempts to account for crime-rate changes should not look first to varying criminal behavior patterns. Instead initial (and, usually, the more successful) hypotheses should focus upon elements of the criminal justice system as the major force behind changing crime rates. Only when these elements are discounted can we legitimately attribute rate changes to criminal behavior changes. The ability of the criminal justice system to shape the nature of its product never should be underestimated.

The remainder of this chapter will concentrate on the determinants of criminal justice system decisions as they influence the official criminal population. That is, the characteristics and behaviors of those in the pool of potential labeled criminals will be held constant, and all changes in population of those with criminal status (C) will be treated as functions of criminal justice system discretion (B). In order, we shall examine the police, the courts, and the corrections system.

THE POLICE

In many ways, policing remains as it was in 1829 in London when Sir Robert Peel initiated the first centralized police patrols as we now know them. The only major changes in policing since Peel's day have occurred with the development of the automobile and two-way radio communications. Motor vehicles provide greater mobility for police officers and increase the size of the areas they can patrol. The radio puts the patrolling officer in better touch with headquarters and allows for faster response time in emergency situations.

Together these two technological innovations have made foot patrols a rarity. On the negative side, they have also served to divorce the police from the public. Police officers are generally not regarded as members of the communities they serve (Rubinstein, 1973:3–25). Despite this alienation, much of police work today involves providing services—escorting ambulances, investigating accidents, answering suicide calls, searching for lost children, and so on (Cumming et al., 1965)—and regulating traffic. In line with the interests of this chapter, however, we wish to concentrate on three primary products of police organization: crime rates, arrest rates, and clearance rates. These three elements are of prime importance in public conceptions of crime and the success of the criminal justice system in fighting it.

Crime Rates

Crime rate refers to the number of crimes committed per a given number of people within a designated population (for example, number of crimes per 100,000 U.S. citizens). Officially, crime rates are computed on the basis of offenses discovered by the police and substantiated complaints made by citizens. People often treat these rates as approximations of the amount of crime in this society, but they may or may not be correct. Practically speaking, official crime-rate figures are nothing more than creations or products of the police. Much crime does not come to the attention of the police. Police and citizen activity regarding crime will greatly determine the number of crimes recorded. Yet Black (1970) argues that we cannot trust official crime statistics as indicators of crimes encountered by or reported to the police. The police do not officially record all crimes they hear of or discover.

Black analyzed data on 554 cases of police encounters with citizen complainants in crime situations in which the suspect was not present. He was interested in what influenced the responding officers to make an official report of the incident. Among the factors shaping the police officer's decision was the legal seriousness of the offense. Police wrote reports in 72 percent of the felonies and 53 percent of the misdemeanors. The complainant's preference also influenced the officer's actions. Even in some felony cases—for example, assault by a friend—the citizen had cooled down by the time the police arrived, and he or she no longer wished to file a complaint but only to see an informal warning given to the offending person. In 84 percent of the felony cases and 64 percent of the misdemeanor cases, the police complied with the complainant's request.

When the citizen requests official action, two additional factors enter into the police officer's decision: (1) the relational distance between the complainant and the suspect, and (2) the complainant's deference to the police officer. Police more readily comply with requests for official action when the complainant and the offender are strangers; less readily when they are friends, neighbors, or acquaintances; and least readily when the offense involves members of the same family. Further, the complainant's behavior toward the police officer determines the officer's willingness to file a report. The less civil or more antagonistic the complainant, the less likely the officer is to file a report.

Finally, Black found that white-collar complainants received greater compliance from police in felony cases than did blue-collar complainants but found no evidence of racial discrimination in police report filing. Interestingly, in more recent work, Black (1980) has revised his view of the race issue, now arguing that race does enter into the police-citizen encounter in fairly complex ways (see also Hepburn, 1978; Sherman, 1980).

It is noteworthy that Black's results concern only the immediate situational determinants of official crime-reporting decisions. Officers in the field may also be influenced by organizational directives and by personal biases. It is not uncommon for police departments to order, formally or informally, their officers to "lay off" certain offenses. Thus, citizen complaints about marijuana use may not result in official reports because the police department feels these reports will inflate the city's drug-violation statistics. Similarly, a department may direct officers not to file official crime reports in assault cases involving spouses. These cases increase the assault rate but rarely result in official indictments, thus making the criminal justice system appear inefficient. In somewhat similar fashion, police may file reports that downgrade the offense in question—for example, from robbery to theft.

Seidman and Couzens (1974) discovered this practice occurring in a situation in which police commanders' jobs rested on a promised decrease in serious crime in their districts.

Personal biases of investigating officers also influence their decisions in the field. Attitudes about the types of persons believed to be involved in crimes may affect reports. In years past, for example, fist fights between whites were recorded as crimes (assaults) while fights between blacks were simply treated as normal behavior. Today, the extent to which an officer will report marijuana offenses may be linked to the extent to which he himself (or she) smokes marijuana.

In sum, since government and public perception of crime is based in large part on official crime reports, it is fair to say that these perceptions are the products of police activity and decisions. Whether or not the rates and perceptions reflect the reality of the crime situation depends on the types of decisions the police are making. Also important, police decisions to report crimes influence arrest rates, since much arrest activity is based on follow-ups of initial crime reports.

Arrest Rates

A second product of police discretion and activity is the arrest rate—that is, the number of arrests per 100,000 population in the area serviced by a police department. Arrest statistics often are used to evaluate police department effectiveness and to learn the characteristics of persons committing crimes. The extent to which the statistics are useful for either purpose depends on the extent to which police departments and individual officers employ discretion in arrest situations. Available research suggests that arrest discretion is extremely prevalent.

Like crime rates, arrest rates simply do not occur; they are manufactured. Although existing laws do not specifically allow for nonenforcement, police departments and their employees have considerable latitude in making arrests. For both parties, the latitude is the result of relatively high levels of autonomy. Although somewhat responsive to political and social pressures and occasionally monitored by civilian review boards, police departments by and large police themselves (Wilson, 1968:227–77). Similarly, though answerable to superior officers, individual police officers are relatively unsupervised in the field. The following factors seem to influence police departments in their arrest policies:

Orientation of the Department toward Policing. J. Q. Wilson (1968: 140–226) suggests that styles of policing are tied to the types of communities being served. Some communities perceive themselves to be plagued by crime. The police department may respond in legalistic fashion, using little discretion and making an arrest in every possible arrest situation. Other communities demand order and are given a watchman-style department, one that exercises a considerable amount of discretion in an effort to achieve order without involving citizens in legal problems. Finally, a service-style department often occurs in communities without a serious crime problem and provides such services as emergency medical care.

Political Pressures. Police departments are political organizations that, while avoiding day-to-day interference, must also avoid serious conflicts with the more powerful leaders of a community who choose the police chief and control the police budget. These leaders may influence arrest policies. District attorneys and judges, by virtue of their ability to embarrass a police department in the news media, also affect arrest policies. Recent attempts to implement police-community relations programs testify both to the increasing political power of lower socioeconomic groups and to the need to cultivate the cooperation of these groups in enforcing the law (Manning, 1975).

Technical Sophistication. Clearly, arrest rates will be influenced by the technical expertise of police departments. The training of officers and the equipment employed in police work vary by department. Arrest rates vary in some degree with the differences in technical sophistication.

Perceived Need for Nonarrest. At times, investigations into criminal activity seem to dictate a nonarrest policy. An attempt to break an organized crime syndicate or a narcotics ring might be hindered, for example, by arrests at lower levels. Hence, it is common for police departments to trade an arrest for information about upper-level criminals. This practice, of course, never allows the effects of full enforcement of the law to be determined (Goldstein, 1960).

Procedural Law. The criminal justice system must operate under rules of due process. That is, there are procedural rules that define *how* the police and other criminal justice agencies may investigate and arrest a citizen (see Chapter 2). Police may not search a home without a warrant, for example. Police officers currently treat procedural laws as technical hindrances and generally attempt to circumvent them when possible. Skolnick (1975) argues that police work (including the number and types of arrests made) would change if police orientation to procedural law were changed.

As noted above, individual police officers lead a relatively autonomous existence in the field. They are subject to a number of pressures that influence their decisions on the job, such as the following:

Organizational Pressures. Much of police field work is structured by the department in the sense that directives are given, arrest records are monitored, and superiors' wishes are made known. Promotions are based on evaluations of the officer's performance in the field. Considerable emphasis is placed on the "good pinch," the arrest that results in charges filed by the district attorney. Rubinstein (1973:26–68) argues that a police officer's immediate superior, the sergeant, exerts the major influence on his or her work in the sense that the superior evaluates the officer's performance in the territory to which he or she is assigned.

Personal Biases. In addition to the normal prejudices every individual harbors, the police officer gradually develops stereotypes of criminals and crime situations. Although these images sometimes facilitate police work, they also sometimes form the basis of discriminatory arrests and police brutality. Based on a study of police encounters with juveniles, Piliavin and Briar (1964) suggest that the major determinants of police decisions to arrest a youth for a minor crime are the youth's appearance and demeanor. To the extent that the youth was disrespectful and looked like a "tough guy," the police were likely to arrest him. Studies of police brutality indicate that police are most likely to harass segments of the population thought to be "problems" by the majority (Chevigny, 1969).

Seriousness of the Crime Investigated. Clearly, there are some offenses that the police officer cannot ignore. In general, arrest discretion occurs more frequently regarding lesser offenses and vice crimes.

Situational Factors. As with the police officer's decision to file an official report for a crime incident, immediate situational factors affect decisions to arrest. These include the physical setting in which the police-citizen interaction occurs, the number of witnesses present and their involvement in the interaction, and the presence of a complainant. Also of considerable importance in police-citizen encounters is the quality of interaction between the two parties. To the extent that the citizen assumes a differential stance toward the officer, the citizen reduces the chances of arrest—all else being equal (Sykes and Clark, 1975). Citizen cooperation with police officers also depends upon the citizen's perception of the seriousness of the offense to which the encounter relates (Sheley and Harris, 1976; Wiley and Hudik, 1974).

Procedural Law. Apart from departmental policies regarding due process in arrests, the individual officer also develops attitudes toward procedural law. Officers vary in the extent to which they are willing to circumvent (and to lie about circumventing) the rules. The question of entrapment in prostitution arrests provides an example. Arrests cannot be made unless the prostitute first quotes a price for prostitution services. If the police officer cites the price first, subsequent arrest of the prostitute constitutes entrapment. Entrapment in this situation cannot be controlled since there are generally no witnesses involved. Whether or not the officer is willing to entrap will in part determine whether an arrest occurs (Skolnick, 1975:91–111).

Corruption. Nonenforcement of laws may occur because police accept payoffs to "look the other way." Corruption represents more than a few "bad apples" on a police force. Most graft is related to vice crimes, and most police officers receive some form of encouragement to accept payoffs. A number of factors provide the encouragement: lack of community consensus regarding the morality of the vices, relative community apathy regarding enforcement of vice laws, a demand for vice services, lack of control over the police department by honest powerful citizens, low visibility of police graft, greater monetary rewards for graft than for its avoidance, lack of sanctioning from the police hierarchy, explicit encouragement by fellow officers, the occasional usefulness of graft to gain order within a given police territory, and constant offers of payoffs from every form of business (Rubinstein, 1973:373–434; Gardiner, 1970:93–104).

In sum, we again note that arrest rates are a product of police activity and discretion, some of which is departmentally encouraged. As such, arrest rates may or may not constitute a representative sample of arrests that could be made by police. Regardless, arrest statistics are used to make evaluative and police decisions. Departmental efficiency is judged partially by arrest records. Individual officers are also evaluated in large part on arrest performance. Finally, decisions about anticrime strategies often are based on arrest trends and characteristics of arrestees. As De Fleur (1975) has demonstrated in reviewing Chicago's drug arrest trends over a twenty-nine-year period, apparent changes in populations using drugs, areas of drug use, and amounts of drug use over time actually reflected police decisions about when, where, and against whom drug laws were enforced.

Clearance Rates

The major criterion of effectiveness by the police department and a standard measure of performance by detectives is the clearance rate—that is, the percentage of known crimes that the police feel they have solved. Like crime and arrest rates, clearance rates are products of police activity and discretion, not simply measures of these elements. That is, police clear crimes through decisions about whom to arrest and, in clearing crimes apart from arrest, about the validity of the information used to classify a crime as "solved" (Skolnick, 1975:164–81).

Clearance statistics are highly problematic. The ordinary citizen often assumes that they represent actual arrests. In fact, crimes are often labeled "cleared" when detectives feel they can attribute them to identified individuals either through confessions or on the basis of method of operation. Thus, the police become convinced by similarities in a number of crimes that one person committed them. Upon the person's arrest, those crimes may be labeled "cleared" whether or not the suspect admits to them. We should also not assume that all offenses cleared by arrest result in criminal prosecution. District attorneys often refuse to press charges either because of weak evidence or procedural rights violations. Nonetheless, the crimes are classified as "solved" or "cleared" in police files.

Pressures on police departments to increase clearance rates undoubtedly result in some rather liberal classifications of crimes as "cleared." Since the FBI publishes monthly clearance statistics for major cities, poor clearance rates are seen by police departments as negative indicators of their performance. The resultant pressure placed on individual investigators to produce higher clearance rates often results in compromises of justice. Police officers bargain with suspects, promising no arrest in return for information leading to clearances or a single charge in return for confessions regarding a number of crimes. In some respects, the multiple-offense arrestee has an advantage over the single-offense arrestee, for the former has more bargaining power with respect to information leading to clearances.

In sum, it is difficult to know exactly what a police department's clearance rate represents: it may or may not mean that a department is energetically fighting crime; it may or may not signify a high number of arrests; it may or may not reflect a high level of convictions for offenders. However, it *does* represent a set of decisions made by police investigators in a political context. For this reason, we must view clearance statistics with great skepticism.

The Police Dilemma. We noted in an earlier chapter the inherent tension between this society's substantive and procedural laws. On the one hand, we demand order—enforcement of substantive law. On the other, we demand that order be achieved under the umbrella of procedural law. The police feel the weight of both types of law. Given the nature of police work (viewing the damage wrought by substantive law violations) and the considerable public pressure on the police to control crime, police departments and individual officers understandably grant more importance to substantive law than to procedural law.

The police themselves are in large part responsible for the pressure they receive. As Manning (1971) forcefully argues, the police long ago created for themselves a crime control mandate. That is, they convinced the public that they and only they should assume the responsibility for crime prevention and the apprehension of criminals. In assuming and perpetuating this mandate, the police have developed an aura of professional and technical expertise: a highly developed bureaucracy; elaborate statistics; "technologies" of patrol and processing criminal suspects. But it is likely that they would prefer now to soften their mandate for it is impossible to fulfill. Goldstein (1977) notes that even the most highly developed and sophisticated police department lacks the capacity to cope well with violent crime rates as they have occurred during the past fifteen years. Crime apparently has risen faster than the ability of the police to convince the public that they can control it. Thus, public pressure on police and politicians has increased dramatically and politicians have worsened matters by promising to push the police harder to fight crime.

Though pressure to fulfill the impossible mandate has grown tremendously in recent years, court-initiated pressure on the police to observe procedure law has not slackened; it has, in fact, increased. Where once a citizenry was unaware of its rights and thus open to unchecked police abuses, segments of that same citizenry are now more aware of and more vocal in demanding their rights. The police, therefore, perceive themselves in an untenable situation. They are told to catch criminals and to prevent crime but see themselves as severely hampered in their attempts to do so. Interestingly, available research suggests that neither observance of nor ignorance of procedural law has an impact on crime levels in this society (Kamisar, 1965; see also discussion of the exclusionary rule in Chapter 2). Though they view their claim of unreasonable procedural constraint as valid and not simply tactical, it is clear that the police have made procedural law the scapegoat in their effort to justify their unfulfilled mandate. In the final analysis, until both the police and the public begin to understand the impossibility of the police mandate and the importance of procedural law, we can expect police to honor that law only to the extent to which they are coerced to do so.

The same impossible mandate that encourages abuses of procedural law underlies much of police misuse of force and authority. In addition to violations of procedural rights, the police break the law by lying to coverup those violations, in bringing false charges to assure prosecution or to hide abuse cases, and in the physical brutality and harassment of members of the public. These problems, in some instances, result from the assertion of individual officers' prejudices and bad tempers. More likely, however, excessive force and abuse of authority represent tools to maintain control over a specific territory and the persons within it by police who are frustrated in their attempts at control through legal means. If police define their role as providing order within a community, they will use the means at their disposal to make crime less visible to the community. Thus, the department seeks control of the city's "high crime" areas and individual police officers seek control of the territories within those areas. One means of control is intimidation. Brutality and harassment sometimes accomplish this end.

Departments do not vigorously attempt to prevent brutality except when forced to do so—usually in the wake of a publicized brutality case. They are geared toward discovery of only the most blatant abuses. Nor do the segments of the population less often touched by police misconduct (those segments less in need of "control") generally pressure the police to abandon their illegal control tactics. Police officers feel that they have the implicit approval of the general public to keep the "criminal" (lower) classes in line by

NEWSPRINT AND COMMENT

Police Had a Tough Time Firing the 'Jawbreaker'

By Dean Baquet

In the early morning hours of Aug. 27, 1974, on a dimly lit French Quarter street, New Orleans police officer Patrick Branighan beat Warren Mayes Jr. until he fell to the ground, then threw his calling card down and dared Mayes to make a complaint, a federal court jury recently concluded.

Two weeks ago, a federal court jury ordered Branighan to pay Mayes $12,500. The city has already settled with Mayes for $5,000. . . .

The federal court fine was the latest in a series of official actions prompted by Branighan's behavior.

Two years after the incident with Mayes, during the night of Sept. 20, 1976, Branighan threw Jose Pagan into an unmarked police car, drove him to a quiet French Quarter street and beat him unconscious, according to an account of the incident in police files.

Two weeks later, Branighan punched out two fellow 1st District police officers, the files show. One of the officers had accused Branighan of trying to get him a date with a prostitute so Branighan could blackmail him.

The Police Department's Internal Affairs Division file on Branighan shows how difficult it was for police officials to fire him after the incident in which he allegedly attacked two 1st District police officers. And, along with interviews with various sources and a review of the Mayes lawsuit, the file describes the career of an officer who became known on the streets of the French Quarter as "Jawbreaker."

In the late 1960s or early 1970s, Branighan, who had been a boxer in the U.S. Marine Corps, joined the Police Department for a brief period, then resigned.

When Branighan tried to return to the force, Maj. James Arnold, the commander of the department's Internal Affairs Division told then-Superintendent Clarence Giarrusso that Branighan should not be rehired because he had been involved in several incidents allegedly involving the use of excessive force, according to Civil Service Commission records.

At first, Giarrusso went along with Arnold's recommendation, Arnold told the Civil Service Commission. But the superintendent "finally relented and let Mr. Branighan come back to the police department," Arnold said.

There were 12 complaints involving Branighan over the next few years. Arnold later told the Civil Service Commission that Branighan had been involved in more brutality complaints than any other police officer. But there was one incident, according to police records, that compelled the department's top officials to begin their efforts to dismiss Branighan.

The incident took place on the night of Oct. 4, 1976.

Only a handful of police officers was on duty in the 1st District station at 10:10 p.m. that night. Officer Victor Manale has told various investigators that he decided to confront Branighan with allegations that Branighan had tried to set him up to be blackmailed.

Manale claimed that several French Quarter prostitutes had told him that Branighan wanted them to have sex with Manale so that Branighan could burst into the room and take pictures. Manale said he did not know why Branighan would have wanted to blackmail him. Manale said he threw a camera flash cube on Branighan's desk and told him he was aware of the alleged blackmail scheme.

In a letter to Branighan outlining the Police Department's conclusions about what followed, Giarrusso wrote that Branighan "began beating him (Manale) with your fists, knocking your brother officer to the floor. Officer Manale struggled to his feet and attempted to grab you. You broke loose from his grasp, again beating the officer with your fists and knocking him to the floor in a semi-conscious state."

When another policeman intervened, Giarrusso wrote, Branighan struck that officer, too.

Three weeks later, Branighan was dismissed from the Police Department. His appeal to the

Civil Service Commission generated more than 1,000 pages of transcripts.

Giarrusso testified that Branighan is "big, good-looking, strong" and "has a lot of charisma." But he also told the commission that the former officer "would not make a good policeman because if he disagrees with you he will strike you and put you in the hospital. . . ."

The Civil Service Commission ruled 4-1 that the firing of Branighan was too strict a punishment. Police officials had dismissed Branighan because of his past record, not because of the fight, the commission decided.

The commission ruled that Branighan should be suspended for 120 days.

After the incident involving Officer Manale, police officials got another opportunity to try to remove Branighan from the department.

Shortly after 2 a.m. the night of Sept. 20, 1976, according to police files, a light blue, unmarked police car pulled up to the corner where Jose Pagan was arguing with a woman. Inside the car were 1st District officers Branighan and Joseph Waguespack, according to a description of the incident in police files.

According to Pagan's account, which was supported by at least seven witnesses who gave statements to the Police Department's Internal Affairs Division, Branighan apparently heard Pagan say the word "pig." The policeman, who has said his weight varies from 210 to 220 pounds, beat Pagan and put him in the back of the police car and drove away, according to a letter Giarrusso later wrote to Branighan.

Branighan stopped his police car in the 900 block of St. Philip Street, dragged Pagan from the car and beat the man until he fell unconscious to the sidewalk, according to a description of the incident in police files.

Later that morning Pagan stumbled into 1st District headquarters on North Rampart Street and lodged a complaint. In his letter to Branighan, Giarrusso wrote, "When you learned that you had been described as the perpetrator, you, along with others involved, altered your appearance by shaving your moustaches and cutting or changing your hairstyles."

However, Pagan was later able to identify Branighan's photograph from police files.

Giarrusso wrote a letter of dismissal to Branighan on Sept. 20, 1977, exactly a year after the police officer's alleged encounter with Pagan. Five days before the letter was written, Branighan had met with the superintendent and denied Pagan's allegations. Giarrusso wrote that he did not believe Branighan's denial.

Branighan appealed his firing on Oct. 20, 1977. In December 1978, the Civil Service Commission upheld his dismissal.

Source: © Times-Picayune Publishing Corp., 1981. Reprinted by permission.

Comment: "Bad Cops"

What exactly is a "bad cop?" The answer to this question carries considerable meaning for our understanding of police corruption and brutality. There is no question that the officer described in the news item reprinted above is a "bad cop." Nor that he is worse than other officers. Nor that his department tries to rid itself of persons like that. But those facts can mislead us toward an incomplete picture of police violations of the law. In short, the article suggests that violations are the products of a few "bad apples" that the department wishes to cull despite bureaucratic red tape.

Perhaps police deviants of the caliber of the "Jawbreaker" are rare "bad apples." But police officers who violate the law more generally are not rare. And they cannot be controlled through better screening processes which keep potential "bad cops" out of the police academy. More often than not, "bad cops" are produced *after* academy training. Corruption in the form of extortion and accepting bribes generally is learned by officers in the course of constant "incentives," ranging from cups of coffee to large cash payments, to pay more or less attention to particular situations. Police brutality is, in large measure, not of the "Jawbreaker" variety but more situational. That is, it is unplanned and arises in dispute situations wherein tempers flare and officers perceive their position of authority to be threatened. In their view, it is this authority that stands between social order and chaos. In both corruption and brutality cases, the rookie officer is encouraged explicitly and implicitly by the deviance of more experienced officers and the fact that police culture condemns protest against and reporting of police infractions of the law.

The purpose of this comment is not to indict all police as "bad cops" nor to dismiss police deviance as "something most cops do—it comes with the job." Instead, its purpose is to locate the source of police corruption and violence, both serious problems on any scale, not in individual "bad apples," but where it belongs: in the structure of policing itself.

whatever means necessary. But in the day-to-day fight against criminals, they feel isolated, a final wall of defense against the dangerous elements. In this fight, police officers tend to develop stereotypes of "symbolic assailants"— often minority persons and political dissidents—who must be attacked before they can attack the officers (Skolnick, 1975). These stereotypes clearly are rooted in community prejudices. Finally, officers view their role as the apprehension of criminals and feel that their work is thwarted by lenient courts that too quickly return offenders to the streets. Thus, the notion of control is extended through the dispensation of "street justice," the punishment of offenders by the police without due process or trial. Again, until both the public and the police understand the futility of the police mandate and the true importance of procedural law, these abuses will continue. They are built into the police role.

The above discussion of the police dilemma, clearance rates, arrest rates, and crime rates gives us a sense of what it means to say the criminal justice system is a production rather than a processing organization. The organization *creates* a product; it does not simply stamp and process an already existing product. Changes in the structure, goals, or methods of police agencies will likely be reflected in their end products: officially defined crimes and officially designated persons to be moved into the court system. The following description (Sheley and Hanlon, 1978) of the consequences of a police decision actively to seek certain arrests graphically illustrates this point.

An Example: Factoryville's Antiheroin Campaign

In 1974, an older northern industrial city called Factoryville (a pseudonym) was embarrassed by a state official's accusation that the city was the heroin distribution center for a multistate region. The claim received extensive news coverage and caused considerable political and public pressure on the police to rid Factoryville of heroin traffickers. The police responded with an antiheroin campaign designed to increase the number of heroin arrests in the city. To this end, narcotics unit personnel were doubled, overtime hours were greatly increased, and investigation funds were more than doubled. The campaign was to last six months.

In light of this chapter's often-stated hypothesis that policy changes in the criminal justice system will alter the characteristics of a community's official criminal population, we might expect Factoryville's official criminal rolls to swell with heroin traffickers. Yet, at first glance, the hypothesis seems unsupported. Heroin arrests increased only 9 percent during the campaign. The publicity surrounding the campaign apparently disrupted normal heroin patterns in the city, driving distributors and users further underground.

A second look at changes in Factoryville's official criminal population during the six-month campaign suggests that the campaign was not without impact. The number of arrests for possession of stolen goods and illegal weapons rose as police increased drug raids and subsequently encountered other offenses. Prostitution arrests declined as plainclothes undercover officers were transferred from the sex offenses unit to the narcotics unit. Arrests for disturbing the peace rose as uniformed officers employed that charge to arrest prostitutes. However, the greatest effect of the antiheroin campaign was a drastic increase—228 percent—in arrests for possession of marijuana. Though not actively seeking such arrests, the police encountered more marijuana violations through increased "street work," more frequent drug raids, and drug tips from the public in response to the antiheroin publicity.

In sum, though there were no apparent changes in the size and composition of Factoryville's marijuana-user population, the police antiheroin policy produced a "marijuana problem" for the city. It also greatly altered the characteristics of its arrest population—the same population from which the prosecutor selected persons for potential labeling as the community's official criminals.

THE COURTS

Although police arrest decisions create a population from which officially labeled criminals will be drawn, the court system performs the actual selection and labeling of official criminals. Despite popular notions, the courts do not simply weigh evidence and determine guilt or innocence. Rather, like the police, they produce a product—labeled criminals—through a series of decisions. Were the structure of this decision-making process altered, the product would also be changed; we would see different numbers or types of persons granted criminal status.

Orientation of the Courts

Ideally, American courts employ an adversary model in evaluating the merits of state-imposed criminal charges against a defendant. This model pits the prosecution against the defense and uses a judge or jury to determine the winner of the conflict. The prosecution and defense do not cooperate in any way. Instead, within legal limits, they do everything in their power to thwart each other's efforts.

Since the state is more powerful than the individual it prosecutes, the adversary model somewhat favors the defense in our system. Defendants need not be proven innocent of the charges against them; they need only show that the prosecution has not proven them guilty beyond a reasonable doubt. Procedural law also limits the manner in which the prosecution builds a case against defendants. Defendants have a right to counsel, and if they cannot afford counsel, one will be provided. There are time limits within which the prosecution must bring the case to trial. Illegally obtained evidence cannot be introduced against defendants. Defendants cannot be retried if acquitted of an offense. Ideally, then, defendants are considered not guilty until proven otherwise.

Many critics argue that the operation of our present court system deviates radically from the adversary ideal. They claim that we have developed a crime-control or cooperative model that downplays conflict between prosecution and defense. The crime-control model processes individuals assumed to be guilty by virtue of arrest and pretrial investigations (Packer, 1968; Blumberg, 1967). With guilt presumed, critics argue, the prosecution, defense, and judge cooperate to move cases through the courts as quickly as possible. Characteristic of this attempt at efficient processing are a reliance on negotiated pleas, avoidance of trials, conservative rulings on procedural rights, and the conduct of trials in a manner favoring the prosecution.

Clearly, the pure crime-control model is no more a reality than is the pure adversary model. Courts in America vary in the extent to which they lean toward either model. Their variation greatly shapes differences in communities' crime situations and the size and composition of their official criminal populations. Changes in orientation within court systems should bring changes within those criminal populations. Greater reliance on the adversary approach should cause decreases in the numbers of official criminals. The numbers should increase as the cooperative approach gains favor. Different approaches will also change the composition of the criminal population. A move toward the cooperative model may, for example, result in the convictions of members of organized crime who have avoided conviction by using safeguards in the adversary model. In sum, then, criminal status is largely a function of the orientation of a court system.

Prosecution and Defense

Within the court system, the key figures in determining the outcome of a criminal case are the prosecuting and defense attorneys. We are presently interested in the factors that influence their decisions regarding criminal cases.

The office of prosecutor is, first and foremost, a political position.

Whether elected or appointed, district attorneys must assure the public that the community is safe, that criminals are being tried and punished, and that justice is being dispensed. Prosecutors face a number of decisions in trying to maintain this image. They must first decide whether or not to bring charges against a suspect. If they do bring charges and they are accepted by a grand jury, prosecutors must choose between negotiating a plea (discussed below) and taking the case to trial. Going to trial also involves decisions about when the trial should take place and how best to present the state's case to a judge or jury.

Among the important factors governing these decisions are: (1) the potential impact of the successful handling of the case on the prosecutor's reputation, (2) the seriousness of the offense considered, (3) the perceived dangerousness of the defendant, (4) the quality of evidence in the case, (5) the cooperativeness of victims and witnesses, (6) the courtroom credibility of potential witnesses, (7) the cooperativeness of the defendant and defense attorney, (8) the potential usefulness of the defendant in a criminal justice system role (such as police informant), (9) community pressure to crack down on certain forms of crime, and (10) the need to placate other members of the criminal justice system, such as the police, who may complain to the news media that the prosecutor is refusing to prosecute the criminals they apprehend (Cole, 1970; Myers and Hagan, 1979; Skolnick, 1967). These decisions are typically made within an organizational framework marked by a large number of cases. If all cases went to trial, the court system would be so overwhelmed that it would cease to function.

The Grand Jury. In Chapter 2 we raised the issue of grand jury abuses in a discussion of the Organized Crime Control Act of 1970. The grand jury is a group of citizens chosen from the community and generally untrained in legal matters. Conceptually, the jury is a two-edged sword. On the one hand, it is a crime fighter, a body whose task it is to investigate suspicious situations to determine whether or not a crime has been committed. Such investigations often focus on possible corruption of public officials and on organized crime activities. On the other hand, the grand jury is the protector of the citizen. In this role, the jury stands as a check on overzealous, arbitrary, or capricious attempts by district attorneys to prosecute members of the public. Prosecution is viewed as costly to anyone, in terms of legal defense and social status losses. Thus, the grand jury seeks to permit prosecution only when the evidence at hand truly merits it.

Critics argue that the grand jury fails to fulfill the second of its roles, the protection of the public (Clark, 1975; Cobden, 1976; *U.S. News & World Report*, 1978). They assert that the prosecutor *owns* the grand jury and that the jury's structure and operation promote this ownership. Few standards govern selection of grand jurors beyond minimum educational and residence criteria. Grand juries generally are empaneled to sit for no more than eighteen months. Their proceedings are nonadversarial; prosecutors are not saddled with having to prove guilt beyond a reasonable doubt. Hearsay evidence is admissible. There are no constraints on topics covered by the prosecutor. The prosecutor chooses all witnesses and none may have legal counsel in the jury chambers. The jury has the power to jail uncooperative witnesses and those who refuse to testify after being granted immunity from future prosecution. In some states, a written transcript of the proceedings is not required.

In sum, as one empirical study of the grand jury in action has found, grand juries give little deliberation time to cases, experience little conflict during deliberations, and overwhelmingly accept the district attorney's position on each case (Carp, 1975). Thus, prosecutors enjoy fairly free reign in their conduct of grand jury proceedings. It follows that the ability of the jury to protect citizens from prosecutorial harassment is nearly nonexistent.

The grand jury abuse problem became particularly noticeable during the late 1960s and throughout the 1970s. The U.S. Justice Department began systematically to put together a federal grand jury network to undermine political activist organizations in this country. Grand juries were used not only to gather information about suspected crimes but more generally to gather intelligence about political dissenters. Typical of prosecutors' fishing expeditions is the following question put to a Los Angeles woman called before a grand jury in Tucson, Arizona, to testify in a case concerning a man's illegal purchase of dynamite in Tucson (Winograd and Fassen, 1973:16):

> I want you to tell the Grand Jury what period of time during the years 1969 and 1970 you resided at 2201 Ocean Front Walk, Venice [Los Angeles], who resided there at the time you lived there, identifying all persons you have seen in or about the premises at that address and tell the Grand Jury all the conversations that were held by you or others in your presence during the time that you were at that address.

In one three-year period in the 1970s, one Justice Department office gained approximately 400 indictments from over 100 grand juries. Among those investigated by the juries were the Viet Nam Veterans Against the War, Daniel Ellsberg (of "Pentagon Papers" fame), the Black Panther Party, the American Indian Movement, and the Los Angeles Antidraft Movement. That the cases represented more intelligence gathering and political harassment than attempts at criminal prosecution is suggested by the fact that, though the normal conviction rate stemming from grand jury indictments is 65 percent, only 15 percent of the 400 indictments written of here resulted in convictions. The problem caused one federal appeals court to note that such abusive practices are intolerable and that "It would be a sorry day were we to allow a grand jury to delve into the membership, meetings, minutes, organizational structure, funding, and political activities of unpopular organizations on the pretext that their members might have some information relevant to a crime" (U.S. News & World Report, 1978:66).

Numerous proposals have been suggested to address some of these problems. Some wish to have the grand jury witnesses be given more rights, including legal representation. Others would be satisfied if the witnesses were more explicitly apprised of their current rights and better informed about the case related to their testimony. Some want the prosecution to be bound by certain procedural rules and to be required to present to the grand jury any evidence favoring criminal suspects, as well as evidence against them. None of these proposals will end prosecutor abuses of the grand jury unless the provision of more rights to a witness results in grand jury proceedings becoming adversarial in nature. While any of the proposals may make the prosecutor's job more difficult, the fact is that he or she will remain in the best position to influence the outcome of grand jury proceedings.

The Negotiated Plea. Once the grand jury has returned a true bill, or the prosecutor has otherwise obtained an indictment, the issue becomes whether or not the defendant will go to trial. Between 60 and 90 percent of convictions in major urban court systems result from negotiated pleas rather than trial verdicts. The negotiated plea or plea bargain generally involves concessions made by the prosecution in return for information from a defendant or a guilty plea. Most negotiated pleas involve reducing the charges (for example, from burglary to criminal trespassing), dropping some charges, or promising lighter sentences. Most court observers argue that plea bargaining has become second nature for the attorneys involved, that it occurs so often that pleas are decided in minutes—almost by recipe (Mather, 1974). The key factor in this process is the development of notions of "normal crimes," stereotypes of offenders, offense situations, and standard charge reductions developed through experience in the courts. So common are these stereotypes, Sudnow argues (1965), that prosecutors and defense attorneys begin to "force" cases into them, ignoring individual qualities of a case; the result is a form of assembly-line justice.

A similar thesis is offered by Heumann (1978). His research results indicate that prosecutors are socialized into a culture of plea bargaining in which superiors, defense attorneys, and judges expect negotiation to occur. The negotiation is not shaped by caseload size but by three factors: (1) judges leave negotiation almost entirely to prosecutors, making them, in effect, the "judges"; (2) prosecutors perceive nearly all defendants as both factually and legally guilty; and (3) prosecutors feel that trial outcomes are unpredictable and that trials, therefore, should be avoided. Given these factors, prosecutors view their job as making certain offenders receive "appropriate" sentences. Thus, negotiations become structured by prosecutors' definitions of what is and what is not a serious crime.

Defense attorneys are also subject to a number of pressures that influence decisions regarding their clients. Public defenders feel primarily organizational pressures. They are given large numbers of cases to represent and are encouraged to process them as quickly as possible. Although they do not automatically assume that their clients are guilty, public defenders are likely to try to fit a client's case into their conception of a "normal crime" in order to process it more easily. The fact that public defenders are members of the "system," constantly interacting with prosecutors and judges and seeking to minimize tensions with these persons, encourages them to negotiate pleas for their clients. It should be noted, however, that Skolnick (1967) argues effectively that the degree of cooperation between prosecuting and defense attorneys often is exaggerated and that a certain adversarial quality always characterizes pretrail interactions.

Private defense attorneys are influenced primarily by the economic features of their practices. Those few attorneys who represent wealthier clients will likely take an adversary approach in building a defense—pushing the prosecution and using every legal loophole available to the interests of their clients. If this approach fails, the attorneys will attempt to obtain the best deal possible for their client.

The practice of criminal law is generally not lucrative, however, for most persons charged with crimes are from the lower classes. Attorneys generally charge a flat fee for representation, and it is therefore to their advantage to minimize the amount of work on a given case and move on to another. To become involved in a trial is to lose money. Hence, the pressure to negotiate a plea of guilty for the client. This pressure is further increased by the need to maintain good working relations with other members of the court whose favors may be required in future cases (Blumberg, 1967).

In sum, the size and composition of a community's official criminal population is in large part shaped by the structure of the practice of criminal law. Changes in this element of the criminal justice system should be reflected in the population of those labeled criminal. For example, U.S. Supreme Court decisions about boundaries of plea bargaining could significantly alter the number and types of cases that result in criminal charges and trials. Similarly, changes in the practice of divorce law may drive more lawyers to the practice of criminal law. The resultant competition for criminal cases will certainly affect the quality of representation a defense attorney provides a client.

The Trial as Image Management

As we previously noted, relatively few criminal cases are decided by trial. Those that are are in some ways special, because they are sensational, because the attorneys involved stand to profit from the trial, because the defendant is unusually stubborn (or foolish) in refusing to accept a negotiated plea, because the defense attorney is relatively certain of acquittal, or because the defendant has nothing to lose and everything to gain by trial (Mather, 1974).

Through courtroom enactments in the entertainment media, the public has formed an impression of the trial as a fact-finding endeavor. In reality, if "the truth will out" in the trial, it will probably do so accidentally, for the adversary-trial model does not actually emphasize facts. The prosecutor is already convinced of the defendant's guilt and will be intent on gaining a conviction. The defense is interested in discrediting the prosecutor's case. Both parties seek to make a favorable impression upon their audience—the judge and jury, which will reward the performance of one side or the other with the verdict it desires. If, in creating the desired impression, an attorney feels that the facts are useful, the facts will be pursued. Sometimes the impression is best managed when the facts are downplayed or ignored.

If a defense attorney feels the prosecutor's case is technically weak, generally the client will be advised to seek a trial before a judge. If, however, the attorney feels the prosecutor's case is technically strong, the client will be advised to choose trial before a jury—a group that is more impressionable. In selecting a jury prior to a trial, both the prosecution and the defense are allowed a number of free challenges by which they may exclude individuals from the jury. Beyond this, they may have an individual excluded on such grounds as racial prejudice or pretrial exposure to the case. In selecting jurors, both attorneys seek persons they feel will be susceptible to the image they wish to project. Generally, they do not seek the best "fact finders."

The attempt by attorneys to choose an impressionable jury is best highlighted by the recent use of scientific surveys and computer analysis in selecting jurors for highly publicized trials (for example, the trials of Angela Davis, John Mitchell and Maurice Stans, and Joan Little). Social scientists are hired to survey the population from which the jury will be chosen. From the survey data, the researchers attempt to find correlations between demographic characteristics and attitudes favoring the defense. From the findings, the researchers develop a profile of the juror most likely to acquit. The defense attorney uses the information in selecting jurors. To date, the method has been extremely successful (Tivnan, 1975). It also lays to rest any doubt that trials are more a matter of image building than fact finding (Van Dyke, 1977).

In the actual trial situation, attorneys choose their witnesses carefully. They are chosen, not on the basis of the information they have, but on the basis of the impression they will make on the jury. Jurors are known to give more attention to witnesses' confidence than to the content of their statements (Erlanger, 1970). Hence, lawyers carefully select the order of appearance of witnesses and the content and order of the questions asked of them. In addition to their concern with witnesses, attorneys are aware that jurors are also influenced by the dress and demeanor of defendants and attorneys. Strategies for image management are thus also planned around these factors.

Social-status characteristics of jurors also seem to influence their collective deliberations and decisions. High-status jurors are more likely to engage in jury deliberation; they are also more likely to be chosen jury foremen.

Strodtbeck and Mann (1956) suggest that the more educated juror is more active in deliberations and female jurors are less active than male jurors. Whether or not deliberating jurors follow the judge's instructions and concern themselves with questions of evidence is debatable. While some researchers (Kalven and Zeisel, 1966:162) report that jurors are attentive to facts and instructions, many observers tend to agree with Frank's claim (1949:108–25) that juries create law by applying their own rules to their selective interpretation of the facts of the case.

In sum, the trial situation differs little from other elements of the criminal justice system. It is an organizational enterprise that produces a product: officially labeled criminals. As we have seen, the influences on the creation of that product extend beyond the facts of criminal cases and the quest for justice. In line with the theme of this chapter, we also realize that changes in the structure of the trial will alter the characteristics of its product.

Sentencing

A criminal conviction (whether through trial or plea) necessitates sentencing. Occasionally, the legislature specifies the exact sentence for an offense. This is done by means of a "flat" or fixed sentence that specifies a nonnegotiable penalty for an offense while negating the possibility for parole, or, to a lesser extent, by specifying a mandatory minimum sentence which a judge may impose for an offense type (see Chapter 12). Generally, however, judges have a number of options in determining a sentence. They may place an individual on probation for a specified time. They may suspend the sentence they impose. They may levy a fine in addition to or in lieu of imprisonment. They may send an offender to a prison, a jail, a work farm, or any number of community-based halfway-house programs.

In sentencing an individual to prison for most offenses, judges may impose a specific sentence within the minimum and maximum number of allowable years determined by the legislature. In some instances, they may structure the availability of parole opportunities. Most often, judges impose an indefinite sentence, assigning the minimum and maximum years to be served and leaving the actual number of years served to be determined by the state parole authority.

Judges vary in the severity of the sentences they impose. For the most part, these differences are linked to variations in world view and penal philosophy—the result of the judges' personal and professional backgrounds (Hogarth, 1971; Nagel, 1962). Sentences also partially reflect the ideas of the community in which a judge sits. Thus, we see "inconsistent" sentences: a judge in one community sentencing an offender to a few years in prison while a judge in another community imposes a more severe sentence on a similar offender. As Richard Quinney notes (1970:167), this sentence disparity occurs even in federal judicial-circuit courts. In 1966, for example, a forgery conviction in the 1st Federal Judicial Circuit brought an average prison sentence of 13.7 months, but the same conviction in the 10th Circuit resulted in an average sentence of 36 months.

Although the public notices sentencing disparity, it generally does not realize that in most large court systems today judges rely on presentence reports and recommendations based on probation department investigations of convicted offenders. Carter and Wilkins (1967) report that the probation officer's recommendations for probation are honored by judges about 95 percent of the time. The courts follow the probation officer's recommendation for imprisonment in 80 to 85 percent of the cases.

Ideally, the presentence report should include a thorough investigation of the offender's background, criminal justice record, and special treatment needs; that is, a suggested sentence should be tailored to the individual offender. Yet it is doubtful that this occurs. The number of cases requiring presentence reports is generally too large to allow such individual attention. Further, as with other members of the court system, probation officers tend to develop notions of "normal cases," stereotypes to which they fit cases, generally ignoring their unique aspects.

The major concern regarding sentencing disparity is that it reflects systematic discrimination, especially against racial minorities. The U.S. Supreme Court in *Furman* v. *Georgia* (408 U.S. 238, 371 [1972]) found that capital punishment had been imposed discriminatorily against the poor and racial minorities. Since that date, states have written and rewritten their capital punishment statutes until, in the early 1980s, most states have met the Supreme Court's definition of fairness in the assignment of the death penalty (see Chapter 12). The only problem remaining for a few states is the development of a process of review for "proportionality," the determination that a sentence is not out of line with those given like offenders.

In terms of empirically grounded knowledge, the question of discrimination in capital punishment and other types of sentencing remains unanswered. Historically, some studies have claimed to have discovered racial discrimination in sentencing (Bullock, 1961); others have reported no links between sentences and such extralegal factors as sex, age, and race when other factors such as seriousness of offense are held constant (Green, 1961). Hagan's (1974) review of sentencing disparity studies suggested that given the poor methodologies employed in past sentencing disparity studies, there was no sound evidence of discrimination in sentencing. This conclusion was supported a short time later by Chiricos and Waldo's (1975) finding of no evidence to support a charge of socioeconomic status bias in the sentencing of 10,488 inmates in the southeastern U.S.

At present, much attention is being devoted to methodological questions in the study of sentencing disparities (better conceptualization of extralegal factors that might influence sentences, better distinctions among types of sentences, and so forth). The results are mixed. Lizotte (1978) reports that, all else equal, laborers and nonwhites receive longer prison sentences than do higher SES groups. In a review of published research on racial bias in sentencing, Kleck (1981) concludes that the death penalty generally has not been imposed for murder in a manner discriminatory toward blacks, except in the South, that death sentences for rape (when such sentences were legal) were highly racially discriminatory (again in the South) and that little evidence exists that widespread discrimination against blacks occurs in noncapital cases. Spohn et al. (1981) counter that, according to their analysis of a large data set, blacks are more likely than whites to be incarcerated, all else equal, though there is no evidence of disparity in length of sentence. Against this last finding, Thomson and Zingraff (1981) report that their review of 1977 sentencing patterns suggests that race is a factor in length of sentence given to offenders. In sum, Kleck's findings notwithstanding, more sophisticated research seems to be pointing to race as a factor in sentencing but the exact form of its influence seems difficult to pinpoint.

In conclusion, the court system reflects a matrix of legal philosophies, political orientations and pressures, bureaucratic tendencies, and personal interests. The ideal adversary model to which it aspires is largely absent. It is eroded by a tendency toward a cooperative, crime-control model that places efficient organizational processing of assumedly guilty persons above due process. As such, it structures the characteristics of our current population of official criminals. Changes in various aspects of the present system (for example, a renewed emphasis on due process or a change in plea bargaining formulas) can be expected to alter the size and characteristics of that population.

AN EXAMPLE: BAIL DECISIONS AND THE PRODUCTION OF OFFICIAL CRIMINALS

Our discussion of the courts has argued that the court process represents a series of organizational decisions that produce a product: officially labeled criminals. One of the better examples of this production phenomenon lies in bail decisions. *Bail* refers to the practice whereby people arrested are allowed to go free pending trial after they (or a bondsman who receives a fee) have given the court a specified sum of money, to be forfeited if they fail to appear for trial. The bail concept strikes a compromise between two conflicting rights: (1) the right of the accused to be treated as innocent until proven guilty (that is, the right not to be incarcerated until proven guilty) and (2) the right of the state to expect that all who are charged with crimes will appear for trial.

Bail would appear primarily designed to benefit the accused. Ideally, the amount of bail is determined solely on the basis of the seriousness of the charge against the accused and the likelihood that he or she will abscond or commit another crime while awaiting trial. However, exorbitantly high bail is often used by the state to harass individuals who are difficult to bring to trial (such as members of organized crime) and to hold persons in jail in the hope that they will cooperate with the state (become police informers, for example) in return for freedom or other considerations (Wice, 1974). Further, high bail reflects attempts by judges and district attorneys to protect their reputations. If the district attorney does not request high bail and the judge does not set high bail, any bail jumping that occurs will be attributed to their "coddling" of criminals (Suffet, 1966). Finally, the bail process may be criticized as economically discriminatory: the wealthier citizen can buy a better brand of justice than can the poorer citizen (Foote, 1959; Goldkamp, 1980).

Regarding this last point, bail decisions would appear at first glance to have little impact on the eventual outcome of a criminal case. These decisions cannot alter the facts that determine verdicts. In reality, however, the accused benefits greatly if he or she receives bail. The ability to make bail influences case outcomes in a number of ways (President's Commission on Law Enforcement, 1967:131):

1. It provides accused persons with the opportunity to work and raise money for their defense.
2. It affords defendants and their lawyers greater access to each other.
3. It allows defendants to participate to a greater degree in the preparation of their defense (for example, finding defense witnesses).
4. It avoids the possible self-fulfilling prophecy that may occur when a jury, seeing that the defendant is not free on bail and is therefore probably "dangerous," votes a verdict of guilty.
5. It discourages guilty pleas out of desperation; at times defendants who do not raise bail are encouraged to plead guilty in return for applying to their sentences the time already spent in jail awaiting trial.

Bail statistics seem to support the claim that ability to raise bail influences case dispositions. One early bail study (Foote, 1954) found that 58 percent of defendants out on bail were acquitted, whereas only 18 percent of those held in jail were acquitted. Another study (Roberts and Palermo, 1958) reported a 31 percent rate of acquittal for defendants on bail as opposed to a 20 percent rate for those held in jail. A study of 1960 New York City bail decisions found higher acquittal rates for persons on bail in six or seven crime categories (Ares et al., 1963). The same study reported that those free pending trial received suspended sentences if found guilty more often than did those held in jail. More recent findings of a study of influences on the legal disposition of homicide cases suggest that bail produces less severe dispositions (Swigert and Farrell, 1977).

Findings such as these have fostered research concerning the effects of non-bail types of pretrial release. In an attempt to discover a means of releasing defendants that did not necessitate raising bail money, staff members of the 1961 Manhattan Bail Project (Ares et al., 1963) interviewed defendants to determine (1) if they had lived at the same address for six months or more, (2) if they were currently employed, (3) if they had close relatives in New York City, (4) if they had no previous conviction record, and (5) if they had resided in New York for at least ten years. If at least one of these questions was answered affirmatively and the answer verified by the staff, the names of the defendants were placed in a pool for possible pretrial release without bail. After a more rigorous second screening by the staff, the remaining defendants were randomly assigned to either of two groups. One group received recommendations for pretrial release without bail. The other received no recommendations and was subjected to the traditional bail decision process.

Analysis of the results of the experiment indicated that 59 percent of those in the group released without bail received acquittal verdicts or had charges eventually dropped, whereas only 23 percent of those detained in jail received similar dispositions. Among those found guilty in the pretrial release group, most received suspended sentences. Ninety-six percent of those in the jailed group who were found guilty were sent to prison. Release without bail also seemed a superior method to release by bail. Only 14 percent of those who were eligible for the project release program but were not given recommendations eventually were released on bail. Fewer persons in the pretrial release group failed to appear for trial than persons who received bail.

Research building on the findings of the Manhattan Bail Project supports its emphasis on the employment and criminal history but reconceptualizes its notion of community ties and argues also that the ease with which a defendant can be contacted (by phone, for example) influences future court appearance behavior (Ozanne et al., 1980). In terms of the community ties, variable length of time in a community is relatively unimportant in predicting appearance behavior. Homeownership, not given specific attention in the Manhattan Bail Project, now seems important. But the key to community ties appears to be whether or not defendants are married and living with their spouses. Ozanne et al. (1980:154–55) argue that this variable reflects a stage in the life cycle (particularly that of the male) that signifies stability and effective social control potential, thus making a defendant a strong bail risk.

In sum, court decisions are instrumental in shaping the size and composition of the official criminal population. This is evidenced by viewing the results of bail decisions. Changes in bail decisions—organizational changes—will alter the products of the court process, and different numbers and types of persons will be defined as criminal in this society.

SUMMARY

In this chapter, we explored the criminal justice system, not as a simple processing organization, but as a production system. Criminal justice agencies are all linked to the creation of a population of persons with official criminal status. The police initiate the production by their selection of certain persons for arrest. Prosecutors further the production process by selecting persons to be charged from among those arrested. The court system completes the process by selecting from among those charged a number of persons to be labeled "guilty."

The key to the production of official criminals is discretion by members of the criminal justice system: police discretion to arrest, prosecution discretion to bring charges and negotiate pleas, and court discretion in determining guilt and in sentencing. As this chapter has emphasized time and again, the influences on use of discretion are often extralegal. That is, the size and composition of today's official criminal population are shaped by political and organizational factors. As these factors change, the size and composition of the criminal population is altered. In sum, criminal justice is not simply the processing of criminals or the sorting of the guilty from the innocent. Rather, it is the creation of a criminal population that, in turn, shapes the public's view of crime and the types of people committing crimes.

REFERENCES

Ares, C. E., A. Rankin, and H. Sturz. 1963. The Manhattan Bail Project: An interim report on the use of pre-trial parole. *NYU Law Rev.* 38:76–86.

Becker, H. S. 1963. *Outsiders: Studies in the Sociology of Deviance.* New York: Free Press.

Black, D. J. 1970. Production of crime rates. *Am. Sociol. Rev.* 35:733–48.

———. 1980. *The Manners and Customs of the Police.* New York: Academic Press.

Blumberg, A. S. 1967. The practice of law as a confidence game: Organization cooptation of a profession. *Law & Society Rev.* 1:15–39.

Bullock, H. A. 1961. Significance of the racial factor in the length of prison sentences. *J. Crim. Law Criminol. & Pol. Sci.* 52:411–17.

Carp, R. A. 1975. The behavior of grand juries. *Soc. Sci. Q.* 55:853–70.

Carter, R. M., and L. T. Wilkins. 1967. Some factors in sentencing policy. *J. Crim. Law Criminol. & Pol. Sci.* 58:503–14.

Chevigny, P. 1969. *Police Power.* New York: Vintage Trade Books.

Chiricos, T. G., and G. P. Waldo. 1975. Socioeconomic status and criminal sentencing: An empirical assessment of a conflict proposition. *Am. Sociol. Rev.* 40:753–72.

Clark, L. D. 1975. *The Grand Jury: The Use and Abuse of Political Power.* New York: Quadrangle Books.

Cobden, L. 1976. The grand jury—its use and misuse. *Crime & Delinq.* 22:149–65.

Cole, G. 1970. The decision to prosecute. *Law & Society Rev.* 4:313–43.

Cumming, E., I. Cumming, and L. Edell. 1965. Policeman as philosopher, guide, and friend. *Soc. Prob.* 12:276–86.

De Fleur, L. B. 1975. Biasing influences on drug arrest records: Implications for deviance research. *Am. Sociol. Rev.* 40:88–103.

Erlanger, H. S. 1970. Jury research in America: Its past and future. *Law & Society Rev.* 4:345–70.

Foote, C. 1954. Compelling appearance in court: Administration of bail in Philadelphia. *Univ. Penn. Law Rev.* 102:1031–79.

———. 1959. The bail system and equal justice. *Fed. Probat.* 23:43–48.

Frank J. 1949. *Courts on Trial.* Princeton, N.J.: Princeton University Press.

Gardiner, J. 1970. *The Politics of Corruption: Organized Crime in an American City.* New York: Russell Sage.

Goldkamp, J. S. 1980. Philadelphia revisited: An examination of bail and detention two decades after Foote. *Crime & Delinq.* 26:179–92.

Goldstein, H. 1977. *Policing a Free Society.* Cambridge: Ballinger Publishing Co.

Goldstein, J. 1960. Police discretion not to invoke the criminal process: Low visibility decisions in the administration of justice. *Yale Law. J.* 69:543–94.

Green, E. 1961. *Judicial Attitudes in Sentencing.* London: Macmillan Publishing Co.

Hagan, J. 1974. Extra-legal attributes and criminal sentencing: An assessment of a sociological viewpoint. *Law & Society* 82:357–83.

Hepburn, J. R. 1978. Race and the decision to arrest. *J. Res. Crime & Delinq.* 15:54–73.

Heumann, M. 1978. *Plea Bargaining.* Chicago: University of Chicago Press.

Hogarth, J. 1971. *Sentencing as a Human Process.* Toronto: University of Toronto Press.

Johnson, W. T., R. E. Petersen, and L. E. Wells. 1977. Arrest probabilities for marijuana users as indicators of selective law enforcement. *Am. J. Sociol.* 83:681–99.

Kalven, J., and H. Zeisel. 1966. *The American Jury.* Boston: Little, Brown and Company.

Kamisar, Y. 1965. When the cops were not "handcuffed." *New York Times Magazine,* Nov. 7, 34–35 and *passim.*

Kleck, G. 1981. Racial discrimination in criminal sentencing: A critical evaluation of the evidence with additional evidence on the death penalty. *Am. Sociol. Rev.* 46:783–804.

Lizotte, A. 1978. Extra-legal factors in Chicago's criminal courts: Testing the conflict model of criminal justice. *Soc. Prob.* 25:564–80.

Manning, P. 1971. The police: Mandate, strategies, and appearances. In *Crime and Justice in American Society.* Edited by J. D. Douglas. Indianapolis: The Bobbs-Merrill Co.

———. 1975. Survey review. *Contemp. Sociol.* 4:481–87.

Mather, L. M. 1974. Some determinants of the method of case disposition: Decision-making by police defenders in Los Angeles. *Law & Society Rev.* 8:187–216.

Myers, M., and J. Hagan. 1979. Private and public trouble: Prosecutors and the allocation of court resources. *Soc. Prob.* 26:439–51.

Nagel, S. 1962. Judicial backgrounds and criminal cases. *J. Crim. Law Criminol. & Pol. Sci.* 53:333–39.

National Institute of Law Enforcement and Criminal Justice, Law Enforcement Assistance Administration, U.S. Department of Justice. 1976. *Improving Witness Cooperation.* Washington, D.C.: U.S. Government Printing Office.

Ozanne, M., R. A. Wilson, and D. L. Gedney. 1980. Toward a theory of bail risk. *Criminology* 18:147–61.

Packer, H. L. 1968. *The Limits of Criminal Sanction.* Stanford, California: Stanford University Press.

Piliavin, I., and S. Briar. 1964. Police encounters with juveniles. *Am. J. Sociol.* 70:206–14.

President's Commission on Law Enforcement and Administration of Justice. 1967. *The Challenge of Crime in Free Society.* Washington, D.C.: U.S. Government Printing Office.

Quinney, R. 1970. *The Social Reality of Crime.* Boston: Little, Brown and Company.

Roberts, J. W., and J. S. Palermo. 1958. A study of administration of bail in New York. *Univ. Penn. Law Rev.* 106:726–27.

Rubinstein, J. 1973. *City Police.* New York: Random House.

Seidman, D., and M. Couzens. 1974. Getting the crime rate down: Political pressure and crime reporting. *Law & Society Rev.* 8:457–93.

Sheley, J., and J. Hanlon. 1978. Unintended effects of police decisions to actively enforce laws: Implications for analysis of crime trends. *Contemp. Crises* 2:265–75.

Sheley, J., and A. Harris. 1976. On police-citizen encounters—a comment. *Soc. Prob.* 23:630–32.

Sherman, L. W. 1980. Causes of police behavior: The current state of quantitative research. *J. Res. Crime & Delinq.* 17:69–100.

Skolnick, J. 1967. Social control in the adversary system. *J. Conflict Resolu.* 11:52–70.

———. 1975. *Justice Without Trial.* 2nd ed. New York: John Wiley & Sons.

Spohn, C., J. Gruhl, and S. Welch. 1981. The effect of race on sentencing: A re-examination of an unsettled question. *Law & Society Rev.* 16:71–88.

Strodtbeck, F. L., and R. D. Mann. 1956. Sex role differentiation in jury deliberations. *Sociometry* 19:3–11.

Sudnow, D. 1965. Normal crimes: Sociological features of the penal code in a public defender office. *Soc. Prob.* 12:255–76.

Suffet, F. 1966. Bail setting: A study of courtroom interaction. *Crime & Delinq.* 12:318–31.

Swigert, V., and R. Farrell. 1977. Normal homicides and the law. *Am. Sociol. Rev.* 42:16–31.

Sykes, R., and J. Clark. 1975. A theory of deference exchange in police-civilian encounters. *Am. J. Sociol.* 81:548–600.

Thomson, R. J., and M. T. Zingraff. 1981. Detecting sentencing disparity: Some problems and evidence. *Am. J. Sociol.* 86:869–80.

Tivnan, E. 1975. Jury by trial. *New York Times Magazine,* Nov. 16, 30–31 and *passim.*

U.S. Department of Justice. 1982. *Criminal Victimization in the United States, 1980.* Washington, D.C.: U.S. Government Printing Office.

U.S. News & World Report. 1978. Are grand juries getting out of line? June 19, 65–67.

Van Dyke, J. 1977. American jury. *Center Magazine* 10:36–48.

Wice, P. 1974. *Freedom for Sale.* Lexington, Mass.: D. C. Heath & Company.

Wiley, M., and T. Hudik. 1974. Police-citizen encounters: A field test of exchange theory. *Soc. Prob.* 22:119–127.

Wilson, J. Q. 1968. *Varieties of Police Behavior: The Management of Law and Order in Eight Communities.* Cambridge: Harvard University Press.

Winograd, B., and M. Fassen. 1973. The political question. *Trial* 9, 16–20.

SUGGESTED READINGS

Criminologists have conducted extensive research on the police, especially as interest in the conflict and labeling perspectives has risen. Three of the best works on the police are *Justice Without Trial,* 2nd ed. (New York: John

Wiley & Sons, 1975) by Jerome Skolnick; *City Police* (New York: Random House, 1973) by Jonathan Rubinstein; and *The Manners and Customs of the Police* (New York: Academic Press, 1980) by Donald Black.

One of the clearest looks at the operations of our courts comes in semi-novel form. Arthur Rosett and D. R. Cressey have written a hypothetical account of a defendant's movement through the court system following an arrest for burglary. The book, *Justice by Consent* (Philadelphia: J. B. Lippincott Co., 1976), offers the reader without a technical, criminological orientation an understanding of the plea-bargaining process and where it fits into our court system. Howard James provides a similarly effective discussion of the courts in his *Crisis in the Courts,* rev. ed. (New York: David McKay Co., 1977); and Milton Heumann gives insight into the role of prosecutor in *Plea Bargaining* (Chicago: University of Chicago Press, 1978).

11

THE CORRECTIONS SYSTEM

A criminal justice system that produces officially labeled criminals must develop a subsystem to deal with such persons. The products of our court system—convicted offenders—are subjected to various degrees of supervision, punishment, and treatment. Some receive suspended sentences and probation and must report regularly to a probation officer. Some are placed in minimum-security facilities and are sometimes allowed temporary leaves. Some are totally confined in maximum-security prisons. Depending on their records in prison, some offenders may be placed back into society before the completion of their prison sentences through supervised parole.

In this chapter we will examine the subsystem of the criminal justice system that supervises, punishes, and attempts to aid offenders—namely, the corrections system. We will present an overview of orientations toward punishment and correction of offenders and devote attention to the institutions and places where these activities occur: jails, prisons, and community corrections programs. Finally, we will discuss the failure of attempted rehabilitation of offenders and suggest the future direction of the corrections system.

WHAT IS "CORRECTION"?

"Correction" implies repair or alteration. Regarding criminals, correction theoretically refers to changing or correcting an individual's inclination toward or pattern of law violation. Though, as we shall see below, correction takes many forms—punishment, behavior modification, counseling, job as-sistance—all forms involve some degree of deprivation of liberty. Thus, we may define "correction" as *the deprivation of an individual's freedom in or-der to alter his or her behavior from criminal to conventional.*

Not everyone will agree that all correctional actions imply deprivation of freedom. Some will argue that deprivation of freedom constitutes punish-ment whereas modern correctional philosophy emphasizes treatment that aids the offender. Stated another way, can we really be punishing people if we are helping or curing them? The answer is yes. No matter what its form or its motive, the fact remains that correction is activity in which offenders are *forced* to engage. They would not be undergoing correction had they not been caught committing a crime, and they would not choose correction if given the option of "no correction." As one report puts it (American Friends Service Committee, 1971:23–24):

> There is an easy test that can be applied to any purported abolition of pun-ishment or imprisonment [in favor of "nonpunitive correction"]. Is the pro-posed alternative program voluntary? Can the subject take it or leave it? If he takes it, can he leave it any time he wants? If the answer to any of these ques-tions is "no," then the wolf is still under the sheepskin.

CHANGING CORRECTIONS ORIENTATIONS

The history of dealing with law violators in the U.S. reflects ongoing attempts to reconcile three primary objectives: (1) punishment of offenders, (2) reha-bilitation of offenders, and (3) custody of offenders for society's protection. Though rehabilitation efforts always have characterized the prison system, punishment and custody orientations predominated until the 1950s. Prisons, in fact, were developed relatively recently as substitutes for "less humane" forms of punishment such as mutilation, beatings, or placement in such de-vices as stocks and pillories. Imprisonment of offenders also was seen as nec-essary for society's protection when other forms of punishment failed.

Punishment of offenders generally has been justified on the grounds that it is a deterrent to further criminal behavior by the offender, is a general de-terrent to other members of society contemplating crimes, and is a source of revenge or justice. Emphasis on these different functions has shifted through-out the years, but the use of punishment, either by itself or combined with treatment techniques (such as vocational training), was a constant until fairly recently. The Auburn System (named after a New York penitentiary opened in 1817) served as the model for American prison systems for 150 years. It emphasized discipline designed to break a prisoner's spirit and force him or her to conform. Prisoners worked and had meals together but were never al-lowed to speak or communicate with each other. The inmates were housed in individual cells within a fortresslike structure with many tiers—much like the design of maximum-security prisons today. Corporal punishment was used to enforce prison rules (Rothman, 1971).

Strong humanitarian ideals, increasing confidence in the behavioral sciences' ability to predict and change individuals' behavior, and a growing frustration with the ability of the prison system to reform prisoners combined in the late 1940s and early 1950s to produce subtle changes in prisons. The *punishment model,* which viewed the offender as evil, began to give way to a *medical* or *treatment model,* which viewed the offender as sick or maladjusted and in need of rehabilitation.

The medical or treatment model gained prominence in the late 1950s and early 1960s. Penal institutions became "correctional facilities." A number of individual and group counseling and therapy programs were introduced into prisons. Guards were labeled "counselors." Educational and vocational training programs were expanded. Indeterminate sentences were widely used; that is, offenders were sentenced to prison for as long as it took to be judged "rehabilitated." It was in this atmosphere that punishment for reformation, revenge, justice, and general deterrence became deemphasized. "Corrections" came to represent attempts to remake, not to break, prisoners. The source of their illness (their criminality) would be diagnosed and treated (Kassebaum et al., 1971).

For reasons we will discuss later in this chapter, most experts now consider the in-prison treatment model a failure. This failure and public fear of crime in the late 1960s and early 1970s have led to a renewed emphasis on the custody orientation to corrections. That is, the major function of the corrections system is seen as the protection of society from criminals. Questions of justice and rehabilitation have become secondary. What is left of the rehabilitation theme exists in the concept of community-based corrections. Community corrections programs attempt to submit the offender to noninstitutional treatment.

Basically, any form of corrections that occurs outside of prison may be called community oriented. These alternatives to prison take the form of probation and parole, halfway-house residential treatment centers, and release and furlough programs, which are all described in this chapter. The programs seek to provide offenders with a full range of social services and, more importantly, to enlist the aid of the community in encouraging conventional values and behavior from the offenders. Because of community concern with safety, most community-based corrections efforts are directed toward lower-risk, lesser offenders. Thus, the value of the community-based corrections model lies not so much in the correction of lesser offenders as in removing them from the corrupting influences of the prison setting.

In sum, the corrections system has been and remains multioriented. At various times, it has operated within a punishment framework; at other times, a rehabilitation framework; and at still other times, a custody frame-

NEWSPRINT AND COMMENT

Judge Puts Lid on Jail Population

By Jack Wardlaw

BATON ROUGE—Parish jail populations must be limited to 602 in Jefferson and 105 in Plaquemines, a federal judge here has ruled. The parishes' sheriffs have signed a federal court order agreeing to comply with the limits.

Similar orders are expected for Orleans, St. Charles and St. John the Baptist parishes from U.S. District Judge Frank Polozola, who was given the job of deciding jail population limits throughout Louisiana by the 5th U.S. Circuit Court of Appeals.

Polozola, Jefferson Sheriff Harry Lee and Plaquemines Sheriff Herman B. Schoenberger signed the orders late Monday. The clerk of U.S. District Court made the orders public Tuesday.

The judge also issued an order barring double bunks for prisoners at the reception center at Elayn Hunt Correctional Center at St. Gabriel. That decision could have far-reaching effects on the state prison system if it is applied to the system as a whole.

The Jefferson order stipulates that no more than 456 prisoners may be held at the Community Correction Center in

Gretna and no more than 146 in the old Parish Prison there.

However, the order permits people to be detained for 72 hours without being counted in the total, up to 41 at the correction center and 11 at the old jail.

Some officials had expressed fears that Jefferson would be unable to comply with the new state drunken driving law that goes into effect Jan. 1 because of limitations on jail space, but the order appears to permit people with short sentences to go in under the 72-hour rule.

All the orders provide that the state fire marshal and state health officer can proceed in state court to close jails exceeding the limits.

Polozola is expected to finish handing out orders on parish jails this week and begin work on city jails before taking up state prisons.

In what may have been a preview of what is in store for state prisons, the judge ordered Hunt officials to dismantle double bunks at the reception center where convicts are examined, tested and shipped off to serve their time.

If the judge bans double-bunking throughout the system, it would threaten Gov. David

C. Treen's policy of avoiding prison construction by increasing prisoner populations at existing facilities.

Treen's plan calls for adding 2,000 prisoners to penitentiaries through fiscal year 1987–1988 by double-bunking and building dormitories at the maximum security prison at Angola.

Should the double-bunking ban be made statewide, the Legislature would have to find money for a $120 million prison construction program.

Treen has declined to speculate on court rulings in the prison cases, but has endorsed the use of double-bunking to house prisoners.

The use of bunk beds has been criticized by many inside and outside the corrections field. Critics claim the procedure amounts to the warehousing of prisoners and leads to security problems and increased chances of violence. However, state officials said proper security would curtail that problem and that there is nothing constitutionally wrong with double-bunking.

Source: © Times-Picayune Publishing Corp., 1982. Reprinted by permission.

Comment: The Jail Squeeze

During the past several years, prisons in this country have overflowed with inmates as judges send more persons to prison for longer terms. The result has been overcrowding of local jails as well. Local jails house inmates for whom prisons have no room. Many prison and jail administrators have tried crowding more prisoners into cells and dormitories. Beds have been placed in hallways and in rooms intended for other purposes. Some inmates are housed outdoors in tents. Institutions at times take on the air of concentration camps.

As the above news item indicates, the courts have ordered state and local governments to remedy overcrowded conditions in their correctional institutions. While losing some of their rights, prisoners have not lost the right to basic dignified treatment as humans and clearly retain their Eighth Amendment protection against cruel and unusual punishment. State and local governments thus find themselves with three unpleasant alternatives.

1. They can build new facilities. This is unattractive in today's economy, especially since demographic projections indicate that added space will not be needed in another twenty years.
2. They can free some prisoners. This has occurred in some jurisdictions, though not on a grand scale. It is certainly not a politically popular choice.
3. They can sentence fewer offenders to prison. Again, this is hardly a popular strategem.

As state financial situations worsen, it is clear that fewer new facilities will be built. Interestingly, the source of prison overcrowding is not increased crime or arrests. Rather, it reflects prosecutors' decisions to take more cases to trial and to plea bargain less freely. We can expect to see other members of the criminal justice system pressuring prosecutors to be more selective in pursuing court cases.

---

work. The constant shift in orientations signifies responses to a number of influential parties: the public that demands protection, the moralists who demand justice, the humanitarians who seek humane treatment of offenders, corrections "scientists" who are attempting to find what "works," and rehabilitation advocates who are convinced that offenders can be turned into conventional citizens. In the early 1960s, rehabilitation advocates prevailed. Today, the custody orientation predominates, though the treatment model exists in community-based corrections. Perhaps the best understanding of present-day corrections can be achieved through a description of current "places of correction." To this end, the bulk of this chapter is devoted to discussions of jails, prisons, and community-based corrections as they currently exist.

JAILS

Jails are local detention and correctional facilities run by city or county administrators, often the sheriff's department. They are designed primarily as holding centers for persons awaiting trial, sentencing, or appeal decisions. However, jails also are utilized as short-term correctional institutions for "small-time" offenders who might be sentenced to serve a few months to a year in jail. Jails also serve as short-term holding facilities for community problem cases such as drunks, the mentally ill, and individuals with drug problems.

According to a June 30, 1982 survey of local jail populations (U.S. Department of Justice, 1983), about 210,000 persons were confined in our nation's jails on that day—nearly 33 percent more than were counted in a similar survey in February, 1978. Table 11–1 offers data indicating that 60 percent of those in jail on that 1982 date had not been convicted of a crime. They were awaiting arraignment, pretrial release, or trial itself. Convicted persons in jails were awaiting sentences, transfers to other custody situations, or parole or probation violation hearings. The prisoners had been in jail an average of eleven days.

The majority of jail inmates (93 percent) are males. As Table 11–2 indicates, about 58 percent of the inmate population are white, 40 percent are black, and 2 percent represent other races. Though efforts have been made in most states to remove juveniles from jails and to place them in separate detention facilities, they have not been fully successful. Over 1,700 juveniles were in jails in 1982. Most inmates, young and old, have not completed high school. The vast majority claimed earning less than $5000 per year during the year preceding their incarceration. Most were unemployed at the time they were admitted to jail (U.S. Department of Justice, 1976a).

Because jails have been considered short-term or temporary holding facilities, they generally have been ignored by the public and by correctional reformers. Recently, however, jails have received severe criticism (see U.S. Department of Justice, 1975; Goldfarb, 1975; Pileggi, 1981). Locally controlled, they receive inadequate financial support. Most jails are overcrowded, poorly maintained facilities whose conditions endanger physical and mental health. Cells are small and cagelike. Sanitary equipment is poor

TABLE 11–1

Jail inmates by detention status, June 30, 1982

	Total	Male	Female
All inmates	209,582	195,730	13,852
Adult	207,853	194,153	13,700
Awaiting arraignment or trial	118,189	110,078	8,111
Convicted	89,664	84,075	5,589
Juvenile	1,729	1,577	152
Awaiting preliminary hearing			
or adjudication	1,274	1,145	129
Adjudicated	455	432	23

Source: U.S. Department of Justice, Bureau of Justice Statistics, *Jail Inmates 1982* (Washington, D.C.: U.S. Department of Justice, 1983), p. 1.

or nonexistent. Adequate medical and recreational facilities are rare; vocational and recreational programs rarer still.

Unlike prisons, which generally maintain at least minimal standards for employment, local jails are extremely poorly staffed. Employees are few in number and generally untrained. Often they are sheriff's deputies who perform many other jobs besides jail duties. In some areas, assignment to jail duty is viewed as a punishment or demotion by deputies. The possibility of rehabilitative services is precluded by the lack of trained staff and by inadequate funds with which to hire professional rehabilitative personnel. Changes in staff qualifications and capabilities are unlikely, given community reluctance to allocate tax money toward jail improvements.

The major criticism leveled at local jails is that they do little screening and segregating of inmates. Thus, persons awaiting trial often share cells with convicts serving time. An individual serving a short sentence for drug possession may share a cell with a person charged with murder or rape. Young first offenders are thrown in with hardened criminals or mentally disturbed persons. With minimal supervision of prisoners, physical, sexual, and emotional assaults are common. It is no mere coincidence that jails are sometimes used by district attorneys to encourage defendants to plead guilty or somehow aid the state in return for a transfer to a state prison or community corrections program.

A number of reforms currently are being suggested or implemented in a few local jails, especially those in large, urban areas. More attention is being paid to staff qualifications; inmates are being segregated by detention status (that is, awaiting trial or serving time), by past record, and by current charge. Educational, recreational, and rehabilitation programs are being introduced.

TABLE 11–2
Inmates of local jails, June 30, 1982

	All inmates	White*	Black*	Hispanic	Other†
Total	209,582	98,688	84,346	23,617	2,931
Adult	207,853	97,732	83,684	23,555	2,882
Male	194,153	91,721	77,750	22,075	2,607
Female	13,700	6,011	5,934	1,480	275
Juvenile	1,729	956	662	62	49
Male	1,577	859	635	47	36
Female	152	97	27	15	13

*Excludes persons of Hispanic origin.
†American Indians, Native Alaskans, Asians, and Pacific Islanders.
Source: U.S. Department of Justice, Bureau of Justice Statistics, Jail Inmates 1982 (Washington, D.C.: U.S. Department of Justice, 1983), p. 1.

Many types of prisoners formerly kept in jails now are being assigned to community-based correctional facilities (for example, drug rehabilitation programs).

The key to the success of these reforms is financial backing. However, most reform programs are now sponsored by federal grants. If and when federal support ceases, local communities must assume support. Their historical reluctance to use community funds for local jails points to a bleak future for serious, long-term jail reform.

PRISONS

Prisons are state- or federally-operated penal and correctional institutions. Three general types of prisons exist: maximum security, medium security, and minimum security. These classifications reflect both the criminal justice system's perceptions of the dangerousness of inmates and the extent to which security measures are used to confine inmates.

Maximum-security prisons most closely approximate the public's view of the prison (usually formed from movies). They generally resemble fortresses, with great walls separating prisoners from the outside world. Some guards patrol the walls of the prison while others keep watch within the various cell blocks. Dining, sanitary, recreation, work, and social activities are regimented and highly supervised. In essence, the prisoner rarely is unobserved.

Medium-security prisons generally resemble enclosed campuses. Dormitories replace cellblocks, and buildings are more clearly separated from each other. Recreational, vocational, and counseling facilities and programs exist in greater numbers. Still, prisoners are highly supervised and controlled. Guards man the perimeter of the institution, and prisoners are under relatively constant surveillance. The major difference between maximum- and medium-security prisons is that inmates in the latter institutions are considered more "reformable" and somewhat less dangerous.

Minimum-security prisons, more often called "correctional centers," differ greatly from maximum- and medium-security institutions. They are generally open, with few walls or fences and little perimeter supervision. Nearly all such facilities demand some form of work (for example, cutting lumber) from inmates. Some provide rehabilitation programs, but these are the exception since most prisoners in minimum-security facilities are not seen as needing rehabilitation. Most are small-time offenders or persons of social or political stature who have been caught in such crimes as embezzlement or accepting bribes. They are in prison not because they are considered dangerous but because they are seen as being in need of some form of just punishment. Since the Watergate scandal, which resulted in sentences in minimum-security prisons for several high-level political figures, the public has become more aware of minimum-security institutions.

There are about 45 federal and 350 state correctional facilities in the U.S. Of the state prisons, about one-third are maximum security facilities, one-third medium-security, and one-third minimum-security. Among the leading states in prison populations are Texas, California, New York, Florida, North Carolina, and Ohio (U.S. Department of Justice, 1983:2). Surprisingly, when the prison population is divided by region, the South accounts for nearly half of all prisoners, though it accounts for only 31 percent of the FBI Index crimes reported in the U.S. and contains only 33 percent of the country's population (see Table 11–3).

As of December 31, 1982, state and federal correctional facilities housed 414,462 inmates, serving sentences of at least one year. Of this number, 90 percent were confined in state prisons (U.S. Department of Justice, 1983:2). On this date, the number of prisoners in America was the largest in the nation's history. As Figure 11–1 illustrates, the number of inmates in prisons rose from 1925 to 1939, dropped steadily through the war years, and then began an upward climb until 1960. The early 1960s saw a steady decline in prison populations. However, with rising public concern about crime in the 1960s and 1970s, the trend was again reversed and prison populations now have grown larger than ever.

Prison populations increased dramatically in 1975 and 1976. The pace of growth then slowed somewhat through 1980 but surged ahead again with record gains of 12 percent in both 1981 and 1982. This growth has been so sudden that some prisons now face problems of overcrowding, a shortage of staff, and difficulty in maintaining adequate health conditions. So great has the problem become that some prisons have refused to accept, or have been ordered by the courts not to accept, more inmates. This in turn places burdens on other facilities such as local jails. Although the public wishes to see

TABLE 11–3

Distribution of state prisoner population, FBI Index offenses, and U.S. population by region (1980)

Region	*Percent of prisoner population*	*Percent of FBI Index offenses*	*Percent of U.S. population*
Northeast	16	21	22
North Central	22	24	26
South	47	31	33
West	15	24	19
Total	100	100	100

Source: U.S. Department of Justice, Law Enforcement Assistance Administration, *Prisoners in State and Federal Institutions on December 31, 1980* (Washington, D.C.: U.S. Government Printing Office, 1982), p. 35; and FBI, *Uniform Crime Reports—1980* (Washington, D.C.: U.S. Government Printing Office, 1981), p. 39.

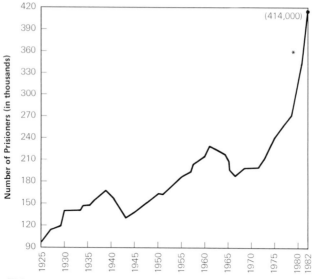

FIGURE 11–1

Number of Prisoners in State and Federal Institutions at Year
End, 1925–1982.* *Source:* U.S. Department of Justice,
Bureau of Justice Statistics, *Prisoners at Midyear 1983*
(Washington, D.C.: U.S. Department of Justice, 1983), p. 1.
*Since 1979, the figures presented in the graph reflect
prisoners out on bail (pending appeals outcomes), work
release, or furlough. These figures were not addressed in
previous reports.)

more criminals behind bars, it is not willing to increase financial support of
correctional facilities.

Most prisoners are male and constitute about 96 percent of prison inmate
populations, though the percentage of female prisoners has been increasing
in recent years. According to a survey of inmates in state institutions in 1974
(U.S. Department of Justice, 1976b:24–25), prison populations were composed of 51 percent white inmates and 47 percent black. Two-thirds of the
inmates were between the ages of twenty and thirty-four. Most had not completed high school and 9 percent had attended college. Most inmates had
been employed in the month prior to arrest, though the majority had earned
less than $6000 during the year prior to arrest. Most had held jobs such as
truck driver, welder, service worker, or laborer.

The Inmate Social System

A major characteristic of total institutions such as prisons and mental hos-
pitals is the inmate culture: a set of rules, roles, and statuses that shape the
lives of inmates (Goffmann, 1961:66–70). Until recently, the inmate culture

was thought to arise from the fact that inmates bring into prison from the outside world a need for guidelines for everyday living. It was considered a direct response to what Sykes (1958:65–78) has labeled "the pains of imprisonment." Sykes argues that prison strips inmates of most aspects of individual identity and self-worth and deprives them of conventionally valued goods and services (for example, nonuniform, self-expressive apparel), heterosexual relationships, autonomy (personal control over one's life), and security (a feeling of personal safety).

Responding to an environment that is characterized by such deprivations and that seeks to reduce individuality among prisoners (through such devices as shaved heads, uniforms, and identification by number), inmates develop their own social system and culture. As Cressey (1973:118) notes, the complexity of this system never can be fully appreciated by the outsider. However, Sykes and Messinger (1960:5–19) report that it contains an elaborate value system, with explicit behavioral codes and social roles and statuses.

Inmates become part of this social system through the process of *prisonization* (see Clemmer, 1958:298–301; Wheeler, 1961:697–712; Garabedian, 1963:139–52). This is the socialization process by which an inmate is assimilated into the inmate culture—that is, comes to think and act in terms of the prison social environment. The process is characterized by "acceptance of the inferior role, accumulation of facts concerning the organization of the prison, the development of somewhat new habits of eating, dressing, working, sleeping, the adoption of local language, the recognition that nothing is owed to the environment for the supplying of needs, and the eventual desire for a good job" (Clemmer, 1958:299). In sum, Clemmer notes, "prisonization is the taking on, in greater or lesser degree, of the folkways, mores, customs, and general culture of the penitentiary." Although prisonization occurs in varying degrees and proceeds at different rates among prisoners, no prisoner is totally untouched by the process.

Sykes and Messinger (1960) divide the inmate social rules, or the "inmate code," into five general categories. The first cautions against interfering with the interests of other inmates; in short, it demands loyalty and the minding of one's own business. The second involves "keeping cool"; that is, staying out of trouble with other inmates and doing nothing to bring on the attention of the prison staff. Third, prisoners are not to exploit each other, either by force or trickery; in short, they are not to lie to, steal from, or cheat each other. Fourth, prisoners are made to "stand tough"; they must not weaken or give in to staff pressures. Finally, prisoners must maintain a social distance from the staff; although they must obey direct orders, they must not overtly cooperate or socialize with guards or administrators. In sum, inmate rules— *don't squeal, be cool, be loyal, be tough, don't break your word, be right, don't be a sucker*—serve both to set the inmate world apart from the administration and to govern relations among inmates.

As in any social system, the inmate system is characterized by a number of social roles and statuses stemming from the needs of the prisoners and the degree to which various inmates adhere to "the code." Cressey (1973:135–38; see also Irwin and Cressey, 1962) describes three inmate subcultures that reflect role and status differences in prison. The first subculture is that of the thief. This subculture has ties to the outside world in that professional thieves hold high status in the criminal world. They are viewed as persons dedicated to crime and a cut above the common criminal. This status is carried over into the prison world, where such criminals are called "right guys" or "real men"—inmates who adhere to the inmate code and neither seek out trouble nor run from it. As Sykes and Messinger (1960:8) put it, "A *right guy* sticks up for his rights, but he doesn't ask for pity: he can take all the lousy screws can hand out and more. ... " In brief, the "right guys" are not prison-oriented but simply do their time while awaiting reentry into the outside criminal world.

Cressey speaks as well of the "convict" subculture, which, unlike the "thief" subculture, is oriented toward prison life. Within this subculture are a number of roles, each accorded varying degrees of social status and each reflecting a degree of deviation from "the code." "Politicians," "peddlers," "shots," and "merchants" are all persons who successfully manipulate the system so that they gain a greater share of prison-valued goods and services. For example, a "merchant" may be assigned to a food-preparation unit and may sell or trade portions of food or coffee in return for some other valued item or favor.

In addition to economically manipulative prisoners, the inmate culture is composed of physically manipulative or coercive prisoners known as "gorillas" (or "toughs," "hoods," "ballbusters"). "Gorillas" exploit other inmates through threats and violence. They are likely to attack both weaker prisoners and staff. They sell "protection" in return for goods and services. They are considered more dangerous than other prisoners by both inmates and staff. More than any other inmates, "gorillas" depart from "the code."

Finally, Cressey points to a third subculture, that of the "square John," "straight," or "do-right." These persons are basically noncriminal, fitting in with neither the "thieves" nor the "convicts." Although they undergo some degree of prisonization, "square Johns" remain relatively isolated from other inmates. They serve their time quietly, waiting to return to the conventional world, and are little bother to the prison staff.

Most prisoners probably overlap somewhat in their membership in the above subcultures. All offer at least some allegiance to the "inmate code," though members of the "convict" subculture tend selectively to base their allegiance on the extent to which "the code" allows them to better their positions in prison. For example, merchants violate "the code" in exploiting other inmates but expect to be left alone in their endeavors because "the code" commands prisoners to mind their own business. Most prisoners definitely are influenced by the values of the high-status "thief" subculture. Yet strict imitation of the "thieves"—that is, strong allegiance to "the code"—

may place an inmate in a poor position if most other inmates violate it. There are scarce goods and services to be had and, if one is to obtain them, one must play the "convict" subculture game to some degree.

Importantly, Irwin (1980) recently has challenged the traditional description of prison organization and inmate culture. He argues that the description may have pertained to most prisons during the first half of this century, but that the many exceptions to it then, and especially now, have been ignored. Irwin claims that the traditional view of the prison did not account for such features of the Southern prison as chain gangs and the use of prisoners as overseers of other prisoners. Nor did it account for racial segregation of prisoners both in and out of the South. The dominant view of inmate culture failed to recognize the extent to which prison culture was imported into the institution by prisoners rather than arising within the prison as an adaptive response to it. Thus, the prison perhaps was not the well-integrated social system it has been reputed to be. Irwin argues that it clearly is not today. The 1960s witnessed the introduction into the prison of political and racial conflict that left it changed and, in many ways, chaotic.

Politicization of Prisoners

In many ways, the politics of the prison mirror those of the outside world. As blacks in the larger society began to assert themselves politically in the late 1950s and throughout the 1960s, blacks in prison began openly to reject their second-class status within the inmate society. In so doing, they began to define their imprisonment and their treatment in prison in terms of political conflict in society. Rather than viewing themselves as criminals and orienting themselves toward the traditional inmate culture, some black prisoners came to view themselves as being politically oppressed and to orient their prison life toward political activism. The late George Jackson (1970:35) wrote from prison:

> Growing numbers of blacks . . . have become aware that their only hope lies in resistance. They have learned that resistance is actually possible. The holds are beginning to slip away. Very few men imprisoned for economic crimes or even crimes of passion against the oppressor feel they are really guilty. Most of today's black convicts have come to understand that they are the most abused victims of an unrighteous order . . . [and] have been transformed into an implacable army of liberation.

The militant posture of black prisoners produced a number of tensions within the prison. One, obviously, was racial. Racial violence began to appear among black, white, and, in some prisons, hispanic inmate groups. But beyond the effects of the racial issue, the political issue posed problems for prison administrators. Black political awareness spread to other inmates and, though still racially divided, inmates began to define their imprisonment as a form of political oppression and to resist the administration in political terms. The result was the imposition of stricter, no-nonsense repressive measures by authorities upon inmates. This served not only to stifle political dissent but also to weaken the traditional inmate social structure. The many social roles that once characterized the prison now decreased in number and importance so that the dominant role became something roughly akin to that of the traditional "tough guy" or "gorilla."

Irwin (1980) argues that the "gorilla" social role that developed in prisons in the late 1960s and early 1970s differed from earlier versions of the role in that it became interwoven with a "gang" factor. In the past two decades prisons increasingly have housed young, prison-wise, urban, minority gang members. Once controllable by the traditional prison social structure, this newer type of prisoner has grown in number to the extent that the old prison social order has been overwhelmed. Gangs of young toughs, usually racially homogeneous, now control the economy of the prison, fight among themselves for power, and terrorize independent prisoners (whose numbers, of necessity, shrink rapidly). There remains little of the "old ways" that is respected in prison. Life has become a matter of attracting members of other gangs and resisting counterattacks. The result, Irwin claims, is not chaos but constant tension and danger. He notes further that the "respected" convict of today stands ready to kill to protect himself, maintains strong loyalties to some small group of other convicts (invariably of his own race), and will rob and attack or at least tolerate his friends' robbing and attacking other weak independents or their foes. He openly and stubbornly opposes the administration, even if this results in harsh punishment. Finally, he is extremely assertive of his masculine sexuality, even though he may occasionally make use of the prison homosexuals or, less often, enter into a more permanent sexual alliance with a "kid" (Irwin, 1980:195).

Sex in Prison

Part of the inmate social system and culture involves sexual customs in prison (see Gagnon and Simon, 1968; Johnson, 1971). Some observers estimate that about one-third of most prison populations engage in homosexuality at least occasionally (Johnson, 1971:83). Most sex in prison is adaptive—that is, a response to heterosexual deprivation. Among male prisoners, most of those who engage in sexual acts with other prisoners do not view themselves as homosexuals. This self-definition stems from the fact that they always take what they see as the "male" role in sex. They sodomize other inmates but are not themselves sodomized; other inmates perform oral sexual acts on them but they never reciprocate. In short, they have sex with "female substitutes." Within the prison, persons who participate in these pseudoheterosexual acts are not labeled "queer."

A small number of male prisoners *are* considered homosexual by the rest of the inmates. These persons are viewed as femalelike sex objects; that is, persons who perform fellatio and are sodomized. Some homosexual prisonsers take on the role as a preference; they come to be known as "broads." Others, particularly young, slightly-built inmates, are coerced into the role. Coercion generally takes the form of the rape of a new, unattached prisoner. Once raped, the prisoner is defined as a "punk" and will be treated as a homosexual for the remainder of his time in prison.

The unattached "broad" or "punk" is fair game for gang rapes by "wolves"—sexually aggressive male attackers. To avoid these attacks, homosexual prisoners often will "set up house" with basically heterosexual prisoners. In these relationships, the "male" prisoner will support and protect the "female" prisoner. The homosexual partner will in turn play the role of "wife." This role is based on a very traditional view of the woman in American society: very submissive, highly feminine (especially as a sex partner), and preoccupied with keeping house. In other words, male inmates form marital or steady relationships that correspond closely to nonprison heterosexual relationships. In sum, homosexuality in the all-male prison serves a number of functions. The most obvious of these is the response to the heterosexual deprivation accompanying imprisonment. The "female" role played by the homosexual "broad" or "punk" allows heterosexual prisoners to engage in sexual acts without *absolute* loss of normal sexual identity, though confusion regarding that identity seems certain in the long run.

Despite the fact that prison homosexuality constitutes a response to the deprivation of imprisonment, homosexual rape in prison should not be viewed as functional. Rapes represent the coercion of an inmate into the role of sex object. Thus, while homosexual relations may be functional for the attacker, i.e., compensatory, they are hardly so for the attacked. Beyond this, in the race- and gang-oriented prison of today, rape seems to have become a form of abuse and hatred directed at enemies. Rape represents, for example, the opportunity for the black prisoner to degrade and to conquer the white prisoner, the representative of the white race, by forcing him to yield his "manhood" (Robinson, 1971).

Control of Prisoners

No matter what their orientation (punishment, revenge, rehabilitation), prisons are first and foremost organized to gain control over inmates so that they (1) will not escape, (2) will not harm the typically outnumbered staff, and (3) will not cause disturbances (such as riots) that occasion public wrath and political interference in prison administration. Order—or, more precisely, a tolerable level of disorder—is the chief concern of prison administrators.

The primary mechanism of order maintenance is clearly the threat of force. Although the staff of a prison is generally outnumbered by the inmates, staff weaponry and resources (for example, the state militia) serve as the dominant threat against a prisoner takeover of an institution. Yet not all disorder is of the magnitude that requires "calling in the troops." In everyday attempts to secure order, prison staff rely on two control mechanisms: punishment and strategic concessions.

Until recently, punishment was a very effective control mechanism. Prisoners were beaten to obtain discipline. Some were placed in "the hole," a dark, solitary-confinement cell. These cells were generally very small, devoid of furnishings, and poorly lit and ventilated. Prisoners often were stripped and forced to sleep in these cold cells without blankets. They were fed subsistence diets. The psychological effects of such confinement were as harmful as the physical effects. Although beatings and confinement in "the hole" are no longer routinely permitted, psychological punishment in the form of social isolation of prisoners (confinement to a cell in an isolated cell block) remains common.

Restrictions on the use of corporal punishment and solitary confinement have limited somewhat the prison staff's means of controlling prisoners. Thus, the staff has come to rely more directly on strategic concessions to prisoners. Minor infractions of institutional rules are overlooked in return for compliance with major rules and a refrain from general defiance. In essence, prison guards need cooperation from prisoners, and prisoners are aware of this. The guard whose cell block is a source of constant disruption will not do well in terms of job promotions and salary increases. Thus, guards may curry the favor of inmates or of inmates gangs, especially those who are influential within the inmate social system. These inmates and gangs will "keep the lid on" in return for staff compromises. Prisoners may be placed in cell blocks with their friends. Guards may overlook contraband or even bring it into the prison. Guards may ignore homosexual marriages and rapes. Occasional retaliatory violent attacks by prisoners on other prisoners also may be allowed (McCorkle, 1956). Prisoners also are kept compliant through rewards. These usually take the form of special assignments to prison jobs (such as mail carrier or canteen worker) that place the inmate in a favorable position in the inmate bartering system.

At one time, when the traditional inmate social structure and culture flourished within prisons, administration control over inmates could be accomplished by other, more powerful inmates. Within any total institution, some inmates came to hold a greater share of valued goods and services: certain jobs or duties, favors from guards, high social status, a corner on a given market (such as cigarettes, coffee, new uniforms) that permits trading for other valuables. Prisoners in this position wished to preserve the status quo. To do so, they championed the "inmate code," stressing the commandments regarding not causing trouble and not interfering with other prisoners. Thus, though the inmate culture promoted inmate solidarity, it also preserved the inmate power structure, including existing patterns of inmate exploitation of other inmates.

In silent collaboration with the prison staff, the more powerful inmates—whether "right guys" trying to maintain a system that basically left them alone or "convicts" trying to preserve favorable social and economic positions—attempted to keep other inmates in line. Thus, a good deal of informal social pressure (such as ostracism or attribution of low status) was brought to bear against "gorillas" who, if left to their own devices, would disrupt the inmate social system and cause the kind of chaos that brought on outside interference in the administration of the prison.

Today's prison is without the traditional "inmate code" and, thus, without the potential for strong inmate control over other inmates. The absence of disorder is a matter of the extent to which rival gangs arrive at negotiated truces. While the tension inherent in this arrangement is not the type of order prison administrators desire, the administrators prefer it to unified, organized resistance by prisoners as a group. Internal factional struggles within the prison, if somewhat controlled, keep the inmates from plotting any organized disruption or move against the administration. Racial infighting and territorial disputes among inmates thus actually promote an acceptable level of disorder within prisons by keeping inmates preoccupied with petty squabbles (Irwin, 1980).

In sum, control of prisoners takes both formal and informal shapes. On the formal side, prisoners are kept in line through threats of force and disciplinary action and through offers of incentives for good behavior. More important is the informal side of control, which is brought about by the prisoners themselves. In essence, prisoners accomplish the administration's task through infighting that keeps them too occupied to accomplish concerted disruptions.

Women's Prisons

As Table 11–1 indicated, far fewer women than men inhabit this country's prisons. Only 4 percent of the nation's prisoners are women. Although women's prisons still emphasize control and security, they differ considerably from men's (Chandler, 1973; Giallombardo, 1966; Heffernan, 1972; Ward and Kassebaum, 1965). Structurally, they have fewer perimeter-security devices and guards. They more closely resemble men's minimum-security prisons in design, with dormitories or, often, cottages and many separate buildings for educational and counseling programs. Rehabilitation ostensibly is more heavily emphasized in the women's prison, though, as some observers report, rehabilitation is primarily a matter of attempting to instill in inmates a dedication to the traditional homemaker role (Giallombardo, 1966:7–8). Smart (1977:97) argues that the penal system for women

> . . . creates a situation in which realistic and potentially self-determining educational and vocational courses are intentionally excluded or reduced in importance. . . . [Women's] typically dependent status will be confirmed and

their ability to control or possibly change their life-styles further damaged [in prisons]. Penal policy for female offenders is geared to preserving the typical female role, its intention is to make women and girls adapt to their pre-given passive social role which by definition is thought to preclude deviant behavior.

The women's prison differs most from the men's, however, in its social structure. Missing from women's prisons are the gangs of today's men's prisons and the "thief" subculture of yesterday's men's prison with its "right guy" orientation and the "convict" subculture with its exploitive roles. "Merchants" are rare; "politicians" and "gorillas" practically are non-existent. There is no strong inmate code. Cooperation with staff is common. Female inmates tend to resemble the "square John" type of prisoner of the old-style men's prisons, undoubtedly because so few were hardened criminals before imprisonment.

Female inmates' response to the deprivations of imprisonment involves the development of small groups that protect and sustain their members. These groups are characterized by family and kinship roles: "parents," "husband," "wife," and male and female "children." Inmates tend to form homosexual "marriage" or "steady" bonds that, though violated as in the outside world, serve "who's who's" and "hands off" functions in the prison.

Homosexuality is more pervasive in female prisons than in male prisons. As in the male prison, however, most homosexuality is adaptive—that is, carried on in prison to fulfill both sexual and emotional needs, and then abandoned upon the inmate's release from prison. Female prison homosexuality also is marked by very clear-cut sexual roles. Some women, a minority, assume a male or "butch" role, but the majority assume the more traditional female or "femme" role. For the most part, these roles survive throughout the institutional stay, and occasional wanderings are frowned upon or considered foolish.

In sum, solidarity and identity are achieved in women's prisons through "family" commitments. Solidarity is small-group in nature—one does not exploit or bring trouble to "family" members, though "nonfamily" members may be exploited or troubled. Self-identity and self-worth are not obtained through one's position in prison but stem from the status accorded one's "family."

Rehabilitation in Prison

As we noted earlier in this chapter, in the late 1950s and early 1960s there were large-scale attempts at introducing a treatment or rehabilitation orientation into prisons. Treatment referred to "making the patient better." That is, criminals were viewed as ill (emotionally or socially maladjusted) and in need of rehabilitation. Rehabilitation took two primary forms: (1) psychological counseling or therapy, and (2) educational and vocational training.

Whatever their form, rehabilitation efforts within prison have come to be regarded as failures. This conclusion is based on the results of studies such as that concerned with the effects of numerous group counseling programs in a California prison (Kassebaum et al., 1971). Researchers randomly assigned incoming inmates to one of several counseling programs and evaluated their adjustment to prison and their records three years after release from prison. The researchers eventually concluded that *none* of the various types of counseling reduced hostility toward prison staff, violation of prison rules, parole violations, length of time out of prison, and seriousness of offenses while on parole. According to "the Martinson Report" (Martinson, 1974), a review of 230 pieces of prison research that were relatively methodologically sound, this finding is not uncommon. The report argues that education and skill-development programs and individual and group counseling techniques have been ineffective in reducing post-release failure. It should be noted that this is a general conclusion: *some* programs have been found to be effective for *some* types of offenders, but a general formula for rehabilitating prisoners has not been found (Palmer, 1975).

Before we discuss the reasons for the failure of the institutional rehabilitation model, some mention should be made of what constitutes "success" or "failure." Although all rehabilitation programs strive to make prisoners "better persons" or "more functional members of society," their ultimate goal has been the reduction of post-release criminality or recidivism. Recidivism is sometimes measured in terms of arrests but is more often viewed as conviction for a felony or violation of parole conditions (for example, leaving the state without permission). The "failure" of institutional rehabilitation programs is a failure to reduce recidivism rates below those of prisoners not exposed to rehabilitation programs and those diverted to community-based corrections programs. In short, "failure" means that rehabilitation efforts have simply made no difference. Regardless of correctional programs to which inmates are exposed, approximately 35 percent will violate parole or be convicted of a felony within two years after release from prison. The figure climbs to 63 percent by eighteen years after release (Kitchener, 1977).

The failure of the institutional rehabilitation model can be attributed to a number of factors:

Lack of Political and Economic Support. Some argue that the treatment model was not given a fair chance, that insufficient funds were allocated to it. There is probably some merit to this claim. Legislators have been careful to respond to prison-reform interest groups, but they have made it clear that their priorities lie with pleasing the greater voting public. Hence, legislators resist being placed in a position that leaves them open to accusations of being "soft on criminals." The result has been a lukewarm political commitment to the funding of rehabilitation programs.

Lack of Prison Administration Support. When it was first proposed, many prison administrators resisted implementation of the rehabilitation model, fearing that it would make maintenance of order in the prison and control of prisoners difficult. However, administrators soon learned that without committing themselves to the model, they could selectively employ elements of it to better control prisoners. Chief among these elements was the indeterminate sentence, which left the decision about the length of time to be served solely to the parole board. The ability to keep a prisoner indefinitely (until "rehabilitated") could be used as a potent threat to force prisoners to conform to administration and staff wishes. Thus, parole was granted not on the basis of rehabilitation success but on the basis of a prisoner's ability to stay out of trouble or provide information or services to prison authorities.

Staff Resistance. Although prison staff members were able to make use of certain aspects of the treatment model, for the most part they resisted its implementation. The model placed them in a precarious position. On the one hand, they were told that their major responsibility was maintaining order within the prison. On the other hand, they were told to rehabilitate inmates without receiving instructions as to how to accomplish the task. Given the fact that the staff members had developed means of keeping order through relationships with influential inmates and various forms of rewards and punishments, they would not jeopardize their positions by pursuing a vaguely defined rehabilitation orientation.

Inmate Resistance. In the same manner that the prison staff felt threatened by the rehabilitation model, influential and powerful inmates viewed it as a threat to the status quo inmate power structure. Basically, the model oriented prisoners to the outside world rather than to the "thief" and "convict" subcultures. Thus, stronger inmates actively resisted rehabilitation by stressing adherence to the "inmate code," which forbade cooperation and communication with prison administrators and staff. The treatment model could not survive without these elements.

Lack of Knowledge. The greatest hindrance faced by the rehabilitation model was the fact that it assumed knowledge we do not possess. Generally, we cannot cure ills without knowledge about what causes them. Yet the rehabilitation model tried to treat inmates with inadequate knowledge about the causes of their criminal behavior. The odds against the success of a model that operates only on guesses and good intentions are enormous.

These problems greatly decreased the life of the institutional rehabilitation experiment. Today the custody orientation prevails in prison. Some rehabilitative services (for example, classes for inmates) still exist, but hopes for a totally restructured corrections system are gone. Some argue that the failure represents a blessing in disguise, for it allows the corrections system to begin from scratch and reconstruct a more realistic approach to the custody and treatment of offenders (Conrad, 1973). Some believe that the answer lies in the concept of community-based corrections.

COMMUNITY-BASED CORRECTIONS

Some convicted offenders are kept in the community rather than in the prison. In the 1970s, community-based corrections have been viewed by many as the form corrections must take if rehabilitation of offenders is ever to be accomplished.

Community-based corrections refers to all correctional activities that occur in the community. They are viewed as alternatives to incarceration and include such programs and activities as pretrial diversion and probation, halfway houses, release and furlough programs, and parole. All of these forms are described later. Before reviewing them, however, we should mention the theory and rationale behind community-based corrections.

Those advocating correction of offenders within the community argue first that this form of correction is more humanitarian than imprisonment. Prisons commonly are viewed as being places of human deprivation, exploitation, and danger. They are labeled nonrehabilitative and, some argue, actually further corrupt the criminal. Alternatively, community-based corrections programs are viewed as mechanisms that provide incentive and motivate the offender to avoid criminal behavior. This is accomplished by integrating the offender into conventional activities and values and, especially, by raising his or her stake in the conventional economic system. Thus, one area of community corrections is employment placement. Beyond this, the programs seem to provide the offender with a full range of social services. Finally, community-based corrections work on the assumption that offenders must develop ties to and receive greater pressure from conventional persons. Thus, community-based corrections attempt to involve the offender's family (assuming it is noncriminal) and other members of the community in correcting the offender. In sum, community-based corrections programs represent more than simply moving the offender from prison to the outside world; ideally, they involve the outside world in rehabilitation of the offender.

Pretrial Diversion and Probation

On the assumption that first offenders committing nonviolent crimes may be harmed or stigmatized by exposure to the criminal justice system, some communities have developed pretrial-diversion programs (see Galvin et al., 1977). In this process, defendants meeting specified eligibility criteria have prosecutorial action on their charges suspended for a given period of time (usually 30 days to a year) in return for their participation in a community-based program of rehabilitative services. If the conditions of the diversion program are satisfied, criminal charges against them are dismissed.

Although the selection criteria for pretrial diversion vary somewhat by program, most programs are directed toward persons with no previous convictions. Offenses for which these offenders are charged must be "nonmajor"—for example, vandalism, disorderly conduct, intrafamily violence, theft and shoplifting offenses, and some sex offenses.

Probation differs somewhat from pretrial diversion. The major goal of the latter is reduction of the possible negative effects of criminal justice processing (that is, negative self-esteem, troublesome family relations, and lost employment opportunities). In contrast, probation is designed to supervise and rehabilitate offenders who have been processed and convicted by the court. Probation occurs when a judge suspends an offender's sentence and places him or her under the supervision of a court appointee—usually a state- or county-employed probation officer (see Klockars, 1972).

Depending on the seriousness of the offense and the offender's record, probation may involve simple supervision of the offender, to determine that he or she does not again commit crimes, or it may involve some form of counseling or vocational training. In some instances, the length of probation is quite short; in other cases, it is much longer. Generally, the length approximates the length of the prison sentence the offender would have received. If the conditions of probation are violated, the offender may be sent to prison to serve that sentence.

Probation, especially when combined with treatment programs, is considered the ideal form of community-based corrections. It leaves the offender in the community, takes advantage of family and employment ties, discourages affiliation with undesirable persons (usually as a condition of probation), supervises the offender, and provides assistance in adjustment to conventional life. In short, probation controls and treats offenders without exposing them to the negative aspects of imprisonment.

Halfway Houses

The halfway-house concept offers yet another alternative to traditional imprisonment. *Halfway houses* are correctional facilities that are partly institutional, in that offenders must reside in them under supervision, and partly noninstitutional, in that residents generally come and go freely to work, shop, attend classes, and find recreation in the community. Basically, the facility resembles a home rather than a prison. Offenders may be sent directly to halfway houses upon conviction or may be transferred to them after serving time in prison. Programs within the houses vary considerably. Some are highly regimented, others more loosely operated. Some are primarily supervisory—a form of structured probation or parole. Others are devoted mainly to counseling and therapy on either an individual or a group basis.

Halfway houses offer a number of advantages. The freedom they provide allows offenders to maintain and develop outside relationships and to offset the many deprivations of imprisonment. The facilities and programs also serve as gradual steppingstones to successful parole. Yet the freedom provided by halfway houses also makes supervision of residents difficult, and offenders occasionally commit crimes during the course of their stay in a house. The staff attempts to counter this problem by building close ties with residents and developing in residents a sense of pride in the reputation and success of the facility. In some houses, residents work toward keeping other residents "straight."

It is doubtful that halfway houses will replace prisons to any great extent, though their potential to aid in the correction of lesser offenders has yet to be fully realized. The greatest obstacle in the path of the halfway house is community resistance. Residents of neighborhoods have often obtained court injunctions to block the opening of halfway houses. Conversely, corrections officials have been known secretly to establish halfway houses in neighborhoods that might resist them. As long as the public remains crime-conscious, the future of the halfway-house concept is limited.

Releases and Furloughs

Some prison inmates are allowed to leave the prison during the day to work or attend classes in the community, returning to the prison afterward. Programs that permit these absences are known as *release programs*. Occasionally, prisoners may be given leaves from prison for longer periods of time in order to take care of family problems or business or to prepare for parole or final release from prison. These leaves are called *furloughs*.

Releases and furloughs are seen as important methods of keeping an offender tied to the community even while imprisoned. Work and educational releases provide inmates with job skills or educational attainments that may benefit them after they have been paroled or served their sentences. Furloughs aid in the transition between incarceration and parole or release at the end of sentence, often a traumatic adjustment if not done gradually. Both releases and furloughs aid the corrections system in reducing prison overcrowding and in allowing an evaluation of a prisoner's parole potential.

On the negative side (especially in the eyes of the public), release and furlough programs carry the danger of escape or criminal behavior by the program participant. Occasionally, this does occur and causes a public furor. Yet prisoners given releases and furloughs are generally a select few and the number returning late, absconding, and committing crimes amounts to no more than 7 percent of the total (Holt, 1971).

Despite "high marks," it is doubtful that release and furlough programs will replace total confinement on a large-scale basis. The risk involved with maximum-security offenders is too great. Yet there is no reason for not fully developing these programs for medium- and minimum-security prisoners, especially in attempting to raise the likelihood of parole success.

Parole

Parole is a form of community-based corrections in which prison inmates are released into the community after they have served only part of their sentences. Their activities in the community are monitored by a state parole agent, and they are returned to prison if they violate the conditions of their parole. In theory, parole meets the needs of both the state and the offenders. The state is permitted to reimprison offenders who "are not ready for life on the outside" or who are again "headed for trouble." This option is not available if the offenders have served their full sentence in prison before release. Ideally, parole aids the offender by providing assistance in the transition from prison to life on the outside. In reality, it is the state's needs that are most satisfied by parole.

The conditions of parole vary somewhat by state. In most states, parolees may reside only in homes approved by parole agents and may not change residences or leave the county without an agent's permission. They must maintain approved employment. Every month they are required to report directly or submit reports to their parole agents detailing their activities during the past month. Excessive use of alcohol and any use of narcotics are forbidden. Parolees cannot own or possess dangerous weapons. They must avoid former convicts and persons with bad reputations. They are required to obtain written permission to drive an automobile. Most importantly, they must not violate any laws.

Unofficially, the conditions of parole are matters of the parole agent's definition. In the end the parole agent is responsible for the parolee's behavior and, therefore, he or she sets the real conditions of parole (Irwin, 1970:149–73). Some agents are extremely rule-conscious. They supervise the parolee intensely and do not tolerate violations of parole conditions. Others are somewhat more tolerant and less intense in supervising the parolee. Some are primarily assistance-oriented rather than concerned with supervision. Finally, some agents basically leave the parolee alone, making the only major condition for parole the avoidance of arrest. In the final analysis, it is the arrest record of the parolee that determines the security of the agent's job and ultimately saves the parole board embarrassment. The threat of impending arrest will make the agent consider revoking parole. Arrest itself frequently will guarantee revocation.

Whether or not parolees succeed in remaining free depends in large part on their ability to survive the immediate reentry into the outside world. As Irwin (1970:107–30) notes, parolees are liable to undergo a form of culture shock as they reenter society. Activities that once were taken for granted—making change or crossing streets—now are difficult. Meeting members of the opposite sex and getting along with family and friends become problems.

Parolees who do not do well in readjusting during the early stages of parole are not likely to succeed. Parolees who do succeed in remaining out of prison are those who manage to make it through the reentry crisis and begin "doing good." "Doing good" represents more than simply getting by. It involves holding a job that pays well, developing satisfactory relationships with those of the opposite sex, and avoiding problems with the parole agent. "Doing good," therefore, does not exclude committing further crimes. In this sense society's definition of parole success (becoming "rehabilitated") differs greatly from that of the parolee (Irwin, 1970:131–48, 176–204).

Success of Community-based Corrections

Like prison rehabilitation programs, community-based corrections programs have many goals. They seek to raise the self-esteem of offenders, to reorient them toward conventional values, to provide them with educational and job skills, and to ease the social stigma of conviction. Yet whether or not these goals are accomplished, success or failure for community-based corrections ultimately is determined by the answer to one question: Do these programs produce lower recidivism rates than imprisonment of offenders? This factor is the most crucial in deciding legislative support for community-based corrections.

According to the earlier-cited Martinson (1974) report, community-based corrections programs do no better nor worse than imprisonment. They simply make little difference in recidivism rates. Like Martinson's negative conclusion concerning in-prison treatment programs, this conclusion is a general one. We have not discovered a general formula for community-based rehabilitation. Yet *some* programs do work with *some* types of offenders (Palmer, 1975). These relationships must be specified.

Three major factors account for the failure of community-based corrections programs to improve upon imprisonment. First, such programs generally have been poorly designed, implemented, and evaluated. Few programs are similar enough to allow comparisons. Few are designed with evaluation in mind. For political reasons, many resist evaluations. Second, community-based corrections have proven to be correction *in* the community rather than correction *by* the community. Despite the label, community-based corrections programs have done little to involve the community, and the community has shown little interest in becoming involved. Finally, community-based corrections programs suffer from the same problem that ultimately caused the downfall of the institutional treatment model. Both have attempted to rehabilitate offenders without adequate knowledge of the causes of the offenders' criminal behavior. In so doing, their chances of success rest fully on guesses.

It is important to note that community-based corrections have not fared worse than imprisonment in reducing recidivism. Thus, the final choice between the two must be determined on criteria other than recidivism. Undoubtedly, the decision will involve two immeasurable factors: (1) the potential humanitarian gains of the treatment model versus (2) the potential general deterrent effects of incarceration of law violators. As noble as the sentiments behind community-based corrections are, it is doubtful that they will be used to treat any but low-risk, lesser offenders. These are persons least in need of rehabilitation. Thus, the value of the community-based corrections model will not lie in the treatment of lesser offenders but in the protection of lesser offenders from the negative influence of the prison setting.

THE FUTURE OF CORRECTIONS

Aside from community-based corrections programs focusing on the lesser offender, we can expect little change from the trend toward nonrehabilitative custody of more serious offenders. A "lock 'em up" philosophy is preferred to innovative rehabilitation efforts by the public for two important reasons. First, the public basically is not interested in treatment of the offender. Beyond a humanitarian concern that prisoners not be abused, the public sees little reason to spend any more tax dollars on "crooks" than is necessary. Further, the institutionalization of offenders serves the purpose of keeping them out of sight and out of mind; thus, we are spared any reminder that we may be implicated in either or both the cause and the cure of criminal behavior.

The second, and more crucial, reason for a lack of innovative correctional policies lies in the American public's conservative approach to risk taking. Above all else, this society cannot long abide disorder. Short-term disorder will accompany nearly all innovations. Within prisons, for example, increased freedom or self-government for prisoners surely will be met with abuses of privileges and of prison staff. If we could guarantee the public that these forms of disorder will only be temporary, public support for correctional innovations might be found. However, such guarantees cannot be made, and the public is not willing to risk the possibility of long-term disorder. Custody seems preferable.

The result of the return to the custody model is, in a very real sense, the self-perpetuation of the criminal justice system. The criminal justice system produces a product—officially-labeled criminals. In failing to rehabilitate offenders and likely corrupting them further through exposure to the prison setting, the criminal justice system assures itself of a steady flow of easily selected candidates for reprocessing and relabeling.

SUMMARY

In this chapter we described the corrections system, the component of the criminal justice system that controls and, in some instances, attempts to rehabilitate officially-labeled criminals. The chapter examined the constantly changing orientations of the corrections system and its current dual orientation toward protection of society from offenders and community rehabilitation of lesser offenders. The description of jails and prisons offered a bleak picture of correctional institutions. They are clearly places where little correction can occur. Yet in terms of reducing recidivism, correction in the community has not fared much better than imprisonment, even with the assignment of prisoners with greater rehabilitation potential to community-based corrections programs. It seems, then, that this chapter can offer the public little hope that criminals can be made noncriminal. Indeed, the chapter has undoubtedly *encouraged* the average citizen's preference for longer incarceration of offenders. This thought represents a major theme of the following, final chapter of this book.

REFERENCES

American Friends Service Committee. 1971. *Struggle for Justice.* New York: Hill and Wang.
Chandler, E. W. 1973. *Women in Prison.* Indianapolis: The Bobbs-Merrill Co.
Clemmer, D. 1958. *The Prison Community.* New York: Holt, Rinehart & Winston.
Conrad, J. 1973. Corrections and simple justice. *J. Crim. Law Criminol.* 64:208–17.
Cressey, D. R. 1973. Adult felons in prison. In *Prisoners in America.* Edited by L. Ohlin. Englewood Cliffs, N.J.: Prentice-Hall.
Gagnon, J. H., and W. Simon. 1968. The social meaning of prison homosexuality. *Federal Probation* 32:23–29.
Galvin, J. J., W. H. Busher, W. Greene, et al. 1977. *Instead of Jail:* Vol. 3, *Alternatives to Prosecution.* Washington, D.C.: U.S. Government Printing Office.
Garabedian, P. 1963. Social roles and processes of socialization in the prison community. *Soc. Prob.* 11:139–52.
Giallombardo, R. 1966. *Society of Women: A Study of a Women's Prison.* New York: John Wiley & Sons.
Goffman, E. 1961. *Asylums.* Garden City, N.Y.: Anchor Books.
Goldfarb, R. 1975. *Jails.* Garden City, N.Y.: Anchor Books.
Heffernan, E. 1972. *Making It in Prison.* New York: John Wiley & Sons.
Holt, N. 1971. Temporary prison release. *Crime & Delinq.* 17:414–30.

Irwin, J. 1970. *The Felon.* Englewood Cliffs, N.J.: Prentice-Hall.

———. 1980. *Prisons in Turmoil.* Boston: Little, Brown & Company.

Irwin, J., and D. Cressey. 1962. Thieves, convicts, and the inmate culture. *Soc. Prob.* 10:142–55.

Jackson, G. 1970. *Soledad Brother.* New York: Bantam Books.

Johnson, E. 1971. The homosexual in prison. *Soc. Theory & Pract.* 1:83–95.

Kassebaum, G. G., D. A. Ward, and D. M. Wilner. 1971. *Prison Treatment and Parole Survival.* New York: John Wiley & Sons.

Kitchener, H. 1977. How persistent is post-prison success? *Fed. Probation* 41:9–15.

Klockars, C. B. 1972. A theory of probation supervision. *J. Crim. Law Criminol. & Pol. Sci.* 63:550–56.

McCorkle, L. W. 1956. Social structure in a prison. *Welfare Reporter* 8:5–15.

Martinson, R. 1974. What works? Questions and answers about prison reform. *Pub. Interest* 35:22–54.

Palmer, T. 1975. Martinson revisited. *J. Res. Crime & Delinq.* 12:133–52.

Pileggi, N. 1981. Inside Rikers Island. *New York* June 8, 24–29.

Robinson, B. 1971. Love: A hard-legged triangle. *Black Scholar* 3:29–48.

Rothman, D. 1971. *The Discovery of the Asylum.* Boston: Little, Brown & Company.

Smart, C. 1977. Criminological theory: Its ideology and implications concerning women. *Br. J. Sociol.* 28:89–100.

Sykes, G. 1958. *The Society of Captives.* Princeton, N.J.: Princeton University Press.

Sykes, G. M., and S. L. Messinger. 1960. The inmate social system. In *Theoretical Studies in Social Organization of the Prison.* Edited by R. A. Cloward, D. R. Cressey, G. H. Grosser, et al. New York: Social Science Research Council.

U.S. Department of Justice. 1975. *The Nation's Jails.* Washington, D.C.: U.S. Government Printing Office.

———. 1976a. *Survey of Inmates of Local Jails, 1972.* Washington, D.C.: U.S. Government Printing Office.

———. 1976b. *Survey of Inmates of State Correctional Facilities, 1974—Advance Report.* Washington, D.C.: U.S. Government Printing Office.

———. 1983. *Prisoners at Midyear, 1983.* Washington, D.C.: U.S. Department of Justice.

Ward, D. A., and G. G. Kassebaum. 1965. *Women's Prison.* Chicago: Aldine Publishing.

Wheeler, S. 1961. Socialization in correctional communities. *Am. Sociol. Rev.* 26:697–712.

SUGGESTED READINGS

Two collections of readings in the area of corrections will provide the interested student with a satisfactory introduction to the topic: R. M. Carter, D. Glaser, and L. T. Wilkins' *Correctional Institutions,* 2nd ed. (Philadelphia: J. B. Lippincott Co., 1977), and R. G. Leger and J. R. Stratton's *The Sociology of Corrections* (New York: John Wiley & Sons, 1977). Neal Shover provides a good general text on corrections: *A Sociology of American Corrections* (Homewood, Ill.: Dorsey Press, 1979).

Beyond this introduction, Lloyd E. Ohlin has edited an excellent collection of papers by leaders in the field of sociology of corrections: see his *Pris-*

oners in America (Englewood Cliffs, N.J.: Prentice-Hall, 1973). Tom Murton's *The Dilemma of Prison Reform* (New York: Holt, Rinehart & Winston, 1976) offers an insider's look at innovations in the corrections system. John Irwin similarly points up dilemmas in the area of parole in his book, *The Felon* (Englewood Cliffs, N.J.: Prentice-Hall, 1970).

Finally, for more radical critiques of corrections in America, the reader is referred to Leonard Orland's *Prisons: Houses of Darkness* (New York: Free Press, 1975), Jessica Mitford's *Kind and Usual Punishment* (New York: Vintage Trade Books, 1974), and John Irwin's *Prisons in Turmoil* (Boston: Little, Brown and Company, 1980).

CONCLUSION

So far, this book has attempted
to provide a framework by
which readers can ask
reasonable questions about the
effects of crime and anticrime
strategies on their lives. Chapter
12 summarizes this framework
and applies it to some recent
crime-control issues.

12

SUMMARY AND OBSERVATIONS ON CRIME CONTROL

This book opened with three questions that must be asked in formulating any anticrime policy, whether at the personal or governmental level:

1. What is the nature and scope of the problem at hand? (That is, how accurate are the assumptions and figures relating to the problem?)
2. Will the proposed remedy actually aid in solving the problem?
3. What incidental side effects may accompany the implementation of the proposed remedy?

The major portion of this book has been devoted to question 1; questions 2 and 3 cannot be addressed confidently unless the first question is laid to rest. The key to answering question 1 lies in bringing together what we know about crime—its forms, its causes, its consequences. In exposing our taken-for-granted assumptions and stereotypes about crime to critical challenges, we gain a better sense of what we know and, perhaps more importantly, what we do not know about crime. The history of crime policy in America is a history of repeated attempts to fight crime in the absence of knowledge about it. In assessing the limitations of our present knowledge, we must wonder how we can begin even to consider responding to questions 2 and 3.

SUMMARY

What have the chapters in this book told us about crime? Let us review our earlier discussions.

Crime in America

The increase in crime fears in the U.S. during the 1960s and 1970s was not entirely groundless. Crime *did* increase in those years. It seems to have leveled off recently. We cannot simply attribute such changes to differences in crime-reporting practices. Yet it is difficult to get a fuller handle on the dimensions of the "crime problem." Better victimization and self-reported criminality research techniques have sharpened our focus somewhat, but our crime statistics remain badly flawed. Most citizens rarely are given a sense of their actual chances of becoming crime victims. Their picture of crime generally is distorted and highlights violent crime and downplays property and white-collar offenses. In fact, even our flawed statistics are accurate enough to indicate that most citizens have little chance of being violently victimized, and their chances of falling victim to a thief really are only somewhat greater. That they lose money to various white-collar offenses is a certainty.

America's sense of its "crime problem" is shaped by more than its crime statistics and media attention to sensational crime. Crime is political, not only in the sense of addressing it through politically structured channels, but in terms of defining it as problematic in the first place. Crime is a political liability for some interest groups and a political tool for others. Power at times is gained or lost in a group's ability to shape public opinion about what should and should not be criminalized and about how much crime threatens the public at any given time. It is no accident that the American public does not appreciate the seriousness and the level of white-collar crime in this society. Without an understanding of these phenomena, the public cannot make fully informed decisions about personal and governmental policy to combat the "crime problem."

Criminals

Victimization surveys and self-reported criminality studies have provided better information about the characteristics of people committing FBI Index offenses than we had previously. We still know little about persons committing non-Index offenses. Index crimes seem more likely to be committed by young, lower-class males. "Lesser" offenses are more evenly distributed among other socioeconomic classes, though not necessarily among other age and sex categories. Indeed, age and sex seem the most unambiguous correlates of criminal behavior. Youth is consistently associated with most offenses. Males commit more crimes than females do, though the gap appears to be narrowing. The relationship between criminal behavior and race and income is more complicated. Blacks and members of the lower classes appear to have higher rates of criminal behavior. The dispute about the relation between class and crime has heightened in recent years, and the race-crime issue clearly is implicated in the class-crime issue. In and of themselves, these correlational issues do not offer a sound platform for anticrime policy (because they do not address the reasons for the correlations), though specification of the correlations is necessary to anticrime policy.

Crime Victims

The picture of crime is incomplete without inclusion of the victim factor. That is, we are finding that victimization is not randomly distributed—some categories of people are more likely to be victims of crime than others are. Beyond this, victim involvement in some types of offenses seems to extend beyond random victimization of the passive individual. At present, we know little else about victims. We must learn more if we are to combat crime effectively.

Causes of Crime

The most pressing of criminological questions will always be: What causes criminal behavior? Our inability to provide an answer also makes it the most frustrating of criminological questions. Beyond the fact that we have discounted some biological and psychological factors (for example, the XYY-chromosome pattern) as causes of any more than a few isolated crimes, we know very little about the causes of crime. This is not surprising, given the sketchy knowledge of crime correlates upon which we build our causal theories. We suspect that certain structural and cultural elements of society (for example, poverty) cause or encourage crime, but we cannot say precisely how these factors operate. In the final analysis, anticrime policy formulation becomes a guessing game at best.

The Criminal Justice System

In many ways, the very agencies we employ to fight crime actually create crime or, at least, the official picture of crime that shapes our fears. Official crime rates and official criminals are products of criminal justice organizational activity and discretion. Although we know that crime has indeed increased, we cannot always know which dimensions of the "crime problem" are real and which are purely organizational products.

RESPONSES TO CRIME

Assuming that we can answer the first of our three questions to the extent that we agree that crime is problematic enough to warrant some type of response, we may ask: Can we solve the "crime problem"? One school of thought of the crime-panicked 1970s suggests that if solution is dependent upon locating the causes of crime, we shall be waiting forever, "fiddling as Rome burns." If solution means addressing the "fact" that crime is an inexplicable given whose only remedy is "getting tough" with criminals, then perhaps something can be accomplished: criminals who are caught will be given no more chances to violate the law, and those not caught will be deterred from further crime when they view the fate of their unsuccessful peers (van den Haag, 1975; Wilson, 1975). This simplistic approach to crime control is the typically frustrated response to a social problem. Unsolved social problems signal to many of our citizens an America grown soft.

We cannot blame the public for seriously fearing crime and for growing frustrated. However, neither should we encourage fears and the "crackdowns" they inspire. Two important factors govern the need for calm. First, although our knowledge about crime is limited, the state of the art of criminology is sophisticated enough to allow more systematic testing of hypotheses underlying anticrime policy than is presently the case. We can give question 2 ("Will the remedy be effective?") far more scrutiny than we currently do. Thus, there is no excuse for panic policy.

Second, most of the remedies now proposed to deal with crime carry potentially costly liabilities that may not be acceptable even if the remedies work and are definitely unacceptable if they do not. Thus, we argue that any attempt to curb crime is not better than no attempt. More attention to question 3 ("Will negative side effects accompany the proposed remedy?") undoubtedly will lead to the abandonment of many policy ideas.

With questions 2 and 3 in mind, we may take a critical look at six anticrime strategies currently in effect or suggested: (1) limited procedural rights, (2) pretrial preventive detention, (3) capital punishment, (4) increased penalties for noncapital crimes, (5) lengthy incarceration of habitual offenders, and (6) gun control. Each of these responses to crime represents a "containment" approach. That is, each suggests that if we cannot eliminate the causes of crime, we can make it more difficult for people to commit crimes.

LIMITED PROCEDURAL RIGHTS

As we indicated throughout this book, a common response to the problem of crime is the attempted elimination of legal "technicalities" that stand in the way of arrest and prosecution of suspected offenders. The "technicalities" are, in fact, constitutional rights that protect citizens from such governmental excesses as unreasonable search and seizure and denial of counsel at the time of arrest. In the 1960s, the Warren Court wrote many decisions that affirmed such procedural rights. Presently, as the current Supreme Court responds to the public and governmental definition of crime as a severe social problem, we note a trend toward conservative redefinition of some of these rights. Many of these changes have involved search-and-seizure laws (see

U.S. Supreme Court Digest, 1978, 1979). The U.S. Supreme Court has ruled in recent years, for example, that:

1. Criminal defendants have no constitutional right to appeal state court convictions to federal courts, even if evidence used against the defendants in their trials was illegally seized.
2. Border-patrol officers at highway checkpoints can stop cars at random without suspicion and question passengers to discover illegal aliens or smuggling.
3. The Internal Revenue Service can use gambling money and records illegally seized in criminal cases as evidence in civil tax cases.
4. Police can routinely search impounded cars without a warrant and use as evidence in criminal cases whatever may be found in a glove compartment.
5. Evidence seized under a statute later held unconstitutional nevertheless can be used at trial against a defendant, so long as the police acted in the good faith belief that the statute was constitutional.
6. Police use of a device to keep track of the telephone numbers dialed by a citizen does not violate that citizen's right to privacy.

Effectiveness

As is the case with the exclusionary rule, described in Chapter 2, the above rulings may provide easier prosecution in certain isolated cases, but they will have little overall effect on the crime situation. Most deal with vice crimes rather than with the more serious offenses that concern the public. Rarely are robbers or burglars convicted on the basis of physical evidence seized in a search of their home or car; convictions generally stem from apprehension of offenders in the act of committing a crime (though other evidence may be used to buttress the prosecution's case). Indeed, few of the procedural "technicalities" affirmed by the Warren Court and modified by the current Supreme Court will influence the crime situation to any major degree. Even the famous *Miranda* decision, which placed limits on the police's ability to elicit a confession from a suspect, has had little to do with an increase or decrease in crime since so few suspects are prosecuted on the basis of confessions.

Negative Effects

Although the procedural-rights rulings may have little impact on the overall crime picture, they are nonetheless important. The Fourth Amendment ban on unreasonable search and seizure and other constitutionally defined rights were intended, as the late Justice William O. Douglass so often argued, "to keep the government off our backs." Historically, the state has shown itself willing to go to great lengths to catch criminals, including abusing the average citizen. Rulings like those described above erode Fourth Amendment protections and make the right to privacy less secure. In return for establishing these conservative precedents, we have gained little or nothing in the combating of crime.

PRETRIAL PREVENTIVE DETENTION

Closely related to the issue of limited procedural rights is that of pretrial preventive detention. In the late 1960s, public fear of crime as a serious social problem led to a rethinking of a number of earlier bail-reform acts. In an effort to restore to criminal suspects the full implications of the presumption of innocence, bail had been made easier to obtain and more persons had been released on their own recognizance. The result was a greater number of suspects free from jail pending trial. In 1970 the public began to be concerned that "dangerous criminals" (so defined by the fact of arrest) were free to commit other offenses while awaiting trial on their original charges.

The response of Congress to this fear was to include, in the 1970 District of Columbia Court Reform and Criminal Procedure Act, a provision for the pretrial detention (incarceration) of persons "likely" to commit crimes if free pending trial: persons charged with dangerous crimes such as rape, arson, burglary, heroin sale, and voluntary manslaughter or with obstructing justice. Passed with virtually no debate, the act required that persons who met certain criteria were to be kept in jail for up to sixty days before their trials. In deciding whether an individual should be detained, Congress ruled that judicial officials were to consider (1) the nature and circumstances of the alleged offense and weight of the evidence against the suspect, and (2) the suspect's family ties, employment situation, financial resources, character and mental condition, past conduct, length of residence in the community, record of convictions, record of previous court appearances, attempted flights to avoid prosecution, and past failures to appear in court (see Baridon and McEwen, 1979).

Effectiveness

The pretrial preventive detention act basically subordinates the individual's right to pretrial release to the state's right to protect itself from possible criminals. The act assumes that pretrial crime is a problem, that much pretrial crime is committed by people charged with dangerous offenses, and that the criteria specified in the act can identify which among the dangerous offenders will commit pretrial crimes. In an effort to determine the validity of these assumptions, a team of Harvard law students in 1970 studied Boston pretrial crime for a six-month period in 1968 (Angel et al., 1971). Their aim was to determine what impact the 1970 act would have had on 1968 pretrial crime.

An examination of official police and court records disclosed that there were 427 individuals who could have been eligible for pretrial preventive detention at the time of their arrests. After reviewing these cases, the Harvard team concluded the following:

1. Pretrial crime is rather low. Only 17 percent of the potential offenders committed pretrial crime.
2. There is no correlation between the original alleged offense and the seriousness of the pretrial crime.
3. Most pretrial crime does not occur in the first 60 days following release, but during 120 to 240 days after release.
4. The criteria for determining who should be detained were not linked to pretrial crime, nor could the criteria be converted to scales to predict pretrial offenders.

The Harvard study's results have been supported for the most part by a recent Department of Justice evaluation of pretrial release and detention programs in eight sites throughout the county (Toborg, 1981). The study found that only 16 percent of all released defendants had pretrial arrest records. Pretrial arrests usually were for less serious offenses than were original arrests. Only eight percent of all released defendants eventually were convicted of pretrial crimes. None of those originally charged with homicide was convicted of a pretrial offense. Only 7 percent of those charged with rape, robbery, or asssault eventually were convicted of a pretrial offense. The Department of Justice study's results differed from those of the Harvard study only in that most pretrial arrests were found to occur before, rather than after, sixty days following pretrial release.

It is assumed that the pretrial behavior of those persons studied by the Department of Justice could be predicted no more easily than could that of the persons studied by the Harvard researchers. It appears, then, that the pretrial preventive detention is ineffective as a crime control mechanism and that, in utilizing it, we forfeit a basic individual right for no gain.

Negative Effects

The notion of pretrial preventive detention cuts deeply into our traditional view that an accused person is considered innocent until proven guilty. Bail and other forms of pretrial release acknowledge the sacredness of that view. Pretrial preventive detention qualifies our right to freedom pending a guilty verdict. It states, in essence, that we have the right *only sometimes*. In qualifying the right once, lawmakers have opened the door to further qualification—most likely through extension of the concept of dangerousness (which could include, at some future date, "political threat"). All this, as we suggested above, for no apparent gain in the fight against crime.

CAPITAL PUNISHMENT

In 1953, two-thirds of the American public favored the death penalty for convicted murderers. In 1966, the proportion had dropped to two-fifths. By 1981, it had risen again to two-thirds (Gallup, 1981). As Figure 12–1 indicates, at present there are over 800 inmates on death row (U.S. Department of Justice, 1982). Since 1930, about 3900 people have been executed in the U.S. No executions occurred between 1967 and 1977, a period during which the U.S. Supreme Court declared all state capital punishment laws invalid. As states have brought their laws into line with Supreme Court guidelines, and as some prisoners have exhausted all avenues of appeal, executions have begun again. Unless opponents of the death penalty find some new challenge to its constitutionality or, fairly unlikely, persuade legislatures to outlaw it, the large number of persons now sitting on death row quickly will be the principals in a rash of executions in the 1980s.

For a variety of reasons, the renewal of executions has been good news to many people. Many support the death penalty for moral reasons, arguing that killers deserve death in return. Some feel that execution is preferable to the cost involved in maintaining a person in prison. Both arguments, of course, are matters of personal moral values, discussion of which exceeds the scope of this book. But two arguments favoring the death penalty do relate to the purposes of this book—thoughts on crime control. Some view capital punishment as a device to protect society from a proven danger. Some argue that the death penalty deters would-be killers from taking lives. We may examine these arguments in terms of their crime-control effectiveness.

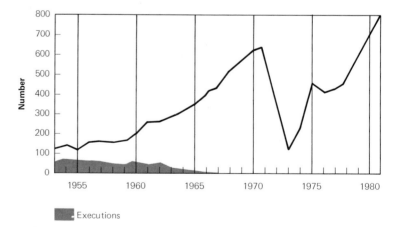

FIGURE 12–1

Death-Row Inmates and Executions at Year End, 1953–1981 (*Source:* U.S. Department of Justice, *Capital Punishment 1981* (Washington, D.C.: U.S. Government Printing Office, 1982), cover.)

NEWSPRINT AND COMMENT

Asked to Testify a Third Time, Trial-Scarred Widow Gives Up

By Richard Boyd

Two years after it happened, Joyce Waites remembers. "There is no way to explain it to anyone. . . . It was the first time I had ever known fear, I mean total, cold-blooded fear. . . . They just walked in and cocked those guns. . . . I felt we would die. . . . I heard the noise but I could not believe a gun went off, and I raised up and I looked and I knew Garland was dead and he put a gun to my head and said I would be next. . . . Then they were gone and I don't know why they didn't shoot me. . . . The way Garland went was horrid. It isn't fair that the last image of him I have is with a bullet in his head, bleeding."

The first two times Waites told in public what happened that day, she was in a witness chair in a Jefferson Parish courtroom.

Both times she broke down, sobbing uncontrollably. Both times, a judge had to call a recess to let Waites compose herself.

The first time was January 1981, when 24-year-old Jimmy R. Robinson of New Haven, Conn., was tried and convicted of murdering her husband, 55-year-old Garland Waites. Robinson was sentenced to die in the electric chair.

The second time was Jan. 28 this year, when another jury convicted Robinson's companion of second-degree murder. Keith Stewart, 17, was sen-tenced to life in prison without parole, probation or suspension of sentence.

Now Waites, emotionally exhausted, says she can't go through another session on the stand. It makes her a victim all over again. But because she is exhausted, the man who killed her husband will escape the electric chair—for a few weeks ago the state Supreme Court overturned the death sentence against Robinson, and without Waites' powerful testimony, the state cannot get it back.

In October the state Supreme Court, in an unanimous opinion written by Justice Harry T. Lemmon, upheld the murder conviction but overturned the death penalty.

The justices found that prosecutor Loeb, in closing arguments to the jury during the sentencing phase of the trial, minimized the jurors' role by stressing that Robinson inevitably would appeal a death sentence. The court considered that a fatal error.

"I was stunned. I was angry. I can't begin to describe the anger and frustration I felt," Waites said.

Capital crimes are tried in two parts in Louisiana. In the first part, a jury determines whether the defendant is guilty or innocent. In the second, the same jury, after hearing more arguments and more testimony, considers whether the crime merits death or life imprisonment.

In Robinson's case, the Supreme Court decision meant the conviction would stand. Only the sentencing phase of the trial would have to be repeated.

"But it's a lot more difficult than that," Loeb said. "In order for a new jury to have enough information to intelligently consider life versus death, they must have the facts of the case; they must hear testimony," he said.

"The new jury must hear as much of the testimony of the guilt and innocence phase of the case as did the first jury, although they aren't deciding guilt or innocence; only a life or death sentence," Loeb said.

In short, that meant Waites, for a third time, would have to go before a jury and recount her nightmare.

"I couldn't do it. I trembled when I thought about doing it again. I was just beginning to come to terms with the loss and they wanted me to go through it all over again. I couldn't do it," Waites said.

On Nov. 7, with her consent, Loeb told the court the state would not retry Robinson on the sentencing phase. Judge Joseph Grefer sentenced him to a mandatory term of life in prison.

What did Loeb do that resulted in the death penalty reversal?

In his closing arguments, he repeatedly referred to the fact that even if the jury recommended death, the sentence would not necessarily be carried out.

He told the jurors that Robinson's conviction and sentence would be appealed.

" . . . this case will be reviewed by the seven justices of the Louisiana Supreme Court and they also will review your recommendation of death," Loeb said.

" . . . there is a very strong possibility—probability—that this case will be reviewed by the federal court system and possibly eventually by the United States Supreme Court," Loeb said.

And if Robinson failed to escape the death sentence at all these steps, the governor could still step in and halt his execution, Loeb informed the jury.

But he argued that the death penalty was important "to send a message that we cannot sit idly by and be murdered in our own homes during the middle of the day, and I'm not going to even argue to you that it will make a significant contribution to that, but ladies and gentlemen, we've got to do something."

The justices decided that such remarks "may suggest to a conscientious juror that his awesome responsibility is lessened by the extensive system of subsequent review."

And Waites is bitter. "It isn't fair. I'm a nobody. I have no political power," she says now.

"If the wife of a justice had been murdered, I wonder if Loeb's remarks on review would have seemed to be in error. He just told the truth; he just told a jury what they obviously know anyway; that the case would be appealed and that the death verdict might at some future point be overturned. What is wrong with that?" she asked.

Source: © Times-Picayune Publishing Corp., 1982. Reprinted by permission.

Comment: Due Process and Capital Punishment

It is clear in the above story that a murderer whom the convicting jury sentenced to die will not be executed. His victim's widow understandably is distraught (though her testimony in a new trial regarding the sentence could produce another death penalty verdict). The case raises two issues addressed in the present chapter: capital punishment and due process.

The public is convinced that killers long have forestalled or even escaped execution through "abuse" of the appeals process. Yet, the possibility of appelate review of a lower court decision was created to aid killers only in the sense that it was aimed to protect every member of society. Our system of justice was constructed to avoid conviction of an innocent person, even at the risk of freeing guilty persons. Further, we value human life so greatly that we make it difficult to take the life of even the worst of offenders. That is, an execution can occur only after an offender has exhausted every reasonable chance to convince us not to execute him. The offender in the above story was able to convince the state supreme court that he should not die—at least until a jury received proper instruction prior to a death penalty decision.

Critics contend that the killer in the story received a reprieve through technical nitpicking. However, we have noted many times in this book that the "technicalities" that outrage the public are hardly minor. Indeed, they are the very rules that protect all of us from criminal justice system error, whimsy, and malice. Critics would do better to direct their anger at the officials who violate the rules—usually in ways that could be avoided.

It is clear in the present case that the prosecutor erred in no small way. He suggested to the jury that their deliberations concerning the death penalty had no real meaning in the final analysis, that appeals courts likely would reverse their decision. We must wonder, as the supreme court justices did, if the jury would have chosen the death penalty had they been told that their decision carried more weight than any others and that the offenders' fate truly was in their hands.

We return again to a major theme of this book. We have choices but none comes without some cost. We can abandon due process to catch and punish the criminal but, in so doing, forfeit the protection due process affords us against criminal justice malpractice. Or we can suffer the occasional loss of punishment to the criminal because we hold due process sacred. Is there, in fact, a choice?

Effectiveness

That the death penalty protects us from crimes that people condemned to die might otherwise commit cannot be disputed. But we might dispute the necessity of the death penalty in accomplishing this end. Could not the same end be achieved by a sentence of life imprisonment without the possibility of parole? (While the possibility of a governor's pardon of a murderer would still exist in theory, it is an unlikely possibility. Persons who do not favor the death penalty are not likely to be elected governor; those that are elected still must face the political ramifications of such an unpopular move as the pardoning of a murderer.) In terms of protecting the public, then, capital punishment seems excessive.

The most hotly contested point of the capital punishment debate is its deterrent effectiveness. Some argue that fear of the death penalty dissuades persons from committing capital offenses. This stand never can be proven, strictly speaking, since we never can estimate the number of people who might have murdered but chose not to because of the death penalty. However, since we gauge the depths of our "crime problem" in terms of official statistics, we may judge the deterrent effect of capital punishment in terms of its relation to trends displayed in those statistics. In this regard, it can be stated with certainty that no evidence exists to support the claim that the death penalty deters homicide (Bowers, 1974; Kleck, 1979). No reasonably methodologically sophisticated research can demonstrate a significant negative correlation between homicide rate and capital punishment sentences or executions—whether the research focuses on comparisons of states with and without the death penalty or on before-after time periods relating to executions.

These findings should not be surprising given the general deterrence literature's emphasis on certainty of punishment. Several studies suggest that perception of certainty of punishment is a stronger deterrent factor than is perception of severity of punishment (Grasmick and Bryjak, 1980; Hollinger and Clark, 1983; Tittle and Logan, 1973; Zimring and Hawkins, 1973). To the extent that homicide can be deterred, it is through the certainty that a reasonably severe prison sentence would result for the killer. That certainty is missing at the moment; killers do not expect to be caught. Even were certainty present, most killings to which the death penalty applies—those committed during the course of a robbery or other felony—are unplanned. The offender enters the crime situation assuming that threat of force will suffice. When threat does not, the offender becomes a potential killer. In short, given the dynamics of felony-related homicide and the perceived unlikelihood of apprehension for it, the death penalty does not serve an effective crime-control function.

Negative Effects

Among the negative effects of the use of the death penalty is its potential for discriminatory application. Historically, capital punishment has been applied to blacks in discriminatory fashion, especially in the South (Kleck, 1981). Much has been done to correct this situation, but the concern that it continues more subtley and that it will reappear in its former shape are reasonable. Even more obviously negative is the irreversibility of the death penalty, once applied. Bedau (1964:434–52) has documented numerous cases of unjust execution. The possibility of an incorrect trial verdict never can be discounted. A mistake cannot be rectified if its victim has been executed. Finally, the death penalty may be viewed negatively in that it reflects frustration and hysteria—at least in terms of its application as a crime-control measure. Capital punishment discourages us from addressing crime in any constructive fashion.

INCREASED PENALTIES FOR NONCAPITAL CRIMES

Perhaps more than any other society, ours turns to the law to settle its problems. As crime increasingly has become defined as problematic, the legislature has responded by passing new laws or by making existing penalties harsher. This practice rests on the assumption that the greater the potential penalty for an act, the less likely an individual will be to commit the act.

Effectiveness

As noted above, the deterrence issue is a complex one. The death penalty does not seem to deter homicide. But most murders are crimes of passion in which little thought is given to the consequences of the act. Generally, when murder accompanies some other felony such as robbery, the murder is not really planned and the consequences not really contemplated.

Can increased criminal penalties deter noncapital offenses? As we suggested in the discussion of the death penalty, available research suggests that they can when we consider three important elements of punishment: its severity, its certainty, and the public's perception of severity and certainty. It

does little good to increase the penalty for a crime if the certainty of apprehension and punishment for the offense is very low. And certainty is of little
consequence if a punishment is meaningless. Neither element is important
unless the public is aware of it. Once public awareness is assured, certainty
seems more important than severity.

Although criminologists appear increasingly willing to accept the deterrence doctrine, most are reserving final judgment until a number of theoretical and methodological problems are addressed (see Tittle and Logan, 1973;
Gibbs, 1975). First, no one has yet provided an explicit theory of crime deterrence that specifies how penalties affect behavior and under what conditions. Second, we must find a way to measure an essentially immeasurable
concept. Since we cannot really know how or when persons choose not to
commit crimes, we must infer deterrence from changes and differences in official crime rates. Third, really to test the deterrence theory, we eventually
must systematically graduate the penalties for a crime and include a "no penalty" situation. Fourth, in comparing communities with different penalty
structures, we must be able to control for such extralegal factors as differences in informal community condemnation of the crime in question and differences in crime-conducive situations such as unemployment.

Negative Effects

If criminologists are somewhat inclined to believe that punishment deters
crime, should we not legislate stronger penalties for crimes? Again, this policy is not without its costs. It encourages an overreliance on legislation to
cure all social ills. It fosters a repressive atmosphere. It threatens the boundaries of what we now consider "just punishment" for a crime and forces us
to contemplate trading justice for crime control. Finally, increasing mandatory minimum sentences for offenses undercuts the possibility of individualized justice, mercy, and rehabilitation. Judges are robbed of the discretion to
make the punishment fit the crime and the ability to deal with the unusual
case that really does not merit prison.

LOCKING UP CAREER OFFENDERS

Many people feel that even if harsher punishments do not deter crime, they
should be enacted nonetheless to remove dangerous felons from society for
longer periods. The "lock 'em up" philosophy is based on evidence that a
large portion of our crimes are committed by a small number of habitual or
career offenders. One study of 10,000 juveniles whose criminal records were
followed until they were eighteen years old revealed that 6 percent of the
sample was responsible for 53 percent of its violent attacks, 71 percent of its
robberies, and 62 percent of its property crimes (Wolfgang et al., 1972). An-

other study of three birth cohorts in Wisconsin reports that about 5 percent of the persons in each cohort was responsible for approximately 75 percent of the felonies (both juvenile and adult crimes) committed by the respective cohorts (Shannon, 1982). A recent Rand Corporation study of 49 imprisoned, habitual armed robbers attributes to these felons, resulting from an average of twenty years in crime (half of which was spent in prison), a total of over 10,500 crimes. These include 1,492 auto thefts, 993 grand thefts, 2,331 burglaries, 855 robberies, 995 forgeries, 3,620 drug sales, 25 purse snatchings, 188 aggravated assaults, and 6 rapes (Petersilia et al., 1978:vii).

Believing that most serious crimes are the products of career offenders, critics of the criminal justice system are calling for harsher criminal penalties, greater concentration on repeat offenders by prosecutors (National Institute of Law Enforcement, 1977), and a reduction in probations and paroles given to offenders (Wilson, 1975). The Rand Corporation study cited above concludes that the armed robbers it studied are beyond rehabilitation and that their incapacitation through imprisonment may be the most effective means of reducing crime. Greenberg (1975) argues that no more than 12 percent of Index crime over a three-year period could be prevented by increasing to three years the average prison sentence of two years served by inmates in the early 1970s. Shinner and Shinner (1975) counter that, assuming that most crimes are committed by career offenders, our crime rate could be cut by two-thirds if every person convicted of a serious crime were given a three-year sentence. The "lock 'em up" sentiment inherent in such estimates has become especially apparent in recent years in "multiple billing" laws enacted in some states. Here, a convicted offender's sentence is doubled, tripled, or quadrupled on the basis of the number of prior felony convictions on his or her record (Sleffel, 1977).

Effectiveness

It is difficult to argue with the logic of preventing persons from committing crimes by incarcerating them. Yet we should not readily assume that this practice will greatly reduce crime when applied to repeat offenders. As noted earlier in this book, there may be limits on criminal opportunities in a community or neighborhood; not all would-be criminals may be able to operate at a given time. The criminal opportunity structure is determined in large part by such factors as the number of readily available victims and situations without witnesses, the offender's familiarity with the area in which he or she contemplates committing a crime, and the effectiveness of police anticrime strategies. If, indeed, there are more potential criminals than criminal opportunities, the imprisonment of repeat offenders will not alter the amount of crime in the community. Others will fill the void left by the habitual offenders.

Some readers will argue that the "limited opportunity" hypothesis is too simplistic, that opportunities to commit robberies abound ("All one has to do is get a gun and stick someone up!"). Yet if crimes are so easily committed, we wonder why career offenders do not commit more. Surely it is because there are some limits on their opportunities. Capture is not a total impossibility. Professional burglars and robbers, for example, take great pains to plan their crimes and caution against becoming too greedy ("going to the well once too often") (see Letkemann, 1973). If we assume that criminal opportunities are limited and if we accept our theories that social conditions such as poverty produce great numbers of potential offenders, we may expect some competition for exploitation of the opportunities. Career criminals may be the current exploiters; they can also be replaced.

Although we have no solid evidence to support the above contention, we can point to the territorial wars of organized crime mobs, youth gangs, drug dealers, and pimps that continually indicate that criminal opportunities are not unlimited. However, we suggest that the "limited opportunities" hypothesis is no less plausible than the "lock 'em up" hypothesis. Neither has been adequately tested.

Negative Effects

The costs of the "lock 'em up" approach are roughly the same as those for the deterrence approach. Both eliminate the possibility for individualized justice and treatment. Both suggest that we trade just punishment for crime control. The "multiple billing" concept carries the additional liability of negating the legal ideal that individuals can pay for their crimes. "Multiple billing" of repeat offenders constitutes making them pay for the same offense twice.

GUN CONTROL

Gun control is one of the more controversial of proposed responses to the crime problem (see Newton and Zimring, 1969; Sherrill, 1973; Wright et al., 1983). Those who favor gun control argue that outlawing private ownership of guns will reduce serious violent crime. Opponents claim that gun control penalizes the noncriminal gun owner for the abuses of guns by criminals. To simplify the present discussion, we will equate gun control with making private ownership of handguns illegal, and we will focus on the possible effects of gun control on crime. (There is, of course, a strong anti-gun lobby which argues that gun laws will reduce gun accidents in the home. This position raises the issue of government determination concerning into what "dangerous" situations persons or families may place themselves. If guns are outlawed to "protect" citizens from harming themselves, the same logic might apply to "protecting" citizens from the potential harm in football, skydiving, race-car dr:ving, and so forth. Reasonable attention to this issue exceeds the scope of this book.)

Effectiveness

Advocates of gun-control legislation attribute a great deal of our "crime problem" to the fact that Americans own between 30 and 40 million handguns. Nationwide, handguns are used in approximately 50 percent of all homicides, and firearms (presumably handguns for the most part) are involved in 40 percent of robberies and 24 percent of assaults (FBI, 1981). Gun-control proponents argue that in order to curb these crimes (or at least to reduce the deaths and injuries associated with robbery and assault), handguns must be made less available. To accomplish this, they seek to outlaw ownership of handguns, thereby eliminating any legitimate reason for the manufacture or importation of handguns.

Critics of gun control counter with a number of arguments. They point to the general ineffectiveness of previous local and state attempts at gun control. They argue that citizens need guns to defend themselves and their property, that gun-control laws will not stop criminals from obtaining guns, and that persons who wish to kill will do so with other weapons if guns are unavailable. Some argue that if we must have gun control, it should be directed at the "Saturday night special," the small, cheap, imported handgun thought by many to be used in most serious crimes.

Most of the criticisms of gun-control legislation are easily rebutted. It is unfair to use past gun-control laws to evaluate the potential effectiveness of currently proposed laws. Previous laws were not uniformly written and enforced. They also were not universally enacted; it accomplishes little to outlaw guns in one city or state when they are readily available in neighboring cities and states.

Undoubtedly, many of the guns used in crimes have been stolen from citizens who bought them for protection. The frontier approach implicit in the purchase of guns for protection is misguided. Statistics indicate that the presence of guns in the home is more likely to lead to the death or injury of a family member or friend than to the wounding of an intruder. Since home intrusions generally are sudden and surprising, gun owners rarely have the chance to use their weapons. In only about 2 percent of home robbery cases is a robber shot by an intended victim. Indeed, the use of a weapon to resist a crime seems to increase the victim's risk of injury (Yeager et al., 1976).

It is true that some criminals always will find guns to commit crimes. Yet gun-control laws may decrease the availability of guns enough to prevent the marginally committed, unprofessional criminals from obtaining a gun. It is those criminals who are most likely to "lose their cool" and use a gun in panic during a crime. Further, when other types of weapons are used in crimes, the risk of death to the victim decreases. The knife wound is more easily healed than the gunshot wound. Were guns less available during household disputes, fewer family members would die.

Finally, according to Sherrill (1973), the "Saturday night special" issue is manufactured. The campaign against this form of weapon, he argues, is sponsored by American gun manufacturers who wish to be rid of the competition from importers. Classification of guns used in crimes by police also has been erratic. Some departments have classified any small gun, even if American-made and expensive, as a "Saturday night special." Sherrill's statistics indicate that the "Saturday night special" is not so related to crime as we sometimes believe. More recent research indicates that, of guns confiscated by the police, 25 to 33 percent are "Saturday night specials" (Brill, 1977; U.S. Bureau of Alcohol, Tobacco, and Firearms, 1976a, 1976b; Wright et al., 1983). Thus, many believe that the disappearance of the "Saturday night special" will do little to alter the crime situation.

In sum, arguments against gun control do not ring true. However, in fairness it must be noted that gun-control advocates have yet to prove their case. Deterrence research suggests that gun-control laws will work only if apprehension and punishment for illegal gun possession are certain—an unlikely possibility. Gun-control advocates argue that the prohibition of guns eventually would decrease the supply of guns, thus decreasing gun-related crimes. But, given the number of guns now in the public domain, it will take a *very long time* to accomplish such a diminished supply.

The results of recent, fairly stringent gun-control laws in a few jurisdictions have been mixed. Washington D.C.'s 1975 gun law, dealing primarily with gun sales, and Detroit's 1976 law, which mandated a two-year add-on sentence for felonies committed with guns, seem to have had no serious impact on violent crimes in these cities (Jones, 1981; Loftin and McDowell, 1981). Massachusetts' 1974 law, which set a one-year mandatory sentence for the possession of an unlicensed firearm, seems linked, however tentatively, to decreases in assaults with guns, armed robberies, and gun-related homicides. But it also seems related to increases in non-gun-related assaults, and the decrease in armed robberies appears to have been short-lived (Pierce and Bowers, 1979). It will be years before we can understand the full impact of any recent gun-control legislation. Further, until a standardized, universally employed gun-control law is enacted, we cannot assess the true effectiveness of gun control on the "crime problem." Is gun-control legislation worth attempting without a guarantee of success? The answer lies in our assessment of potential negative side effects of gun control.

Negative Effects

Were gun control to have no effects other than possibly to curb crime, the risk of legislation would be minimal. Yet, as gun owners argue, there is a side effect; gun owners are being penalized for the crimes of a few. Although there is some question about the constitutionality of gun-control laws, we need not concern ourselves with it at present. Suffice it to state that gun-control laws represent one more intrusion of the government into the private lives of citizens. In this instance they are being told what they may own. Each such intrusion sets the precedent for further intrusions. If a reduction in crime is the result of gun-control laws, some will term the laws worthwhile government interference. If crime is not reduced, we likely will not be allowed to go back and begin again, reinstituting private gun ownership. Thus, we had best be certain of our picture of the "crime problem" and the relationship of handguns to it before we enact gun-control legislation.

CONCLUSION

No aspect of the crime problem is simple. Crime's dimensions are complicated. Its correlates are difficult to identify. Its causes are frustratingly puzzling. Why, then, do we find ourselves so often approaching the crime problem simplistically? We insist on seeing ourselves as under siege by a horde of barbarians, and we search for one-step policies to lop off their heads. If this book has accomplished anything, it has, hopefully, given its readers reason to pause before they panic. As this chapter has demonstrated, all of our anticrime policies carry potential liabilities. We owe ourselves the time and effort to weigh these losses against the gains in fighting crime.

REFERENCES

Angel, A. R., E. D. Green, H. R. Kaufman, et al. 1971. Preventive detention: An empirical analysis. *Harvard Civil Rights–Civil Liberties Law Review* 6:289–396.

Baridon, P., and T. McEwen. 1979. Preventive detention: A matter of balance. *Criminology* 17:22–33.

Bedau, H. A. 1964. *The Death Penalty in America*. Garden City, N.J.: Doubleday & Company.

Bowers, W. J. 1974. *Executions in America: Discrimination and Deterrence and an Inventory of 5,769 State-Imposed Executions*. Lexington, Mass.: Lexington Books.

Brill, S. 1977. *Firearms Abuse*. Washington, D.C.: The Police Foundation.

Federal Bureau of Investigation. 1981. *Uniform Crime Reports—1980*. Washington, D.C.: U.S. Government Printing Office.

Gallup, G. H. 1981. *The Gallup Poll, March 1*. Princeton, N.J.

Gibbs, J. 1975. *Crime, Punishment, and Deterrence*. New York: Elsevier Science Publishing Co.

Grasmick, H., and G. Bryjak. 1980. The deterrent effect of perceived severity of punishment. *Soc. Forces* 59:471–91.

Greenberg, D. 1975. The incapacitative effect of imprisonment: Some estimates. *Law & Society Rev.* 9:541–80.

Hollinger, R. C., and J. P. Clark. 1983. Deviance in the workplace: Perceived certainty, perceived severity, and employee theft. *Soc. Forces* 62:398–418.

Jones, E. D. 1981. The District of Columbia's Firearms Control Regulations Act of 1975: The toughest handgun control law in the United States—or is it? *Ann. Am. Acad. Pol. Soc. Sci.* 455:138–49.

Kleck, G. 1979. Capital punishment, gun ownership, and homicide. *Am. J. Sociol.* 84:783–804.

———. 1981. Racial discrimination in criminal sentencing: A critical evaluation of the evidence with additional evidence on the death penalty. *Am. Sociol. Rev.* 46:783–804.

Letkemann, P. 1973. *Crime as Work.* Englewood Cliffs, N.J.: Prentice-Hall.

Loftin, C., and D. McDowell. 1981. "One with a gun gets you two": Mandatory sentencing and firearms violence in Detroit. *Ann. Am. Acad. Pol. Soc. Sci.* 455:150–68.

National Institute of Law Enforcement and Criminal Justice, Law Enforcement Assistance Administration, U.S. Department of Justice. 1977. *Curbing the Repeat Offender: A Strategy for Prosecutors.* Washington, D.C.: U.S. Government Printing Office.

Newton, G. D., and F. E. Zimring. 1969. *Firearms and Violence in American Life.* Washington, D.C.: U.S. Government Printing Office.

Petersilia, J., P. W. Greenwood, and M. Lavin. 1978. *Criminal Careers of Habitual Felons.* Washington, D.C.: U.S. Government Printing Office.

Pierce, G. J., and W. J. Bowers. 1979. The Impact of the Bartley-Fox Gun Law on Crime in Massachusetts. Paper, Northeastern University, Center for Applied Social Research.

Shannon, L. W. 1982. *Assessing the Relationship of Adult Criminal Careers to Juvenile Careers: A Summary.* Washington, D.C.: U.S. Department of Justice.

Sherrill, R. 1973. *The Saturday Night Special.* New York: Penguin Books.

Shinner, S., and R. Shinner. 1975. The effects of the criminal justice system on the control of crime. *Law & Society Rev.* 9:581–611.

Sleffel, L. 1977. *The Law and the Dangerous Criminal.* Lexington, Mass.: Lexington Books.

Tittle, C. R., and C. H. Logan. 1973. Sanctions and deviance: Evidence and remaining questions. *Law & Society Rev.* 7:371–92.

Toborg, M. A. 1981. *National Evaluation Program, Phase II Report: Pretrial Release.* Washington, D.C.: Department of Justice.

U.S. Bureau of Alcohol, Tobacco, and Firearms. 1976a. *Project Identification: A Study of Handguns Used in Crime.* Washington, D.C.

———. 1976b. *Project 300.* Washington, D.C.

U.S. Department of Justice. 1982. *Capital Punishment, 1981.* Washington, D.C.: U.S. Government Printing Office.

United States Supreme Court Digest: 1978. St. Paul: West Publishing Company.

United States Supreme Court Digest: 1979. St. Paul: West Publishing Company.

van den Haag, E. 1975. *Punishing Criminals: Concerning a Very Old and Painful Question.* New York: Basic Books.

Wilson, J. Q. 1975. *Thinking about Crime.* New York: Basic Books.

Wolfgang, M. E., R. M. Figlio, and T. Sellin. 1972. *Delinquency in a Birth Cohort.* Chicago: University of Chicago Press.

Wright, J. D., P. H. Rossi, and K. Daly. 1983. *Under the Gun: Weapons, Crime, and Violence in America.* New York: Aldine Publishing.

Yeager, M. G., J. D. Alviani, and N. Loving. 1976. *How Well Does the Handgun Protect You and Your Family?* Technical Report 2. Washington, D.C.: U.S. Conference of Mayors.

Zimring, F., and G. Hawkins, 1973. *Deterrence: The Legal Threat in Crime Control.* Chicago: University of Chicago Press.

SUGGESTED READINGS

Chapter 12 has been concerned primarily with "reasonable" responses to crime-control issues. Thus, the suggested readings for Chapter 2 again are appropriate. Beyond this, however, two books in particular and a collection of criticisms of them seem exceedingly valuable in a discussion of potential solutions to the "crime problem." James Q. Wilson and Ernst ven den Haag's rather conservative attacks on traditional criminological research and criminal justice agencies (especially the courts) apparently have done much to promote a "lock 'em up" anticrime approach: see Wilson's *Thinking about Crime* (New York: Basic Books, 1975) and van den Haag's *Punishing Criminals: Concerning a Very Old and Very Painful Question* (New York: Basic Books, 1975). A number of critical reviews of Wilson's book serve to counterbalance it nicely: see *Contemporary Sociology,* July 1976, pp. 410–18. Finally, H. Pepinsky offers a systematic approach to combatting crime in *Crime Control Strategies* (New York: Oxford, 1980).

AUTHOR INDEX

SUBJECT INDEX